CITIES & ECONOMIC CHANGE

'An invaluable text for all those interested in cities and economic change. Empirically grounded, theoretically informed, and written in a highly accessible way to help students understand processes underlying the changing urban economy, urban governance, and the role of place. In a world of many texts, this one deserves a place on the bookshelves.'

Lily Kong, Professor of Geography, National University of Singapore

'This exciting and informative volume provides a series of accounts on the organisation of economic activity in a globalized world. Editors and contributors leave readers in no doubt about the extent of the transformations coursing through urban economies in the global north and south, and the theoretical and methodological challenges that arise in trying to make sense of them.'

Kevin Ward, Professor of Human Geography, University of Manchester

'This book provides a timely, critical and compelling overview of some of the major economic concerns of the early twenty first century. It will be an essential read for anyone interested in the role of cities in the changing global space economy.'

Professor James Faulconbridge, Lancaster University

'At a time when cities have harboured the majority of the human race and the main of the global economy, there is nothing more significant than understanding the intertwine of cities and economic change. This is an assemblage of cutting-edge scholarships in urban studies contributed all by experienced writers with authoritative expertise. It addresses the issue of cities and economic change in such an incredible breadth and depth that students of urban studies are led to new horizons of navigation and enquiry. I have found the documentation and interpretation stimulating, provocative, and extremely well-articulated. Theoretically informed and empirically grounded, this is a collection of essays that makes a timely and path-breaking contribution to the urban literature. It stands out as an excellent addition to the expanding urban library and a key reference on urban issues I would highly recommend to anyone interested in urban and economic development.'

George C.S. Lin, Chair Professor of Geography and Associate Dean of Social Sciences, Hong Kong University

'*Cities and Economic Change* offers a lucid and fearless look into the wide-ranging challenges posed by the on-going restructuring of urban economies in a globalizing world and leaves the reader with sober and level-headed assessment of a generation of policy change in international urban political economic development.'

Roger Keil, York University, Canada

'This collection shows how imperatives of capital and state have wrought dramatic transformations in cities around the globe, supplies timely data on urban employment, occupations and labor markets and provides critical assessments of on-going experiments in policy and governance.'

Michael L. Indergaard, St. John's University Jamaica

'The world's cities continue to expand, sometimes with and sometimes without economic growth; urban-economic transformations are not what they used to be, either in form or effect. Charting these shifting conditions, *Cities and Economic Change* brings together newly commissioned essays from leading researchers in the field. It's an excellent collection'.

Jamie Peck, University of British Columbia

'Encompassing the Global North and the Global South, this book re-examines the rich scholarship on urbanization and cities with a twenty-first century perspective. Through a multipolar global framework, the book gives colourful accounts of capitalism's polarizing and politicizing outcomes, the reimaging and place-marketing of cities, and the economic and cultural reproduction of space and place in the post-industrial era.'

C. Cindy Fan, UCLA

SAGE was founded in 1965 by Sara Miller McCune to support the dissemination of usable knowledge by publishing innovative and high-quality research and teaching content. Today, we publish more than 750 journals, including those of more than 300 learned societies, more than 800 new books per year, and a growing range of library products including archives, data, case studies, reports, conference highlights, and video. SAGE remains majority-owned by our founder, and on her passing will become owned by a charitable trust that secures our continued independence.

Los Angeles | London | Washington DC | New Delhi | Singapore

CITIES &  ECONOMIC CHANGE

RESTRUCTURING AND DISLOCATION IN THE GLOBAL METROPOLIS

Edited by
Ronan Paddison & Tom Hutton

Los Angeles | London | New Delhi
Singapore | Washington DC

Los Angeles | London | New Delhi
Singapore | Washington DC

SAGE Publications Ltd
1 Oliver's Yard
55 City Road
London EC1Y 1SP

SAGE Publications Inc.
2455 Teller Road
Thousand Oaks, California 91320

SAGE Publications India Pvt Ltd
B 1/I 1 Mohan Cooperative Industrial Area
Mathura Road
New Delhi 110 044

SAGE Publications Asia-Pacific Pte Ltd
3 Church Street
#10-04 Samsung Hub
Singapore 049483

Editor: Robert Rojek
Assistant editor: Keri Dickens and Matt Oldfield
Production editor: Katherine Haw
Copyeditor: Kate Harrison
Proofreader: Derek Markham
Indexer: Jackie McDermott
Marketing manager: Michael Ainsley
Cover design: Francis Kenney
Typeset by: C&M Digitals (P) Ltd, Chennai, India
Printed and bound by Henry Ling Limited, at the
    Dorset Press, Dorchester, DT1 1HD

Editorial arrangement and Chapter 1 © Ronan
    Paddison and Tom Hutton 2015
Chapter 2 © Kenneth E. Corey, Mark I. Wilson and
    Peilei Fan 2015
Chapter 3 © John Harrison 2015
Chapter 4 © Stefan Krätke 2015
Chapter 5 © Ivan Turok 2015
Chapter 6 © Danny MacKinnon 2015
Chapter 7 © Colin C. Williams 2015
Chapter 8 © Iain Deas and Nicola Headlam 2015
Chapter 9 © Mario Polèse 2015
Chapter 10 © Marguerite van den Berg 2015
Chapter 11 © Edgar Pieterse 2015
Chapter 12 © Mark Whitehead 2015
Chapter 13 © K. C. Ho 2015
Chapter 14 © Tom Hutton 2015

First published 2015

Library of Congress Control Number: 2014937465

British Library Cataloguing in Publication data

A catalogue record for this book is available from
the British Library

ISBN 978-1-84787-938-7
ISBN 978-1-84787-939-4 (pbk)

MIX
Paper from
responsible sources
FSC
www.fsc.org   FSC® C013985

Contents

List of Figures and Tables

About the Contributors

Kenneth E. Corey is Professor Emeritus of Geography and Urban & Regional Planning at Michigan State University, East Lansing, Michigan, USA. His principal research and practice interests are in planning intelligent development regional strategies and policies that seek to take advantage of the new realities and opportunities of the globalized networked information society. These dynamics are addressed in his most recent research that examines a new ongoing social entrepreneurship experiment that is under way on Fogo Island, Newfoundland as a model for rural development. His 2013 book is *Global Information Society: Technology, Knowledge and Mobility*, published by Rowman and Littlefield and co-authored with Mark Wilson and Aharon Kellerman.

Iain Deas is a Senior Lecturer in Planning and Environmental Management at the University of Manchester. He is co-director of the university's cross-disciplinary Centre for Urban Policy Studies. He has published widely on the politics of urban regeneration and the governance of territorial policy, including recent articles on post-politics and city-regions (in *Urban Studies*, 2014), policy actor networks and economic development agencies in England (*Local Economy*, 2013), and 'agglomeration boosterism' and regional policy (*Environment and Planning A*, 2014).

Peilei Fan is Associate Professor of Urban and Regional Planning at Michigan State University. Her research focuses on innovation and economic development in emerging economies and Asia's urban sustainability. She has served as a consultant/economist for United Nations University – World Institute for Development Economics Research (UNU-WIDER) and Asia Development Bank.

John Harrison is a Senior Lecturer in Human Geography at Loughborough University, UK, and an Associate Director of the Globalization and World Cities (GaWC) research network. His research examines how new, generally more networked urban and regional spaces, are being produced in globalization, focusing in particular on the implications for planning and governance. He has recently co-edited *Planning and Governance of Cities in Globalization* (Routledge, 2014), *Megaregions: Globalization's New Urban Form?* (Edward Elgar, 2014), and a special issue of *Urban Studies* on city-region governance. He is currently a co-editor of the journal *Regional Studies*.

Nicola Headlam is a post-doctoral researcher based within the Heseltine Institute for Public Policy and Practice at the University of Liverpool. With a professional background in regeneration and economic development, her research is about the relationships between neighbourhood networks and metropolitan co-ordination.

K. C. Ho is Associate Professor of Sociology at the National University of Singapore. Dr. Ho's research interests are in the political economy of cities, urban communities, and higher education. He is co-author and co-editor of *City-States in the Global Economy*, (Westview, 1997); *Service Industries, Cities and Development Trajectories in the Asia-Pacific* (Routledge, 2005); 'Globalization and Southeast Asian Capital Cities' (*Pacific Affairs*, 78(4), 2006); 'Capital Cities and their contested roles in the Life of Nations' (*CITY*, 13(1), 2009); *New Economic Spaces in Asian Cities* (Routledge, 2012); 'Globalising Higher Education and Cities in Asia and the Pacific' (*Asia Pacific Viewpoint*, 55(2), 2014).

Tom Hutton is Professor in the Centre for Human Settlements, School of Community & Regional Planning, Faculty of Applied Science at the University of British Columbia, Vancouver. His principal research interests are in the 'new economy'. Besides editing (or co-editing) special journal issues dealing with the new economy, his recent publications include: *The New Economy of the Inner City* (Routledge, 2008/2010); *Cities and the Cultural Economy* (Routledge, 2014) ; and *New Economic Spaces in Asian Cities: From Industrial Restructuring to the Cultural Turn* (Routledge, 2012; co-edited with Peter Daniels and K. C. Ho).

Stefan Krätke is Professor of Economic and Social Geography at the European University Viadrina in Frankfurt (Oder), Germany. His research focuses on comparative urban studies, the world city network, and the role of creative industries in urban development. He is author of *The Creative Capital of Cities. Interactive Knowledge Creation and the Urbanization Economies of Innovation* (Wiley-Blackwell, 2011), and has published articles in a range of international journals such as *Urban Studies, International Journal of Urban and Regional Research, Global Networks*, and *European Urban and Regional Studies*.

Danny MacKinnon is Professor of Regional Development and Governance in the Centre for Urban and Regional Development Studies (CURDS) at Newcastle University. His research focuses on the institutions and politics of urban and regional development and questions of urban and regional adaptation and change. He is the author or editor of four books and has published over 40 journal articles and book chapters since 2000. He is also an editor of the *Urban Studies* journal.

Ronan Paddison is Emeritus Professor of Geography at the University of Glasgow. His research interests focus on the political processes driving urban change and, in particular, under what conditions local participation can contribute to the making of more inclusive and democratic cities. Recent projects have included the role of community participation in the installation of public art, and the limitations to public participation in the post-political city. He is Managing Editor of *Urban Studies* and of *Space and Polity*.

Edgar Pieterse is holder of the South African Research Chair in Urban Policy. He is founding director of the African Centre for Cities (ACC) and is Professor in the School of Architecture, Planning and Geomatics, both at the University of Cape Town. He is co-founder and consulting editor for *Cityscapes* – an international biannual magazine on urbanism in the global south. His most recent co-edited books are: *Africa's Urban Revolution* (Zed, 2014); *Rogue Urbanism: Emergent African Cities* (Jacana, 2013); *African Cities Reader II: Mobility & Fixtures* (Chimurenga, 2011).

Mario Polèse is Professor at INRS (University of Quebec), Centre Urbanisation Culture Societé in Montreal and holds the Senior Canada Research Chair in Urban and Regional Studies. Books include: *The Wealth and Poverty of Regions* (University of Chicago Press, 2010); *Connecting Cities with Macroeconomic Concerns* (World Bank, 2003); *The Social Sustainability of Citie*s (University of Toronto Press, 2000). Mario Polèse writes regularly on issues of urban economics. He has held research and teaching positions in the U.S., Latin America, Switzerland, and France.

Ivan Turok is Deputy Executive Director at the Human Sciences Research Council in South Africa and Honorary Professor at the Universities of Glasgow and Cape Town. He is Editor-in-Chief of *Regional Studies*, a Board member of the Regional Studies Association, and an adviser to the United Nations, OECD, European Commission, African Development Bank and South African Government. He has authored over 150 academic papers on aspects of urban and regional development, labour markets, the green economy, resilient cities, urban transformation and national urban policies.

Marguerite van den Berg is an Assistant Professor of sociology at the University of Amsterdam, the Netherlands. She defended her dissertation 'Mothering the Post-Industrial City – Family and Gender in Urban Re-Generation' in 2013. For this dissertation, she researched parenting guidance policy practices in Rotterdam, the Netherlands for 14 months. Marguerite's work is positioned where urban studies, gender studies and sociologies of culture overlap. She has published on paternalism, sexualities, policy practices, urban revanchism, city marketing and genderfication.

Mark Whitehead is a Professor of Human Geography at Aberystwyth University. His research interests include the politics of sustainable development, urban geography and environmental citizenship. He is the author of several books including *Spaces of Sustainability: Geographical Perspectives on the Sustainable Society* (Routledge, 2006) and *State Science and the Skies: Governmentalities of the British Atmosphere* (Wiley-Blackwell, 2009). He is the Managing Editor of the journal *Environmental Values*.

Colin C. Williams is Professor of Public Policy in the Sheffield University Management School at the University of Sheffield in the United Kingdom. His research interests include the informal economy, work organization and the future of work, subjects on which he has published some 20 monographs and 300 journal articles over the past 25 years. He currently holds a four-year Marie Curie grant that investigates how to tackle the undeclared economy in Croatia, Bulgaria and Macedonia.

Mark Wilson is Professor of Urban and Regional Planning in the School of Planning, Design and Construction at Michigan State University. He also serves as Chair of the

International Geographical Union Commission on the Geography of Global Information Society. Research and teaching interests address urban and regional economic development, information technology, and mega events. Current projects include mega event planning for world's fairs, innovation and information technology access in Michigan, and the development of Massive Open Online Courses (MOOC).

Acknowledgements

The idea for this book – and its sister volume *Cities and Social Change* – owe much to the encouragement of Robert Rojek of SAGE. Besides planting the idea, Robert offered continuing assistance in helping to guide our initial thoughts on the structure and contents it should adopt. Fleshing out the contents and deciding on key authors was achieved between the two of us, initially in the convivial surroundings of English Bay in Vancouver and subsequently through numerous emails.

In multi-author volumes much is dependent on the contributors as well as the editors. We have enjoyed working with the contributors, appreciating their responsiveness to requests as to how chapters might be written and revised as well as in the patience they have shown in the production of the volume.

Ronan would particularly like to thank Tom for his never-ending enthusiasm for the project and for the ingenious ideas he is capable of producing to overcome the problems that typically arise in editing. He would also to thank the numerous colleagues that he discussed the proposal with in Glasgow and beyond.

Tom has greatly enjoyed this collaborative project, and thanks Ronan for the invitation to be a partner in thematic selection, recruitment of contributors, and manuscript editing. He would also like to extend his gratitude to the contributing authors who have succeeded in generating a wealth of new ideas and insights on economic change in cities (and, as a corollary, the role of cities in economic change). The result is a highly original book which should prove instructive in the quest to better understand increasingly complex problems of urbanization and urbanism among both advanced and transitional societies.

We owe a particular debt of gratitude to those at SAGE who helped to bring the book to fruition – to Keri Dickens for overseeing the process, to Katherine Haw for attending so professionally to the processes of copyediting and proofing and to Michael Ainsley for promoting and marketing the book.

Ronan Paddison, University of Glasgow
Tom Hutton, University of British Columbia

1

Introduction: Cities and Economic Change

Ronan Paddison and Tom Hutton

While the urban imaginary may often be expressed in social and symbolic terms, the variable fortunes of cities continue to be shaped largely by economic change. Issues concerning why cities exist in late capitalist societies, why urbanization accounts for more than half the world's population and why mega-cities, with populations of more than ten million, dwarfing earlier cities, have recently emerged is first and foremost rooted in their economic role. It may be that over the long durée cities exist (and have existed) to serve several functions, as the loci of control over a political territory, as (in Christallerian terms) 'central places' within regional markets, or more symbolically meeting social and cultural needs. Indeed, some cities, those which were to become the capital city or centres of religious pilgrimage, were to gain their pre-eminence, or at least their early growth, for reasons other than the economic. Yet, in pre-industrial societies, and much more emphatically following the onset of industrial capitalism in the global north, cities became the key sites through which economic growth and accumulation was to be focused.

The narrative of urban change, the growth and decline of cities, has been and remains, then, fundamentally intertwined with economic change, in effect the progression of capitalism, its dynamic quest for accumulation and the spatial ramifications of creative destruction, of growth and dislocation, to which this gives rise. These connections were apparent from the early onset of industrial capitalism – the rapid development of cities such as Manchester ('Cottonopolis') in the early phases of industrial capitalism in the UK were to be the harbinger of a trend that transformed – urbanized – the first industrial nations. For Engels (1844, 1969), as an early and perceptive observer of urban-industrial growth, it was the very rapidity of Manchester's growth, as well as its stark social inequalities, that was so striking. Industrial capitalism, allied to and spurred on by technological advances, was to unleash profound changes in the space economy in which cities were to play a pivotal role.

Dynamism has been an abiding trait of cities. The dynamic nature of cities and of the role economic change has played in underpinning urban change is immediately apparent from a comparison of the configuration of urban development in the early twenty-first century with its counterpart just one or two generations earlier. In many of the early industrial nations of the global north those cities and urbanized regions that had been prime actors in the development of industrial capitalism were being peripheralized in the new spatial fixes of late capitalism. This was to become reflected at different spatial scales, inter-regionally as well as intra-metropolitan. In the US the shift towards the sunbelt cities and the emergence of rustbelt cities (Storper, 2013) was matched by similar developments in Germany and the UK, albeit at a different scale. Further, new industries have sought different locations within metropolitan areas, contributing to the development of edge cities and challenging the economic logic of the old industrial districts. Added to these shifts in the global north were those linked to the deepening processes of capitalist globalization, the emergence of new economies in the global south in which both the scale and speed of urban growth has been trans-formative. In the space of little more than 20 years, for example, Shenzen, targeted early on in China's endorsement of economic liberalization, was to grow from less than one million to over ten million, and has spectacularly transitioned from a regional territory of crude manufacturing to a place of advanced services, finance and cultural experience, shaping a distinctive identity within the urban systems of East Asia.

Where the dynamism of capitalist development is so graphically captured by the phrase 'creative destruction', its corollary in urban terms is matched by the unevenness of urban development and the unfolding processes of urban growth and decline. Understanding these shifts – why cities grow and become economic successes, why some grow more than others, why some cities experience economic decline – are key questions not just for urban scholars but increasingly for urban policy professionals, and ones which have spawned considerable debate. Both growth and decline bring their own problems of governance, of shifts in the labour market, of social change yet, perhaps arguably, it is the dislocations that follow from capital mobility – and in par-ticular the devalorization of space – that are the more problematic and have become the subject of so much policy attention. Reversing the processes of decline has become a policy industry in its own right, frequently drawing on practice developed in other cities and emphasizing the mobilities that increasingly define how cities are being regenerated. In other cases it is the *revalorization* of space which creates or exacerbates policy challenges, as seen in the sequences of property market inflation, social upgrad-ing and dislocations common within the central and inner city areas of cities such as London, Barcelona and Chicago.

These arguments may resonate with the experience of cities in the global north yet in fundamental ways may have less relevance to urban development taking place in the global south. In the currently most rapidly urbanizing region in the world, Africa, the rapid growth of cities is only loosely connected with economic development. Rather, as Mike Davis (2006) graphically portrayed in *Planet of Slums*, African cities are defined by their poverty and squalour, their crumbling public services, as places of despair rather than they are of hope. Such a view has been challenged, not least by those who have sought to unravel the intricate and ingenious ways in which infor-malization is used to ensure urban survival in cities that are otherwise dysfunctional (Simone, 2010). Further, where for some writers on African cities their rapid develop-ment is linked to the production of poverty (Turok, 2014), the encouragement of urban development precisely because of its promise in encouraging economic growth is advocated as a key policy the state should adopt (World Bank, 2009).

What these debates demonstrate is that even an argument as fundamental as to whether urban growth can be necessarily linked to economic growth may not be as clear cut as it might appear and can become contested. In turn, such doubts reflect the diversity of cities and the growing recognition amongst contemporary urban theorists that extrapolating the experience of cities – those in the key economies of the global north, for example – to elsewhere is questionable. The uniqueness of cities challenges how we can generalize the economic processes underlying their growth, as well as their decline. This is not to deny that there are powerful forces at play – deepening globalization and the harnessing of neoliberal policy tools to foster how cities grow, the transnational mobility and adoption of 'universal' policy tropes, for example – that appear to have universalizing effects on the paths urban growth in otherwise different economies is taking. Rather, there is growing awareness that how such developments influence how urban economies unfold needs to be contextualized and take account of the diverse typology of cities. In the remaining part of this introductory chapter we offer some basic economic arguments linked to the growth of cities before turning in the final section to outline the rationale and structure of this volume.

CITIES AS ECONOMIC SPACES

Any appreciation of the economic processes linked to the city will rapidly encounter a number of issues which stem from the complexities of the urban economy. Firstly, there are problems with defining the nature of an urban economy and what factors are important in stimulating the economic growth of the city. These definitional problems are compounded by epistemological considerations, the different emphases given to economic explanations by different disciplines and theories. Economists, economic geographers, economic historians, not to mention political economists will emphasize different processes that underpin the city's economic growth and change. Neo-classical explanations have sought to identify the economic advantages of the city. Marxist explanations, challenging neo-classical arguments, have shown how urban development has been linked to the accumulation of capital and the exploitation of labour. Each tradition has generated its own ideas on urban economies which themselves are often contested. Even the basic connection made between urban and economic growth, as we have suggested earlier, can be contested, reflecting the diversity of cities and their economic trajectories. Finally, both cities and their economies are dynamic, further challenging our ability to understand their nature and the effect of wider contextual changes on their performance. Small wonder, then, that our understanding of the urban economy is diverse in the disciplinary traditions from which it draws, frequently the subject of heated debate and evolving in an attempt to come to grips with its dynamic nature.

This dynamism, the changing fortunes of cities in recent decades – deindustrialized and new industrial spaces – has forced us to rethink our ideas on how to explain the economic growth of cities. In some cases the conceptual repositioning has had

to be radical with a shift in emphasis towards supply-side from demand-side explanations. An influential, essentially simple, explanation of urban economic growth
from the past and one which continues to hold currency, has been the idea that to
grow, cities need to be able to export tradeable goods. Cities able to produce such
goods based on some comparative advantage may in turn be able to harness competitive advantage which, in turn, will underwrite the ability of the city to trade
successfully. But what constitute tradeable goods? In the basic/non-basic representation of urban economic growth, basic industries were those on which export was
based, whose significance to the economy was expressable in terms of the employment associated with the sector. The sector would need supporting through a range
of non-basic activities, including banking, construction activities, public services,
cultural facilities, the employment which was generated by the needs of the basic
sector. Expressed as a ratio the model was seductive for its simplicity – cities able
to compete successfully through exporting tradeable goods would in turn generate
further growth which could be expressed through the changing profile of employment. The model had its obvious drawbacks, not least the emphasis that it gave to
demand-side explanations, over-looking key considerations of human capital and
the soft assets of cities, as well as the under-accounting of the export potential of
services, notably intermediate services, as disclosed in the work of Peter Daniels,
Saskia Sassen and others. Further, the calibration of the model gave rise to definitional problems on the distinction between what constituted basic and non-basic
activities. Yet, such problems were rarely to stretch to the inclusion of, for example,
cultural amenities as being tradeable. In other words, activities which current orthodoxy, urban policy in particular, singles out as significant as tradeable goods were
considered in a wholly different light in earlier theories used to explain urban economic growth.

If these shifts in our ideas of the explanations of urban economic growth reflect the
wider shifts in the contexts in which cities are located over half a century later, con-
tinuities in the ideas used to explain why cities play such a fundamental role to economic growth are apparent and, particularly for those championing the city in the
present phase of economic restructuring (Glaeser, 2011), these ideas are being revisited
and re-invested with importance. Many of these ideas centre on the economic advantages associated with the city drawing from neo-classical economics.

Cities, then, as spaces in which economic activities become clustered are able to
harness agglomeration economies (Baldwin and Martin, 2004; Storper, 2013) in
which the advantages of proximity for firms and labour as well as for consumers
outweigh the disadvantages created by concentration and linked to urban congestion
(Duranton and Puga, 2004). For firms it is not just that by virtue of being in a city
demand may be bigger, but that they are able to take advantage of the transport
advantages cities offer. As transport hubs, cities are able to offer lower transport costs;
allied to historical trends in falling transport costs their effect, more evidently in the
advanced nations at least over the longer term, has been to facilitate economies of
scale in production, extending the trading hinterlands of cities and further concentrating economic activities. Such gains are uneven, smaller cities tending to be advantaged
less than larger cities.

The advantages of agglomeration, and their differential impact between cities, become spelt out in other ways. Critically, cities become, by virtue of their high densities and its propinquities, centres of knowledge circulation, of innovation and of networking. Besides helping to raise productivity in existing industries, their contribution is to foster specialization. Combined with other advantages – a shared and skilled labour pool, the fostering of backward and forward linkages between local firms – the spillovers of knowledge and information on a localized basis is linked to the appearance of industrial clusters. Such factors were used by Alfred Marshall (1920) to explain the emergence of regional clusters in the 'old industrial districts' of the global north. The re-emergence of clusters in the post-Fordist economy – the development of high technology clusters as well as of those linked to the new cultural economy – continues to emphasize the benefits of agglomeration through the operation of specific processes including entrepreneurship, knowledge spillovers, networking and innovation.

As is widely recognized, alongside these economic benefits resulting from spatial clustering, agglomeration imposes costs – negative externalities which challenge the productivity of cities as an economic space. Typically these include the ability of infrastructural capacity to meet the growing demands placed on it, congestion costs, rising land and house prices, air pollution, social inequalities and social order including crime. Some may be addressed through technological advances or policy initiatives. The adoption of underground systems of circulation – with London's pioneering Underground a full century and a half ago as progenitor – was an early initiative adopted in major cities in the global north in the nineteenth century aimed at reducing congestion which had already become a major brake on the ease of movement within the city. Increasing levels of motorization exacerbate other externalities, notably air pollution, congestion and pollution (as in China, where car-ownership is rising rapidly); the latter being acknowledged as leading to significant health problems in the cities.

Other negative externalities emphasize the social consequences of urban development and the contradictions arising from continued growth. Contemporary cities are characterized by deepening social inequalities, a trend which is neither novel nor unexpected, but which is re-emerging as a profound outcome of urban economic growth. Social inequality was a hallmark of early urban-industrial development just as it has become in contemporary cities. Some of these inequ(ali)ties arise simply from urban growth. Thus, growth will tend to lead to rises in land rents with direct consequences on housing costs and, in turn, on housing affordability. Besides the equity problems raised by housing affordability, the lack of ensuring the supply of affordable housing opportunities poses a challenge for the planning of cities in which globalization has contributed to their economic resurgence and potentially to their continued economic vitality (see, for example the Introduction by Alain Bertraud (2013) to the 10th Annual Demographia International Housing Affordability Survey, 2014).

The recitation of the benefits and disbenefits linked to agglomeration obscures the reality that significant research gaps exist in our understanding of the urban economy and that the relative importance linked to the factors linked to urban economic growth is often contested. Further, what evidence base there is tends to be drawn from the experience of cities in the global north and from a select number of major southern cities, particularly those that have attained global status. If we understand the key factors in explaining *why* cities function as key economic spaces, *how* this unfolds – the processes at play – is less well understood. Why have some cities, as opposed to others, been able to (re)build their economies more successfully? What factors are able to foster growth? These typify the questions that remain the subject of considerable academic, and policy, debate. Added to these are questions linked to an understanding of the implications of globalization and neoliberalism in late capitalism including the uneven nature of urban growth, the role of capital mobility in the global arena opening up new centres of production able to tap into cheap labour, the impact of speculative capital particularly in processes of financialization, the restructuring of labour markets, and the changing configuration of state–market relations.

We can also cite as relevant to the agglomeration discourse changes in the traditional structure of the 'firm' as the basic unit of the urban economy, exemplified in Gernot Grabher's work (2002a, 2002b) on fluid 'project ecologies' in creative industries such as advertising. In fields such as architecture, urban design and consultancy, 'practice' often encompasses consortia which extend beyond the bounds of specific 'place'. Then, there are questions concerning the association between traditional urban agglomeration economies and the burgeoning digital economy, including sales and distribution (Amazon, eBay) and social networking (Google, Facebook, Twitter) as well as production (Microsoft, Apple, Nokia). *Prima facie* digital technologies might appear to reduce the urban advantage of agglomeration, as sourcing, recruitment and marketing are increasingly conducted on a global scale. But as we saw in the earlier phases of telecommunications innovation, where some prognosticators envisioned the 'death of distance' and the marginalization of 'place', cities such as San Francisco, Seattle, Singapore and Munich have if anything experienced growth in the most advanced areas of technological research, innovation and associated production.

As much as more critical analyses of contemporary urban restructuring has been able to unravel its 'darker side', not least the multiple inequ(al)ities both socio-economic and political with which its unfolding can be linked, revitalizing the urban economy has become a key policy concern under neoliberalism. The contribution cities can (and often do) make to the national economy is considered reason enough to the goal of ensuring and enhancing their competitive position (see, for example, Centre for Cities, 2014). Its achievement has been sought through an expanding battery of projects often market-inspired including property-led development, city marketing and branding, the fostering of entrepreneurialism and of flexible labour markets.

It is a quest that has spawned a litany of policy tropes that seek to spell out the conditions under which urban economic development can be fostered. Some – Richard Florida's (2002) ideas on the significance of ensuring cities are attractive to the new creative classes is certainly one such trope – have attained 'policy orthodoxy' in their global adoption, in spite of the critical analysis they have attracted, including, notably, the deep critiques of Ann Markusen (2006), Allen Scott (2008) and more recently Stefan Krätke (2011) which have served to seriously undermine both the diagnostic and prescriptive bases of the creative class concept. But to Florida can be added 'creative cities' (Landry, 2008; G. Evans, 2009; Hietala and Clark, 2013), 'cultural regeneration' (Paddison and Miles (2007), the role of mega-events in branding and other policy 'solutions' that are championed as the means of reinstating or enhancing the economic position of cities. Urban policy itself has become transnational in its adoption to the point that particular initiatives – the 'Bilbao effect' (Plaza, 1999; McNeill, 2009) following the opening of the iconic Guggenheim museum in what was an old industrial city – have been emulated by other cities eager to harness the perceived impacts of such innovation. The reality is that many have been the subject of critical analysis where their adoption glosses over their equity implications, Jamie Peck's critique (2005) of Florida for instance, or their effects in crowding out developments that might have otherwise occurred had policy intervention not been so focused. Policy experimentation has emerged as a dynamic element of urban neoliberal governance; the appeal of policy tropes as powerful stimulants to how to structure urban economic policy is undeniable. That said, though, policy 'experimentation' increasingly takes the form of a superficial mimicry of generic 'best practice', rather than true 'innovation' derived from a serious engagement with cities and communities. Critical aspects of local-regional contingency, including both the specific potentials (and problems) of place, as well as local values, needs and aspirations, are often glossed over in the pursuit of what Jamie Peck calls 'fast policies' and the regressive syndrome of 'policy mobility'.

A PATH THROUGH THIS VOLUME

Our intention in this volume is to explore the changing nature of the urban economy in an empirically grounded and theoretically informed discussion. Indisputably, the world in which the analysis is undertaken is one of profound change; abbreviated, it is closely associated with deepening globalization, the emergent hegemony of neoliberalism as the means of steering economic growth, the effects of which are translated through the changing economic configuration of cities and the development of new technologies that underwrite shifting geographies of production and the creation of novel industries. Whether or not the claims made by those championing the city are adopted, the last two decades have been witness to rapid economic restructuring in which cities have played a major role defying the pessimistic assumptions surrounding the future of cities in the early stages of the current round of globalization and the predicted impacts of new technologies. This final section outlines the structure of the book and provides a brief rationale for the essays.

The volume is divided into three parts, the first detailing key processes linked to the changing nature of the urban economy, following which we unravel the governance frameworks through which city economies are being steered. In the final section we offer certain reflections on change, the restated role and positioning of place as a critical factor underwriting how shifts in the urban economy are emergent at different spatial scales and a backwards gaze to the multiple ideas and arguments raised by authors.

Making an initial cut into the processes underpinning urban change courts the risk of suggesting a priority which may be more apparent than real. In opening with the role of technological innovation there is the risk of explaining change through technological determinism. In opening through the role of technology neither argument is intended. Even so, the influence of technological advance and urban change, both long term and at the current moment, is undeniable. Basing himself on the role of technology and using Toffler's wave explanation of the transformation of American society, Ruchelman (2007) identified three waves of urban development and change, pre-industrial to industrial and post-industrial. Each underpinned successive waves in the development of capitalism and was marked by profound changes in the forms of urban development and economy. In a provocative discussion, Peter Hall (1988) sought to show that successive technological innovations could be linked to long-term (Kondratiev) cycles of growth and decline in industrial capitalism and the changing economic geographies of production – based on the case of the UK he was able to argue that key technological advances had catalysed new economic activities, helped stimulate a new phase of economic growth and that this had been contributory to the creation of a new spatial fix.

The harnessing of new technologies has multiple consequences for the (urban) economy, both in production and for the labour market. Formulating their discussion around the developments of new ICTs, Corey, Wilson and Fan, in Chapter 2, develop its implications for the urban economy against the backdrop of globalization, the premise of which is that these new technologies underpin knowledge and its potential usage in developing new economies.

The influences of technological advance, in playing itself out in different aspects of urban economic restructuring, is contributory to the contemporary rescaling of cities at the supra-national as well as sub-national scales. Of course, neither rescaling, nor its close ally globalization, are new, though a defining feature of contemporary globalization, again as in the past, is its ongoing ability to favour particular cities within the world economy. Fundamentally too, the process of urban rescaling is rooted in the search by capital for more favourable conditions for accumulation within which the harnessing of new technological capacity can become a powerful means through which to achieve competitive advantage (see Chapter 3). What is salutary here is not just the selectivity of globalization to favour particular cities but the speed of change, reflected in turn by the emergence of mega-cities. To the three world cities identified by Sassen (1991) (New York, London and Tokyo), the last two decades has witnessed the growth of other global cities particularly in Asia, while recent growth in economies such as Turkey harbour the emergence of a new rung of global cities in the international urban hierarchy.

Economic change is rooted in the development of new economies and of new economic spaces. The new urban economy is associated with a diverse of activities – cultural, media, bio-engineering and high-tech – the common denominator of which is their dependence on knowledge networks and, often, the advantages of propinquity. Their geographical imprint, as Stefan Krätke shows in Chapter 4, has resulted in the production of new economic spaces at the intra-metropolitan scale, including cultural quarters and edge industrial developments. The emergence of these new economic activities represents the latest stage in the ongoing role creativity has had in the stimulation of urban growth. For Peter Hall in his pioneering work *Cities in Civilisation: Culture, Innovation and Urban Order* (1998), creativity, either cultural or artistic, had underwritten the growth of cities from medieval Florence through to late twentieth-century

Tokyo. Arguably, what distinguishes the adoption of culture in the contemporary city, compared to its historical counterpart, is that it is not only a reflection of the city's wealth and status but has become more directly employed as the means of generating new economic growth in its own right.

The advent of the new economy and of new economic spaces represents a new spatial fix around which accumulation can be fostered. Its corollary is the abandonment of old economic spaces. Ivan Turok takes up the theme of the unevenness of capitalist economic growth in Chapter 5, looking at redundant and marginalized spaces. The symptoms are familiar, whether in Cleveland, Glasgow or industrial sites in the post-Socialist economies, and have become a key locus for urban policy. Marginalized spaces, as Turok shows in the case of the Thames Gateway project, can also become the focus of economic regeneration, aided admittedly by the proximity of a burgeoning world city. Yet the redundancy or marginalization of cities and of city spaces, particularly through rescaling processes, remains a powerful force linked to the changing fortunes of cities.

The remaining two chapters in the first part of the book look at how economic restructuring has become linked to the reshaping of labour markets, and the persistence and development of informal and alternative economies. Both reflect how the urban economy intersects with the social structure (and life) of cities. The reshaping of the labour market has been profound, whether through new work and employment shifts, through demographic changes including migration, both nationally and across national boundaries. Some of these shifts have become well-established – the restructuring and increasing polarization of the labour force, its casualisation, and its deepening inequalities. Nor are there signs that the restructuring of the labour force has reached an 'end point' – precarity, more a characteristic of employment among the less and unskilled, is becoming a growing feature of professional middle-class employment in the advanced economies following ongoing processes of corporate restructuring, as elucidated in Chapter 6 on 'Splintering Labour Markets' by Danny MacKinnon. In the global south the precariousness of urban employment has been an enduring feature, with urban survival for the majority in cities in Africa being dependent on informal activity. Yet, from an initial understanding of the informal sector that emphasized its negative features (by comparison with employment in the formal sector), there has been a growing recognition not just of the role of the informal sector – to retail trading, for instance – but for the opportunities it creates for entrepreneurial initiative. Further, rather than being or becoming residual, as Colin Williams shows in Chapter 7, informal employment is both a persistent and important element of the urban economy which is by no means confined to the global south or to transitional economies.

Few if any of these processes linked to urban economic restructuring are not, to a greater or lesser degree, influenced by the actions of the state. In the second part of the volume we focus on the multiple ways in which the state has become, and is, deeply enmeshed with steering the urban economy. The role is in some ways ironic: that with the adoption of neoliberalism as the driving force underpinning globalization and economic restructuring, and given as an ideology its commitment is to ensuring the play of market forces in restructuring, that the state should be so active. Whether as facilitator, (de)regulator, as partner with the private sector, and in spite of the predictions of the hyper-globalists, the state is (often pro-)active in influencing the trajectories of the urban economy.

In a seminal paper Harvey (1989a) mapped out the rationale for and techniques of entrepreneurial urban governance. As a new and increasingly adopted style of govern-ance it centred on the ambitions of city governments, acting with an enhanced private sector and often involving para-state development agencies, to attract mobile capital, thereby bolstering the local economy and raising the competitive position. In some advanced economies, neoliberalism had already become entrenched in urban policy and governance by the early 1980s. By the turn of the century the shift had become so entrenched that Harvey (2005) was able to describe it in hegemonic terms and as hav-ing 'pervasive effects on ways of thought to the point where it has become incorporated into the common-sense way many of us interpret, live in and understand the world' (p. 3). The argument provides the backdrop for Iain Deas and Nicola Headlam's discussion in Chapter 8 of contemporary urban governance in a post-political age.

Steering the urban economy within the tenets of neoliberalism has been achieved through an expanding repertoire of models and techniques. Many have, through emulation, become part of policy orthodoxy – waterfront regeneration, the fostering of gentrification and the adoption of city marketing to name a few, comprising what Russell Prince describes as 'policy assemblages'. Such techniques have the immediate aim of ensuring cities enhance or revive their competitive position, although experi-ence suggests that 'quick fixes' that ignore local needs and contingency rarely succeed. But they also provide the means of cities meeting more fundamental objectives, the harnessing of resilience, the reimaging of the city, of addressing inclusivity and envi-ronmental sustainability – though how their adoption has been broached by cities varies, each has become instrumental to the contemporary understanding of how the urban economy should be steered.

Applied to the city the notion of resilience may be a relatively new entrant to the policy lexicon, but in its aim of spelling out why and how the urban economies of some cities rather than others are able to withstand shocks, the reasons for its appeal are obvious. Mario Polèse (in Chapter 9) identifies two types of resilience, the ability to survive shocks and to not only survive but also change in the face of shocks – spelt out through the experience of different cities, the analysis provides insight as to what makes for the successful urban economy.

Resilience is one of a number of discourses through which steering the urban economy is rationalized. In Chapter 10 Marguerite van den Berg explores why and how imagineering the city is a pervasive and evolving strategy of urban neoliberalism. The need to reimage the city may be a greater priority for some cities in particular – Rotterdam rather than Amsterdam, Pittsburgh rather than San Francisco – yet the reality is that imagineering has become universalized in its policy adoption although as van den Berg demonstrates the selectivity exercised by many local governments occludes harsh social realities of inequality and marginalization. Inclusivity, too, as Edgar Pieterse shows, as an assault on the inequalities that characterize urban growth, South and North, has become a key policy discourse. Finally, in Chapter 12, Mark Whitehead explores the opportunities and tensions surrounding urban economic development and environmental sustainability.

In the final section of the volume we offer some reflections. K. C. Ho begins Chapter 13 with an 'old question' – Does place matter? – but specifically in relation to production. The question has a long pedigree but is worth revisiting if only because of the early, now refuted, assumption that new technologies had overcome geography. The reality is that context continues to be important to the new economic geographies of production, but it does so in sufficiently different ways that a revisiting of its theorization, as well as a gaze across disciplinary boundaries as to how place is conceptualized, is warranted. The final chapter by Tom Hutton provides a synthesis of the volume, as well as conjecture on the shape of emergent urban development trajectories, drawing on the major arguments advanced by our contributing authors, and an interrogation of relationships between urban growth and economic change over the long durée as well as within cities of the contemporary world.

Our aim in this volume is to unravel the connections between cities and contemporary change. It is comprehensive rather than exhaustive in its scope. Being an edited volume, it is important to draw attention to the threads that run through the book. Essentially these are encapsulated in the subtitle of the text, 'Restructuring and dislocation in the global metropolis'. Both major sections highlighted in the volume, the processes underpinning urban economic change, and the steering mechanisms linked to it, together with the reflective comments concluding the text, address how urban economies in the global south and north are undergoing rapid change. Deepening globalization, the ratcheting of urban neoliberalism and of accelerating competition between cities challenge our ability to come to terms with the dynamism that underpins contemporary urban economic change.

SECTION 1

PROCESSES

2

Cities, Technologies and Economic Change

Kenneth E. Corey, Mark I. Wilson and Peilei Fan

Technologies have been instrumental in the formation and growth of cities since the dawn of urbanization (Childe, 1950). 'Technologies' are a wide-ranging, nearly all-encompassing concept that can span such innovations as the plow, irrigation, writing, record keeping, and the transmission of information through time and space to the point today whereby electronic innovations permit personal and targeted interactive networking and the ability to tap into seemingly infinite sources of information. This chapter examines some of the principal developmental relationships of these new information and communications technologies (ICTs) to city-regions and resultant economic change in the context of today's globalized economy. Often, technologies, especially material infrastructure, and information technologies (IT), are conceived as development ends in their own right. However, ICTs should be seen as means to the more strategic ends of creating innovative knowledge for the marketplace and the societal advancement of Intelligent Development of places, city-regions and national territories.

Technological innovation is a critical instrument for changing places. The basic thesis of this chapter is that knowledge can be used by stakeholders to take informed action and influence decision-making to improve the development of places – especially city-regions where most people live and work today. Such development, to be intelligent and effective, requires a working understanding of the roles and impacts that contemporary information and communications technologies have had and can have.

In order to plant the seeds of mobilization for the practice of intelligent urban regional development, five substantive points are discussed: (1) technopoles; (2) deepening of urban technological change; (3) competitive advantage; (4) resulting new urban spaces; and (5) impacts on urban labour markets. The chapter concludes by discussing some over-arching issues about technology-based urban development. Thereby, the reader is challenged to use the understandings that have been gathered from the chapter to make informed and on-going contributions to the improvement of their own city-region's future development and to an improved civic society.

The chapter is framed and referenced with the intent that readers, students and teachers might derive knowledge and follow a pedagogic strategy to learn the content and issues raised in this discourse; the goal is for readers to devise, perfect and practise their own self-designed learning strategy for customizing and selective application. Given the limitations of space, the Asia-Pacific region of the global economy is used as a principal touchstone and empirical source for grounding the discussion. In the Asia-Pacific, the developed global north would include Japan, Korea, Macau, Hong Kong, Taiwan, Singapore, Malaysia, Australia and New Zealand, while the emerging global south would include all remaining countries, such as India, China, Indonesia and others. The Reference section includes a deep selection of resources that facilitate readers to emulate the chapter's approach for analyzing the urban, technological and economic relationships within and across other major regions of the global economy. Refer to the box on 'Pedagogy and Learning' below.

Pedagogy and Learning

For the learner, the new economy has yet another critical meaning; we are in a globalized information society. This also brings the challenge of path dependence. The legacies of the old economy's muscular mindset shape dated interpretations and expectations, and require us to revisit concepts and issues in light of the new economy. Whether teaching, learning, or researching cities, technology and economic change today, it should be remembered that these subjects and relationships are complex and highly dynamic. Therefore, *it helps to have a framework to impose some working conceptual order*. For example, the ALERT Model and the concept of comprehensive Intelligent Development strategy are suggested as organizing frameworks for aiding understanding and the taking of informed collective civic action (Corey and Wilson, 2006; Wilson and Corey, 2008). An additional useful approach is to select theory-driven organizing strategies such as growth poles, or life-cycle concepts, clusters, or technopoles as means to understand complex empirical realities and in the process be positioned to take informed action as a result of improved understanding (Plummer and Taylor, 2001a, 2001b).

One might design such a self-learning and or pedagogic process first by selecting a city-region as a *benchmark* and *'good'* practice against which comparisons might be made (Vettoretto, 2009; Corey and Wilson, 2010; Ward, 2010). Another approach could be via a manageable set of criteria such as per capita income or internet penetration per 100 population (Table 2.3) across the Asia-Pacific. These can serve as basic organizing means for identifying and learning about socio-economic development issues, places, their spatial organization and changing relationships across a range of development from developed global north economies to emerging global south economies and selected gradations in between.

To begin an exploration analogous to the research that produced this chapter, one might study data and narratives on the global knowledge economy and global information society as a whole for context and then drill down into such country aggregations as Latin America, the Middle East and North Africa, Sub-Saharan Africa and parts of the less technologically developed countries of Asia; such studies will provide insights into the global south. The global north, at varying levels of technological development, might be studied similarly by exploring Western Europe, North American data and narratives; Eastern Europe and Russia will reveal different levels of technology-based development measures. For data (Table 2.3) and analysis, see: Taylor and Walker, 2004; World Bank, 2006; Huggins et al., 2008; Foster and Briceno-Garmendia, 2010; International Telecommunications Union, 2010; Internet World Stats, 2010; Taylor, 2010; and World Bank, 2010. For selective narratives, see Hall and Pain, 2006 for some city-regions of Western Europe; for the tropical internet, see Warf, 2007; for the Arab internet, see Warf and Vincent, 2007; for Australia, see Plummer and Taylor, 2001b; West, 2001; Yigitcanlar et al., 2008.

CITY-REGIONS AS CENTRES OF TECHNOLOGICAL INNOVATION

The reasons for exploring these relationships are: (1) to *understand* the dynamics that underlie informational technologies and their interaction with the development of city-regions; and (2) to engage in informed decision-making and planned *actions* to contribute to a more civil society. As citizens of an increasingly interdependent global economy and fragile global environment, each of us has a responsibility to contribute to the common good.

Today, half of the world's population lives in cities (Seetharam and Yuen, 2010). Urban places have been dominant as locations where information-based technologies, intelligence and knowledge have been combined to generate economic growth that has been characterized as the *new economy*. William Beyers has offered thoughtful analyses on defining the new economy (Beyers, 2002), which he concludes is one with: (1) relatively high multi-factor productivity growth; (2) relatively high levels of capital investment in information technologies; and (3) structural changes in production and consumption of ICT (Beyers, 2008).

The term 'city-region' is used here as a reminder that we are concerned with cities, the functionally connected areas and places nearby, and the distant locations linked remotely by networked information technologies. This more encompassing concept of the city-region better represents the 'city' realities of today's highly connected and layered global knowledge economy and network society.

These new-economy dynamics have produced complexities that are understood more effectively when *conceptual frameworks* are used for organizing and analyzing urban dynamics. For example, in the British framework for sustainable communities:

> City-Regions are the enlarged territories from which core urban areas draw people for work and services such as shopping, education, health, leisure and entertainment. The city-regional scale also plays a significant role for business in organizing supply chains and accessing producer services. The City-Region is therefore an important *functional* entity. (Office of the Deputy Prime Minister, 2006)

City-regions also have been used by scholars to identify issues and possible implications for local development as a result of the new-economy forces of globalization (Scott, 2001b). In the context of economic globalization, the city-region is the principal working local unit of observation.

THE TECHNOPOLE THESIS

In 1994, Manuel Castells and Sir Peter Hall published their book, *Technopoles of the World: The Making of 21st Century Industrial Complexes*. This timeframe coincided with the widespread adoption and dissemination of the internet. It also was an ideal time for researchers to assess the shift from traditional manufacturing production to more high-technology production of not only goods but also advanced services (compare Scott, 1993; Hutton, 2004; Daniels et al., 2005). *High-technology* production may be defined as having significant investment in research and development (R&D) related occupations and employment, as well as significant investment in the creation and production of new technologies, new products and new kinds of services (Corey and Wilson, 2006: 202–03). Conferring priority on such innovation is intended to transform production processes and result in higher economic productivity, greater profit, wealth creation and enhanced competitiveness for the participating stakeholders, investors and the place and country hosting these clusters of such science and technology (S&T) based and R&D functions.

The French and Japanese have framed such hosting environments for technology-facilitated R&D as 'technopoles'. Castells and Hall adopted the term and the concept of technopole to organize and focus their research and findings, which they portray as the:

> social, institutional, economic, and territorial structures that create the conditions for the continuous generation of synergy and its investment in a process of production that results from this very synergistic capacity, both for the units of production that are part of the milieu and for the milieu as a whole. (Castells and Hall, 1994: 9)

Castells and Hall used four empirical classifications for technopoles: (1) '*industrial complexes* of high-technology firms that are built on the basis of innovative milieu. These complexes, linking R&D and manufacturing, are the true command centers of the new industrial space' (Castells and Hall, 1994: 10). Examples include Silicon Valley, California and Route 128 in the Boston region; (2) *Science cities* are complexes not necessarily co-located and directly connected to informing manufacturing innovation. Tsukuba, Japan is an example; (3) *Technology parks* and science parks that seek to attract high-technology manufacturing firms to city-region space set aside and planned specifically for such development, such as Sophia-Antipolis in southern France; and (4) The case of *an entire national-scale developmental programme of technopoles planned for Japan*. The purpose of Japan's Technopolis Program was to de-concentrate Tokyo-region development and in turn to enhance development of other targeted regions (Malecki, 1997: 265–6). Additionally, (5) Castells and Hall discovered that beyond the spontaneous and planned technopoles, they concluded that '*the great metropolitan areas of the industrialized world*' should be studied for their innovative milieux and role as advanced manufacturing centres; such as Tokyo, Paris and London (1994: 11, italics added).

The Asia-Pacific region is already heavily urban, containing most of the world's largest urban regions. Asia includes 63% of the world's urban population and 253 major metropolitan areas (Seetharam and Yuen, 2010). Much of global urban growth in the future will be in Asia. The emerging economies of population and areal giants China and India in particular will generate significant urban growth. By 2030, China will be 65% urban, bringing up issues of housing, quality of life, and sustainability (UN-Habitat, 2010b).

Table 2.1   Major technology policy initiatives in China since the reform

Year	Policy initiative
1978	First National Science Congress, held on 18 March
1982	Key Technologies Research and Development Program
1985	Decision on the Reform of the Science and Technology System, issued after the National Working Conference of Science and Technology
1986	High-Tech Research and Development Program (Program 863)
1988	Torch Program
1990	First group of 27 high-tech parks set up
1991	The first high-tech park (Zhongguancun High-Tech Park) established
1993	Technology Progress Law enacted
1995	Decision on Accelerating Science and Technology (S&T) Development announced by the State Council
1995	211 Program to construct 100 top universities in the 21st century
1996	Technology Transfer Law enacted
1997	National Program for Priority Basic Research and Development (Program 973)
1998	Knowledge Innovation Program (1998–2010) to improve the scientific performance of the Chinese Academy of Sciences and build it into China's pre-eminent S&T centre for innovation capability
1999	Decision on Enhancing Technology Innovation, High-Tech Development and Industrialization issued
2006	Medium- and Long-Term National Plan (MLTP) for Science and Technology (S&T) Development 2006–2020 to promote a S&T development strategy and enhance innovation capacity. Selective development is to occur in energy, water resources, environmental protection, innovation in information technology, new materials, advanced manufacturing technology, and bio-technology
2006	The 11th Five-Year Plan on Western Region Development
2006	National S&T Development Plan for the 11th Five-Year Period (2006–2010)
2008	China Association for Small & Medium Commercial Enterprises to enhance innovation capacity and market competitiveness of domestic firms
2008	The Thousand Talents Program to connect domestic scientists with global first-class researchers by bringing to China overseas expatriates
2008	Framework for Development and Reform Planning for the Pearl River Delta Region (2008–2020)
2011	The 12th Five-Year Plan (2011–2016) will have many technology, science and knowledge initiatives that build on and extend current technology policies

Source: Summarized by the authors; see Fan and Wan (2008: 11); and CORDIS (no date)

China, India and other Asia-Pacific places can illustrate the dynamics and relationships of the technopole (Phillips and Yeung, 2003; Koh et al., 2005; and Walcott and Heitzman, 2006). To stimulate science and technology-facilitated and knowledge-based economic growth for the future, *research and development-centred policies* (see Table 2.1) have been planned and implemented in numerous locations across China. One of these important programmes was the early development of technopoles in the forms of high-technology zones and high-technology parks. What are some of the key lessons to be taken from these first-generation Chinese technopoles?

In the late 1980s, 52 High and New Technology Industry Development Zones were established throughout China. Researchers found that these technopoles or 'the high-tech zones in coastal provinces, perform only slightly better than those in interior provinces' (Wang et al., 1998: 293). It was found that interior provincial capitals can compete with coastal cities in the development of high technology industries. *Distinct Chinese characteristics* were attributed to this counter-intuitive finding. Because of their political status, provincial capitals are privileged by government investments as construction of infrastructure for communications, international airports, and logistics facilities. Such capitals often have research institutes and higher education institutions in proximity. Producer services and business services in capital city-regions are needed to support research and learning institutions as well as government; so banks and financial services, along with other services such as management consultancy, market research, advertizing and legal counsel, are attracted to capitals.

Among the range of six types of ownership and as measured on a per employee basis, *overseas-invested, joint-stock* and *privately owned* enterprises outperformed the other three types, which included the *state-owned*, the *collectively-owned* and *other enterprises* of different ownership types, such as co-operatives, with no overseas investment (Wang et al., 1998: 293 & 295).

ADVANCED TECHNOLOGY AND THE 'TECHNOLOGICAL DEEPENING' OF THE CITY-REGION ECONOMY

The early adoption of technopoles laid the R&D groundwork for much of China's science and technology based economic growth. In this section, recent technological deepening and the evolution of the urban knowledge economy are examined. How has the technopole thesis fared as an early organizing and inspirational concept for urban-regional economic growth in China?

Early technopole initiatives were characterized by interdependencies with manufacturing, and more recently a mix of high-technology manufacturing-oriented R&D and knowledge-oriented advanced services R&D (Malecki, 1997: 265). First generation science parks did not seem to create the synergies necessary to be self-sustaining; spin-offs and local linkages had not yet emerged in various high-tech centres in the United Kingdom, Germany, Japan and Korea (Malecki, 1997: 270–1). French technopoles also experienced mixed results as they matured (Chordá, 1996). In contrast, South Korea's mature technopole, Taedok Science Town, has been judged to be successful (Oh, 2002).

Returning to the case of China's technopoles, Hu's research into High- and New-Technology Parks illustrates more recent (1992–2000) performance in high-tech R&D based economic change and growth in China. Hu's research results:

> provide no evidence that firms benefit from concentrating in technology parks or being close to a large metropolis. However, I do find that these firms are more productive when their host city receives more FDI [foreign direct investment], although this may not necessarily be in the form of spillover. (Hu, 2007: 86)

His analyses also revealed that in their early development stages, these technology parks slowed the regional inequality divide between the interior technology-park technopoles and their coastal-region counterparts. However, this effect was not strong enough to reverse the trend of regional inequality. Without evidence of knowledge spillover and with a strong trend of fast converging labour productivity growth, the high growth of Chinese technology parks seems influenced by preferential policies such as tax breaks that operate to generate the return on investment. These conclusions raise the question of whether the growth of these technology parks can be sustained once policy supports are ended and if no external economies are captured.

In the aggregate, China's full range of technology, science and knowledge based urban places, including the various types of Chinese technopoles, have combined to

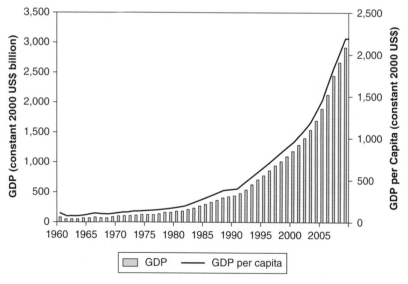

Figure 2.1   China's economic development 1960–2009

Source: World Bank (2010)

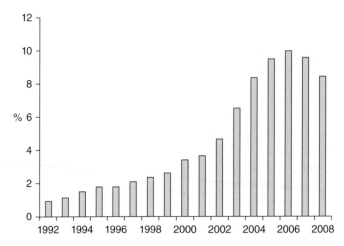

Figure 2.2   High-tech exports as a percentage of China's GDP

Source: World Bank (2010)

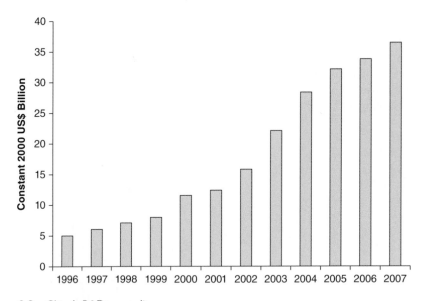

Figure 2.3   China's R&D expenditure

Source: World Bank (2010)

produce high rates of economic growth. Its great city-regions' high- and new-technology industrial and knowledge complexes, plus China's local-government technology parks have contributed to GDP growth, high-technology exports and increasing R&D input and output. Refer to Figure 2.1 China's Economic Development 1960–2009; Figure 2.2 High-tech Exports as a Percentage of China's GDP; Figure 2.3 China's R&D Expenditure; and Figure 2.4 China's R&D Expenditure as a Percentage of GDP.

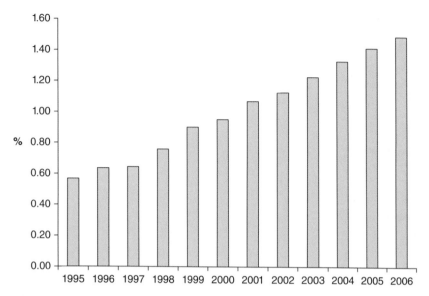

Figure 2.4   China's R&D expenditure as a percentage of GDP

Source: World Bank (2010)

In 2007, there were 56,047 certified high-tech companies in China (Zhou and Yang, 2010) and 48,472 of these enterprises were in high-tech zones (National Bureau of Statistics, 2009). Thus, 86% of China's high-tech companies were located in high-tech zones in 2007. This and the economy's overall performance have enabled China, over the last decade, to grow its R&D expenditures at a dramatic 19% in inflation-adjusted dollars (National Science Board, 2010: 4–5).

Technology has been a significant part of GDP growth. Using the production function to explain the sources of growth for China, Fan and Wan (2008) decomposed the growth of GDP into three parts: capital, labour and technology. Over 1981–2004, technology contributed on average 49% economic growth (Fan and Wan, 2008: 10–11); ranging as high as 72% and as low as 39%. See Table 2.2 which decomposes the GDP growth into the three factors: capital, labour and technological progress. The details of the Total Factor Productivity decomposition method are described by Fan and Watanabe (2006: 305–7; Fan, 2011).

In recent years, these patterns have been characterized as *new economy*; 'this paradigm is based on the notion that productivity increases observed since the mid-1990s have been based (in part) on the cumulative impact of information technologies, which have finally raised multi-factor productivity levels for a window of time' (Beyers, 2008: 1). In addition, to the relatively high multi-factor productivity growth, the new economy has high levels of capital investment in IT and the new economy manifests structural changes in production and consumption of IT, including growing consumer demand in services.

China's state-led macro-economic strategic planning and policies implementation have allowed it to accelerate and modernize the science and technology (S&T) capacity

Table 2.2 Contribution of technology progress to economic growth in China 1981–2004

Time Periods and Sectors	% Contribution
1981–1985	
Technology Progress	41.0
Labour	18.0
Capital	42.0
1986–1990	
Technology Progress	52.0
Labour	19.0
Capital	29.0
1991–1995	
Technology Progress	43.1
Labour	05.7
Capital	49.6
1996–2000	
Technology Progress	72.1
Labour	08.1
Capital	19.8
2001–2004	
Technology Progress	38.8
Labour	06.1
Capital	55.1

Source: Calculations based on data from World Bank, 2006

of its economy. China's technology and scientific knowledge have been and can be expected to be advanced and extended by means of continued major R&D investment. Since the initiation of the reform period in the late 1970s and early 1980s, central government economic development policies have been dominant. The policies also demonstrate increasing interest in investment shifts that reflect both internal maturation of high-technology development and more targeted and selective new-economy investment strategies. See Table 2.1 'Major technology policy initiatives in China since the reform', e.g. note the 2008 Thousand Talents Program.

Already China has more researchers than any other country. By means of such initiatives as the Thousand Talents Program and other targeted development policies, China is competing globally for human capital, commodities and other resources that are needed to continue its drive toward prosperity. After many generations of having been exploited by foreign powers, China now is on the economic and political ascendancy and is regaining its former position as a world power.

Technology, infrastructure and place qualities will be even more critical as China pursues its high-technology development goals. As other countries have learned, China will perfect its planning and implementation for the next generation of high-tech centres and technopole hubs. The US National Research Council foresees China preparing for the realization of these high-tech development goals by establishing 'modern facilities built around innovation-technology-education clusters' (2010: 31) and investing in education, infrastructure, and ICT networks and databases (National Research Council, 2010: 26).

Such developments might be located not only in the larger city-regions of the eastern and coastal provinces, but also in interior locations in secondary and third-tier city-regions. The intent might be to stimulate high-technology development and R&D investment with growth-pole (Plummer and Taylor, 2001a: 222–3) aspirations in mind. In the meantime, foreign and outside investors will continue to be interested in less risky locations such as the Pearl River Delta region (Wei, 2007: 29–30). Recently, for example, Guangzhou and Singaporean investors signed a contract to establish a joint venture to create Guangzhou Knowledge City. The ultimate multi-billion yuan city project is intended to attract knowledge-based industries, skilled personnel and talent in eight sectors: information technology; bio-technology and pharmaceuticals; energy and environmental technology; advanced manufacturing; creative industries;

Table 2.3 Internet penetration as a percentage of population selected Asia–Pacific economies. *Updated 30 June 2010 and 30 September 2010

Political-Economy	% Population
New Zealand*	85.4
South Korea	81.1
Brunei Darussalam	80.7
Australia*	80.1
Japan	78.2
Singapore	77.8
Taiwan	70.1
Hong Kong, SAR, China	68.8
Malaysia	64.6
Macao, SAR, China	49.5
China	31.6
Philippines	29.7
Vietnam	27.1
Indonesia	12.3
Pakistan	10.4
Sri Lanka	08.3
Laos	07.5
Bhutan	07.1
India	06.9
Nepal	02.2
Cambodia	00.5
Bangladesh	00.4
Myanmar	00.2

Source: Internet World Stats, 30 June 2010 and 30 September 2010*

education and training; health and wellness; and research and development. By 2015, the development should host 500 companies and contribute 20 billion yuan to the GDP; by 2030, the Knowledge City should house 300,000 residents and generate 300 billion yuan for the economy (Low, 2010).

TECHNOLOGY AND COMPETITIVE ADVANTAGE WITHIN URBAN SYSTEMS AND HIERARCHIES

This is a useful place to remind ourselves that our mindset for analyzing and planning informed action for cities, technologies and economic change is derived from applicable theory and best practices (Vettoretto, 2009). Competitive advantage is an aggregate of behaviours and processes that 'endow some regions, places, and nations with more success than others (Plummer and Taylor, 2001a: 226–7). Such behaviour is practised by business enterprises, institutions, governments and individuals. Regional competitive advantage can be earned from the sum of these behaviours leading to successful productivity, effective strategy, rate of creativity, responsiveness to demand, focus of demand, return on investment, and among other attributes, the integration of the firm and or a locational clustering of related and supporting enterprises into the city-region's agglomeration of externalities of skilled labour availability, learning, technology, and innovation (Plummer and Taylor, 2001a: 227).

As competitive advantage is considered in the context of the interdependencies of city-regions, technologies and economic change, it is imperative to employ a *relational mindset*. Henry Wai-chung Yeung counsels not to put sharp edges on our conceptualizations (Yeung, 2002). Yeung offers a visual framework of three relationalities that portray the interactions and connectivities among: (1) actors and their various institutional structures; (2) hierarchies of scale – local, regional, national and global; and (3) socio-spatial themes that may be framed as economic, social and political (Yeung, 2005: 43–4). The latter element may be extended thematically to include culture and creative enterprises, the natural environment and so on. It is through the continuous practice and application of relational theory to the empirical contexts of cities, technologies and economic change that one will uncover stimulus-response understandings and be positioned to offer insight into the possible actions and interventions needed to enable imaginative and responsive planned futures scenarios to be constructed so as to realize Intelligent Development (Corey and Wilson, 2006, see especially pp. 214–16; and 131–8).

Competitive advantage within the context of the global knowledge economy has been explored by Robert Huggins, Hiro Izushi and their colleagues at the Centre for International Competitiveness, University of Wales Institute in Cardiff. This work offers us some operational insight into the comparative *competitive advantage* of 145 city-regions across 19 knowledge economy benchmarks. The places span the wide range of knowledge-based and technology-facilitated city-regions from one end of the global north to the other end of the global south. These data were used to construct a composite index of the global economy's leading sub-national urban regions. The

Huggins and Izushi group now has generated five editions of the *World Knowledge Competitiveness Index* (WKCI). They define competitiveness as:

> [the] capability of an economy to attract and maintain firms with stable or rising profits in an activity, while maintaining stable or increasing standards of living for those who participate in it. ... Competitiveness ... involve[s] balancing the different types of advantages that one place may hold over another – the range of differing strengths that the socio-economic environment affords to a particular place compared to elsewhere. (Huggins et al., 2008: 1)

High technology and information technology indicators, among others, were used to take the pulse of and to monitor the regions. Focusing on these benchmarks, the WKCI framed three as 'Knowledge Capital Components', including government and business R&D spending and patents registered. In recognition that local investment in ICT infrastructure is critical in today's economy, the WKCI has framed five 'Knowledge Sustainability' indicators, including secure servers, internet hosts, broadband access, and public spending on education.

The Index is composed of three additional categories of indicators including 'Human Capital Components' of employment levels in IT, bio-technology, automotive and mechanical engineering, instrumentation, high-tech services, and management. 'Regional Economy Outputs' include labour productivity, earnings and unemployment, while 'Financial Capital Components' are represented by private equity investment.

Some of the highlights of the 2008 *World Knowledge Competitiveness Index* (WKCI) include the leadership role of Silicon Valley (San Jose-Sunnyvale-Santa Clara city-region) followed by the Boston region. Among the top 20 knowledge-competitive urban hubs are: three additional New England city-regions (two from Connecticut and one from Rhode Island); five more from California; two from Sweden; two from Japan; two from Michigan; and one each from Iceland; the Netherlands and Finland. The global south city-region representatives are from the emerging economies of China and India, including eight from China/Hong Kong and three from India.

Additionally, the WKCI-2008 digs deeper into China's urban knowledge-hub concentrations. Special analyses were provided for the three principal regional clusters of the Bohai Gulf Region (cf., Zhou, 2008), the Yangtze Delta Region and the Pearl River Delta Region. A special insightful feature of Chapter 8 of the WKCI-2008 document is an integrated discussion of the policy mechanisms, the performance outcomes that are attributable to the particularities and unique enterprise cultures of these three regions as their development paths have evolved to date (Huggins and Luo, 2008: 34–46).

Huggins, Izushi and colleagues have developed a *body of findings* that enables us to delve deeper into some of the dynamics of competitive advantage within city-regional systems. A selection from this body of work includes: Huggins, 2000; Huggins and Izushi, 2002; Huggins and Izushi, 2007; Huggins et al., 2007; and Huggins, 2008.

TECHNOLOGY AND ITS ROLE IN SHAPING THE CITY-REGION SPACE-ECONOMY: CONCENTRATION AND DISPERSION

Since Castells and Hall published *Technopoles of the World* (1994), it was clear that technopoles could be attributed to several sets of forces and results. Using the life-cycle of French technopoles, Chordá has framed the dynamics producing technopole outcomes as: (1) the pole model; and (2) the agglomeration model.

The *pole model* is a land and building-property initiative to create a locationally focused cluster of supplier and user enterprises of high value-added technology-centred R&D activities on a site with strong investment and financial support from sponsors. 'The "pole" model is a top-down supply-led and purposeful approach, usually starting from scratch.' The *agglomeration model* seeks to take advantage of a spatially wide set of existing local and regional technological and R&D talents and occupations engaged in producing new and advanced services and new and advanced products. Multiple technological poles are usually established as parts of the agglomeration across the designated territory being branded (See Chordá, 1996: 147; and compare with Plummer and Taylor, 2001a, 2001b).

In this age of information society and the knowledge economy, what are the processes that stimulate concentration responses and dispersion responses? *Codified knowledge* principally is information that can be written and electronically transmitted easily – even over long distances via the internet. In contrast, *tacit knowledge* is impossible or much more difficult to write down; indeed it requires skilled experts or knowledgeable people to communicate and interpret the often nuanced meanings of such innovative knowledge. One of the principal characteristics of new economy interactions was that it 'still demanded face-to-face meetings and that structural change was favoring non-standardized production processes requiring such meetings' (Beyers, 2008: 2).

Over time however, tacit knowledge is increasingly becoming more codified. When there is familiarity and commonality of experience or even trust, more routine codified information can substitute for some tacit knowledge. Even though codified knowledge renders distance less critical to proximity in the era of the internet, tacit knowledge will continue to be more highly valued. With tacit knowledge, 'it is much easier to enjoy the rents attached to ownership of the knowledge, precisely because its tacit nature makes it harder for it to spill over to competitors' (Swann, 1999: 187). As a consequence, today's digital technologies and capitalistic networks 'cannot yet undermine all agglomeration economies' (Swann, 1999: 188).

Peter Swann uses the dispersion properties of codified knowledge and the concentration properties of tacit knowledge to differentiate broad categories of economic activity: '*innovation* is the most tacit process; followed by *production*'. *Trade* in goods and services are more codified than production processes (Swann, 1999: 188). He modeled the relationships between economies of scale, economies of scope, agglomeration economies and the effects of information technologies and observed that ITs do not seem 'to erode economies of scale, and indeed bring economies of scope in line with economies of scale' (Swann, 1999: 192). As a consequence, economies of agglomeration advantages remain and the 'forces for concentration remain potent' (Swann, 1999: 192).

The location of innovation is at the heart of the concentration and dispersion discussion. Audretsch and Feldman (1996) have examined the critical locational factor of the technologically facilitated business of creativity. They used a quotation from Glaeser, Kallal, Scheinkman and Shleifer that captures the essence of understanding these issues and their related concepts – 'intellectual breakthroughs must cross hallways and streets more easily than oceans and continents' (1992: 1127). In exploring the locational factor of innovation, Audretsch and Feldman observed:

> The location of innovative activity might not matter in the absence of what has become known as *knowledge spillovers*. New economic knowledge is said to spill over when the unit of observation which utilizes that new economic knowledge is distinct from the one that produced it. These knowledge spillovers do not, however, transmit costlessly with respect to geographic distance. Rather, location and proximity matter. That is, while the costs of transmitting *information* may be invariant to distance, presumably the cost of transmitting *knowledge* and especially *tacit knowledge* rises along with distance. (1996: 256, italics added)

From their research of 4,200 manufacturing innovations, they noted that as industry matures its innovative activity may be dispersed to existing production capacity in the same region. Specifically, '…what may serve as an *agglomerating influence* in triggering innovative activity to spatially cluster during the introduction and growth stages of the industry life-cycle, may later result in a *congestion effect,* leading to greater dispersion in innovative activity' (Audretsch and Feldman, 1996: 271). Technopoles are dynamic. Now that technopoles across the global economy have functioned for over a generation, one generally may assess their stages of evolution and the processes of concentration and dispersion upon which they are premised.

Scholars have expressed some dissatisfaction with the simple concentration-dispersion binary relationality. For example, Bathelt et al. have formulated a buzz-and-pipeline model of cluster competitiveness that reflects the need for a more relational perspective. They have explored 'why firms can gain *competitive advantage* by being co-located in a cluster with many other firms and organizations which are involved in similar and related types of economic activity' (2002: 20). They argue four points to answer this question.

1. 'A milieu where many actors with related yet complementary and heterogeneous knowledge, skills and information reside, provides a perfect setting for dynamic interaction' (2002: 21).

2. 'The more developed the pipelines between the cluster and distant sites of knowledge, the higher the quality (and value) of local buzz benefiting all firms in the local cluster' (2002: 21).

3. In order to manage effectively *both* the inward-looking and the outward-looking information flows, informal channels of communication and interpretive schemes need to be put in place so that the cluster buzz is sufficiently intense to insure that it gets to the units 'where it could be transformed into commercially useful knowledge' (2002: 21).

4. Lastly, the authors hypothesize 'that a large number of independent firms in a cluster can manage a larger number of pipelines than one single firm alone' (Bathelt et al., 2002: 22). This may explain why spatial clustering of many complementary and heterogeneous firms stimulate *competitive advantage*.

In discussing collective innovation and open networks, Anna Lee Saxenian has observed that 'co-location is a tremendous asset, as are shared language, culture and worldwide view' (Saxenian, 2006: 43). She cites Stan Shih, founder and CEO of Taiwan's Acer corporation who summarized the innovative benefits of location in Taiwan's Hsinchu Science Park (Lin, 1997; and Lee and Yang, 2000):

> Industry clustering speeds up the pace of innovation. Once … clustering is established, working within its disintegrated structure can allow an individual business to concentrate its capabilities on a certain task and share risks with other companies. If there are risks associated with a larger initiative, tasks can be appropriately allocated and coordinated among upstream, midstream and downstream satellite businesses; and if by chance the direction is wrong, everyone involved can communicate and the plan [can be] adjusted quickly. Even if some losses are incurred, they are shared by all the parties involved, and the loss for individual companies is minimized. (Saxenian, 2006: 43)

Other scales of re-shaping the urban space-economy include changes that occur for districts within city-regions. Suburban technopoles in Japan have been elaborated. The *international campus-garden-suburban style* approach has been analyzed as one that results in pleasant environments that are supportive of and conducive to innovation and creativity. Given the low density of this style, it may accommodate relatively large numbers of knowledge workers and residents (Forsyth and Crewe, 2010).

Technopole development in Japan's Kansai region has revealed that seeming failure of business site developments branded as high-technology hubs have the foundation of potential success built into past experience. The initial promotional behaviour and approach of the business and political elites of Osaka City and Osaka Prefecture demonstrated that if technopole locations are to attract high-technology and knowledge-intensive activities – especially international enterprises – then the basics of *innovative milieu and capacity* need to be there. Advanced business services and local synergies that integrate spin-offs and start-ups into new sites need to be evident in attracting IT firms. For example, cost-benefit analyses, focused attention to such requirements and demands as logistics, telecommunications and supportive institutional synergies are essential. Thus, in the business context, if reality and rhetoric can become one and the same, then successful technopole development is more likely to be realized (Anttiroiko, 2009).

As the era of technologically-enabled high-technology developments mature, new spatial patterns are being exposed. Stephen Graham and Simon Marvin have introduced us to the concept of *splintering urbanism* which sees a parallel process of unbundling due to infrastructure networks. 'Such a shift … requires a reconceptualization of the relations between infrastructure services and the contemporary development of cities' (Graham and Marvin, 2001: 33).

Some of these dynamics were illustrated by Graham and Guy (2002) by means of their analysis of downtown San Francisco and this central city district's relationships to the dot-com era. They raised the critical issues of contestation and inequalities that often surround the then-emerging neoliberal practices of *digital capitalists*. Such actors include: urban IT entrepreneurs, technology firms and local government politicians committed to succeeding by aggressive steering of the public purse toward the acquisition of land and the building of premium infrastructure in support of these preferred technology stakeholders.

It is valuable to distinguish between the locational concepts of digital *space* and urban *place* and contrasts between elite digeratis (Brockman, 1996: xxxi) and ordinary people (Friedmann, 2010). Politicians and business elites join forces to enable for-profit enterprises to be privileged with world-class infrastructure provision such as highways, ICTs, and airports. Such special provisions enable knowledge-economy business formation to the city-region that otherwise would not likely occur. However, too often infrastructures, the land, space and basic service needs of the area's poor and vulnerable are bypassed in the process of attracting new-economy investments as part of development visions and strategies to enable the locality to compete in the global knowledge economy. In the global south, Bunnell and Das (2010) have illuminated these neoliberal processes in the Kuala Lumpur Multimedia Super Corridor (MSC) in Malaysia, and the Hyderabad-Andhra Pradesh, India city-region. Further, they have made the connection of the role that the MSC strategy played for inspiring analogous high-technology development approaches to be taken by the state of Andhra Pradesh in Hyderabad city-region. The effects on the ground in and around Hyderabad have been documented as object lessons of neoliberal practices (Biswas, 2004; and Kennedy, 2007).

The boxed text below documents the critical role that computer gaming played in transforming the South Korean broadband technology environment into one of the most creative of the globe's economies. There is widespread recognition around the world that culture can be a driver and creator of new spatial organization. Among urban-regional economies of the West a 'new cultural economy' and related spatial organization are being driven by new media, video game production, and computer graphics and imaging, shaped by interdependencies of technology, creativity, talent, and attributes of 'place', in locations such as London, New York, San Francisco, Paris and Los Angeles (Scott, 2000). These fusions of technology and other factor inputs are changing the economic landscape of Asian cities such as Tokyo (Shibuya, Ropponggi), Seoul (Kangnam and the 'Teheran Valley'), Shanghai (Suzhou Creek and many other 'cultural quarters'), Beijing (District 798), and Singapore (Esplanade–Theaters by the Bay). This cultural-space dimension of economic innovation has become a noteworthy force throughout the Asia-Pacific region from New Zealand's 'Frodo Economy', to

India's 'Bollywood Economy', and its many other regionally-based language, music and dance cinema industry manifestations. These and many other culture-economy forms, industries and emerging new spaces have recently been researched and compared (Izushi and Aoyama, 2006; Kong and O'Connor, 2009; Yamamoto, 2010). Learning about such dynamics in the increasingly globalized economy is important for understanding the ability of diverse places 'to support the development of indigenous content and local idioms in artistic work' (Kong, 2009: 1). These diverse cultural-economy functions and clusters attract external interest such as tourists and conventioneers; they are also important complements to the local hosting environment for retaining and attracting technology- and knowledge-based production talent as new-economy enrichments to the quality of life and amenities of the city-region (refer to Corey and Wilson, 2006: 126–8).

For follow-up, consult *New Economic Spaces in Asian Cities* by editors Peter Daniels, Kong Chong Ho and Thomas Hutton (2011). It includes Asian cities case studies, and a theoretical and normative discussion of the emergence of the new cultural economy. The cases include: Tokyo, Seoul, Shanghai, Beijing, Shenzhen and Singapore.

South Korea's Leap-Frogging to Global Prominence in Broadband and Internet Penetration

Prior to the Asian Financial Crisis of 1997–1998, South Korea's performance in broadband and internet services was undistinguished. However, the crisis and its serious negative impact on South Korea's economy was a spur to government, business and citizen stakeholders to re-think the country's competitive position on the consumption side of telephony and IT services.

Three sets of factors were identified for action: (1) Public-sector supply-side actors moved to liberalize the regulatory framework to spur the internet market and create a more competitive and less monopolistic marketplace. Demand for fast, accessible and affordable broadband was stimulated through IT literacy programs targeted to home-makers, elderly, military personnel, farmers, low-income families, and the disabled, among others. High-density high-rise housing was exploited to lower connectivity cost while cyber building certificate programs and inter-building competition operated to speed up broadband adoption among households and businesses alike. (2) For-profit actors formulated new business strategies to take advantage of the deregulated market place. The increase in additional small and large competitors resulted in lower-priced broadband services. (3) The social and cultural factors of South Korean society converged to produce a climate of receptivity and demand that had not existed earlier. The citizenry and business community were reeling under the various remedies that were being imposed on the economy to address the Asian Financial Crisis issues. There was high demand, especially among young people, to engage in *computer gaming*; much of this *demand* was being met by cyber cafés called PC Bangs. Family and parents, however, preferred children to use computers in the home where responsible use could take place. For this to occur, residents needed IT literacy training.

The convergence of factors allowed for demand and supply to be matched and addressed relatively quickly. The core demand, in the form of high bandwidth online gaming provided the 'killer application' that was needed to shift from too-slow home dial-up, thereby creating the huge household demand that enabled the now-multiple internet service providers to respond to the newly-created demand within the context of fierce competition. Refer to: Lee et al., 2003; Kim et al., 2004; Lau, Kim and Atkin, 2005; and Kim, 2006.

TECHNOLOGY AND URBAN LABOUR MARKETS

Over the last several human generations, structural shifts in the ways that economic production have evolved have been significant. How do city-regions develop within the production system of modern capitalism? Allen Scott answered this question by analyzing these structural shifts from industrialization to urbanization by means of the division of labour (Scott, 1988b: 1–2). Beginning in the 1960s, scholars and policy actors began paying more attention to the rise of the role of services in economies (Hutton, 2004; and Daniels et al., 2005). 'Changes in the way production is organized carries with it major social, economic and political change for work, workers and the places where we live and work' (Corey and Wilson, 2006: 12).

Jean Gottmann's urban-centric regional research into the processes that generated *Megalopolis* (1961) was some of the earliest that examined the structural shifts in industries and occupations as national and local economies moved more into services from manufacturing (Corey and Wilson, 2006: 7–11). This 'white-collar revolution' (Gottmann, 1961: 565–630) at its core depended on the integral role of information, characterized by Gottmann as the 'life blood of commerce anywhere' (p. 576). Further, he discriminated employment in 'tertiary' services such as retail sales, from more advanced 'quaternary' economic services such as 'transactions, analysis, research or decision-making, and also education and government' (p. 575).

Over the following decades, the differentiation between such routine services and advanced services became the object of research and reflection. For example, William Beyers derived a definition of the *new economy* as one:

> ...changing the mix of industrial outputs, the ways of producing across the economy, with related shifts in consumer and business demands, changes in occupational structure, and the emergence of some new lines of industrial activity. While measurement is difficult, particularly in services that have been heavy purchasers of information technologies, it appears as though one of the important attributes of the New Economy has been an increase in productivity. (Beyers, 2002: 5)

Beyers and Gottmann identified the path dependence problems of actual structural economic changes out-pacing the capacity of society and governments to achieve a widespread working consensus within and across national economies on responsive classification schemes to measure and thereby accurately portray the structural shifts from old economy to new economy (Beyers, 2008). To this day, structural shifts and their associated fuzzy definitions and lack of widely accepted and used measurements continue to plague researchers and policy analysts alike (De Roo and Porter, 2007). As a consequence, case studies and their life-cycles enable us to continue learning about the dynamics, patterns and variances of high technology places and spaces, i.e. technopoles.

The Cambridge high technology industry cluster in the United Kingdom is one of the global knowledge economy's most successful and reputed technopoles (Keeble, 1989). A recent key research question was to what extent R&D workers benefit from being in the cluster? The study found that many of these researchers do not believe that their work benefits from being in the cluster. However, the research revealed that there were labour market advantages, such as job mobility within the cluster, along with an indirect benefit – 'the global image or "brand" of Cambridge as a place of excellence in science and technology' (Huber, 2010: 20). Another advantage of the Cambridge cluster is that many R&D workers rely on alternative sources of knowledge from other enterprises within the cluster. At this mature stage of the cluster's life-cycle it may be necessary to re-set policy priorities to manage the brand and emphasize labour market activities that retain and attract a critical mass of R&D workers (Huber, 2010).

Since each technopole cluster around the world has its own unique mix of characteristics, it is prudent and strategic to monitor a technopole's empirical status. Turning to North America, Wolfe and Gertler (2004) have conducted a national study of 26 knowledge-intensive clusters across Canada, using four indicators: inflows; outflows; local social dynamics; and historical path dynamics. Both commonly shared experiences and unique local circumstances were identified to reveal the forces shaping each cluster. Five themes were derived; one, labour, is the focus here. 'Inflows of people are, in our view, an especially robust indicator of local dynamism. It is increasingly well established that highly educated talented labor flows to those places that have a "buzz" about them – the places where the most interesting work in the field is currently being done' (Wolfe and Gertler, 2004: 1084). In particular, the importance of local 'talent' drawn to the area is noted along with the need for a critical mass of talent to maintain and grow the region.

Global-scale human capital and social capital networking are also important relationships to understand. The mobility of science and knowledge workers is significant. In addition to the benefits that receiving countries derive from educating and training knowledge workers (many of which stay on), the sending countries also benefit. Foreign degrees and post-doctoral experience can promote and sustain science, technology and development collaborations by means of social capital network building that link regions and support knowledge hubs. Among respondents from six Asia-Pacific countries, i.e. Australia, China, India, Japan, Korea and Taiwan, they documented strong relationships among those with foreign post-doctoral positions and knowledge-producing collaborations. Further, such networking was found to persist through time (Woolley et al., 2008: 180). The above recent research findings suggest that again, both local market forces and trans-national forces play important roles among highly skilled workers in the global knowledge economy.

LOOKING BACK TO MOVE FORWARD

The above five lenses and their relationships have been used in this chapter to demonstrate the importance of technology in influencing urban economic change: (1) technopoles or high-technology R&D locations; (2) the technological deepening of the recent urban economy; (3) competitive advantage within urban systems and hierarchies; (4) reshaping the urban space economy in terms of concentration and dispersion; and (5) impacts on urban labour markets. By way of drawing conclusions from the discussion above, several over-arching issues may be posed and elaborated. These elaborations may be taken as benchmarks from which informed future expectations may be made.

Technological innovation-based development has been used as a strategic tool to stimulate economic take-off and sustain economic growth by countries of the Asia-Pacific, specifically Japan (Freeman, 1987), the Newly Industrialized Economies (Hobday, 1995; Wong and Ng, 2001) and the more recently emerging China and India (Lal, 1995; Gu, 1999; Mahmood and Singh, 2003). For instance, for the two most distinguished periods of Japan's economic development, the Meiji Period (1868–1890) and Post World War II (1956–1986), the Japanese government involved itself directly in the country's industrial development by identifying national priorities and providing guidance and direction. Improving Japan's technological capability was emphasized particularly (Freeman, 1987). Similarly, to enhance their innovation capabilities, China and India have invested heavily in R&D expenditure and R&D personnel in recent decades. Consequently, innovation capacity has contributed significantly to the economic growth of China and India, especially in the 1990s (Fan, 2011).

Economies of the Asia-Pacific, especially Japan, South Korea, Taiwan, China, and India, have adopted a 'walking on two legs' strategy to import technology from the West and to develop indigenous R&D capacity simultaneously (Johnson, 1982; Kim, 1998; Lall and Teubal, 1998; Fan, 2006; Fan and Watanabe, 2008). For instance, while Japan sent a large number of students overseas to European countries in the Meiji Period, the country also diligently worked on improving the technological capacity of its own nascent enterprises. In the post World War II period, the government not only relied on technological transfer, but also organized research consortiums for various strategic industries, such as super-computing and energy, so as to promote indigenous capability of Japanese companies as technological leaders in these industries (Johnson, 1982). Further, evidence shows that developing indigenous R&D, together with technology transfer from the West, is crucial for China and India to catch up in the telecommunication equipment industry and biotechnology industry, respectively (Shen, 1999; Fan, 2006; Fan and Watanabe, 2008). Such domestic R&D capacity building should be expected to continue.

Technology-based development, like other growth-pole development strategies, has different implications for different cities and regions. Those places that have possessed or invested heavily in technological and science assets, such as research institutes and universities and skilled technological labour force, will be able to grasp the development opportunities. Other places which do not possess these assets will not be able to take advantage. Many cities and regions in the Asia-Pacific that had a strong base in traditional manufacturing have invested heavily in their technological assets and utilized industrial upgrading to shift the focus of local economies towards technology-intensive industry. For instance, Shanghai experienced significant industrial restructuring in recent years. While certain labour-intensive sectors such as textiles, have relinquished their dominant positions, other technology- and capital-intensive sectors such as electronics, telecommunication equipment, transportation equipment, and petrochemical, have become major new players, contributing 75% of Shanghai's industrial growth from 1996 to 2000 (Gong, 2003). Correspondingly, many people who worked in traditional manufacturing for decades, such as state-owned textile enterprises, lost their jobs, whereas white-collar migrants who are highly educated have continued to flow into the city to take up various new positions in Shanghai's emerging technology-intensive industries.

Increasingly, the Asia-Pacific has played an important role in a *new* international division of labour (Fröbel et al., 2000), not only in labour-intensive industries, but also in technology-intensive industries. Due to large reserves of knowledge workers available in the region, a significant amount of global R&D has been attracted to the region, especially in Japan, and the Newly Industrialized Economies, and China, and India. A survey by the Economist Intelligence Unit (2004) has demonstrated that China and India are two of the top ten destinations for foreign R&D expansion; this is attributable to their rich endowment of low-cost and well-trained scientists and engineers, accompanied by fast growing domestic markets and the increasing foreign investment in manufacturing (Sun et al., 2007). By 2005, multinational companies had set up 750 foreign R&D centres in China, growing five times since 2003 (Walsh, 2007). Further, certain cities became the concentrated location for global R&D Beijing, Shanghai, and Shenzhen have attracted over 84% of foreign R&D centres in China (Yuan, 2005).

Historically, economies such as Japan, South Korea, and Taiwan have benefited from the returnees who studied and worked in technology-intensive industries in the West to establish their own high-tech industries such as steel, machinery, electronics, semiconductor, and the automobile industries in the Meiji Period and the 1960s (Freeman, 1987; Kim, 1998; Amsden and Chu, 2003). China and India started to send a large number of students overseas only in the last three decades. Already, they are both benefiting from returnees who set up ventures in biotechnology, the internet, semiconductor and other technology-intensive industries (Saxenian, 2006; Fan and Watanabe, 2008). Asian cities have joined other city-regions in the West to lead or participate in various global R&D networks of technology-industries. For instance, Singapore has become a global hub for biotechnology R&D, attracting top-tier scientists in the field from all over the world, including the Atlantic realm; Seoul has become the global R&D centre for the digital wireless technology Code-Division Multiple Access (CDMA) mobile phone technology and gaming software; Bangalore is considered the IT outsourcing centre and the software development capital of the world.

More than a generation ago, the late communication guru and opinion setter, Everett Rogers planted the seeds for a new development paradigm. He envisaged a more equitable form of development that included economic growth and material advancement, but had matured to also incorporate 'a widely participatory process of social change' in a society that intended to seek social advancement and the freedom for the majority of people to gain 'greater control over their environment' (Rogers, 1976: 225). Further, his prescience foresaw an important facilitative role for communications and information in the realization of this new development paradigm. With today's global knowledge economy based on an increasingly pervasive distribution of personal, mobile and other powerful multi-media ICTs, we have the option, and indeed the social and civic responsibility, to inform ourselves individually and collectively to engage in purposeful change toward the kind of places that the stakeholders of a city-region and its country want.

Lastly, the reader, including the teacher and learner alike, are challenged to use the five lenses of this chapter to construct their own learning strategies. Thereby, their knowledge capital may continue to grow and their world will expand as other macro regions of the global knowledge economy are explored. See the boxed text within this chapter. These selections are intended to provoke continuous general learning and illustrate selective focused lessons, i.e. the catalytic role that technological demand and close attention to the needs of consumers can play. Such particularized empirical lessons may be revealed by drilling down via individual researches into selected city-regions and their host countries of the Asia-Pacific, e.g. places in China and India – and in other regions of the world economy. Regardless of the regions being researched, it is imperative to ground the material and technological realities and cultural particularities of the city-region's place and space (Yeung and Lin, 2003). Looking to the future is important; for example, the role of science and the city-region (Matthiessen et al., 2006; Nature, 2010; Van Noorden, 2010) and the central role of network connectivities and advanced services (Taylor and Walker, 2004; Taylor, 2010) both will continue to expand and deepen. Rigorous empirical research, as informed by applicable theory can be blended to produce intellectual growth, generalizable results, and the preparedness and capacity to engage in Intelligent Development (Corey and Wilson, 2006: 205–6).

Engaging in Intelligent Development may be facilitated by consulting a recently published book entitled, *Global Information Society: Technology, Knowledge, and Mobility* (Wilson, Kellerman and Corey, 2013). By presenting the intellectual and regional empirical underpinnings of the globalized information society and the roles that urban-regional technologies perform to enable information networking, the core narrative of the book leads the inspired reader to demonstrate ways for collaborating with other local and regional development stakeholders in order to take advantage of the new economic and social opportunities offered by today's global technological change. Ongoing digital education and pervasive social media, especially as framed by relevant concepts and tailored strategies, can empower and stimulate imaginative approaches to harness the development potential of today's cities and other places and regions. Relying on fact-based informed decision making, this resource is a means to extend the knowledge introduced in this chapter and this book into shaping the life of your community and your future.

3

Cities and Rescaling

John Harrison

Rather than promoting 'balanced' urban and regional development within relatively autocentric national space-economies, the overarching goal of urban locational policies is to position major cities and city-regions strategically within supranational circuits of capital accumulation.

(Brenner, 2009a: 125)

INTRODUCTION: CITIES IN RETROSPECT AND IN PROSPECT

The last two decades have been dominated by discourses claiming a resurgence of cities, which as Brenner (2009a) points out has captivated policy élites keen to capitalise on the latent geoeconomic power of globalising cities. Yet in the early stages of globalisation the prospects for cities looked bleak. The breakdown of the Bretton Woods monetary agreement, the ensuing oil crisis, global economic recession, and dissolution of the Fordist-Keynesian institutional compromise left those cities in the North Atlantic rim which had prospered most from Fordist mass production on the verge of bankruptcy by the late-1970s. Triggering an accelerated, crisis-induced phase of industrial restructuring, cities which had been expanding as a result of Fordist accumulation in the post-war period – in particular its unquenching demand for inputs and reliance on a deep reservoir of local labour – came under threat, globally, from increased foreign competition, capital mobility and labour migration, and were undermined, locally, by labour-management disputes and stagflation. The result was major urbanised zones of Fordist accumulation (the German Ruhr district, the 'snowbelt' cities of northern and northeast United States, northern England and the midlands) were no longer drivers of nationally-specific systems of production. Rather mass unemployment, unprecedented levels of social upheaval, and general urban decay resulted in those industrial cities and regions which benefited most from Fordist accumulation becoming a serious drag on the national economies within which they were embedded.

The long-term outlook for cities also looked bleak. In the two decades following the collapse of Fordism, consensus suggested how advances in technology and communication were inducing an era of global deconcentration and with it a diminishing role for cities. Yet for all that new technologies have undoubtedly extended our capacity to interact and transfer information and commodities more freely and more frequently across space in capitalist globalisation, the predicted decline of cities never materialised. In fact, the propensity of economic activity to cluster in dense agglomerations has seen consensus go the other way, as by the late-1980s mounting evidence affirmed how a distinctive group of cities, that is, metropolitan clusters of socio-economic activity, were forging ahead as important command and control posts in the new global economy.

This propensity for globalisation to crystallise out in nodes of dense social and economic activity led urbanists such as Saskia Sassen to popularise the view that cities were not disappearing in globalisation; rather globalisation entailed the emergence of a new type of city, the global city (Sassen, 1991)[1]. In short, while capitalist restructuring under conditions of globalisation is rendering distance less of a barrier to the exchange and transfer of knowledge, commodities, and information in new global systems of production and consumption, cities enact a key strategic role in organizing and structuring globalised forms of capital accumulation. Giving rise to the dominant global city discourse of the late-twentieth and early twenty-first century, many have since ascribed a hierarchy of importance to cities based on their geo-economic power in creating, shaping, and orchestrating the operation of the global economy (Beaverstock et al., 1999). Some commentators even go so far as to attest that concentration of geo-economic power in cities is so profound that major urban regions have now superseded national economies as the fundamental unit of the capitalist economy (Ohmae, 1995; Storper, 1997; Scott, 1998, 2001b). Whether you agree with this assertion or not, the essential point is that in globalisation, capital is freeing itself from the shackles of historically entrenched nationally scaled regulatory systems which had kept capital accumulation contained within, and constrained by, territorially demarcated national economies during the epoch of Fordist industrial growth. We are witnessing, as many writers have noted, the rescaling of capital under globalizing conditions.

Most crucially for this discussion, it is cities and metropolitan regions which have been foci for the crystallisation of globalised capital accumulation insofar as localised agglomeration economies foster and harbour the conditions, assets, and capacities upon which leading sectors of transnational capital depends (Brenner, 2004). In short, the rescaling of capital has seen globalizing cities prosper. Part and parcel of this discourse is how processes of global economic integration, rescaling of capital, and crystallisation of capital accumulation in subnational production complexes are fuelling a second

---

1 I use 'popularise' deliberately because other authors had previously noted a new role for cities in globalisation (see Friedman and Wolff, 1982; Timberlake, 1985), however, it was Sassen who crystallised these thoughts into a concise research agenda and it is this which became the antecedent to what we know today as the global city discourse. Interestingly, other authors felt this presumptuous at the time. In their 1989 book, Richard Knight and Gary Gappert write: 'THE TITLE OF THIS VOLUME, *Cities in a Global Society*, is rather presumptuous because it anticipates the global society; but it is less presumptuous than the original title, "Global Cities", which implies that global cities already exist' (p. 11).

defining feature of globalisation – rapidly accelerating urbanisation. In stark contrast to the consensus of two decades ago, which signalled the demise of cities, today more than 50% of the world's population are living in cities for the first time (UNFPA, 2007). With forecasts predicting this to rise to 70% by 2050, globalisation is thus, on the one hand, fuelling claims of a resurgence of cities as drivers of economic development (and expected growing affluence). Yet, on the other hand, substantive expressions of rapidly accelerating urbanisation are increasingly challenging existing urban economic infra-structures and urban-regional governance, particularly as metropolitan landscapes now stretch far beyond their traditional territorial boundaries. The extraordinarily rapid urbanisation underway in China, especially the Pearl River Delta, for instance, offers a vivid example of the challenges posed by city expansion into larger city-regions com-prising multiple functionally interlinked urban settlements. To be sure, this is a process which disturbs our established conceptions of the city as a distinctively coherent phe-nomenon in its own right (Wachsmuth, 2014), but also its place in the wider context of regional, national and international relations.

Stirred into action by these developments, this century has seen a whole raft of research into the emergence of a new and critically important kind of geography and institutional form on the world stage, the global city-region. Showcased as a new scale of urban organisation, the global city-region discourse extends the logic which saw global cities being defined by their external linkages during the 1990s to consider both the external *and* internal linkages of these rapidly expanding, increasingly multi-clustered, metropoli-tan areas. Linked to their vigorous expansion and ever increasing economic activity as dense nodes of human, social, and cultural capital, many commentators purport these large-scale complex urban formations to 'function as territorial platforms for much of the post-Fordist economy'; constitute the 'dominant leading edge of contemporary capitalist development'; and thereby represent what many now believe to be the 'basic motors of the global economy' (Scott, 2001a: 4).

Providing added impetus to this emergent global city-region discourse has been the emergence of trans-national, trans-regional and trans-frontier economic spaces in glo-balisation: prominent examples include Europe's 'blue banana', a discontinuous urban-ised corridor of industrial growth running from northern England to northern Italy; the Dutch-German EUREGIO cross-border region; the Singapore-Johor-Riau growth tri-angle in south-east Asia; and the 'Cascadia' region in the Pacific north-west of North America. This is further supported as, among others, UN-Habitat (2011) move to rec-ognise the merger of global cities and global city-regions to form even larger urban spaces as an indicator that there is a new and critically important socio-spatial forma-tion on the world stage. Stretching for thousands of kilometres (often across national boundaries) and home not to tens of millions of people but hundreds of millions of people, these *super-urban areas*[2] are coming to represent this century's competitive

---

2 Various other titles have been ascribed to these social formations, including 'mega reg-ions', 'urban corridors', 'megapolitan cities' and 'endless cities', but I would argue that in so doing each serves to stretch, and by implication blunt, established concepts such as 'region', 'corridor' and 'city' to identify these new spaces. For this reason I prefer to use the term super-urban areas.

territories *par excellence,* a foci for and driver of wealth creation, and loci for new forms of territorial cooperation and competition on a previously unimagined scale (Harrison and Hoyler, 2014b). Moreover, and of particular note is that many of these super-urban areas – certainly the most dynamic – are located outside of the traditional capitalist heartlands of North America and Western Europe. Some of the most prominent examples include the Pearl River Delta, Yangtze River Delta and Bohai Economic Rim, Beijing-Pyongyang-Seoul-Tokyo, Tokyo-Nagoya-Osaka-Kyoto-Kobe, Mumbai-Delhi, Rio de Janeiro-Sao Paulo, and Ibadan-Lagos-Accra (see box below).

Selected Examples of Dynamic Super-Urban Areas in Newly Industrialised and BRIC countries[3]

Pearl River Delta (PRD): China's southern-most and largest super-urban area, it is estimated that a growing population of 120 million live in the area around Hong Kong, Shenzhen and Guangzhou. Here, Hong Kong has emerged to be an important service-oriented hub and gateway to the PRD, where Guangdong Province is one of the world's most important manufacturing bases. The PRD administrative area covers 42,824 km^2. There have been suggestions, albeit refuted by the Guangdong Provincial Authority, that they plan to merge the nine mainland cities (current population c.40 million) to create one urban metropolis.

Yangtze River Delta (YRD): China's second largest super-urban area, the YRD administrative area covers 110,115 km^2 and has a population of 90 million. Located on the East China Sea, the YRD is centred on 16 cities of which Shanghai, Nanjing and Hangzhou are the most prominent. Shanghai is mainland China's financial centre, but where the PRD focuses on light consumer goods, the YRD is more focused on heavy industry. The Ports of Shanghai and Ningbo are the world's first and fourth busiest cargo ports respectively.

Bohai Economic Rim (BER): Although the least heralded of China's three super-urban areas, the BER is emerging as an important economic hotspot to rival the PRD and YRD. Situated around the Bohai Sea, China's northern-most super-urban area has a growing population of c.60 million. Centred on the cities of Beijing and Tianjin, the BER has traditionally been involved in heavy industry and manufacturing, but one of the issues was always the lack of integration between cities in the rim and the BER to Shanghai (mainland China's financial centre). The Beijing-Tianjin Intercity Railway (the world's fastest conventional train service which, on opening in 2008, reduced travel times from 70 to 30 minutes) and the Beijing-Shanghai High-Speed Railway (opened June 2011, halving the travel time to 4½ hrs) are examples of how the Government are prioritizing the integration of the BER and, in so doing, are uncorking its economic development potential.

Beijing-Pyongyang-Seoul-Tokyo: On a much larger scale, the Bohai Economic Rim is also part of a super-urban area with Pyongyang (North Korea), Seoul (South Korea) and Tokyo (Japan). Connecting 77 cities with populations over 200,000, over 97 million people currently live in this super-urban area which stretches for 1,500 km.

(Continued)

---

3 The source of much of this data is the UN Habitat (2011) *State of the World's Cities Report 2010/2011.*

(Continued)

Tokyo-Kobe-Osaka-Kyoto-Nagoya: Like Beijing, Tokyo is also located in a second super-urban area. Unlike the former which connects four megalopolises in four countries, this super-urban area is located solely within Japan. But with a population predicted to hit 60 million by 2015 this is double the size of the largest global city-region.

Mumbai-Delhi: Another 1,500 km urban corridor stretches from Jawaharlal Nehru Port in Navi Mumbai on the west coast to Dadri and Tughlakabad in Delhi at the very northern edge of India. This industrial corridor connects two cities with populations currently in excess of 40 million and is seen as an emerging economy with the potential to become Central Asia's super-urban area.

Rio de Janeiro-Sao Paulo: More than 43 million live in Rio de Janeiro, Sao Paulo in Brazil and the area inbetween. This 430 km urban corridor is also seen as an emerging economy with the potential to become a South American super-urban area.

Ibadan-Lagos-Accra (ILA): The 600 km ILA urban corridor is the engine of West Africa's expanding economy. Actually linking five cities (Ibadan, Lagos, Cotonou, Lome, and Accra), each separated by 100–125 km and spread across four countries (Nigeria, Benin, Togo Ghana), conservative estimates suggest around 25 million people live in this industrializing economy. Perhaps more foresight is required in this example, but with 20 million people living in the major cities and with an emerging and expanding economy, this economic hotspot could one day represent sub-Saharan Africa's super-urban area.

Irrespective of whether you perceive these spaces to be real or imagined, the mere fact these cross-border regional networks of interlinked cities are in the social consciousness as a result of their rapid expansion in number, size, and scope, is doing much to advance the claim that cities at the heart of major urban-regional industrial production complexes are acting quasi-autonomously, that is, outside territorial structures formally administered or governed by the nation-state (Scott, 2001a, 2001b). Giving rise to 'unusual' or 'unbounded' regionalism – the recognition that city-regions and/or regional networks of cities often do not conform to any known territorial entities but are constructed in ways that appear to defy hierarchical control (Deas and Lord, 2006) – it is hard to escape the conclusion that, while cities are back, it is not as we once knew them.

Against the background of deepening globalisation the purpose of this chapter is to highlight the shifts accompanying the changing configuration of the urban economy, in particular those linked to the rescaling of the city and the emergence of new forms of urban economic space. To put work on cities and rescaling in context, we first need to distinguish between cities as we once knew them and cities as we now know them. To do this, the chapter explores the drift of cities away from national urban systems toward the orbit or gravity pull of international systems and global circuits of capital accumulation. In particular the chapter draws on Brenner's (2004) distinction between 'rescaling the geographies of capital' and 'rescaling the geographies of statehood' to emphasise how the rehierarchization of the urban and regional system is only partly

explained by economic factors (crisis-induced industrial restructuring, the rise of flexible production systems, new spatial divisions of labour); just as important are political
factors (centrally orchestrated state strategies to promote transnational investment in
major urban regions, governmentalised remapping of state spaces, the political-
construction of an 'elite' top hierarchy of cities and urbanised regions within national
and international circuits of capital). So in the next section the chapter explores the
changing configuration of the urban economy before critically examining the role of
the state as facilitator, orchestrator and enabler of changes to the urban economy in
the second half of the chapter.

CITIES AS WE ONCE KNEW THEM, CITIES AS WE NOW KNOW THEM: THE CHANGING CONFIGURATION OF THE URBAN ECONOMY

Technological innovation, the rise of flexible production systems, and processes of
deterritorialization have all contributed in eroding the stability of historically
entrenched urban and regional hierarchies under globalizing conditions. During the
era of Fordism, these urban and regional hierarchies were largely internalised by
nationally-specific systems of production[4]. Today this is what we might call the 'old
order', with areas designated according to their status as *inter alia* growth areas
(those benefitting from Fordist accumulation), over-growth areas (satellite towns,
suburbs), and depressed areas (those problem areas in need of assistance). In nationally-specific contexts, this spatial hierarchy was then utilised by the state to redirect
capital employment from growth areas to depressed areas according to the principles
of spatial Keynesianism, that is, the need for state intervention in redistributing
resources to promote balanced urban and regional development through national
scaled regulatory control of the space economy.

Strategies of spatial Keynesianism were dominant during the Fordist period, particularly in Western Europe. In the United Kingdom, for example, the 'post-war consensus'
which followed the 1940 Royal Commission on the Distribution of Industrial Population's placement of a national duty on the UK government to control capital so as to
prevent socio-spatial inequality in general, and the over-heating of London and the
south east in particular, offers a vivid example of how strategies of spatial Keynesianism
provided the backdrop for state-led urban and regional planning during the Fordist
period. Similarly in France, indicative planning in the post-war period was implemented
with the over-arching aim of identifying potential over-supply, bottlenecks, and shortages in order that state investment decisions could be spatially targeted in a more timely

---

4 A fantastic visual representation of this national hierarchy of cities and regions can be
found in Robert Dickinson's book *City and Region – A Geographical Representation*
(1964: 388). It identifies a hierarchy of 1st, 2nd, 3rd and 4th order cities in each national
territory of Western Europe. Reprinted in Brenner (2004: 122).

way to reduce market disequilibrium. While in Germany, the first federal law on spatial planning (the 1965 *Bundersraumordnungsgesetz* or ROG) established the basic aim of enabling territorial equilibrium; planners interpreting this to mean further accumulation of resources in major cities should be avoided and should be targeted instead at those so-called 'lagging' rural and border zones which are not primary sources of capital accumulation.

Dominant in the period 1940–1970, the relative stability afforded by the Fordist-Keynesian institutional compromise was violently ruptured by the rapid decline in traditional manufacturing industries, a process which starved the Fordist growth dynamic of its life-blood. Despite this, not all urban areas experienced the collapse of Fordism and its impacts to the same extent. But why was this? Well the answer rests, first, in the rise of flexible or 'lean' production systems (Harrison, 1994). The crisis of Fordism saw firms forced to switch from mass producing single products to a model of flexible specialization. This involved the production of diverse product lines targeted at specific groups of customers, requiring the use of non-specialist machinery and multi-skilled labour able to respond quickly and efficiently to market change. As part of a wider strategy to enhance efficiency and externalise risk, flexible specialization led to parts of the production process being outsourced or subcontracted on short-term contracts to a network of suppliers. In the first instance then, those traditional manufacturing firms, sectors, and locations which were able to restructure and quickly adopt flexible production systems were able to foreshorten the crisis and its effects. The classic example of this is the automobile industry – 'the mass production industry *par excellence*' (Dicken, 2010: 339) – where mass production techniques were displaced by a system of lean production, led by highly efficient and cost-competitive Japanese automobile firms (Toyota, Honda, Nissan) in the 1970s and copied subsequently by US and European car producers (Ford, GM, Fiat, Volkswagen, Renault). Nonetheless, this is only part of this particular story for, in addition, flexible production systems were also at the heart of three sectors which came to characterise, perhaps even determine, capitalism's post-Fordist economic and geographic form – (1) high-technology manufacturing; (2) revitalised design-intensive craft production; and (3) advanced producer and financial services (Storper and Scott, 1990).

While the collapse of the Fordist mode of traditional mass production sent shockwaves through older industrial urban regions, these events were countered by the emergence of 'new industrial spaces' (Scott, 1988a). Industrial regions such as Silicon Valley, Orange County, and Route 128 in the United States, along with Baden-Württemberg, Catalonia, Lombardy, Rhône-Alpes (the so-called 'Four Motors of Europe'), and more recently Bangalore (the 'Silicon Valley of India') proved beacons of hope, demonstrating how certain industrial locations were successfully bucking the trend of national economic decline to emerge as 'winners' in the period after Fordism. Initial endeavours to account for these industrial developments chronicled wholesale shifts from Fordist mass production to post-Fordist flexible specialization (Piore and Sabel, 1984), old industrial spaces to new industrial spaces (Scott, 1988a), and national economies to regional economies (Sabel, 1989). What they suggested was that owing to mass production technologies never being widely adopted in these exemplars of the post-Fordist growth dynamic, and their economies being vertically disintegrated and flexibly organised around high-levels of inter-firm coordination in high-technology sectors, their urban-economic form and infrastructure secured these regions a competitive territorial advantage in the new global economy. Nevertheless, these accounts proved too narrowly economistic in their search for explanation, often guilty of overlooking important social and political factors upon which the post-Fordist growth dynamic relies.

In an insightful account into the formation of these new regional economic spaces of capital accumulation, Michael Storper highlights how equally important in globalizing forms of capital accumulation are those 'soft', 'untraded interdependencies' (such as rules of action, customs, conventions, understandings and values) which constitute the 'non-material assets in production' (Storper, 1997: 192). Critically, this chimed with research being conducted by other economic geographers at the time – most notably Phil Cooke and Kevin Morgan's work on 'regional innovation networks' in Europe. Their research into regional development in Baden-Württemberg, Emilia-Romagna, Wales, and the Basque country pinpointed how successful regional economies were those governed less by vertical relations of authority and dependence but by horizontal relations of cooperation and reciprocity (Cooke and Morgan, 1998). Echoing much of what Storper articulated in relation to 'untraded interdependencies', Cooke and Morgan believed horizontal relations of cooperation and reciprocity relied on those very same societal conventions. Trust, solidarity, loyalty and tolerance between the state, economic actors, and civil society stakeholders thereby came to be perceived as key to fostering dense local networks, where sharing trade and business information, technology and training becomes commonplace – a necessary component for post-Fordist capital accumulation. With this in place, it was argued, 'intelligent' regions were formed, that is, regions which are able to exploit the transition toward globalizing forms of capital accumulation to their own advantage. One important consequence of this argument was the suggestion that regions were operating as quasi-independent 'actor spaces', able to mobilise themselves to have a decisive influence on economic development, wealth distribution, and consolidating a sense of inclusiveness (Amin and Thrift, 1995).

Giving rise to what we have come to know in retrospect as the 'new regionalism', this body of literature established strong support for nationally-specific production systems being superseded in globalisation by more localised industrial districts and regional innovation systems. This emerging political-economic orthodoxy suggested post-Fordist capital accumulation required networked hubs comprising both 'hard' institutional structures and 'soft' institutional processes; the latter being best developed at local and regional levels because 'this is the level at which regular interactions, one of the conditions for trust-building, can be sustained over time' (Morgan, 1997: 501). In regional studies, leading proponents of the 'new regionalist' orthodoxy were so convinced that major urban regions were the fundamental building blocks of economic and social life after Fordism they prophetically announced that we were coming to live in a 'regional world' (Ohmae, 1995; Storper, 1997).

Under conditions of globalisation, areas which are well-resourced (containing large concentrations of transnational corporations, highly-skilled workers) and well-connected (within existing transportation and communications networks) have successfully exploited these crucial locational advantages to consolidate, increase, and further concentrate high-level economic and industrial activity, alongside flows of foreign direct investment, skilled migrant labour and tourists at the expense of other less favoured locations (Brenner, 2009b). For this reason, alongside those new urban and regional industrial zones, global cities have likewise proved to be loci for industries with flexible production systems. One sector in particular locates almost exclusively in global cities, and that is the advanced producer and financial services sector. Advanced producer and financial service functions (advertising, banking, financial consultancy and management, insurance, real estate) give elite global cities a monopoly over what is the indicator of choice for most analyses into the functionality of global cities, that is, the measure by which cities are ranked according to their command and control over global circuits of capital accumulation[5]. This monopoly is reinforced by recognition that not only do advanced producer and financial services cluster in global cities, these industries which serve the demands of transnational capital and its thirst for enhanced command and control over space on a global scale have expanded rapidly over the past 40 years. In this way, advanced producer and financial services are a classic example of how for all the talk of deterritorialization, the collapse of distance, and transition to a borderless world, what we are witnessing is the emergence and consolidation of a series of global command and control points that are assuming greater importance as power is localised in an increasingly select number of place-specific, wealth-generating locations.

The essential point here is that even in an era of global economic integration, characterised by increased capital mobility, the expansion of transnational finance capital, and formation of global production networks, capital will exploit favourable local and regionally specific conditions of production to secure competitive advantage. Such arguments have given rise to what we have now come to recognise as the rescaling and reterritorialization of capital under globalizing conditions (Brenner, 2004). This is the notion that for all capital has been able to release itself from the shackles of national scaled regulatory control, it is forced to (re)produce new and/or modify existing socio-spatial infrastructure at supra-national and sub-national scales to create the conditions necessary for capital accumulation. It is here, for reasons noted above, that major urban cores and new regional industrial districts are able to exploit their place- and territory-specific location advantages to prosper in globalisation.

---

5 It must be noted that this data can only be used as an indicator. It does not equate that the most connected cities are necessarily those with the most power over global circuits of capital accumulation, but it is the closest researchers have come to interpreting the changing geography of the world economy through a critical lens.

CITIES IN GLOBALISATION – THE CHANGING URBAN ORDER

Much of the last two decades has been spent documenting the impacts this rescaling of capital has had on particular geographical location across the globe. Specifically, research has been documenting how the rescaling of capital has been highly uneven, leading to even more pronounced forms of spatial division (any social and economic inequality), at every scale. Three are worth mentioning here. Firstly, the tendency toward metropolitan polarization described above has ensured that being a national and major region centre is not enough in the era of globalised capital accumulation. As urban competitiveness becomes increasingly reliant on the demands of transnational capital, in turn dependent on the presence of specialised producer and financial services, the formation of a network of global cities in which command and control functions are centralised have created a new tier of highly connected, elite level cities. Over the past decade, the Globalization and World Cities (GaWC) research group have developed a world city network model which deepens our understanding of how cities are increasingly connected across space as part of capitalist strategies to position cities within global circuits of capital accumulation[6].

What the GaWC analysis shows is that even within this tier of highly connected, elite-level cities there are distinct tendencies of developmental/growth divergence. The first observation to make is the general rise of connectivity in this network of upper-tier cities (Taylor et al., 2010). The second is how London, New York and Hong Kong remain the most connected cities, in effect the 'capital' global cities to the three major networks of global cities in the world city network – the west European (London, Paris, Milan, Madrid), north American (New York, Toronto, Chicago) and Pacific-Asian (Hong Kong, Singapore, Tokyo, Sydney, Shanghai, Beijing). Below this, and not represented by the table, there is a Latin American network (Buenos Aires, Sao Paulo, Mexico City) and an emerging east European network (Moscow, Warsaw, Istanbul). Highlighting the global dimension of these city networks, Africa is the only area one might suggest is 'off the map' with Johannesburg the sole representative in the top 50 (cf. Robinson, 2002). Nevertheless, this does not mean African cities are disconnected from the global economy, just less well connected. This is evidenced in the latest findings which highlight how 11 African cities have global connectivity scores more than

---

6 While the GaWC methodology arguably represents the most comprehensive approach to mapping and analysing inter-city relations and their importance in globalisation, it does not go uncontested. In the context of this chapter, perhaps the most notable critique comes from Jennifer Robinson (2006) who, writing from a post-colonial perspective, identifies how a focus on global cities does not adequately represent, and thereby under emphasises the importance of, cities of the global south. For more on this and other critiques, plus how the GaWC methodology has been revised over time, see Beaverstock et al. (2011: 190–1).

'Top 20' Most Connected Cities in Terms of Their 'Global Network Connectivity' (GNC) in 2000 and 2008

2000			2008		
RANK	**CITY**	**GNC**	**RANK**	**CITY**	**GNC**
1	London	100.00	1	New York	100.00
2	New York	97.10	2	London	99.32
3	Hong Kong	73.08	3	Hong Kong	83.41
4	Tokyo	70.64	4	Paris	79.68
5	Paris	69.72	5	Singapore	76.15
6	Singapore	66.61	6	Tokyo	73.62
7	Chicago	61.18	7	Sydney	70.93
8	Milan	60.44	8	Shanghai	69.06
9	Madrid	59.23	9	Milan	69.05
10	Los Angeles	58.75	10	Beijing	67.65
11	Sydney	58.06	11	Madrid	65.95
12	Frankfurt	57.53	12	Moscow	64.85
13	Amsterdam	57.10	13	Brussels	63.63
14	Toronto	56.92	14	Seoul	62.74
15	Brussels	56.51	15	Toronto	62.38
16	Sao Paulo	54.26	16	Buenos Aires	60.62
17	San Francisco	50.43	17	Mumbai	59.48
18	Zurich	48.42	18	Kuala Lumpur	58.44
19	Taipei	48.22	19	Chicago	57.57
20	Jakarta	47.92	20	Taipei	56.07
Cities that rise into the top 20 in 2008			**Cities that fall out of the top 20 in 2008**		
22	Buenos Aires	46.81	21	Sao Paulo	55.96
23	Mumbai	46.81	22	Zurich	55.51
27	Shanghai	43.95	25	Amsterdam	54.60
28	Kuala Lumpur	43.53	28	Jakarta	53.29
29	Beijing	43.43	31	Frankfurt	51.58
30	Seoul	42.32	40	Los Angeles	45.18
37	Moscow	40.76	46	San Francisco	41.35

Source: Taylor et al. (2010: 339)

10% that of London (Wall, 2010); a point which repeats earlier findings leading Taylor et al. to conclude 'all cities can be characterised to some degree as both "world" and "global" in nature. Hence, they are all "cities in globalization".' (2007: 15). A third observation is that while the top level remains relatively constant, with London, New York, and Hong-Kong occupying positions 1 to 3, and

Paris, Singapore, and Tokyo in positions 4 to 6, there has been remarkable fluctuation elsewhere in the top 20. The European cities of Frankfurt, Zurich and Amsterdam have all dropped out of the top 20, along with the US cities of Los Angeles and San Francisco. They are being overtaken and replaced by the Pacific-Asian cities, Shanghai, Beijing, Mumbai, Seoul and Kuala Lumpur, showing that services are rising fast to complement the regions established manufacturing prowess as the new 'workshop of the world'. Other cities making a notable rise are Moscow – spearheading a revival of cities emerging from their communist past to become well connected in international circuits of capitalist accumulation – and Buenos Aires, emerging as the major economic gateway to Latin America. One important consequence of this is functions once located in national capitals and major regional centres are being concentrated in a select number of global cities whose function is as a gateway to the global economy for what are now much larger, increasingly transnational, networks of national capitals and major regional centres (Brenner, 2009b).

All of which has produced a new elite level of cities that act as important gateways, articulating regional and national economies into the global economy. But the rescaling of capital has also seen a development and growth divergence among cities within national urban systems. For the observed shift from what we come to identify as the 'old' industrial spaces of Fordist accumulation to 'new' industrial spaces of post-Fordist capital accumulation has led national urban hierarchies to be recalibrated as industrial production polarised in the most economically advantageous sub-national production complexes. In the US, this saw industrial production, and as a result urban development, switch from the 'snowbelt' cities of Detroit and Pittsburgh in the north and east to the rapidly expanding 'sunbelt' boomtowns of Houston and Tucson in the south and west. This was mirrored in Europe. In Germany, for example, the boom regions were no longer those centred on the cities of Cologne, Essen, and Hamburg in the north but those newly dynamic cities of Frankfurt, Munich and Stuttgart to the south. In England, the same situation saw the traditional industrial heartlands of the Midlands and the North eclipsed by the rise of Cambridge and the M4/M11 corridors in the south east, while in Italy, dynamic post-Fordist economic growth is centred on a rapidly expanding industrial triangle around Milan, Turin, and Genoa in the north of the country. The second process where the rescaling of capital has led to more pronounced forms of spatial division is, that emerging in each national space economy is an inter-urban network where industrial activity and urban development is increasingly polarised. Of late, the extension of this observed pattern of inter urban polarization sees Inter-Urban networks which are transnational in nature: as evidenced by Europe's 'blue banana', which connects London at its north-westerly apex with *inter alia* Amsterdam, Brussels, Frankfurt, Stuttgart, Strasbourg, before reaching its south-easterly apex in Milan; NY-LON/PAR-LON, concepts used by commentators to emphasise strong transnational ties between particular cities in this network of cities, in this case New York–London and Paris–London; and super-urban areas, most notably in Newly Industrialised and BRIC countries (see the box earlier in this chapter).

A third important process sees divergence in the levels and/or degrees of primacy in different national urban systems. If we again use the most recent GaWC analysis as a starting point, a number of important observations can be made (Taylor et al., 2010). Firstly, there is a strong tendency towards primacy in many of the traditionally advanced capitalist nations. In the United Kingdom, for example, London remains the most globally connected city but the next city in line, Manchester, is only ranked 113th with a connectivity of 22% that of London. A similar picture emerges in France with Paris fourth but the next most connected city, Lyon, ranked 145th with a connectivity only 18% that of London. These are the most prominent examples of a primate city system. A very different picture emerges in China, however, where six cities (Hong Kong, Shanghai, Beijing, Taipei, Guangzhou, and Shenzhen) have global connectivity scores 25% or more that of London. Germany also has six cities with a global connectivity 25% or more that of London but what it lacks in comparison to China are cities at the apex of global connectivity. While once firmly established in the top 20, in 2008 Frankfurt once again found itself the highest ranked German city, but only 32nd overall with a proportionate connectivity half that of London. With Berlin (55), Hamburg (60), Munich (67), Dusseldorf (76) and Stuttgart (91), Germany emerges as the exemplar of a 'horizontal' urban system (Hoyler, 2010); albeit one which shows German cities to be experiencing a relative decline in their overall global network connectivity. The US, by contrast, shows evidence of being both a 'primate city' and 'horizontal urban' system: the former evidenced by the second-ranked city, Chicago, having a connectivity score 57% that of New York; the latter by 15 US cities having a global connectivity score higher than Manchester and 20 cities a score higher than Lyon (Taylor et al., 2010).

It is clear from this analysis how the collapse of the Fordist growth dynamic in the 1970s, and the major economic structural changes which have followed, led to a drift of cities away from national urban systems toward the orbit or gravity pull of supra-national circuits of capital accumulation, alongside both a developmental and growth divergence among cities within national urban systems. What is less clear is the role the state has played in this, and it is to this question that the chapter now turns.

WHAT ROLE THE STATE?

For sure, the state's trusted Keynesian macro-economic policy instruments which had proved effective in maintaining regulatory order during the Fordist era quickly became ineffectual in coping with the global economic crises of the 1970s. Quite simply, as national state space became increasingly permeable to untold myriad of transnational flows of capital, knowledge, commodities, labour, and information, nationally-configured regulatory frameworks, institutions and supports which had proved effective foundations for Fordist-Keynesian regulatory strategies were unsettled and forced to undergo major restructuring as the process of capital accumulation was globalised. Where controversy and debate emerges is that there are two schools of thought on what affect this major restructuring to the mode of regulation has had on the state. On one side there are those who believe state power is being eroded as national infrastructures are dismantled and replaced by new forms of political-economic regulation at supra-national (e.g. WTO, IMF, European Union, NAFTA, ASEAN) and sub-national levels (e.g. urban and regional governance). From this perspective the restructuring and rescaling of state power away from the national level to organisations and agencies enforcing neoliberal, market-led strategies at supra-national and sub-national levels signals the extent to which nation states have lost their ability to control and regulate the movement of capital across space, and leads authors such as Ohmae (1995) to proclaim 'the end of the nation-state'. On the other side there are those of us who believe that this major restructuring does not come at the expense of the state; in accordance with some kind of either/or, zero-sum, logic which appears to under-pin arguments made by those signalling the demise of the state. Albeit never for-getting that contemporary processes of state restructuring were crisis-induced, the argument put forward here is that the state is not the victim, but a key architect, of these processes of geo-economic integration. Building on the pioneering work of predecessors such as Bob Jessop, Neil Brenner's attempt to decipher how 'new state spaces' are being produced under contemporary capitalism has opened our eyes to the way in which the state has reconfigured its spatial and organisation structures to maintain control over urban and regional development (Brenner, 2004); in the process disturbing notions of the powerless state and premature announcements proclaiming the death of the nation state. Opening the black box on the rescaling of state power, Brenner's eloquent reasoning on this is worth quoting at length:

> Even as national states attempt to fracture or dismantle the institutional compromise of postwar Fordist-Keynesian capitalism in order to reduce domestic production costs, they have also devolved substantial regulatory responsibilities to regional and local institutions, which are seen to be better positioned to promote industrial (re)development within major urban and regional economies. This downscaling of regulatory tasks should not be viewed as a contraction or abdication of national state power, however, for it has frequently served as a centrally orchestrated strategy to promote trans-national capital investment within major urban regions, whether through public funding of large-scale infrastructural projects, the establishment of new forms of public-private partnerships or other public initiatives intended to enhance urban territorial competitiveness. (Brenner, 2004: 61–2)

Related to this, Brenner goes on to introduce the twin concepts of state spatial projects and state spatial strategies: the former referring to the organisational divi-sions of the state which, albeit increasingly located at multiple scales, are being organised and coordinated to re-establish coherence to the regulatory system; the latter alerting us to how state policies are increasingly spatially selective, with intervention privileging certain spaces over others and bringing about geographical variation among state activities. State spatial strategies are important in this discussion because what we have witnessed since the collapse of Fordism is the widespread abandonment of traditional Keynesian models of regional policy in favour of new national strategies designed to make major urban regions attractive to transnational capital. In short, nation states began to actively encourage, facilitate and shape geo-economic integration. For cities were no longer seen to be passive containers of all the socio-economic ills leftover from the collapse of Fordism but dynamic growth engines at the heart of what Brenner (1998: 8) identified as a new 'city-centric capitalism'. To be sure, the task of positioning cities strategically within global circuits of capital accumulation became an officially institutionalised task and goal for policy elites the world over. But while we can identify much that is uniform in how this task has been approached, some notable differences have undoubtedly contributed to the developmental and growth divergence among cities identified above; differences perhaps best illustrated by the spatial strategies adopted in the United Kingdom and Germany.

During the 1980s, growth in London and the south-east of England was heralded as the 'textbook' example of how major urban regions were able to pull away from the rest of the country due to their locational advantages in being able to attract transnational capital. Nevertheless, this representation of London and the south-east as a successful growth region 'did not simply fall into place; it had to be produced' (Allen et al., 1998: 10). And produced it was. The neoliberal strategies of liberalization and deregulation pursued by Margaret Thatcher and her Chancellor of the Exchequer, Nigel Lawson, proved extremely successful in strategically placing London (as global city) and south-east England (as global city-region) at the apex of the European and global urban hierarchy. It was part of a political strategy, known as Thatcherism, which made the conditions right for attracting transnational capital. Inflation was controlled, taxes lowered, exchange rate controls abolished, trade unionism restrained, state industries privatised, and finance deregulated in the belief that free market competition would see the price of products and services decrease and their quality increase.

All of which propelled London to global city status. But it also saw London and the south-east singled-out for growth, with the central state concerned primarily with promoting London's competitiveness as a world financial centre. Perhaps most famously, the 'Big Bang' reform of 27 October 1986 saw restrictions on financial lending lifted as part of a fundamental reform of the London Stock Exchange. A decision which strengthened London's place as finance capital, the Big Bang became the cornerstone of the Thatcher Government's neoliberal reforms. At home, it encouraged financial lending, which fuelled a housing boom in the south-east, as mortgage lending increased, and a consumer boom, as personal credit became easily accessible. Internationally, it exposed London's financial markets to a more competitive world, which in turn led to more jobs in the financial and professional services, led to an increase in high-wage earners, which in turn fuelled the consumption boom as demand for other products and services increased. In short, it presented London and the south-east as a dynamic growth region when many other regions appeared depressed; a perception constructed both materially and discursively by the state.

Not only did the Thatcher Government's neoliberal reforms prioritise financial capital and single-out London and the south-east for growth, the central state rolled-back regional aid, thereby starving the declining cities and regions of northern and western Britain of the traditional compensatory adjustment measure of regional policy under spatial Keynesianism, and abolished regional government, so as to depower dissenting opposition from industrial capital and manufacturing workers. In place of the former, massive public sector investment was channelled into making London and the south-east attractive to transnational capital, most notably the development of Canary Wharf as a new financial district in London's Dockland. In place of the latter, new local and regional agencies were created in accordance with the state-rescaling thesis; albeit in the case of the UK, one where the state maintained a very dominant and controlling hand. Conceptualised as the states tendency toward centrally orchestrated localism and regionalism (Harrison, 2008), evidence for the state continuing to prioritise London and the south-east can be seen in (amongst other things) recent 'city-region' policy initiatives – with £22 billion of public sector investment pumped into four city-region growth areas in the south-east, while the equivalent project in the north of England received a meagre £100 million (Harrison, 2011).

It is hard to escape the conclusion then that state spatial strategies have played a critical role in producing the UK's primate city system. Nonetheless, the same can be said for Germany which, as noted above, exhibits all the tendencies of a horizontal urban system. For, albeit the Federal State responded to the challenges of European integration and the intensification of globalisation by prioritizing the reconcentration of resources into major urban regions, this growth was to be in multiple urban regions. Two key political factors are important in explaining this. The first relates to Germany's lack of what we might deem an exceptional city. Whereas both London and Paris had by the 1970s acquired exceptional status in their respective national urban hierarchies, Germany had a number of urban regions at the apex of their urban hierarchy. In part this can be explained by German separation and the prevention of Berlin from acquiring a similar exceptional position in the urban hierarchy. Part can also be explained by the Federal Government's 1965 spatial planning law (*Raumordnungsgesetz*) which stated how a spatially equally distributed system of central places should be created to ensure balanced economic growth and territorial equilibrium across Germany. Meanwhile, second and somewhat related to this latter point, Germany has a much stronger decentralized state system than the UK which has meant it is not a politically viable option to prioritise a single urban region to the extent successive UK Government's have done with London. In addition, the Federal Government used this decentralised state system to push each major urban region toward achieving a functional specialization, with Frankfurt establishing itself as finance capital, Hamburg as the centre for print-media, Munich as a centre for publishing and film industry, and so on.

More recently, the decision to reassign Berlin as national capital of the reunified Germany in June 1991 led many to consider whether this signalled the beginning of a process whereby Berlin was being singled out for the reconcentration of functions[7]; further fuelled by the controversial redevelopment of Potsdammer Platz and the construction of the new government district during the 1990s. Nevertheless, the Federal Government's new spatial planning laws reaffirm the critical role played by the state in explaining developmental and growth divergence among cities in national urban systems. Responding to the challenge of positioning major cities and regions within supra-national circuits of capital accumulation, the Federal Government strategically selected six agglomerations (Berlin/Brandenburg, Hamburg, Munich, Rhine-Main, Rhine-Ruhr and Stuttgart) to be 'European Metropolitan Regions', that is, major urban regions deemed to be of 'superior' strategic importance (BmBau, 1995). Quite simply, it was recognition that although these major urban regions assumed various national tasks and formed important clusters in key areas of business activity, human capital, information and technology exchange, cultural experience and political engagement, Germany does not have an exceptional (global) city; what it has instead are a number of cities which are well positioned within European circuits of capital. In other words the inherited institutional and spatial arrangements, themselves the legacy of previous state spatial projects and state spatial strategies, have, in part, produced Germany's horizontal urban system, which in turn is now influencing decisions made by the Federal Government in responding to the task of positioning major urban regions in supra-national circuits of capital accumulation (on this, see Harrison and Growe, 2014a, 2014b). All of which is a sure sign the state has played, is playing, and will continue to play a critical role in encouraging and facilitating geo-economic integration, and as a direct consequence, in positioning cities in national and international urban systems, networks, and hierarchies.

SUMMARY AND CONCLUSION

It is perhaps timely that this chapter is written two decades after Sassen's (1991) *The Global City – London, Tokyo, New York* became the antecedent to the global city discourse and a decade since Allen Scott's (2001a) edited collected *Global City-Regions – Trends, Theory, Policy* did likewise for the global city-region discourse. Against the backdrop of deepening globalisation both came at key junctures, helping us to understand the changing role, form, and function of the major cities in the world in an era of unprecedented economic restructuring. Alongside this, the current chapter has drawn on Brenner's distinction between the rescaling of capital and rescaling the state to reinforce the importance of recognizing that for all capital has been seen to release itself from the shackles of national scaled regulatory control, the very fact it is forced to (re)produce new and/or modify existing socio-spatial infrastructure at supra-national and sub-national scales to

---

7 A similar process had occurred previously when the German Reich favoured Berlin as capital, leading to a concentration of resources in the city and prompting large population growth in the 50 years prior to World War II.

create the conditions necessary for capital accumulation requires a reterritorialization of capital. Simply stated, capital is not as 'free' as many hyper-globalists would have us believe.

What this chapter has shown is how the state actively encourages global economic integration. Evidence suggests that while the rise of neoliberalism and its market-driven approach to economic and social policy has been accompanied by a rolling back of the state, states have not only reconfigured their own institutional form to forge an ability to centrally orchestrate urban and regional development, but where they do intervene is often in response to the challenge of global economic integration and the goal of positioning their major cities and city-regions strategically within supra-national circuits of capital accumulation. This can clearly be seen in the examples of the United Kingdom and Germany described above where the state intervened to create new, or modify existing, socio-spatial infrastructure at the urban and regional level to, firstly, create the conditions necessary for capital accumulation, and secondly, make their major urban region(s) more attractive to transnational capital than their international competitors.

Thus, the future developmental and growth divergence among cities within national urban systems, the rescaling of the city, and emergence of new forms of (transnational) economic spaces will not only be shaped by inherited institutional and spatial arrangements, but by how states reconfigure their institutional form in response to rapid urbanisation and global economic integration continuing apace, related demands for more 'appropriate' (widely understood to mean more flexible, networked and smart) forms of urban and regional planning and governance arrangements, and new *loci* and/or expressions of inter- and intra-urban territorial cooperation and conflict around questions to do with increased competitiveness, resilience, new economic developments, infrastructure, the collective provision of services, and governmentalised remappings of urban and regional space (Harrison and Hoyler, 2014a). In this context then, this chapter highlights how it is timely to ask some searching questions about these new territorial dynamics and politics, to begin the process of developing appropriate vocabularies for mapping and conceptualizing the transforming urban economic landscape, and to explore the successes and failures of responses to the profound practical challenges posed by global economic integration and rapid urbanisation. One important question it re-raises is by whom and for whom these new economic spaces are being defined, delimited and designated as competitive territories *par excellence*. Undoubtedly a daunting challenge, it is one we as researchers need to scale in order to deepen our understanding of both the economic *and* political processes underpinning the contemporary urban condition.

Pedagogic Guide

City Mayors (http://www.citymayors.com). Established in 2003 and maintained by the City Mayors Foundation, this website deals with all aspects of urban affairs, including: city rankings, governance structures, and issues facing cities in areas ranging from economic and investment, business, culture, development, environment, transports, education and health.

City Population (http://www.citypopulation.de/world/Agglomerations.html). Provides an up-to-date list of all agglomerations of the world with a population of one million inhabitants. This was Scott's starting point for identifying the 'global city-region' as the pivotal socio-spatial formation in globalisation, and the data presented here identifies the 525 cities in the world which have a population of more than one million.

Globalization and World Cities (GaWC) Research Network (http://www.lboro.ac.uk/gawc/). Based at Loughborough University (UK), GaWC is the leading academic think-tank on cities in globalisation. The GaWC website contains 430+ research bulletins, 100+ project details, and 25 data sets on cities in globalisation.

Metropolis (http://www.metropolis.org) is the World Association of Major Metropolises. Created in 1985, the Metropolis Association is represented by more than 100 members from across the world and operates as an international forum for exploring issues and concerns common to all big cities and metropolitan regions.

UN-Habitat (http://www.unhabitat.org) is the United Nations agency for human settlements, and publisher of the bi-annual *State of World Cities* report which identifies current and future trends of urban dwelling.

4

New Economies, New Spaces

Stefan Krätke

The breakdown of the neoliberal 'dealer economy' and the finance dominated model of capitalist development at the end of 2008, which led to a worldwide economic crisis, marks the peak of a round of 'abbreviated restructuring' episodes of urban economies since the early 1990s and indicates the need for a review of this period's urban economic development concepts and growth ideologies. A major trend in this period was the rise of 'new economy' sectors like ICT, bio-technology, media and culture industry, etc. and the emergence of new urban space economies focusing on the intra-metropolitan scale. The rise of new 'city industries' (including knowledge-intensive production activities and the culture industries) lies at the heart of the resurgent urban economy. 'City industries' that prefer to locate and expand in the inner-city area were expected to take on the role of core growth sectors which might compensate for the decline of Fordist industries.

This chapter intends to review the most influential urban economic development concepts of the last decades with particular emphasis on the rise of new leading growth sectors. Secondly, it deals with the emerging new economy of the inner city and its impact on the reshaping of the urban regions' spatial fabric. The proliferation of new industrial sites in the inner city can be regarded as a *global phenomenon* that includes cities in Europe and North America as well as cities in the growth economies of Pacific Asia such as Singapore, Shanghai, Tokyo and Seoul (Hutton, 2010).

The rise of new 'city industries', however, entails a marked variation in the particular reindustrialization processes and experiences of individual cities and inner-city districts (Hutton, 2010). The extent to which these new economies and new spaces are reshaping the city varies according to different types of cities (such as metropolis, large city, medium-size city) and is particularly pronounced in large cities and metropolitan regions, where the new city industries can develop a 'critical mass'. The culture industries, for example, are characterized by a highly selective concentration within the urban system, so that the formation of viable clusters of the cultural economy only applies to a limited number of cities. Furthermore, the rise of new city industries varies according to the type of economies in which the cities are embedded:

The 'new economy of the inner city' phenomenon shows a particularly strong dissemination in the industrialized countries of the 'global north'. Secondly, there is evidence of similar developments in major cities of newly industrialized countries (e.g. Singapore, Kuala Lumpur, Seoul) and of transitional economies such as China, Brazil, and India (see below), whereas in developing countries the 'new economy' sectors are comparatively less developed and have not yet exerted a strong impact on urban economic and spatial restructuring.

URBAN ECONOMIC DEVELOPMENT CONCEPTS AND GROWTH IDEOLOGIES

The debate on urban economic development has been shaped by a sequence of generalizing concepts that intended to grasp the respective period's prime 'motors' of urban economic growth in terms of new leading subsectors of the urban economy. These concepts were often transformed into new urban growth ideologies (such as the 'post-industrial city', the 'service metropolis' and the 'creative city') which strongly affected urban economic development strategies.

From the Industrial City to the Post-Industrial Service Metropolis

For a long time, the co-evolution of industrialization and urbanization in Western countries has shaped the vision of the economic base of cities. Hence the 'industrial city' represented the most influential generalizing concept of urban economic development. The focus on the cities' role as manufacturing centres in a 'Fordist' phase of capitalist development (cf. Scott, 1988a) could be combined with the notion of a spatial division of labour within the urban system that corresponded to the rise of a multi-regional organization of large firms and included a distinction between 'headquarter cities' and 'branch plant cities' (cf. Pred, 1977). In the 'global north', economic restructuring accompanied by shrinking employment in manufacturing led to the decline of many cities whose economy was primarily focused on traditional manufacturing sectors.

On the background of secular declines in Fordist production and the rise of a specialized service economy since the 1970s, which had been theoretically articulated by the notion of an emerging 'post-industrial society' (Bell, 1974), the 'post-industrial city' emerged as a new general concept of urban economic development. In the 'binary world' of the post-industrial city concept, manufacturing-based cities were regarded as the losers of structural change, and cities with an expanding service economy appeared to be the winners (cf. Smith and Williams, 1986; Soja, 2000). This simplified concept of structural change has been converted into the new urban growth ideology of the city as a centre of service sector activity, particularly of advanced producer services. As a consequence, large cities in the 'global north' geared their economic and spatial development strategy towards supporting an expansion of the city's service industries, e.g. by new extensions of the central business district; or the reconversion of abandoned industrial sites for new office complexes, etc.

The idea that urban economies are primarily relying on service industries (cf. Daniels and Moulaert, 1991; Bryson and Daniels, 2007) did not take into account that manufacturing activities continued to form a relevant part of most urban regions' economic base. Processes of functional upgrading and structural change within urban regions' manufacturing sectors have been widely ignored. The growth of advanced producer services is to a large extent an articulation of organizational restructuring processes within the manufacturing sector itself, which has increasingly 'outsourced' technology-related service functions (like R&D, technical testing activities, laboratory services, etc.) to autonomous firms in the service sector (Krätke, 2007). Today, the urban economy of prospering cities (such as, for example, Munich and Barcelona) is often based on a comparatively high share of research-intensive manufacturing sectors and technology-related services. This type of sectoral profile differs from those cities which are predominantly relying on knowledge-intensive market-related business services and the financial sector. The concept of the 'city as a service metropolis' widely ignored the fact that urban economies are characterized by quite diverse sectoral profiles (i.e. the particular mix of manufacturing and service sectors) and development paths (i.e. the main direction of restructuring of the urban economy's sectoral mix), so that, for example, the particular path of London or Paris could not be taken as a general model of future urban economies (Krätke, 2007).

The emphasis on the cities' prominent role as providers of specialized corporate services has also exerted strong influence on the 'global city' line of urban research, which represents a most relevant concept of urban economic development in the era of intensifying globalization. This approach places the cities' external economic relations and their positioning within globally extended corporate networks at the centre of analysis. 'Global cities', in which international financial and corporate services are concentrated, are functioning as locational centres for the production of a global control capacity over worldwide extended production networks and market spaces (Sassen, 1991; 2000a). Whereas traditional concepts of the 'service metropolis' have stressed the importance of a city's corporate services for the respective national economic territory, global city research concentrates on the *global* reach of the cities' service capacities. The formation of a world-city network that is based on the organizational networks of global service providers is subject of the research carried out by the 'GaWC' Group (cf. Taylor, 2004).

However, the impact of globalization processes on urban economies cannot be exclusively related to the role played by global service providers. The expansion and diffusion of industrial urbanism on a global scale which is led by the formation of global production networks with local anchoring points in metropolitan regions all over the world is a most distinctive feature of the current phase of globalization (cf. Soja, 2000). Particularly the cities of the 'global south' are characterized by specific profiles of globally connected economic functions, which include manufacturing activities and global production networks' branch plants. In sum, the research on 'cities in globalization' represents an approach to urban analysis that still has great potential for thematic extensions.

The Conceptualization of Urban Economies' Restructuring Since the 1990s

Since the early 1990s, the debate on urban futures has been related to a sequence of 'abbreviated restructuring episodes' of urban economies, and concentrated on diverse aggregates of 'new growth sectors' that seemed to be at the heart of a resurgent urban economy.

The first restructuring period has been shaped by the 'new economy' bubble. The rise of information and communication technologies (ICT) and other new industries has been branded by the term 'new economy' in order to indicate a superior quality and good prospects as compared to the 'old economy' of traditional manufacturing industries (cf. Hübner, 2005). On the level of cities, the related urban growth ideology and development concept emphasized that cities which are able to become prime centres of new economy sectors, particularly the high-tech sectors of the ICT branches and technology-intensive subsectors of the media industries (such as multimedia and the internet business), will be the winners of economic restructuring. Thus many cities focused their economic development strategy on the promotion of ICT activities and the expansion of the new economy. However, this new economy triggered a speculative bubble in the financial sector around new economy enterprises, which broke down in 2001. After the crash, the new economy hype was substituted by new generalizing concepts of the 'lead sectors' of urban economic development.

A second line of debates on a promising strategy of urban economic regeneration has been closely related to the cultural economy of cities. This debate highlighted the strong impact of the cultural economy sector (including activities such as film & TV, music industry, publishing, the performing arts, etc.) on urban economies in the 'global north' (Scott, 2000), and detected its particularly strong embedding in inner-city areas (Krätke, 2000, 2002). The spread of urban regeneration concepts which drew on the cities' cultural economy sector and further cultural assets has fostered an increasing interest in the cultural economy of cities. However, the cultural economy's possible contribution to the compensation of shrinking employment opportunities in traditional Fordist industries is limited in quantitative terms, so that no city can solely count on the culture industries' growth. In recent times, economic development concepts that focus on the city's cultural economy have increasingly been equipped with the new fashionable branding of 'creative industries' (cf. Hartley, 2005) which has artificially 'substituted' the former analysis of the cultural economy of cities.

After the burst of the new economy speculative bubble in 2001, the 'knowledge-based city' became the most influential and still relevant concept of urban economic development and restructuring. This concept is based on the notion that the advanced industrial countries' development path is increasingly shaped by activities of an emerging 'knowledge economy' that bets on the generation and economic exploitation of new knowledge in terms of continued innovation activities (Dunning, 2000; Cooke, 2002). The leading sectors of this model of development are the diverse knowledge-intensive branches of economic activity (including the above mentioned knowledge-intensive producer services, the cultural economy as well as

research-intensive manufacturing activities). The knowledge-based economy represents an account of broad trends in contemporary economic restructuring in the
'global north' which are of particular relevance to urban economies, since the knowledge-intensive sectors are selectively concentrating in large cities and metropolitan
regions (Krätke, 2007). The debate on urban development prospects in the era of the
knowledge economy (cf. Raspe and van Oort, 2006) is strongly related to the role of
cities as major innovation centres for diverse economic subsectors. This debate highlights the relevance of intra-metropolitan knowledge networks and local knowledge
spillovers (Tödtling et al., 2006; Krätke and Brandt, 2009; Krätke, 2010a), i.e. the
relational component of urban regions' innovation systems. The 'knowledge-based
city' still represents a relevant concept of urban economic development and restructuring that focuses on the urban regions' innovation capabilities and the expansion
of knowledge-intensive subsectors of the urban economy.

However, in recent times this approach has been 'overtaken' by the fashionable
concept of the 'creative city' as the locational centre of a 'creative class' (Florida, 2002).
This approach starts from the thesis that creativity has become the essential resource
of contemporary urban economic development. Florida (2005) claims that those cities
which show a strong concentration of members of the 'creative class' (and thus a concentration of 'talent') are revealing a particularly successful economic development in
high technology sectors (Florida, 2002, 2005). Florida's concept exploits the 'cultural
inflection' of contemporary urban analysis (Peck, 2005) and deals with specific attraction factors of cities for the members of the creative class, emphasizing particularly
socio-cultural attraction factors. The 'creative city' concept says that the creative class
is selectively concentrating in those cities that offer the best 'qualities of place' in terms
of cultural amenities of a specific character (such as a vibrant music scene, a 'cool
scene' of clubs, pubs and restaurants, etc). The approach results in a recommendation
to urban decision-makers to take care of providing a high quality of living and leisure
amenities for the creative class members. The concept also combines with a booming
debate on 'creative industries'.

The notion that cities and in particular the large metropoles of the urban system
are functioning as major centres of creativity and innovation, is not a new idea
(cf. Jacobs, 1969). Yet in recent years, the 'creative city' concept has been taken up as a
message of hope and guidance to future successful development. The concept has been
transformed into a new urban growth ideology which is based on the self-glorification of
particular functional elites of the neoliberal model of society, since Florida's creative
class does not only include scientifically, technologically and artistically creative
workers, but also the functionaries of the financial and real estate sector, the managerial class and diverse business service providers. The critique of the 'creative class'
concept can be complemented by the empirical finding that Florida's 'creative professionals' do not have a significant impact on the urban regions' success in developing
sustainable economic structures (Krätke, 2010b). Quite on the contrary, prominent
parts of Florida's creative class, such as the FIRE sector professionals, are the social
actors who just recently have caused a collapse of the finance-dominated model
of capitalist development, which leads to a tremendous economic damage and loss of

jobs worldwide. On the other hand, it makes sense to analyze the role of techno-logically and artistically creative occupations in an urban economy's innovative performance. However, the macro-level analysis of urban regions' creative capacities as presented by Florida (2005) doesn't touch the important question of how creative work is generating successful innovation in the institutional setting of an urban economy. This question is more seriously taken up in the framework of the 'knowl-edge-based city' approach (see above).

The debate on 'creative cities' has for the most part concentrated on a selection of specifically creative subsectors of the urban economy. However, the delimitation of 'creative industries' is contested and still open to debate. The creative capacity of cities cannot seriously be restricted to a narrow range of industries such as the cultural economy and the software industry. On the other hand, the inclusion of all economic subsectors with continuous innovation activity under the term 'creative industries' would be misleading, too, since this term suggests that there are also non-creative industries. An analysis of the creative capacity of cities thus should include both the culture industries and the industrial research & development activities.

Altogether, the rise of new economic subsectors which are strongly based on knowledge-intensive work and creative performance has led to a resurgence of urban economies in the 'global north'. These new urban growth sectors, however, in total could not compensate for the ongoing loss of traditional 'regular' jobs in Fordist industries (due to offshoring, etc.) and the decline of 'regular' low rank service sector jobs (due to rationalization and the exploitation of informal immi-grant labour). Thus, many large cities in the 'global north' today are facing severe labour market pressures with regard to the large population group of less skilled workers and are confronted with related problems of social polarization, even though they can achieve a 'high rank' or positive development in the new economic growth sectors of knowledge-intensive industries and the cultural economy. The urban population still contains large social groups which tend to be excluded from the gains of the 'new islands' of urban growth.

NEW ECONOMIES AND THE RESHAPING OF THE URBAN SPACE-ECONOMY

There is much evidence on the emergence or revival of new production spaces in the metropolitan core in terms of a formation of 'new industrial districts', which draw on diverse types of agglomeration economies. Case studies relating to large cities in the 'global north' include, for example, New York, Toronto, Vancouver, London, Paris, Barcelona, Berlin (cf. Krätke, 2000; Scott, 2000; Bell and Jayne 2004; Indergaard, 2004; Lloyd, 2006; Evans, 2009; Pratt, 2009; Hutton, 2010). The formation of new intra-urban industrial districts of research-intensive activi-ties and the culture industries might be regarded as a local spatial articulation of the broader economic restructuring trend towards an increasingly knowledge-intensive and innovation-driven economy.

As regards the spatial organization of a metropolitan region's economy, for a long time the simplified view prevailed that the urban centre is characterized by an agglomeration of key business services and corporate headquarters. Manufacturing industries, on the other hand, would either concentrate in the urban periphery or relocate to the fringes of the metropolitan region. In recent times, this rough picture of the metropolitan economy's spatial organization has been challenged by two trends. Key subsectors of manufacturing activity are regrouping to form new local industrial districts *within* the metropolis itself (Scott, 1988b; Krätke, 2000). A number of traditional local areas of production activity in the inner-city area of the metropolis are subject to a process of restructuring and 'upgrading' by a new mix of production activities which predominantly enclose knowledge-intensive high-tech subsectors such as the software industry, pharmaceutical industry and bio-technology, medical engineering, and the diverse cultural products industries. These subsectors are forming new 'city industries' which lead to a revitalization of productive activities in the inner-city.

As a consequence, however, there is an increasing number of competing and conflicting claims for the use of inner-city space. Hutton (2010: 18) emphasizes that new city industries are constantly threatened by expanding spatial demands of the commercial-financial sector. 'The role of the latter in driving inflationary pressures within the property market suggests a profile of "precarious reindustrialization" in the metropolitan core'. Particularly the small experimental producers of the cultural economy are prime candidates for displacement in the framework of inner-city redevelopment projects. The inner-city areas of metropolitan regions represent a 'contested' social space not just with respect to residential use and gentrification processes, but also with regard to various production activities.

The restructuring of metropolitan economies' spatial organization corresponds to a trend towards re-agglomeration, particularly in R&D-intensive manufacturing sectors, design-intensive industries and cultural products industries (cf. Scott, 1988a; 2000). New local agglomerations of such industries are on the one hand located in the inner-city area of large cities and metropolitan regions, on the other hand in the peripheral zones of metropolitan regions. Here, the emerging local clusters of knowledge- and research-intensive industrial activities are frequently labelled as new urban 'technology districts' (see below). A recent empirical analysis of industrial location at the intra-metropolitan level (Arauzo-Carod and Viladecans-Marsal, 2009: 556) confirmed that particularly the high-tech industries' new manufacturing firms 'prefer to locate their establishments within, or as close as possible to, the central city itself', in order to maintain fluid communications with the centre and to benefit from its agglomeration advantages.

The formation of new production spaces at the intra-metropolitan scale is fostered by the continued 'unbounding of the metropolis' in terms of the extraordinary expansion of its spatial scale (cf. Soja, 2000) towards the formation of a metropolitan region which might include several secondary cities and urban sub-centres besides the central city and its core area. When we talk about 'globalizing cities' (Marcuse and van Kempen, 2000), we do increasingly mean the expanding spatial scale of a global city region that exceeds former administrative boundaries of the city (Scott, 2001a).

New Industrial Spaces in the Inner-City Area: The Example of Berlin

The Berlin metropolis today contains a series of new local industrial agglomerations, which are distributed over all zones of the city's territory (Krätke, 2000). A first group is located in Berlin's urban periphery (denoting the districts outside the densely built inner-city area that is delimitated by the 'S-Bahn' railway circle). Here, the sectoral profile is characterized by a concentration of firms from both R&D-intensive high-tech and medium high-tech manufacturing industries. These local agglomerations stem from industrial restructuring and 'upgrading' processes which result in an increased share of R&D-intensive industries. The Adlershof 'technology district' is a prominent local industrial agglomeration within Berlin's outer urban area, whose sectoral profile is specifically dominated by R&D-intensive high-tech industries.

A second group incorporates a series of local agglomerations, all of which are located in the inner-city area, particularly in a ring of districts around the East Berlin city centre (as for example the districts of Prenzlauer Berg, Friedrichshain and Kreuzberg; see Figure 4.1). The sectoral profile of these local industrial agglomerations reveals a predominance of culture and media industry firms. However, there are also local agglomerations of research-intensive industries, for example, on the sites of

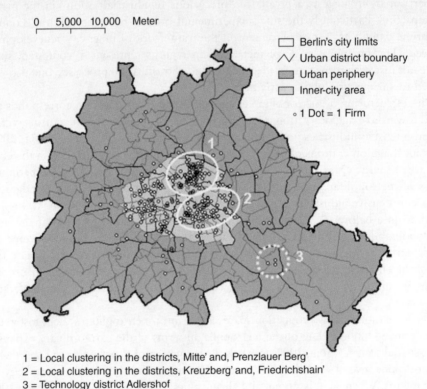

1 = Local clustering in the districts, Mitte' and, Prenzlauer Berg'
2 = Local clustering in the districts, Kreuzberg' and, Friedrichshain'
3 = Technology district Adlershof

Figure 4.1   Local agglomerations of the culture and media industries in Berlin. The example of multimedia firms, 2008

inner urban 'technology centres' (cf. Krätke, 2000). In Berlin, the majority of 'new economy' local agglomerations have developed as new industrial spaces at the intra-metropolitan scale.

Figure 4.2 New production spaces of the culture industry at the 'Media Spree' waterfront site, district of 'Friedrichshain-Kreuzberg', Berlin

Figure 4.3 The former Berlin Wall as an object of cultural production: 'East Side Gallery' in 'Friedrichshain-Kreuzberg', Berlin

(Continued)

(Continued)

The selective concentration of the culture and media industry firms and actors in the inner-city districts of Berlin can be related to several factors: Firstly, the actors prefer 'mixed-use' inner-city districts that allow for a local integration of working and living. This is essential for people who have to work more than 12 hours a day and more than five days a week. Such 'work and lifestyle' needs an infrastructure of services, gastronomic establishments, etc. in close proximity to the work place. Secondly, the inner-city districts of Berlin offer production premises with esteemed stylistic and urban design qualities. Thirdly, the local agglomeration of firms and actors of the same or complementary fields of activity leads to a self-inforcing growth dynamic. In the case of firm relocations to Berlin or start-ups from within, the firms are consciously looking for proximity to other firms of the same or complementary fields of activity. Local clustering creates an economic environment that offers valuable opportunities for inter-firm communication, learning and the spread of innovation impulses. The dense local environment of differently specialized culture and media industry firms is appreciated by the actors in terms of a stimulating 'creative milieu' (Krätke, 2002).

In large cities and metropolitan regions of Europe, a considerable share of 'creative activities' are locally concentrating in the districts of an 'inner urban ring' which surrounds the city's central business district. Particularly the culture industries require urban settings that offer openness and diversity in terms of opportunities for social interchange and cross-fertilization between different activity branches and actors. According to Landry, the inner urban ring districts are usually:

> the home of the less well-established creative and knowledge industries – such as design and Internet companies, young multimedia entrepreneurs or even artists – that provide the buzzing atmosphere on which cities thrive, experimenting with new products and services. (…) Lower prices enable younger, innovative people to develop projects in interesting spaces that in the centre only companies with capital can afford. As these companies grow and become more profitable they move into the hub or gentrify their own areas. This inner ring provides a vital experimentation and incubation zone. (2000: 35)

This quote emphasizes both the spatial dynamic triggered by new economic activities in the inner-city districts and the essential property of urbanization economies, i.e. to enable and enhance the local diffusion of creative ideas in a densely populated local economic area (cf. Storper and Venables, 2004). Activities that are focused on the unfolding of creativity require *stimulating environments*, where face-to-face contacts are convenient and efficient. Urbanization economies include the notion of proximity-based knowledge-spillovers and a fast spread of innovation impulses between different clusters (or subsectors) of the urban economy. The performance of creative and knowledge-intensive industries is also dependent on urbanization economies in terms of urban areas' socio-cultural properties like institutional and cultural diversity. Large cities and metropolitan regions are most likely to offer the socio-cultural diversity which is essential beyond the opportunities of inter-organizational knowledge networking related to the process of local cluster formation.

The basic forces behind the selective spatial clustering of high technology manufacturing activities and cultural industries in large cities and metropolitan regions are economic externalities (cf. Marshall, 1920) in terms of agglomeration economies which can be differentiated into externalities deriving from specialization ('localization economies') and externalities deriving from diversity ('urbanization economies'). The innovative capacity of research-intensive manufacturing sectors is strongly based on knowledge networking and spillovers between the related knowledge bases of specific sectors' cluster firms (Krätke and Brandt, 2009; Krätke, 2010a). In metropolitan regions, these cluster firms are also making use of a diversified economic structure which enables them to draw on and combine knowledge resources from other industries (Simmie, 2003). Urban clusters of the culture industries which particularly rely on artistical creativity are in similar ways making use of externalities that stem from both specialization and diversity. However, the specific properties of artistically creative work seem to privilege the benefits deriving from urbanization economies (Lorenzen and Frederiksen, 2008). Particularly in the culture industries, where production is frequently carried out by project teams and relies on a highly flexibilized and self-employed creative 'freelancer' workforce, knowledge and innovative ideas are not only exchanged between firms, but to a large extent also outside the sphere of inter-firm interaction, i.e. in the sphere of urban social life (cf. Storper and Venables, 2004; Meusburger et al., 2009). Hence we might say that the creative capabilities of large cities and metropolitan regions are based on the 'interaction effects' of urbanization and localization economies.

Besides the impact of 'new city industries' on economic development, the culture industry and its creative workforce are playing a specific role in urban spatial restructuring: The local agglomeration of artists and cultural economy activities functions as a seedbed for gentrification processes in the inner urban ring districts. Local displacement of 'creative industry' firms and workers can also result from processes of industrial upgrading within the sector – e.g. new upscale media firms edging out less affluent artists. Hence the local agglomeration of cultural producers and artistically creative workers in inner-city areas can be interpreted as a *precarious* reindustrialization within the metropolitan core (Hutton, 2010), in which the economically less potent firms and the low income strata of creative workers are constantly fraught with instability and displacement.

It is important to emphasize that the development of a 'new economy of the inner city' in terms of the formation of new local industrial districts at the intra-metropolitan scale is not restricted to cities in the 'global north' – similar developments have been recorded in 'transitional' cities and metropoles of the 'global south' such as Singapore, Beijing, Shanghai, Hanoi (cf. Surborg, 2006; Currier, 2008; Ho, 2009; Turner, 2009; Hutton, 2010). Emergent scholarship in East- and Southeast Asia, however, indicates that the specific socio-economic development context entails a variation of particular reindustrialization processes of cities and inner-city districts in the 'global south' as compared to the 'global north'. Manufacturing industries continue to have a significant share of the urban economy, which is reinforced by the integration of 'transitional' cities into global production networks, and the mixture of new economy subsectors in the inner-city districts shows a different activity profile. Nonetheless, cities in the 'global south' increasingly recognize the potential of culture and media industries for economic development and urban image construction. The creation of Beijing's Dashanzi arts district, for example, initially drew on activities of its resident artists to preserve the industrial area; due to the growing political awareness of the economic potential behind cultural districts, the area then became officially branded as '798 Arts District' in order to promote Beijing as a global city (Currier, 2008).

New Industrial Spaces in the Inner-City Area: The Example of Singapore

Singapore's history as one of the Asian 'tigers' that drew on export-led development and industrial upgrading, and its more recent ascendancy as a global city, has been widely acknowledged. Less attention has been directed towards the growth of new 'city industries' of the creative economy sector, which today in Singapore significantly contributes to employment (Hutton, 2010). Compared to the cities of the 'global north', however, Singapore's creative industries show a stronger share of IT and software services, advertizing, broadcasting media and publishing, i.e. subsectors that

Figure 4.4   Three-storey shophouse and 5-foot walkway, Telok Ayer, Singapore

Source: Hutton (2008: 157)

generate higher revenues and exports than, for example, the performing arts and fashion design subsectors. The new industries of Singapore have brought new districts outside the CBD and the global-scale activity complexes of industrial and science parks into play. New industrial spaces have developed within the centrally located inner-city heritage districts (Ho, 2009).

Particularly in the Chinatown Historical District, the sub-area of Telok Ayer on the edge of the CBD has emerged as 'the most salient site of new industry formation within Chinatown' (Hutton, 2008). The area consists of an attractive built environment of historical two- and three-storey shophouses (see Figure 4.4) and intimate urban spaces. According to Hutton (2008: 159), 'rents were attractive to many small shops and businesses, reflecting the price shadow effect of the proximate CBD, and the earlier migration of former residents to newer ... estates elsewhere in the city and the suburbs produced a substantial stock of shophouses, protected by heritage legislation, for adaptive re-use'.

The new economy in Telok Ayer includes a local agglomeration of telecommunication firms, internet services, software development, digital marketing, digital graphics and art. Since 2000, the area's mix of new economy subsectors has changed in terms of a transition from a landscape of dot-coms to a location of the ascendant urban cultural economy (see Figure 4.5). This cultural production orientation was further augmented by a fresh entry of firms in the 'lifestyle services' sector (gyms, spas, massage, fitness and lifestyle counseling). In the process of restructuring, Telok Ayer has become home of more durable ensembles of creative industries as compared to the initial clustering of technology-intensive New Economy firms.

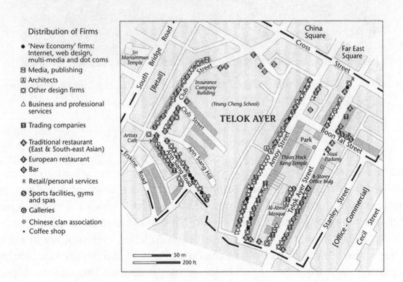

Figure 4.5 Local clustering of media firms, culture and amenity in Telok Ayer, Singapore, 2006

Source: Hutton (2008: 174)

(Continued)

(Continued)

While Telok Ayer developed as a rather 'spontaneous' local agglomeration of creative new economy firms, the adjacent area of the Far East Square entails an example of 'induced' new industry formation, in which a consortium of state and corporate actors drove the reconstruction of Far East Square as 'The Creative Hub' of Singapore (Hutton, 2008). This small area on the edge of the CBD (see Figure 4.6) became the location of some of the biggest global names in the advertizing, internet and multimedia industries. However, the reconstruction measures led Far East Square rents closer to those of the CBD office spaces, so that it will rather serve as a local hub for 'upscale firms' of the new economy and media industry.

Figure 4.6   The crafted landscapes of the 'Creative Hub', Far East Square, Singapore

Source: Hutton (2008: 165)

Beyond the development of a new economy of the *inner-city* core area, the urban regions' space-economy has been reshaped by the formation of intra-metropolitan 'Technopoles' in terms of specialized districts with specific infrastructures for research & technology-intensive new industries that are in most cases located outside the inner-city core area (such as the Berlin Adlershof technology district or the 'cité scientifique' in the metropolitan region of Paris; cf. Scott, 1988a). Furthermore, an increasing specialization of urban economic functions leads to an increasingly polycentric structure of the urban regions' space-economy. Specific functions such as back offices, logistics, large-scale entertainment and sport facilities are relocated within a metropolitan region to decentral locations (Hall, 2001). A particularly important issue is the formation of 'edge cities' (Garreau, 1991) in terms of new sub-centres and local economic growth poles that are often located on the fringe of the metropolitan area (cf. Phelps and Parsons, 2003).

Edge cities might be defined in a broad sense as new intra-metropolitan sub-centres that can take on a variety of forms: Hall (2001) doesn't restrict the usage of the term to suburban spatial environments and distinguishes four types: firstly, the 'external edge city' that is often located on the axis of a major airport (such as, for example, London Heathrow or Paris Charles de Gaulle). Secondly, there are 'outermost edge city complexes' for back offices or R&D functions that are typically located at major train stations in comparatively large distance to the city centre (such as, for example, Reading in the metropolitan region of London). Thirdly, the new sub-centres can take on the form of 'internal edge cities' that are resulting from pressure to expand the traditional urban business centre or from speculative reconversion and development of old industrial sites or redundant harbour areas in proximity to the traditional city centre (such as, for example, the London Docklands or Paris La Défense). Fourthly, Hall (2001) also includes among the different types of edge cities, 'specialized sub-centres' such as new entertainment districts, exhibition and convention centres. Some of these are located on reconverted sites close to the traditional city centre, others are developed in formerly separate towns that have become progressively embedded in the space-economy of a wider metropolitan region. The development of edge cities is often included in the large cities' growth strategies in terms of a spatially focused expansion strategy. In the urban metropoles of Asian growth economies such as China and India, edge cities are quickly emerging as automobile ownership rises and the spatial expansion of these urban regions accelerates.

The reshaping of the urban space-economy also comprises the formation of new spaces of consumption and spectacle in terms of attractive 'shopping districts' and 'cultural quarters' which serve in the inter-urban competition as major consumerist cultural assets. These developments as well as the formation of specialized intra-metropolitan technology districts mentioned above, might be regarded as a specific variant of the formation of new 'specialized sub-centres' of the urban economy. The emergence of edge cities or specialized sub-centres is related to the expanding spatial scale of the contemporary metropolis that induces the development of an increasingly polycentric spatial structure.

Furthermore, the integration of more and more cities in contemporary globalization processes leads to the expansion of the 'world-city network' and constitutes a challenge to further research on the experiences of restructuring and spatial change in 'transitional' cities (Shanghai, Kuala Lumpur) and other cities of the 'global south' (e.g. Sao Paulo, Mexico City). Transitional cities like Shanghai seem to rapidly expand in all dimensions of urban spatial change, i.e. not only in large scale development of new suburban and 'edge city' residential space, but also in intra-urban reconstruction (removal of old quarters for new apartments and office buildings), accompanied by the development of large-scale manufacturing areas on the fringes of the metropolitan region as well as by the planned formation of specialized intra-metropolitan districts for 'new industries' (such as information & communication technology and the media industry). The urban economy of Shanghai is not only functioning as a growth pole of China's urban and regional system (cf. Logan, 2008), but also increasingly linked to the network of global city regions and thus additionally affected by external growth impulses. In other cities of the 'global south' such as

Mumbai and Sao Paulo, the well-known picture of a pronounced divide between the formal and informal economy sectors and an extreme socio-spatial polarization that corresponds with the expansion of the urban poor's informal settlements, the spread of 'gated communities' of the population's affluent strata, and the restructuring of inner-city areas for 'modern' commercial uses is still dominating. However, the economy and spatial fabric of such cities today also includes expanding islands of globally integrated economic activities.

CONCLUDING REMARKS

This chapter started from a review of urban economic development concepts and growth ideologies that reflect a series of restructuring phases of urban economies since the early 1990s. The rise of new growth sectors has been accompanied by the emergence of new urban space economies focusing on the intra-metropolitan scale. The resurgent urban economy was strongly based on new 'city industries' that prefer to locate in the inner-city area. The inner-city districts of large urban regions are not only functioning as a major location of advanced producer services (as suggested by the notion of the 'city as a service metropolis'), but also as a prime location of the culture industries and new R&D-intensive industries' activities. The economic space of large cities and metropolitan regions is functioning as a 'super-cluster' which contains various local clusters with overlapping and partially interconnected activities that allow for a productive interaction of diverse local productive milieus.

The analysis emphasized the significance of dynamic agglomeration advantages for the functioning of urban economies in the framework of an economic development path that is based on knowledge-intensive economic subsectors and continuous innovation activities. The functioning of urbanization economies is related to specifically urban qualities of place and the opportunities of cross-fertilization between a diversity of activity branches and actors. The formation of 'new industrial spaces' at the intra-metropolitan scale draws on interactive knowledge creation within local clusters of particular industries and on the urbanization economies of technological and artistical innovation activities. In this way, the city offers socially produced locational advantages particularly for knowledge-intensive industries and the cultural economy sector.

The current research frontier in the field of new urban economies and new spaces includes the challenge to identify the propulsive sectors of future urban economies with regard to the restructuring of capitalist economies after the worldwide crisis of 2008, and to study the effects of this crisis on the geography of uneven development in the worldwide urban system. Furthermore, we need comparative analyses of the differing economic profiles and development paths of cities both in the global north and south, with particular emphasis on the different modes of urban regions' involvement in globalization processes. On the intra-metropolitan scale, there is need for extended research on the proliferation of new economic activities, the functioning and dynamics of knowledge networks and local creative milieus, and the new economic spaces that are developing in the context of urban economic restructuring processes in different zones of the city. A further challenging area of research concerns the often marginal and everyday spaces in which creativity unfolds, i.e. the development of informal or 'vernacular' spaces of creativity and production in the cities of both the global north and south (cf. Edensor et al., 2009).

Web Source for the Issue of 'Cities in Globalization'

http://www.lboro.ac.uk/gawc/

The GaWC website offers access to a large number of research papers on the formation of a world city network and approaches to global urban analyses.

5

Redundant and Marginalized Spaces

Ivan Turok

INTRODUCTION

Cities throughout the world contain spaces that are run-down and neglected. They include abandoned sites, decayed buildings, boarded-up shop fronts, public facilities in disrepair and blighted neighbourhoods. They seem to have outlived their usefulness to the economy and are by-passed by society. There is little apparent demand from firms to locate there and little interest from people with a choice of where to live. Some cities contain more disused spaces than most, reaching a scale and intensity that can affect the viability of the city as a whole. Swathes of derelict property are portrayed by the media as the symbols of cities caught in a spiral of decline as a result of inexorable forces. Their desolate spaces signify redundant places with bleak futures that should perhaps be abandoned. A variety of former industrial cities across Europe and North America have been characterized in this way from time to time (e.g. Leunig and Swaffield, 2007), damaging their reputation and harming prospects of attracting further investment, jobs and visitor spending.

Of course the reality is more complex than these over-generalized accounts allow. There are many different kinds of marginal spaces and diverse reasons for their existence. In some cases they are caused by systemic economic decline and job loss, giving rise to persistent population decline through out-migration. The effect is an unambiguous lack of demand for land and buildings, reflected in physical deterioration and disinvestment, depressed property values and falling tax revenues. Turning this trajectory around can be a lengthy undertaking. Policy-makers face a classic dilemma of whether to focus on the people or the place. It may be more cost-effective to support residents to move elsewhere (at least those who don't move on their own accord) than to regenerate the place. Examples of settlements that lose their raison d'etre include mining towns built on resources that become depleted and coastal ports deserted by shifting patterns of trade. Decline may be inevitable unless they can develop an alternative economic rationale. Cities with a narrow industrial base are also vulnerable to the technological obsolescence and instability that is a feature of capitalist economies.

It is more common for disused spaces to be localized within cities and bound up with processes of internal economic change or restructuring. Here it is not so much a general lack of demand caused by wholesale economic decline, rather the shifting composition of demand, the rapid pace of change or other circumstances which make it difficult for the supply of land and property in particular districts to adjust to the new requirements. This is partly a function of inherent characteristics of the built environment, including the durability of the fixed capital investment and the slowness of property redevelopment through market mechanisms, given strong private property rights and formal mechanisms for vested interests to contest rebuilding proposals going through the planning system. It also reflects sectoral shifts in the economy, with new business and labour processes requiring different locations and infrastructure from the old. Shifts in transport technologies, demographic patterns and household preferences create additional pressures for change and adjustment problems for the physical fabric of cities.

The state is a key actor in mediating these dynamic interactions. Government policies and regulations can help or hinder property adjustment processes, and thereby contribute to localized decline or hasten renewal and the productive re-use of vacant property. Government is uniquely placed to make difficult decisions about whether neglected spaces represent assets worth renewing or obsolete liabilities to be written-off. It can take a short-term view and respond to market signals, or pursue a longer-term approach and seek to shape and steer the market in order to manage urban land resources more strategically. This may include wide-ranging interventions to stem decline in places thought to offer future opportunities, or where there are compelling social equity arguments. Decisions ought to be based above all on their benefits and costs to people, not places, although people have strong economic and social ties to places so such calculations are not straightforward. The outcomes of state action are not always deliberate since disused spaces can emerge as an unintended consequence of pursuing other objectives. For example, generous state support for home ownership through mortgage subsidies had a major effect on suburban growth and inner city decline in many northern countries during the post-war era, as did state investment in urban freeways to promote household mobility.

Superimposed on this there was, and in some cases still is, an anti-urban ethos that favoured peripheral development and contributed to urban neglect (Beauregard, 2003; Buck et al., 2005; Turok, 2007). For many years, cities in the global north were perceived to be excessively congested, polluted and unhealthy places. They were seen as remnants of an industrial era when transport costs were high, supply chains were local and people lived close to work in over-crowded and unsanitary buildings. In a post-industrial world of low communication costs, people and firms preferred to locate where property was cheaper, congestion lower and environmental quality higher. Radical slum clearance policies rebuilt older neighbourhoods at lower densities to improve living conditions, although the mass-produced housing often became a problem itself subsequently. Derelict spaces had no economic potential, so were cleared, grassed over or converted to car parks or playgrounds. Meanwhile, modern physical and social infrastructure was laid down in surrounding new towns, dormitory suburbs and business parks along motorways to support the deconcentration of jobs and population. Urban policy typically consisted of residual welfare schemes to compensate poorer communities stranded by job loss and selective out-migration.

There has been a remarkable shift in thinking over the last decade or so, with a growing tendency to regard cities as sites of renewed economic dynamism, more inclusive and liveable communities, and places that can help to resolve environmental challenges (Urban Task Force, 1999; Buck et al., 2005; Cochrane, 2007). One argument is that dense, well-connected cities are drivers of productivity growth because of their economies of scale and scope (Parkinson et al., 2006; World Bank, 2009). They contain the cultural vitality and social amenities to attract the skills required to generate knowledge and innovation (European Commission, 2007; HM Treasury, 2006). Compact cities may also make more intensive use of infrastructure, reduce energy consumption and cut carbon emissions (Jenks et al., 1996; Martine et al., 2008; R. Willis, 2008; Ng, 2010). In short, a new urban agenda is emerging internationally that endorses higher density working and living for multiple reasons. It implies a general need to revalue vacant or under-used urban spaces with spare infrastructure capacity because of the opportunities they offer for raising densities through productive re-use. This agenda appears relevant to quite different contexts in the global north and south. It offers the potential to build a stronger consensus in spatial planning and development policy, and should therefore attract greater intellectual scrutiny, elaboration and practical testing of the ideas.

The purpose of this chapter is to delve beneath the surface of disused spaces in order to understand more about why they occur and what might be done about them. The geographical scope is global, although with an emphasis on the north, where cities tend to be older and more vulnerable. The next section considers the patterns and processes of *systemic* urban decline. The subsequent section looks more closely at the reasons why empty and unproductive spaces emerge *within* cities. It also asks whether policy should intervene more actively in enabling property adjustment to economic change. This is followed by a consideration of urban policy, including the potential for the new agenda to provide a more comprehensive rationale for transforming neglected spaces and remaking place.

SYSTEMIC DECLINE AND DERELICTION

How many cities have suffered from widespread decline, disinvestment and dereliction as a result of a deep structural condition? Unfortunately, there have been few international studies of marginal places defined in this way. Most research has involved case studies of particular cities or groups of cities. One of the difficulties with large-scale research is the lack of consistent definitions and comparable data on disused or vacant property. Such data relies on detailed site-by-site analysis and is therefore very costly to collect and update. Remote methods such as satellite imagery and aerial photographs can assist with some basic descriptive information on the extent of undeveloped land across a city, but they cannot capture information on detailed site conditions, historical uses, ownership patterns, price profiles or building occupancy in order to understand the dynamics. There is also a danger of confusing land that is deliberately protected from development for environmental reasons or strategic planning purposes (e.g. flood plains, bio-diversity or future airport expansion), with land that is otherwise available for development but has not been taken up for productive use, or has fallen into disuse.

An alternative approach is to consider surrogate indicators, focusing particularly on the drivers of demand. Data on aggregate economic activity over time at the city level is generally unavailable. The relationship between aggregate indicators such as output or employment and the demand for property is also complicated by wide sectoral variations in the amount of property required (the space used by office activities is very different from manufacturing plants or warehouses) and the changing composition of urban economies over time. Consistent demographic information is more readily available from population censuses. Population change is an important component of the demand for residential property (along with household composition and income), and housing is by far the most extensive user of urban land. Changes in city population are also linked with economic change, both as cause and effect, especially over the longer-term (Turok and Mykhnenko, 2007). Consequently, a city's population trajectory may indicate whether it is facing general, prolonged decline, or a more localized and temporary condition. It is important to define the city boundary carefully to avoid mistaking suburbanization for overall decline.

A recent study examined the population trajectories of 310 European cities with over 200,000 inhabitants over the period 1960–2005 (Turok and Mykhnenko, 2007). It found 116 of these cities had experienced recent demographic decline lasting between five and 15 years. The majority were in Central and Eastern Europe, particularly Russia, Poland, Ukraine and Romania. Indeed most cities in this region were declining, partly through international out-migration and falling fertility rates (Mykhnenko and Turok, 2008). The main cause was the shock of their transition to market economies and European integration, producing a sharp contraction in economic output and employment. The physical outcome has been extensive underoccupation, abandonment and demolition of residential property, summed up in the notion of 'shrinking cities' (Oswalt, 2006; Wiechmann, 2008). In many cases there were signs of recovery during the 2000s, at least until the setback of the global recession. The signs of revival suggested that the problems were more circumstantial than systemic, although there are important exceptions, particularly among single industry cities and towns created by the Soviet regime that are locked into particular products and markets (see box below).

Case Study from Russia

The 700,000 inhabitants of the city of Tolyatti in southern Russia (Figure 5.1) face a very uncertain future. The city's main employer, the car-maker Avtovaz, faces plummeting sales and the threat of bankruptcy. Russia has many towns and cities like this,

(Continued)

(Continued)

called a *monogorod*, or mono-city, where a single industry or factory dominates the local economy. Under pressure from the global crisis, the government is reviewing their future and considering how to restructure local enterprises, replace job losses, or manage their decline and move the people elsewhere. Most are less than 50–60 years old and are spread out across the country as a result of central planning. They have been starved of investment for years, their products are generally uncompetitive, and they are being kept barely afloat by the government's oil and gas revenues.

Tolyatti is Russia's biggest monogorod and home to what remains of the domestic car industry. Avtovaz employs 102,000 workers making Lada cars, down from 160,000 in 2006. Between 17,000 and 27,500 further redundancies are forecast, and huge efforts are being made to avoid complete collapse, including selling a 25% stake to Renault. Avtovaz has already absorbed £500m in state support through interest-free loans, and is currently running just one of two normal shifts, with workers on half pay. The city is a major financial headache for the state, with the largest projected unemployment and highest debts of any monogorod. Shops and restaurants struggle for customers and car dealerships stand empty. Government employment centres and social services offices are unable to cope with rising need. Unemployed factory workers have been given temporary public works jobs with state funding. There are serious frustrations and social tensions in Tolyatti and other single-industry cities, with regular street protests and demonstrations against pay and production cuts. *Source*: Financial Times, 27 October 2009.

Figure 5.1   Tolyatti River Port

Source: Wikipedia Commons

Turok and Mykhnenko's study found only 13 cases of sustained demographic decline lasting 25 years or more. Three are UK cities (Greater Liverpool, Newcastle and Glasgow) and seven are German (located in the Ruhr, Saarbrucken and Leipzig). Profound deindustrialization was the principal cause of the jobs haemorrhage and population exodus. The social and environmental legacy for the former industrial districts of these cities was very costly in terms of derelict and contaminated land, surplus housing, worn-out infrastructure and devastated communities suffering from worklessness, ill-health, family breakdown and behavioural problems among children. The core administrative areas of both Liverpool and Glasgow lost almost half of their populations over a 50 year period. Yet many of these 13 cities have rebounded in recent years, attributable in part to major public investment in new infrastructure and housing, improved services, higher consumer and tourist spending, and the attraction of new industries such as call centres (Parkinson et al., 2006; Turok, 2008; Power et al., 2010). Improved amenities, restored city centres, renewed public spaces, refurbished warehouses and the construction of modern apartments in derelict waterfront locations have also helped to attract younger professionals, students and other small households back to 'city living' (Nathan and Urwin, 2005).

There are other examples of places in Europe facing complex economic and social challenges that have experienced unexpected revitalization in recent years. Physical regeneration and environmental restoration often performed vital functions in rebuilding public confidence, attracting private investment and creating the conditions for new productive activities. British coalfield towns are among them, following several decades of disinvestment and stagnation. Extensive public investment in land reclamation, new business premises and improved housing have achieved a striking physical transformation along with strong employment growth and reduced unemployment (Beatty et al., 2007; Audit Commission, 2008).

'Rustbelt' cities in the United States have also experienced serious environmental and social problems. With less support from the federal government than in Europe, many seem to have suffered steeper and longer decline and more chronic depopulation (Beauregard, 2003, 2009; Power et al., 2010). They also appear to have found recovery more difficult to achieve. North-Eastern cities such as Detroit, Cleveland, Flint, Youngtown, Erie, Camden, Bridgeport and Rochester have witnessed physical decay and dereliction on a bigger scale than in Europe (see, for example, Gillette, 2005, on the plight of Camden). They have also faced stronger suburbanization pressures, partly because more land is available, planning controls are looser, public transport systems are weaker and socio-economic inequalities are larger. Nevertheless, there have been active programmes to reclaim and redevelop brownfield sites, convert old buildings into housing and restaurants, and remodel old ports into waterfront precincts. Limited federal support has forced them to develop innovative financing mechanisms reliant on partnerships with private sector developers, financiers and non-profit organizations (Greenstein and Sungu-Eryilmaz, 2004). Partly through these efforts, many city centre populations have begun to stabilize and recover, and economic activity has returned through new business investment and tourism, although the process is fragile and uneven.

On other continents one can find further examples of systemic decline. Urban population loss is rare in Africa, but it has occurred over the last two decades in the Zambian Copperbelt as a result of job losses in the mines causing poverty and insecurity (Potts, 2009). In Australia, the main spatial problem has been the decline of many county towns in the interior as a result of agricultural mechanization, industrial restructuring and the growing concentration of private and public services in the major coastal cities. Falling property values, deteriorating infrastructure and the closure of local services have affected the savings, job prospects and quality of life of the remaining residents. Declining rural towns are common in many other parts of the world as well. Canada has many abandoned mining settlements and logging towns, some of which have been revived through heritage- or eco-tourism. Chile and Mexico also have many abandoned mining towns. Elsewhere, urban settlements have suffered from the closure of railway lines, the building of road bypasses, or the replacement of old ports by deeper harbours with facilities for containers. These examples demonstrate the importance of connectivity to external markets and centres of population. Natural disasters, climate change and human conflict have also contributed to the abandonment of selected urban areas.

To summarize, the systemic decline of cities and towns is a powerful determinant of property disinvestment and physical decay. It is difficult to stem these forces, especially if the cause is deep-seated economic weakness. Improvements to the physical fabric of the place can help to restore some confidence and establish the conditions for recovery, but the fundamental problem lies elsewhere and requires focused attention. Local knowledge and initiative across the public, private and community sectors may be vital in helping places to identify alternative economic possibilities. But most localities lack the wherewithal to 'go it alone' and are likely to require sustained government support to develop these opportunities effectively. The scope for adaptation and recovery may be greater for diversified cities that possess a range of skills and competences to build new productive capabilities than for places locked into specialized technologies and patterns of trade (Jacobs, 1961; Parkinson et al., 2006; Turok, 2009a).

LOCALIZED DECLINE AND DISINVESTMENT

Localized decline within particular parts of cities is more common than systemic decline. There are many reasons why some parts of the same city show signs of dynamism while others fall into decay and disuse. It is important to distinguish between explanations that relate to (i) the demand of firms and people to locate in a particular place; (ii) the physical structures or supply of land and property in those places; and (iii) intermediary factors such as the role of government.

Some of the demand-side issues have already been mentioned, including the changing property requirements of new industries compared with old. They may need more specialized premises, flexible layouts, ICT capabilities, loading facilities, car parking or a better environment to retain scarce staff. The post-war shift from labour intensive manufacturing processes in multi-storey buildings to semi-automated production using horizontal plant layouts was one of the factors causing inner city sites to be abandoned for fringe locations. Yet, contemporary office-based activities, such as call centres, data processing and 'shared service' functions, often prefer central city locations at the hub of the transport network to maximize access for junior white-collar workers reliant on public transport. Concentrating such functions in one building may be designed to gain economies of scale at the expense of jobs in the original dispersed locations, such as branches of banks. Along with major changes in retailing (such as the growth of superstores and internet shopping), this has contributed to the decline of some high streets. Professional and business services, such as consultants, accountants, lawyers and design firms also tend to locate in city centres, for prestige and to benefit from face-to-face contact with corporate clients.

The residential demands of households reflect their income, space preferences and desire for access to jobs and amenities. As their earnings rise they tend to want to move to neighbourhoods with superior locational assets, i.e. bigger and better homes and amenities. This means leaving behind areas with inferior housing stock or isolated from opportunities. They may be replaced by new or poorer households moving from elsewhere. The patterns of household demand interact with neighbourhood characteristics in complex ways to produce diverse outcomes for people and places (Lupton, 2003). Neighbourhoods that seem equally poor can have contrasting trajectories because of their different attributes. Some function as *escalators* assisting people to gain a foothold in the labour market or housing system because they are well-located and have good schools or strong social networks. They may appear to be poor because of the steady influx of low income residents and departure of those who become better off, but the areas are actually working well. Other places function as poor *enclaves* – people get trapped through isolation and because their services suffer under pressure from concentrated poverty. Renewal policies need to be sensitive to place dynamics and the role areas perform within the urban system, economically as well as residentially. Escalators may have greater potential to reduce poverty through improved personal services, while enclaves may require more comprehensive regeneration on the grounds of need (Robson et al., 2008).

Turning to the supply-side issues, there are many physical attributes of property that can contribute to localized decline. It may simply be the progressive deterioration of the fabric of older urban areas through neglect and its failure to meet rising expectations and standards of health and environmental quality. The underlying condition of the land and infrastructure is clearly fundamental. A legacy of contamination by toxic waste and obsolete concrete structures left by former industrial uses can impose prohibitive remediation and clearance costs on any redevelopment proposals. Stringent environmental regulations designed to protect the purchasers of new housing built on previously developed land can also inhibit redevelopment. Brownfield sites generally present many more uncertainties and technical complications to developers than greenfield sites, as well as risks to future occupiers.

A series of land ownership issues are also relevant (Adams et al., 2001). Fragmented parcels of urban land and entrenched private property rights create considerable assembly costs and bureaucratic hurdles for potential developers. Monopoly owners of strategically-located properties often have no incentive or desire to sell. State entities such as railway operators or the military are often the worst culprits in failing to dispose of substantial tracts of land surplus to their requirements. Once developers have acquired a site, the formal consultative procedures of the planning system can give surrounding owners and residents considerable scope to delay progress.

Many inner urban sites also suffer from out-dated infrastructure and are inaccessible to the motorway network. The environment of old industrial estates is typically very poor, including a lack of maintenance, security problems, tipping and dumping. This discourages upgrading, refurbishment and redevelopment by individual property owners and occupiers. It also deters potential occupiers who make unfavourable comparisons with attractively landscaped business parks with modern services in the suburbs and beyond.

The 'thin' character of some urban property markets, reflected in the lack of transactions or information on prices, can create additional risks for developers. No one may want to be the 'first to jump' because of the uncertainties. They want to see that it is possible to sell or let property before getting involved. The state may unwittingly exacerbate the problem by zoning large amounts of land for industrial, commercial or housing development across the city, thereby causing confusion about priority areas and doubts about the prospects of manageable, phased regeneration in the places that need it most. Low property values may also mean that transactions costs (stamp duty, registration fees, legal costs, etc.) become significant barriers to the willingness of owners to sell – it is simply not worth their while.

Many of these factors would not be decisive in themselves, but in a context of low demand they may become critically important in reinforcing passive behaviour and deterring redevelopment. The concept of 'negative externalities' captures the interacting and cumulative effects of property decline and environmental degradation on business confidence, blight, stigma, rising crime and inflated insurance premiums. Desolate waste ground and boarded-up buildings create a bad impression, attract anti-social activities and heighten anxiety as places to invest. Adverse perceptions of such areas may also mean that vital assets in the form of strategic sites close to arterial routes are written-off, along with older buildings with intrinsic value and heritage potential. It is simply too risky for individual investors and developers to go against the general sentiment and buck the market. This supports the case for tackling decline on a coordinated, area-wide basis rather than site by site. Area renewal programmes based on clear masterplans can signal sustained state commitment to improvement and boost investor confidence through positive demonstration effects. A transformative impact is required, rather than small improvements that may be vulnerable to setback. The second case study (see box below) describes the situation of Medway in the Thames Gateway, where Europe's largest regeneration programme is seeking to turn around the fortunes of a former industrial and dockyard area that has suffered from a poor reputation and physical decay for many years.

Case Study of Medway, Thames Gateway

Medway is a large urban area in SE England about 30 miles east of London and with a population of 250,000 (Figure 5.2). It is one of six priority locations for development in the Thames Gateway. Local socio-economic and environmental conditions are poor by national standards, and the area has been bypassed by rising regional prosperity over the last decade. For many years its economy was dominated by dockyards and port-related industries, but deindustrialization during the 1970s and 1980s destroyed its manual jobs and left a legacy of derelict and contaminated land. Medway's poor image and infrastructure mean it has struggled to attract the high value industries and regional service functions that a city of its size would typically sustain. Proximity to London and poor internal connectivity hamper its ability to operate as a hub of diverse consumer and business services.

Medway has a porous economy with high levels of out-commuting to London. This is reflected in its physical structure: five towns that lack a focal point for the transport network that could have become a viable city centre. Instead there are five railway stations, four separate high streets and three municipal centres. External connections have improved over time, but this may have made the economy more 'leaky' rather than to have encouraged inward investment. Given its strategic location between London and the Channel ports, one would have expected greater buoyancy. Negative external perceptions, the long distance to an international airport and poor workforce skills have discouraged investment. Other towns in Kent are benefitting much more from the high speed Channel Tunnel Rail Link. A strong regeneration case could have been made for routing the CTRL through Medway – a missed opportunity.

Instead, the regeneration plans focus on a big increase in the supply of new housing in order to meet shortages across the South East. Medway was chosen as a priority area because brownfield sites were available and the local authorities were

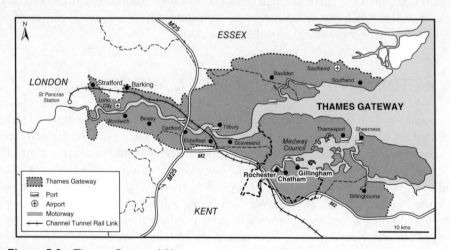

Figure 5.2 Thames Gateway, UK

(Continued)

(Continued)

receptive to development, in contrast to widespread NIMBYism elsewhere. The priority afforded to new housing is inconsistent with the needs of existing residents for
more jobs, skills and community services. The housing emphasis complicates the
task of job creation in reducing the supply of employment land. If local regeneration
was the priority, the focus would be on addressing economic and social weaknesses
directly through improved local amenities, infrastructure and sense of place.

Source: Turok, 2009b

There may be detrimental city-wide effects of localized decay that justify the pursuit
of greater balance. Cities with buoyant property markets in some areas and under-
used land in others make inefficient use of their resources and are vulnerable to
bottlenecks in property supply. Some districts suffer from low demand, neglect of the
building stock and unused infrastructure, while others may experience over-heating
and excessive development pressure as a result of undue constraints on where it is
considered desirable to live, work and invest across the city. Slower economic growth
may result from higher overall property prices discouraging potential incomers and
new firms from starting up, and promoting decentralization of business activity to
out-of-town locations. Pressure to build housing at higher densities and on parks,
playing fields and other open spaces in favoured districts of the city may spoil the
amenity of these areas and cause local resentment. Meanwhile, inadequate maintenance of the physical structures in neglected districts may jeopardize their long-term
prospects of re-use. Imbalanced patterns of development across the city may also
cause more congestion on the transport network than would exist with better-
distributed activities. There are high costs for the city's productivity from congestion
delays and unreliability when transport investment and urban development are
neglected or poorly coordinated (Eddington, 2006).

GOVERNMENT POLICY AND REMAKING PLACE

The state is a powerful intermediary in the workings of the property market.
Through its powers to plan, regulate, finance and manage aspects of the built environment, it can facilitate or frustrate property renewal and redevelopment. The
government is well positioned to make strategic decisions about whether a city's land
and property resources should be abandoned or re-used. Its approach can be to follow the market with a residual role that limits administrative burdens, provides
information on market transactions and perhaps offers minor incentives to encourage private sector investment. Alternatively, it can take a broader view and seek to
steer and stimulate market development as an active participant in the process. This
might involve managing urban regeneration in a more hands-on manner to demonstrate an area's economic potential and create value by assembling coherent land

parcels where existing private and public owners are uncooperative. It might also mean investing to initiate development through 'catalytic' projects where private financiers and developers are reluctant participants – acting as a kind of 'developer of last resort' – and subsidizing non-commercial uses of property, such as social housing or cultural and recreational projects. The state can also add value by improving the functional efficiency of the built environment through sound land-use planning and reducing the risks to other investors through consistent policies.

In recent years, a new urban policy agenda has emerged that supports higher-density, mixed-use development for economic, social and environmental reasons (Urban Task Force, 1999; Newton, 2008; R. Willis, 2008; Ng, 2010; for sceptical views, see Gordon, 2008; Whitehead, 2009). The apparent widespread applicability of these ideas to different national contexts adds to their appeal. Densification could provide a more comprehensive rationale for regenerating under-used areas than earlier urban policies because the arguments go beyond issues of neighbourhood renewal or physical revitalization. The case implies reassessing the value of vacant and under-developed spaces because of the special opportunities they afford to raise densities in well located areas. This is likely to require an integrated and active approach on the part of the state to address the multiple obstacles to redevelopment. Before discussing what this might involve, it is important to consider what density means and why it might be important.

The Meaning of Density

The concept of density is often misunderstood and efforts to promote densification frequently generate negative reactions. Density is equated with over-crowded tower blocks or noisy tenements. People fear the impact of high-rise buildings and migrant populations on their neighbourhood character and the extra pressure on local services. The media fuels fears with images of poor quality, insecure environments in notorious inner city areas. Yet density does not have to mean townscapes dominated by tall structures and congested streets. Densification should be communicated less as an end in itself, and more as a means towards wider ends, with benefits of convenience, connectivity and social vitality. With sensitive urban planning and management, density could arguably improve housing choices, amenities, employment and public services (Tan and Klaasen, 2007; Howley et al., 2009; Newton, 2010; Ng, 2010).

Density is essentially the product of two distinct elements: (i) physical structures (the supply of housing); and (ii) the actual resident population (which reflects the demand from people to live there) (Whitehead, 2009). The former is usually measured by the number of dwellings per hectare, although this neglects important aspects of their size and the number of habitable rooms, which also influence density. The latter is typically measured by the size of the population per hectare.

Physical density gets most attention, especially from urban planners and other policy-makers who have some influence over new development. However, the real objective is to raise the actual population density. The relationship between the two elements is more complex than often assumed, partly because of variations in household size and composition, which evolve over time in response to changes in income, stage in the life-cycle, and social norms. As people's income rises, they typically aspire to more living space, so the density of existing buildings and neighbourhoods tends to decline (Gordon, 2008). The average size of households has been falling in many northern countries, contributing to lower actual population densities in most established urban areas.

The relationship between planned and actual densities is further complicated because new buildings are a small fraction of the existing urban fabric. Their influence on the average density of the area is at the margin. Existing densities also influence the new patterns of occupation (who moves into new housing) through the character of the area, housing costs, and the quality of local schools and amenities. In democratic societies, existing communities may also influence the form of new development directly through advocacy if they perceive that higher densities nearby will affect them adversely. All this makes it very difficult to achieve a step change in density in the short term. An exception is where large sites are available for (re) development that can make a big impact on their own. Public ownership can avoid speculation and market processes causing delays and inhibiting careful density planning. Physical separation from existing built-up areas can also reduce community opposition.

The discussion of new schemes should not deflect attention from the potential of older, established neighbourhoods when trying to raise densities. Many areas may have considerable scope for 'incremental' densification, for example through subdividing properties, building extensions and converting lofts, basements or outbuildings. Higher energy and environmental standards can be incorporated at the same time through upgrading and adaptation ('retrofitting'). Significant economic opportunities may arise from the renewal and refurbishment work, recycling old materials and producing new energy-saving equipment.

The principle of intensification of the built environment can go beyond individual initiatives through the consolidation of adjacent plots, thereby allowing infill development or the demolition of existing structures and redevelopment of higher density, multi-storey buildings. Redevelopment may allow for better integration into the existing urban fabric and transport infrastructure than piecemeal infill. It can permit cross-subsidization of affordable housing and coherent improvements to water and waste treatment systems, local energy generation and the public realm. This can add great value to old and under-capitalized properties (and create many jobs in the process) and is particularly appropriate along public transport corridors and around activity centres. Newton (2010) refers to this as the regeneration of 'greyfield' precincts, whereby tracts of 20 or more old properties are brought together and redeveloped in ways that are technologically and environmentally up-to-date. There are examples in selected Australian and Canadian cities, such as Melbourne and Vancouver. Here rapid population growth creates urgent pressures for this kind of innovation in urban development.

There are three basic approaches to densification, or combinations of the three: (i) through state-driven procedures – such as acquiring and making land available for development, or directly providing new low income housing; (ii) through market mechanisms – using incentives or regulations to encourage new housing developers to build at higher densities; and (iii) through fiscal measures to influence household preferences and location choices. For example, detached houses can be taxed more heavily than flats, or the costs of private car use can be increased through parking fees, fuel duties or road user charges. These may encourage more intense use of the existing housing stock in the central city.

The most effective way to shift prevailing development patterns and household behaviour is likely to involve using all three approaches in combination so that they reinforce each other. This means ensuring that public investment plans, incentives and controls are properly aligned and mutually supportive. The lack of consistency in the spatial policies of different parts of government is a major weakness in many countries.

The Rationale for Densification

There are essentially three arguments for higher densities. The first relates to the creation of cities which will be more sustainable into the future – environmentally and financially. It is increasingly accepted that low density sprawl imposes high environmental costs in energy consumption and carbon emissions from private transport (Newton, 2008, 2010; Ng, 2010). It also imposes extra capital costs through the provision of bulk infrastructure and services such as public transport, health, water and sanitation. Higher density development within the existing urban fabric can help to reduce the rate at which peripheral land with agricultural, bio-diversity and mineral potential is consumed. It might also reduce the need for people to travel to work by car, and make more efficient use of the city's existing infrastructure. Renewing the oldest urban fabric could allow modern energy, water and waste treatment systems to be installed. Public transport, open spaces and arrangements for walking and cycling could be improved. A larger resident population would increase demand for retailing, bars, restaurants and consumer services, and make new and enhanced arts, cultural, educational, sports and entertainment venues more viable. These assets could in turn reinforce a city's position as a magnet for tourism and creative industries.

The second and related argument is that higher economic densities promote learning, creativity, efficiency and growth through positive externalities, information flows and 'agglomeration economies'. There is mounting evidence that large concentrations of firms, customers, suppliers and competitors enhance productivity and innovation, and that the benefits decay quickly with distance from the centre (Rosenthal and Strange, 2004; Carlino et al., 2007; World Bank, 2009). The literature on densification tends to neglect the economic dimension, yet as we have seen, a stronger economic base is crucial for the stabilization and resurgence of cities experiencing systemic decline, such as Tolyatti.

The third argument is that a higher density central city is important for social inclusion and integration. Central cities are unique locations of historic significance at the hub of the transport network, with a sizeable share of jobs in the city.

Disadvantaged groups who move into the inner city will gain better access to employment and training opportunities, and save considerable financial and personal costs of long-distance commuting. A culturally diverse central city with a lively public realm and shared services can function as a model of tolerance, understanding and trust across the city, showing how social cohesion and a common sense of belonging can develop when people from different backgrounds mix successfully (Jacobs, 1961; Parkinson et al., 2006).

The first argument tends to imply that the principal target of densification is middle- to high-income groups working in the city centre who would otherwise live in the outer suburbs. They offer the biggest gains by cutting car-based commuting and economizing on peripheral land. They are likely to demand generous space standards in their homes, well-designed and secure surroundings, and attractive public spaces nearby. High quality schools, health centres, shops and other services may also be required, depending on their age and household composition.

The second argument implies that densification should be driven by economic considerations. The city centre is a special place for activities relying on proximity and face-to-face contact. The priority is to attract, retain and nurture enterprises that will benefit most from a central location. This means making appropriate premises, infrastructure and support services available for higher value activities and small/medium enterprises in creative sectors such as design, ICT, media and music. An expansion of higher education, research, professional services and cultural institutions could strengthen the environment for business formation, innovation and development. Beyond the central city there may also be a case for supporting industrial areas because of the scarcity of well-paid manual jobs.

The priority for the third argument is to accommodate low income groups. Affordability is a major consideration, implying different space standards and levels of design and maintenance of the built environment compared with higher-income residents. For example, walk-up flats of three to four storeys offer better value for money than taller structures served by lifts and requiring more substantial foundations and energy inputs. There is likely to be greater need for subsidized provision of schools, health centres and community facilities.

These distinctions are presented rather starkly. The challenge is to devise ways to balance and combine the objectives in practice. The mixture will differ in different places, reflecting their distinct potential. Nevertheless, there are some inconsistencies which will not disappear. They need to be brought to the fore if density planning is to anticipate and respond to the challenges effectively. They include tensions between the quality and cost of buildings, exclusionary and inclusionary urban design, and residential and employment uses of property. Different priorities will also imply different responsibilities and costs for the public and private sectors.

The task of promoting residential densification can be explored in more detail from two broad perspectives: the desire of people to live in the city centre and the supply of property to accommodate them. Many urban strategies adopt the birds-eye view of the planner in assuming that there is no constraint on demand for central city living. The approach appears to be 'if houses are built, people will come', without questioning which people will come and in what numbers. All the obstacles are assumed to lie on the supply side, so the challenge is to build more homes at higher densities. It is important, therefore, that the issue of demand is examined more closely.

The Demand for City Living

The composition of demand for city living has wide-ranging implications for density planning and service provision. The income of the prospective new residents is a key dimension for consideration – effective demand (backed by the ability to pay the requisite costs) is more significant than a general wish to live in the central city. Age and household structure are two other vital elements. Little is known about the household make-up of the current population of many central cities, and the trade-offs they make between space, location and access to jobs and amenities. Even less is known about these preferences of possible incomers. A better understanding of how inner cities function in the wider metropolitan housing market would help to estimate the potential for growth and the sources of that growth, and therefore the actual densities that might be achieved.

Groups vary in their housing requirements and expectations of local services. Central cities worldwide house disproportionate numbers of students, young working couples, older single people and migrant populations (Nathan and Urwin, 2005). They attach greater importance to access to centrally-located jobs, universities, amenities and opportunities to socialize than to suburban lifestyles. Yet, as people's incomes rise and they have children, it is common for adults in their 30s and 40s to move to the suburbs in search of more internal space, outside gardens, better schools, greater security and access to the countryside and natural amenities (Muth, 1969; Whitehead, 2009). So city centre living may be quite a short-term experience for many people, and more a way of living than a place to live (Nathan and Urwin, 2005).

If central cities are to retain and attract back some of these families to stem sprawl and long-distance commuting, their demands for space and flexibility to cope with additional children will need to be satisfied. It should be considerably easier to attract students, single adults and recent migrants, who have restricted budgets and are more tolerant of living in small flats. However, the benefits for environmental sustainability from accommodating these groups will be more limited, since their alternative is not a suburban house with a pool and car-based commuting.

Another possibility is that many of the new dwellings are bought as second homes for weekday living by people whose main houses are in the outlying suburbs and towns, or even as holiday homes and investments by people living elsewhere in the country or abroad. These outcomes would be more likely if densification was driven by private developers with little consideration to investment in public services, amenities and affordable housing (Unsworth, 2007). It would be a perverse effect of encouraging more housing without considering the source of demand.

Affordability is the critical issue for lower income groups. Central city living tends to be more costly because the value of the land is reflected in property prices and rents. It is also apparent in the price of shops, entertainment and some other services. Some central city strategies seek to cross-subsidize affordable housing from higher income development and encourage publicly-owned land to be sold cheaply. This is laudable, but 'affordability' is often ill-defined and there are limits to what is feasible, especially where developers are cautious about schemes on complex sites with an additional 'tax'. Subsidizing affordable housing will also make developers less willing to share the infrastructure costs, thereby requiring the public sector to shoulder the burden. Research suggests that volume house-builders struggle to adapt their modes of operation to the context of brownfield development and remain wedded to greenfield sites (Adams and Watkins, 2002).

In many southern cities, policy-makers find it difficult to justify additional subsidies to multi-storey housing and new public services for inner-city residents who don't yet exist, in face of pressure to reduce the large backlogs in outlying communities. It also demands considerable powers of coordination to persuade state entities to allocate their well-located vacant land parcels for affordable housing. A detailed case will need to be made, incorporating the long-term, city-wide costs and benefits of different development scenarios.

The Supply of Suitable Property and Amenities

The supply side obstacles to densification are generally better understood than the issues of demand, although much analysis is required to establish their scale and significance in particular cities and localities. Efforts to renew and redevelop marginal areas need to recognize at the outset the importance of creating a stronger sense of place in order to replace their negative image with something more appealing. That will require a compelling vision of the area and how it should function in its wider urban context, along with a clear strategy for its reconstruction. A coherent plan will engender greater certainty among the various stakeholders by providing an over-arching context for individual investment decisions and land transactions. It will be all the more convincing if endorsed by all the relevant public organizations to avoid conflicting development priorities. This is a wide-ranging agenda that can be organized into six broad categories.

Firstly, the capacity of infrastructure – water supply, sanitation, power and telecoms – in the city centre and surrounding nodes and corridors to accommodate additional population and economic activity is fundamental to above-the-ground activity. A step change in demand for services is bound to require substantial investment in additional bulk capacity. This should be a relatively straightforward technical engineering matter, subject to resource constraints and the need to minimize disruption to everyday activities in established areas.

Secondly, bringing forward a supply of serviced sites for development is essential if substantial growth is envisaged. Complex negotiations may be required to release publicly-owned land for development. Acquiring private land in fragmented ownership can be very time-consuming if compulsory purchase procedures have to be used. Some previously-used (brownfield) sites also face substantial remediation costs, including upgrading worn-out infrastructure. Finding new and more intensive uses of old buildings is technically and financially challenging, especially if they have to be preserved for heritage reasons. New planning powers may be needed to consolidate separate properties and allow more intense and integrated redevelopment. Extensive public consultation may be important to build support and legitimacy.

Thirdly, the design of the new housing and surroundings is critical to the long-term success of density plans. If the new homes are too small and inflexible, and outside spaces are neglected, the diversity of the central city and outlying districts could be compromised. Taller buildings raise densities but are more costly to construct and maintain, undermining affordability. The level of income inequality and cultural differences within many contemporary cities complicate the urban design challenges and call for creativity and imagination. Central cities and suburban nodes with historical significance and located in fragile ecosystems (such as water scarce regions) may also struggle to accommodate big increases in population.

Fourthly, combining different forms of housing tenure that mix age groups, cultures and family types is one way to promote social integration. Careful planning and financing are required to support inclusionary housing and avoid obvious segregation by income. Governments need to be demanding of developers and flexible in the use of housing subsidies to create mixed, dense neighbourhoods. There are many positive examples of cross-subsidization and social interaction within mixed tenure communities in European cities, with no apparent negative effect on property values (Bailey and Manzi, 2008). High quality design and careful management of shared spaces seem to be important ingredients of success. Community involvement can help to identify the issues that matter most to people and promote mutual understanding and respect.

Fifthly, higher densities and less living space are more likely to be tolerated if there are attractive external spaces, good public services and recreational amenities. These are also vital arenas for social interaction and engagement, so open access and inclusivity are important. Flexibility is required towards public service standards such as school playgrounds and car parking, bearing in mind the shortage of land and the need for buildings containing mixed uses. A holistic perspective going beyond the provision of more housing units is important to create vibrant communities. Jobs and amenities are important ingredients.

Finally, density plans may fail in isolation of wider changes in policy and practice. Experience shows that developers prefer to exploit simpler greenfield sites. They are even less likely to develop in the inner city if the density plan is perceived to impose additional burdens that don't apply elsewhere. Consequently, it is best conceived as part of a broader effort to reorient the private property market and encourage more innovation in the development process. A city-wide plan should support 'smart growth' (higher densities and mixed uses) in key locations across the city and limit sprawl. Nothing less than a paradigm shift may be required for urban designers, architects, engineers, financiers and developers to accept the primacy of brownfield and greyfield development, and to adapt their methods accordingly.

CONCLUSIONS

The built environment is an integral part of the economic and social life of the city. It reflects the city's prosperity, but also facilitates its ongoing growth and development.

Adapting the physical fabric of the city to periodic shifts in business requirements and household expectations is essential for its continued functionality. This is complicated by the pace and character of economic restructuring, by changes in technology, transport and communications, and by inherent features of the built environment, including its durability, property rights and locational fixity. One of the effects is the fall into decline and disuse of particular sites, buildings and districts of the city, and sometimes the city as a whole.

The state has a vital role to play in overseeing the development and maintenance of the built environment, and intervening in the property market when things go wrong. Through its powers of planning, regulation and positive investment, it can support or hamper renewal and redevelopment. Government is better placed than other actors to make difficult decisions about whether neglected spaces represent assets worth restoring or liabilities to be written-off. It can follow the market with limited actions, or seek to steer and stimulate the market in order to manage urban land resources more strategically. The state can create value through the pattern and intensity of land-uses that is encouraged. It can also participate directly in development as a provider of information, land or capital.

A new urban agenda is emerging internationally that endorses higher density working and living for economic, social and environmental reasons. It suggests revaluing vacant or under-used urban spaces because of their contribution to raising densities through productive re-use and intensification. It also implies a more active and integrated approach to redevelopment and regeneration. This agenda appears relevant to diverse contexts in the global north and south, which makes it all the more important to encourage further research, development and testing of the ideas in practice.

Useful Websites

Australian Housing and Urban Research Institute (www.ahuri.edu.au/)

British Urban Regeneration Agency (www.bura.org.uk/)

European Cities Network (www.inspiringcities.org/)

European Urban Knowledge Network (www.eukn.org/)

Regeneration and Renewal Network (www.regen.net/)

Shrinking Cities International Research Network (www.shrinkingcities.org/)

US think tank – The Urban Institute (www.urban.org/)

6

Splintering Labour Markets

Danny MacKinnon

INTRODUCTION

Labour has been described as the 'most fundamental and the most inherently problematic of all economic categories' by the economic sociologist Fred Block (1990: 75). Whilst conventionally regarded as a factor of production, labour cannot be reduced to this purely economic role. It remains fundamentally human and social in nature, representing an 'irreducible, ubiquitous feature of human existence and social life' (Storper and Walker, 1989: 154). It is in this sense that Karl Polanyi famously termed labour a 'fictitious commodity' which takes on the appearance of a commodity, but does not function like a proper commodity. While the labour market brings together the buyers and sellers of labour through the price (wage) mechanism, labour is not directly produced for sale, but instead emerges from society, through the family and education system. Moreover, labour is reproduced outside the market, relying on broader social and institutional relations associated with family, friendship networks, community and the state (Castree et al., 2004).

Traditionally, labour markets have been regarded as highly localized, reflecting the need for relative spatial proximity between home and work (Peck, 1996). As Harvey (1989b: 19) has memorably expressed it, 'unlike other commodities, labour power has to go home every night'. This has given rise to a patchwork of urban or city-regional labour markets, incorporating a city and its surrounding hinterland, as defined by Travel-to-Work-Areas (TTWAs) in the United Kingdom (UK) for example (see Figure 6.1). Urban labour markets are shaped by a range of factors, including not only the types of employment and wage rates available locally, but also social and institutional conditions relating to the norms and expectations associated with work, the organization of labour through trade unions and the practices of local state agencies in regulating labour (Peck, 1996; Martin, 2000; Castree et al., 2004). As a set of social institutions, local labour markets effectively mediate and coordinate the collision between capital which seeks higher profits and labour which is concerned with improving its wages and conditions through organizations like trade

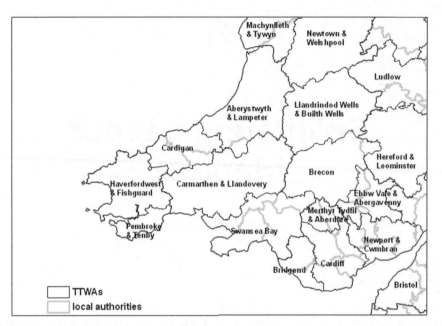

Figure 6.1   Travel to work areas in South and West Wales

Contains Ordnance Survey data © Crown copyright and database right 2014

unions. While many commentators have highlighted the unequal relationship between global capital and local labour (Peck, 1996), it is worth stressing that labour is not wholly immobile and place-bound as shown by the migration of workers to find employment elsewhere (Kelly, 2009).

Urban labour markets in developed and developing countries have been subject to widespread restructuring since the 1970s, reflecting a number of influences such as globalization, technological change, deindustrialization, sub-contracting, the weakened position of organized labour, under-investment and the spread of neoliberal policies of deregulation and liberalization (Peck, 2000; Rutherford and Gertler, 2002). According to Wills et al. (2010: 8), sub-contracting is the paradigmatic form of employment under global neoliberalism and the migrant is the world's paradigmatic worker. Labour has become increasingly globalized through the emergence of a global labour surplus, based upon the development of new labour supplies in developing countries, particularly China and India (Standing, 2009). As a result, workers' share of national income has declined across much of the globe, reflecting a serious weakening of labour's bargaining position relative to capital (Harvey, 2010).

Cities in the global north have experienced the loss of traditional manufacturing jobs through deindustrialization and the growth of service employment, while parts of the global south, particularly in East and South Asia, have undergone rapid industrialization and development. In the remainder of the south, by contrast, rapid urbanization has coincided with prolonged economic stagnation, exerting huge pressures on labour markets. An underlying theme is that of increased inequality between people and places, particularly those in relatively high-status, well-remunerated professional employment and those subject to either low-paid marginal employment or unemployment. As Martin (2000: 457) observes, '[w]ithin most major cities, areas of mass unemployment, poverty and social exclusion co-exist with other areas of successful, high-income professional workers'. It is this kind of social and spatial divide that underpins the notion of 'splintering' labour markets (see Graham and Marvin, 2001) whereby employment processes and work practices for different groups of people become increasingly 'unbundled' and fragmented, resulting in increased polarization between segments of the workforce. In addition to the loss of traditional manufacturing jobs, the polarization of urban labour markets also reflects the restructuring of service work which has involved the de-skilling of clerical labour and the shedding of middle managers through mergers, rationalization and capital substitution (Grimshaw et al., 2002; Goos and Manning, 2007).

The remainder of this chapter is organized in four main sections. Next, I review changing approaches to the study of labour markets by geographers and other social scientists. This is followed by an assessment of key forces which structure urban labour markets, including changing international divisions of labour, demographic factors, particularly migration, and labour market governance. The chapter then examines the restructuring of urban labour markets in developed countries, assessing the 'splintering' effects of deindustrialization and the growth of new types of service employment. Next, I turn to developing countries, highlighting the pronounced inequalities that characterize urban labour markets in the global south. Finally, a brief conclusion draws together the principal arguments of the chapter.

CHANGING APPROACHES TO LABOUR MARKETS

Although extensively critiqued by geographers and others, the neo-classical economic perspective on labour markets remains influential, not least in informing policies of labour market deregulation (Peck, 2000). This approach views the relationship between capital and labour as individual, whereby workers sell their labour power to employers in exchange for a wage (see Table 6.1). The onus is on individual workers as rational economic actors to invest in their skills and human capital so as to command higher wages in the marketplace (Peck, 1996). From this perspective, there is no role for labour as a collective interest organized through trade unions which are viewed as interfering with the operation of the labour market, leading to inflated wages and conditions for workers. Similarly, the role of government should be limited to enforcing legal standards and rights and ensuring that there are few impediments to the operation of market mechanisms.

Understandings of labour markets in geography and related social sciences have diverged from the neo-classical orthodoxy since the 1970s. Marxian perspectives were particularly prevalent in the 1970s and 1980s (Harvey, 1982; Walker and Storper, 1983; Massey, 1984), emphasizing the unequal nature of the relationship between labour and capital. Labour is viewed as the ultimate source of value or profit, according to the labour theory of value, with the extraction of surplus value not only providing the basis for class exploitation, but also underpinning the process of class struggle, giving rise to a collective politics of labour (see Table 6.1). In geographical terms, Marxist approaches stressed the power of mobile capital over place-bound labour by exploiting spatial differences in labour qualities and costs in order to maximize profits through, for instance, the relocation of routine forms of production to regions where costs were lower (Peck, 1996). The key expression of this approach was Doreen Massey's theory of spatial divisions of labour whereby different parts of the production process were being carried out in different regions according to the availability of supplies of labour (Massey, 1984). More recently, the past decade or so has witnessed the growth of a 'new labour geography' which emphasizes the active role of labour in shaping the economic landscape (Herod, 2001). It has focused on the problems of organized labour in confronting the changed circumstances of advanced global capitalism. An important theme has been the re-scaling of industrial relations, as established national-level structures have given way to an array of locally and regionally-specific arrangements (MacKinnon et al., 2008).

Institutional approaches view labour markets as structured by a range of social norms and power relations, drawing on Polanyi's conception of the economy as an instituted process (Peck, 1996). Here, institutions refer to not only formal rules and regulations, such as laws guaranteeing certain legal rights to workers (for example, protection against unfair dismissal), but also to more informal practices and conventions (e.g. attitudes towards low paid work) (Gertler, 2010). Since such practices and conventions vary from place to place, and even formal national rules can be interpreted differently in different places, labour markets are locally constituted (Table 6.1).

Table 6.1 Perspectives on urban labour markets

	Theoretical influences	Basic tenets	Main focus
Neo-classical	Neo-classical economics and the micro-economics of the labour market.	Labour is like any other commodity. Labour markets are like other markets.	Mechanisms of labour market 'clearing'. Failure of urban labour market to clear (e.g. local unemployment) reflects the existence of 'barriers' and 'impediments' (e.g. minimum wage, trade union power) to their free operation.
Marxian	Marxian economics, sociology and geography.	Unequal relationship between labour and capital rooted in the extraction of surplus value as profit. Class politics. Labour as an active agent shaping the economic landscape.	Spatial divisions of labour and the exploitation of place-based labour by global capital. Efforts of organized labour to respond to globalization.
Institutionalist	Institutional economics and economic sociology.	Labour markets are structured by a range of social norms and power relations. Urban labour markets vary in their institutionalized regimes of employment practice, social norms, work cultures and labour traditions.	How institutional structures shape labour market outcomes (employment, wages, etc.). The governance of urban labour markets.

Source: Adapted from Martin (2000: 462–3)

Martin, R. (2000) Local Labour Markets: Their Nature, Performance and Regulation. In Clark, G. Feldmann, M. and Gertler, M. (eds) 2000 *The Oxford Handbook of Economic Geography*. Oxford: Oxford University Press. pp. 455–76.

Questions of labour market governance have attracted particular interest, focusing attention on the role of the different agencies and practices that structure the operation of local labour markets, mediating and regulating the relationships between production, work, social reproduction and consumption (Jonas, 1996).

STRUCTURING LABOUR MARKETS

While the operation of labour markets is structured by a range of forces, I focus here on three sets of factors which relate to the demand for labour, the supply of labour and the regulation of labour markets respectively. Firstly, I outline how changing international divisions of labour in service industries influence the demand for labour. I then turn to assess demographic trends that underpin the supply of labour, focusing on population growth in developing countries and the role of migration. Finally, this section examines processes of labour market governance, emphasizing the spread of neoliberal policies of deregulation and liberalization, and assessing the concept of local labour market control regimes.

Changing International Divisions of Labour and Expertise

The advent of a New International Division of Labour (NIDL) in the 1970s was based on the selective relocation of manufacturing activities to developing countries where costs, particularly labour costs, were significantly lower than in the global north (Fröbel et al., 1980). Since the early 1990s, this rather simple model of the NIDL has given way to a far more complex pattern, characterized by the international re-location of services, increased out-sourcing by MNCs, growing regionalization and cross-investment between the core economies of North America, Europe and East Asia, and outwards investment from newly industrialized countries in East Asia particularly (Coffey, 1996).

Bryson (2007) identifies a 'second global shift' involving the international relocation of certain service activities to developing countries. While this is enabled by new information and communication technologies and is a response to differentials in labour costs, it is not a simple one-dimensional process. Rather, Bryson argues that it is underpinned by 'spatial divisions of expertise' which are characteristic of occupations such as finance, business services and engineering which depend upon embodied expertise (Bryson, 2008). Large firms and MNCs manipulate the spatial division of expertise through either the transfer of managers, and other experts between facilities located in different countries, or by the development of integrated supply chains involving the external sourcing of expertise. Spatial division of expertise are evident in the emergence of educated and expert workers with English-language skills in developing countries. Here, India has emerged as the key 'offshore' destination, accounting for around 25% of out-sourced information technology enabled services globally (Russell and Tithe, 2008: 615–16), and other important sites include South Africa, the Philippines, Malaysia and China.

Demographic Trends

There are estimated to be 3.1 billion workers in the world today of which 73% live in developing countries (Ghose et al., 2008). Every year in the future, 46 million new workers will be joining the world's labour force, primarily in developing countries, reflecting the underlying asymmetry in the distribution of the world's productive resources whereby the labour force is primarily concentrated in developing countries, while capital and skills are concentrated primarily in developed countries (ibid). Absorbing these numbers represents a huge challenge in view of existing problems of unemployment and under-employment in the global economy (Dicken, 2007). Cities in the developing world are characterized by very high levels of under-employment with large numbers of people engaged in low-productivity survival activities in the informal sector of the economy. Unemployment remains a significant problem in most developed countries which are characterized by ageing populations, raising serious policy questions about how to support large numbers of retirees (Blake and Mayhew, 2006).

The global economy is also characterized by high levels of migration, reflecting the underlying inequalities between developed and developing countries. It is difficult to obtain accurate figures on levels of international migration, but the number is thought to have doubled to 190 million between 1970 and 2005 (K. D. Willis, 2008: 212), a figure which is likely to significantly under-estimate the total due to large numbers of undocumented migrants. These migration flows are complex, although the underlying pattern is from the global south to the north, including movements from Asia, Latin America and the Caribbean to the US; from China and India to Canada; and from North Africa, Turkey, Eastern Europe and South America to the European Union (EU) (Castree et al., 2004).

Sassen (2008) identifies two types of transnational labour market in operation, relating to the top and bottom ends of the global economic system respectively. The first is comprised of flows of high-level managerial and professional workers across a range of economic sectors, including finance, business services and engineering (Saxenian, 2006). The second, by contrast, refers to mostly informal flows of lowly paid immigrants from the global south who become employed in the north as cleaners, janitors, restaurant and shop workers, maids and nannies. Remittances from such migrant workers have become a vital source of income and foreign exchange for developing countries such as India, China and the Philippines (Kelly, 2009), linking spatially distant locations within the world economy (Massey, 2007).

Labour Market Governance

Changes in the governance and regulation of labour markets since the 1970s have been widely characterized in terms of a shift from Fordism to post-Fordism (Peck, 2000; Rutherford and Gertler, 2002). Of central importance has been the promotion of flexible labour markets in terms of encouraging workers to perform different tasks and acquire different skills, compared to the rigid hierarchies and divisions of labour that characterized Fordist mass production. At the same time, temporary, part-time and agency-based employment has grown, creating secondary labour markets of workers who can be hired and fired in line with changing market conditions (Pollert, 1991). Employment relations have been individualized, in contrast to the collective labour norms that typified the Fordist era, with unemployment, for example, seen to reflect individual deficiencies in terms of skills, work ethic and responsibility (Crisp et al., 2009). This shift towards more flexible labour markets has been widely interpreted as representing a shift in the balance of power from labour to capital, although organized labour retains the capacity to disrupt production systems in the pursuit of its objectives (Herod, 2000).

The concept of local labour control regimes (LLCR) was developed by Jonas (1996) to emphasize how labour is subject to multiple processes of regulation at the local scale by business interests and state agencies. According to Jonas (1996: 325), the LLCR is a 'historically contingent and territorially embedded set of mechanisms which co-ordinate the time-space reciprocities between production, work, consumption and labour reproduction with a local labour market'. Control is exerted through a range of localized social relations and institutions, incorporating social norms, rules and practices in addition to formal organizations such as local government. In particular, Jonas argues, local growth coalitions often co-opt potential sources of resistance through the development of ideologies of community, emphasizing the needs of the locality and sometimes encouraging labour to make sacrifices in the interests of competitiveness (see Coe and Kelly, 2002). Far from viewing LLCRs as singular and isolated, Jonas stresses how local labour markets are nested within wider production systems and state structures. As such, the LLCR is a valuable concept for examining the restructuring of urban labour markets, although it remains rather structuralist in orientation, tending to privilege the needs of capital over the agency of labour and community groups (Coe and Kelly, 2002; Helms and Cumbers, 2006).

LABOUR MARKET RESTRUCTURING IN DEVELOPED COUNTRIES

Having begun in the 1960s, the speed of deindustrialization accelerated in the 1980s and 1990s with overall manufacturing employment falling by a third in the UK between 1981 and 2001 (Gordon and Turok, 2005: 245). At the same time, cities and city-regions have been identified as key crucibles of innovation and learning within the contemporary, knowledge-based economy (Simmie, 2002), focusing attention on the benefits of 'thick' urban labour markets containing large pools of workers with relevant skills (Gordon and Turok, 2005). Metropolitan regions such as Greater London are particularly advantaged in this respect, offering a range of specialized jobs in business services, financial services and the cultural industries and continuing to act as 'escalators' by offering employment opportunities and upwards social mobility to young migrants (Fielding, 1991).

According to Richard Florida's influential but controversial thesis of the creative classes, cities must compete to attract mobile 'creatives' through the promotion of tolerance, openness and diversity (Florida, 2005). This typically involves the redevelopment of neighbourhoods to develop amenities such as authentic historical buildings, converted lofts, walkable streets, coffee shops, arts and live music spaces, generating a sense of buzz and vitality. As such, creative policies have tended to reinforce and accelerate existing processes of gentrification through which former industrial and working-class inner-city areas have been redeveloped and colonized by middle-class professionals and 'yuppies' (Smith, 1996). This approach seems likely to reinforce problems of inter-urban inequality and poverty as the gentrification of selected urban neighbourhoods results in the further marginalization and displacement of 'non-creative' groups. In this respect, critics have argued that the most creative cities and regions, as measured by Florida's rankings, also tend to be the most socially polarized and unequal (Peck, 2005). In response, Florida has acknowledged this point, attributing it to broader economic shifts which are increasing the returns to higher education and creative ability (Gertler, 2010: 9).

As indicated earlier, employment policy in developed countries over the past couple of decades has been dominated by efforts to promote flexible labour markets (Peck, 2000). This approach has focused largely on the supply-side of the labour market, seeking to ensure that workers adapt their skills and expectations to the needs of the economy, and providing training and incentives for the unemployed to get back into work (Etherington and Jones, 2009). Such 'welfare to work' policies neglect the demand side of the labour market, assuming that unemployment arises from a lack of individual skills and incentives rather than the wider structural factors which have been steadily reducing the demand for low-skilled workers since the 1970s (Ghose et al., 2008). As a result, policies designed to increase labour market flexibility have had very limited success in reducing unemployment and have fuelled the growth of low-paid, part-time and temporary employment (ibid), contributing to the creation of 'splintered' urban labour markets and increased social polarization (Etherington and Jones, 2009; Wills et al., 2010).

The original theory of global cities advanced by Sassen (1991) emphasized the importance of social polarization as a central feature of such cities. This was supported by evidence of income and occupational polarization in US cities such as New York, referring to a divergence in earnings and the growth of employment at the top and bottom ends of the labour market respectively. In response, however, critics accused Sassen and others of over-generalizing from the US experience, pointing to evidence of increased professionalization in European cities like London and the Randstad (Hamnett, 1996). According to Hamnett (1996), the differences between the US and UK could be explained by lower levels of immigration and more generous welfare entitlements in the UK which have prevented the growth of a large low-paid workforce.

More recently, May et al. (2007) have argued that this view is now untenable in relation to contemporary London, due to increased volumes of immigration and the process of welfare reform and labour market deregulation which have moved the UK closer to the US model. Accordingly, recent evidence suggests that London has also been subject to processes of occupational polarization through a growth in the proportion of jobs at the bottom end of the market, with a disproportionate number of these filled by migrant workers (ibid: 153). According to Wills et al. (2010), low-paid jobs have been devalued to the point of becoming difficult to fill, creating new migrant divisions of labour in the service economy of Greater London (May et al., 2007; McDowell et al., 2009). For instance, McDowell et al. (2009) suggest that new immigrants from the eight EU accession countries are relatively well-placed to compete for work in the most precarious sectors of the labour market compared to other migrants and non-migrant poor white and coloured groups. Two-thirds of migrants interviewed in a recent survey regularly sent financial remittances to people in other countries (May et al., 2007: 161), underlining the importance of such flows in constituting a regime of 'transnational urbanism' (Smith, 2001) in contrast to the top-down model of the global city (Sassen, 1991).

Former centres of manufacturing industry have been most severely affected by deindustrialization, creating problems of unemployment, economic inactivity, social deprivation, ill health and physical dereliction (Hudson, 2009). In the US and UK, the growth of service employment, largely in activities such as retail, catering, public administration, tourism and call centres, has barely been able to offset the loss of manufacturing employment, creating a distinct 'jobs gap' (Turok and Edge, 1999). In the UK, employment growth during the 1990s and early-to-mid 2000s resulted in reduced unemployment across all regions, but the problem of high levels of economic inactivity in the deindustrialized northern conurbations, such as Liverpool, Glasgow, Manchester, Newcastle and Sheffield, remained intractable (Industrial Communities Alliance, 2009). Furthermore, recent data indicates that traditional industrial regions such as these and the Mid-West of the US have been worst affected by rising unemployment in the 2008–2010 recession (Dolphin, 2009; Industrial Communities Alliance, 2009).

Labour Market Restructuring in Glasgow

Glasgow lost 68% of its manufacturing jobs between 1971 and 2001, placing the city at the extreme end of city experiences in Europe (Turok and Bailey, 2004: 41). Service jobs increased by 39% over the same period, although this was not sufficient to compensate for job losses in manufacturing (ibid: 41). In addition, many service jobs tend to be part-time and occupied by women, in contrast to the male full-time jobs which characterized manufacturing (Helms and Cumbers, 2006). Employment growth in services continued to be strong through the early-to-mid 2000s, concentrated particularly in retail, catering, financial and business services, public administration, tourism and leisure. Until recently, falling unemployment has disguised high levels of economic inactivity with 27.1% of the working age population

(Continued)

(Continued)

defined as inactive compared to the UK average of 21.2% in 2007–2008 (Cumbers et al., 2009: 11). The labour market is characterized by a divide between qualified and skilled workers and the less skilled and poorly-qualified. In general, working-class residents of inner-city neighbourhoods and peripheral housing estates have lost out from the economic shift outlined above, whilst qualified suburban commuters have gained (Turok and Bailey, 2004: 54).

These economic changes and outcomes have been accompanied and facilitated by shifts in the institutional regulation of the local labour market. While the UK government continues to set the broad parameters of policy, other key actors include: the devolved Scottish Government which has been responsible for areas such as education, health and regeneration since 1999; devolved government agencies such as Scottish Enterprise and Skills Development Scotland, charged with delivering economic development services and skills and training programmes respectively; and Glasgow City Council as the elected local authority. These organizations can be seen as crucial players in an emergent local labour control regime in the city which is particularly focused on addressing problems of inactivity and deprivation (Helms and Cumbers, 2006). Key initiatives include the promotion of call centre employment, attempts to recreate traditional apprenticeships for young people in the construction industry particularly (reflecting the lack of manufacturing employment) and various local intermediate labour market programmes which seek to get the unemployed back into work (ibid). In particular, the city has been in the vanguard of active labour market polices in the UK through initiatives such as Glasgow Works (Turok, 2005). Despite these efforts, however, less qualified groups remain concentrated in low paid and casualized employment, for which they are likely to face increasing competition from more qualified workers made redundant during the 2008–2010 recession (Cumbers et al., 2009).

LABOUR MARKET RESTRUCTURING IN DEVELOPING COUNTRIES

Labour can be seen as the most important asset for poor urban households and it is through employment that they benefit most directly from economic growth (Grant, 2008: 1). Since the 1980s, the effect of global processes of economic restructuring has created increasingly bimodal or splintered labour markets in developing cities (Lyon and Snoxall, 2005). The divide between the formal and informal sectors represent a key axis along which such splintering has occurred, although the informal sector is itself highly heterogeneous (Chant, 2008). The formal sector, comprised of legally-recognized enterprises, has grown rapidly in parts of East, South East and South Asia particularly, driven by the process of export-led industrialization and, more recently, service 'offshoring', reflecting the evolution of international divisions of labour (Daniels et al., 2005; Bryson, 2007). Both manufacturing plants and service facilities such as call centres tend to be concentrated in urban or peri-urban areas, providing investors with access to large pools of labour and links to global transport and communications infrastructure (Kelly, 2002; Hutton, 2004). In large parts of the global south, where urban growth has not been supported by economic growth, the informal sector, made up of various unofficial activities such as street-vending and domestic production which exist outside of the boundaries of the for-mal economy (Hart, 1973), has come to play a key role in absorbing increased urban populations (Chant, 2008).

Export-orientated industrialization is often spatially concentrated in Export Pro-cessing Zones (EPZs) which have spread rapidly since the 1970s from a total of 79 in 1975 to 5,000 in 2003 (Dicken, 2007: 220). Although the *maquiladoras* of Mexico are perhaps the best-known examples, 87% of employment in EPZs is in Asia (ibid). They are generally associated with elaborate regimes of labour control based on the spatial containment of labour, aiming to prevent unionization (Kelly, 2002). Research has shown that labour in EPZs tends to be female, young and often drawn from rural areas (Wright, 2006). In urban Madagascar, for example, 68% of the employees in the *Zone Franche* were women, echoing the wider pattern (Glick and Rouband, 2006: 728). While low by global standards, wages and conditions in EPZs are often better than those in other sectors of the domestic economy. Glick and Roubaud (2006), for instance, found that the growth of export-orientated manufac-turing in the *Zone Franche* was drawing women workers out of the informal sector, leading to significant increases in earnings. More negatively, however, hours of work are very long in *Zone Franche* firms and labour turnover is high, again echoing more general characteristics of employment in EPZs (Wright, 2006). Based on research on three factories in East Asia, another study found that permanent labour had been subject to dismantling in recent years as companies rely on temporary workers and fixed-term contracts, offering greater numerical flexibility (Nichols et al., 2004).

Discussions of a 'second global shift' and new divisions of service expertise (Bryson, 2007, 2008) require that attention is paid to services as well as manufacturing. In the dynamic growth economies of East and South East Asia, advanced services such as finance, business services, call centres, hotels and retail have expanded rapidly, par-ticularly in large metropolitan regions (Hutton, 2004). This has created a new middle class of service workers who tend to adopt Western modes of consumption, reflected in the profusion of shopping malls and global brand outlets (Douglass, 2005). Again, while call centre workers in India earn far less than their equivalents in developed countries – £1,502 per year for a new operative compared to £12,945 in the UK (Bryson, 2007: 386) – such employment tends to be better paid than most other employment in the domestic economy. Indian call centre workers are generally better educated, with university graduation a pre-requisite for work as a 'process executive', but the semi-skilled nature of labour often leads to disillusionment and a high turnover (Russell and Tithe, 2008). In this sense, call centres in developing counties such as India have been characterized as reproducing in exaggerated and culturally-distinctive forms a division of labour that has proved problematic in developed countries like the UK, reflecting the pressures on employees to interact effectively with customers who are geographically and culturally distant (Taylor and Bain, 2005).

The growth of advanced services in the burgeoning cities of the developing world is juxtaposed with the proliferation of informal small-scale service operations in the trad-itional sector, highlighting the persistently dualistic character of urban labour markets

(Daniels et al., 2005). Data on the nature and scale of the informal sector are notoriously unreliable, given its irregular and often clandestine nature, shifting classifications by governments and international bodies and overlap with more formal activities. Nonetheless, informal employment has grown in many parts of the world since 1980, representing a survival strategy for many households (Riddell, 1997). In Latin America, for instance, an estimated seven out of ten new jobs created in the 1990s were in the informal sector, and the proportion of the non-agricultural labour force employed in the informal sector increased from 43% to 51% between 1990 and 2002 (Chant, 2008: 218). In Asia and sub-Saharan Africa, the share of the workforce employed in the informal sector is even higher at 71% and 72% respectively, with countries like Benin and Chad reporting levels of 91% (ibid). Much of this growth reflects the impact of recessions and neoliberal forms of economic restructuring related to high levels of indebtedness and structural adjustment programmes (Sassen, 2008). These have resulted in reductions in public employment, the closure of private firms and growth in subcontracting by formal employers (Chant, 2008: 218–19). In this sense, 'the "top-down" informalisation promoted by governments and employers has been matched by a "bottom up" informalisation stemming from the need for retrenched formal sector workers and newcomers to the labour market to create their own sources of earnings…' (ibid).

In general, chronic poverty is often associated with casual labour and informal business activities (Grant, 2008), with the disproportionate effects on women reflecting the gendering of urban poverty and marginality. Several economically active members of a household may be engaged in the informal sector, reflecting the importance of labour as the main economic asset of the poor, but research from urban Peru and Madagascar indicates that the more household members that are involved in informal employment, the poorer they are, underlining the poor economic returns from this type of work (ibid: 2). Evidence from Ethiopia suggests that 27.5% of the heads of chronically poor urban households work as casual labourers or in female business activities, compared to only 7.7% of those who are never poor, who are far more likely to work for a wage (ibid). In response, there is a need for municipal governments to support entry into the formal labour market and to improve the quality of jobs for the urban poor, particularly through the promotion of labour-intensive growth, something which has been neglected by national Poverty Reduction Strategy Papers in recent years.

The Metamorphosis of Marginality in the Favelas of Rio de Janeiro

The US scholar, Janice Perlman's (2006), study of the changing lives of the poor in the favelas (shanty towns) of Rio involved Perlman returning in 1999–2003 to communities she had originally studied in 1968–1969. Despite the efforts of successive governments to address the problem of urban poverty, Rio's favelas have continued to grow with twice as many existing in the early 2000s as in 1969. Between 1980 and 1990, the overall rate of city growth was just 8% but the favela population grew by

41%. The corresponding figures for the period 1990 to 2000 were 7% and 24%. As a result, 19% of Rio's population lived in favelas in 2000, compared to only 7% in 1950.

Unsurprisingly, Perlman uncovered a complex and mixed picture of how favela dwellers' lives had changed over the 30 years since her original study. One of the most positive findings was that 40% of those who had lived in favelas at the time of the original study had moved to become owners or renters of homes in legitimate neighbourhoods. The type of community in which respondents resided was closely associated with their socio-economic status as the chronically poor were disproportionately comprised of those who had lived in favelas all their lives. The research also showed a huge increase in consumption since 1969, well beyond what would be consistent with income levels. Educational standards and literacy rates have also improved greatly across the generations. A number of negative aspects also emerged. These included high levels of unemployment with 65% of respondents reporting being unemployed for over a month compared with 31% in 1969. As such, higher levels of education had not resulted in stable employment, breeding a sense of hopelessness and alienation among many young people. High unemployment reflects a dramatic loss of manufacturing and construction jobs in the city, affecting thousands of blue-collar workers; technological advances which have replaced labour-intensive jobs with a smaller number of high-skilled positions; reduced demand for the provision of domestic services by women due to changing consumption habits; higher education standards for job entry; and a pervasive prejudice and discrimination against favela residents. The other negative change has been an increase in drug-related crime and violence, resulting in reduced social capital and connectivity as people have become more afraid to leave their homes, reducing their access to information about employment. On these grounds, Perlman argues that the 40 years since 1969 have witnessed a transformation from a 'myth of marginality' to a 'reality of marginality', concluding that the availability of stable employment is the key to improving the lives of the urban poor.

A key underlying theme of this section is the mobility of labour at different scales, particularly the intra-national (or inter-regional) and international. As previously emphasized, high levels of rural to urban migration have led to rapid urban growth and the expansion of the informal sector to meet the daily survival and reproduction needs of poor urban households. At the same time, rapid export-led growth has attracted labour from poorer regions which become dependent upon remittances as a crucial source of income. In the Philippines, for instance, Kelly (2009) shows how many in-migrants to the Cavite province in the region of Southern Tagalog, a centre of industrial growth since the late 1980s, have come from the poor Visayan region in the central Philippines. In addition, developing countries also generate outflows of labour, and remittances have acquired great economic significance as a source of income and foreign exchange (Sassen, 2008), reaching a value of US$233 billion in 2005, compared to a volume of bilateral aid from OECD countries of US$106.48 billion (K. D. Willis, 2008: 212). While the consequences of international migration for source regions have often been viewed as negative, resulting in depopulation and the erosion of human capital, De Hass (2006) suggests, on the basis of research conducted in Southern Morocco, that it can have positive impacts, allowing households to improve their living standards. In the Philippines, Kelly (2009) found that remittances fostered the upward social mobility of recipient households through investments in consumption, production and private education for children, resulting in increased polarization between such households and those which had no remittance income.

CONCLUSIONS

Processes of labour market restructuring in the global north and south are united by a common theme: the splintering of labour markets between those in skilled, high-wage employment and those consigned to precarious low-paid employment or unemployment. This process of polarization is reflected in the social geography of cities, whereby affluent middle-class areas are often closely juxtaposed with poorer working-class neighbourhoods. The so-called urban frontier shifts over time of course, as indicated by the gentrification of many former working-class neighbour-hoods in the cities of the global north (Smith, 1996). Deindustrialization has resulted in a profound reduction in the demand for low-skilled labour (Ghose et al., 2008) with the inability of service employment to fully compensate creating a 'jobs gap' (Turok and Edge, 1999). As research has shown, employment in services is divided between high-skilled work in financial, business and professional services, and pre-carious low-paid work in sectors such as retail, catering, cleaning and entertainment (Sassen, 1991, 2008; May et al., 2007; McDowell et al., 2009). Inequalities have also increased in many of the cities of the global south, shaped by the divide between the formal and informal sectors (Chant, 2008). The formal sector has grown rapidly in a relatively smaller number of rapidly industrializing countries, particularly in Asia, with factories employing largely young female workers in enclaves such as EPZs and information technology-enabled services attracting mainly young graduates. Eco-nomic stagnation has seen the informal sector grow in many countries (ibid), reflect-ing the adverse impact of neoliberal processes of economic restructuring and the need to absorb large numbers of new entrants into the labour force because of population growth and rural-urban migration (ibid).

In addition to the shared, though differentiated, experience of labour market splinter-ing, cities in the global north and south are linked by a variety of economic flows (Sassen, 2008). Changing international divisions of labour have seen capital flow to selected parts of the developing world, particularly in East and South East Asia and Mexico, a pattern that is being extended through a so-called 'second global shift' of service employment (Bryson, 2007). Underpinned by these international divisions of labour and expertise (Bryson, 2008), locations in the global north and south are linked together in global production networks (Coe et al., 2008). Flows of labour represent another key link with levels of international migration, largely from south to north, having doubled between 1970 and 2005 (K. D. Willis, 2008). In most cases, migrants to northern cities – who are disproportionately employed in precarious, low-wage service employment (May et al., 2007) – maintain strong links with their countries and regions of origin, not least through the provision of financial remittances, prompting Smith (2001) to speak of a new regime of transnational urbanism. Cities in the global north and south are also connected by policy initiatives, particularly through their common experiences of labour market deregulation, which has been promoted by a number of international organizations such as the World Bank, IMF and OECD (Peck, 2000). Deregulation has fostered labour market splintering, encouraging the growth of precarious low-wage employment in northern cities and the expansion of the informal sector in the south (Chant, 2008; Ghose et al., 2008). As such, the redressing of labour market inequalities will require a fundamental re-regulation of employment, abandoning the shibboleth of flexibility and emphasizing the creation of stable jobs and the expansion of overall demand.

Useful Websites

ALF-CIO (http://www.aflcio.org): The main US trade union federation.

British trade union confederation site (www.//tuc.org.uk)

Innovation Systems Research Network (http://www.utoronto.ca/isrn/index.html): This site brings together the work of a number of researchers on innovation and labour markets in various Canadian cities and regions.

International Confederation of Free Trade Unions (www.icftu.org): The main website for the umbrella body that represents the international trade union movement.

Independent Global Labour Institute (www.global-labour.org): tends to be more radical and militant than the official trade unions.

International Labour Organization (www.//ilo.org): The UN body that carries out research into global labour issues. Produces data and research papers on a range of labour issues from trade unions membership to trends in labour flexibility.

UK Official Labour Market Statistic (www.//nomisweb.co.uk)

US Bureau of Labor Statistics (http://www.bls.gov/)

7

Informal Economies

Colin C. Williams

INTRODUCTION

A long-standing belief regarding urban economic development is that goods and services have been increasingly produced and delivered via the formal economy rather than on a subsistence or barter basis in the informal economy. The outcome is that informal work has been configured as a leftover from a previous era and as gradually disappearing from view as economic 'advancement' takes hold. In recent decades, however, this reading of urban economic development in general, and the role of the urban informal economy in particular, has been challenged as it has been realized that informal work is a persistent and substantial feature of many urban economies. In this chapter, therefore, the aim is to evaluate the various perspectives that have emerged which explain this persistence and growth of the urban informal economy.

To achieve this, firstly, the long-standing residue thesis, which dominated thought throughout much of the twentieth century, will be briefly outlined, and secondly, we will look at some of the evidence that has led to the refutation of this portrayal of the urban informal economy as a residual disappearing sector. The third section then introduces the current ways in which the persistence of the urban informal economy is being explained whilst the fourth section evaluates these competing perspectives and finds that, although each is wholly valid in relation to specific populations and particular types of informal work, no one articulation fully captures the diverse nature and multiple meanings of the informal economy. The resultant argument in the fifth section is that only by using all the current perspectives will a finer-grained and more comprehensive understanding of the complex and multifarious character of informal work in different places be achieved. A conceptual framework is then presented that synthesizes the contrasting representations, and in doing so provides a more multi-layered and nuanced depiction of the urban informal economy. The chapter then concludes with a discussion of some of the implications for urban economic development and policy.

Before commencing, however, the informal economy needs to be defined. Reflecting the widespread consensus, the 'informal economy' covers all work that is not 'formal employment', that is, paid work registered with the state for tax, social security and labour law purposes. This defining of the informal economy in terms of what it is not, displays not only the ideological centrality of the formal economy but also how informal work acts as a residual umbrella category to catch all work which is left over (Latouche, 1993). As such, diverse types of work are covered. To bring some order, three broad types of informal work are here distinguished: 'self-provisioning' which is the unpaid household work undertaken by household members for themselves or for other members of their household; 'unpaid community work', which is unpaid work conducted by household members by and for the extended family, social or neighbourhood networks and more formal voluntary and community groups, and ranges from kinship exchange, through friendship/neighbourly reciprocal exchanges to one-way volunteering for voluntary organizations; and 'undeclared work' which can be defined as all monetized exchanges that are unregistered by or hidden from the state for tax, social security and/or labour law purposes but which are legal in all other respects (Pahl, 1984; Williams and Windebank, 1998). In consequence, it is not tasks (e.g. cleaning, cooking) that differentiate one form of work from another but rather the social relations within which these tasks are conducted.

THE URBAN INFORMAL ECONOMY AS A RESIDUE

During the twentieth century, the dominant discourse was that goods and services were being increasingly produced and delivered via the formal economy and that informal work was disappearing. The informal economy was read as a leftover from some earlier mode of production. Its continuing presence, especially in majority (third) world urban economies, was thus portrayed as a sign of their 'under-development', 'traditionalism' and 'backwardness', while a large and growing urban formal economy was viewed as signalling 'progress', 'development', 'modernity' and 'advancement' (Boeke, 1942; Lewis, 1959; Geertz, 1963).

Variously referred to as the 'modernization', 'dual economy', 'residue' or 'formalization' thesis (Williams and Windebank, 1998; Chen, 2006; Fernandez-Kelly, 2006; Williams, 2007), this depiction is an exemplar of what Derrida (1967) calls hierarchical binary thought in that it firstly, conceptualizes formal and informal work as separate spheres constituted via negation, and secondly, reads them in a normatively hierarchical manner in which the superordinate (the formal economy) is endowed with positive attributes and the subordinate (or subservient) 'other' (the informal economy) with negative attributes and impacts. The outcome is a temporal and hierarchical sequencing of these spheres in urban economic development.

They are temporally sequenced by reading the superordinate (the formal economy) as extensive and in the ascendancy and the subservient 'other' (the informal economy) as primitive or traditional, stagnant, marginal, weak, and about to be extinguished. Informal work is thus portrayed as a leftover of pre-capitalist formations which is disappearing, and fragmented and scattered in the margins of the urban economic landscape (Latouche, 1993). It is not depicted as resilient, ubiquitous, capable of generative growth, or as driving urban economic change. Nor is it portrayed as part of a multitude of different forms of work co-existing in the contemporary urban economic landscape. Instead, it is characterized as a remnant of the past and 'pre-modern' (Rose, 2005: 26). Running alongside this temporal ordering is a hierarchical sequencing that normatively reads informal work as a sign of 'under-development', 'traditionalism' and 'backwardness' (Geertz, 1963). Formalization, in contrast, is a sign of 'progress', 'development', 'modernity' and 'advancement' (Lewis, 1959). An outcome is to depict cities globally as in a development queue according to their degree of formalization, with Western cities portrayed as more advanced than those in the majority world that have larger informal economies.

They are also depicted as separate realms. This is manifested firstly, in accounts that depict formal and informal enterprises as discrete entities; secondly, and characterized by the 'marginality thesis', in accounts that view informal work as concentrated amongst individuals excluded from formal employment; and thirdly, in depictions of formal and informal work as occupying separate spaces in the urban economic land-scape. At the micro-spatial level, for example, informal work is often consigned to the household while formal work occupies the separate sphere of the 'employment-place'. Scaling upwards, meanwhile, informal work is assigned to deprived neighbourhoods in Western cities and shanty towns in third world cities (Davis, 2006) and formality to more affluent districts.

RE-READING THE INFORMAL ECONOMY AS A PERSISTENT AND SUBSTANTIAL FEATURE OF CITIES

In recent decades, the residue thesis has come under concerted attack as it has been recognized that the informal economy is not only a persistent and substantial fea-ture of cities but, if anything, is growing rather than declining relative to the for-mal economy (ILO, 2002; Mehrotra and Biggeri, 2007; Jütting and de Laiglesia, 2009). Indeed, this has been particularly recognized in cities in the global south where the informal economy is heavily relied on in urban livelihoods and survival practices (Jhabvala et al., 2003; Roy and AlSayyad, 2004; Brown, 2006; Bryceson and Potts, 2006; Davis, 2006; Cross and Morales, 2007; Mehrotra and Biggeri, 2007). Here, some of the methods and evidence used to reach this conclusion is presented.

Although some commentators employ indirect proxy indicators of formalization, such as employment participation rates, caution is required. Analyzing participation in formal employment tells us nothing about whether the balance is shifting between formal and informal work. Increased participation in employment is not always accompanied by a decline in informal work. It may be accompanied by a quicker or slower growth in informal work, a decline in informal work or a similar growth rate resulting in no change in the overall balance of formal and informal work. Unless both formal and informal work is analyzed, therefore, whether formalization is occurring will not be known.

For this reason, direct measures of the changing balance between formal and informal work have been adopted which compare the volume and value of formal and informal work in different time periods using measures of either the inputs into, or outputs of, such work (Goldschmidt-Clermont, 2000). One of the most popular methods is to measure the volume and value of the inputs using time-budget data (e.g. Gershuny, 2000). Here, participants fill in diaries of what they do and the time that they spend in formal employment and in other forms of work is then calculated.

Table 7.1 collates the findings of time-budget studies conducted in 20 countries over the past half century or so. It reveals that unpaid work today continues to occupy just under half of all working time, meaning that the time spent on unpaid work, so long considered a marginal 'other', is only slightly less than the time spent on paid activity. It also displays that it is perhaps presumptuous to talk of a universal process of formalization. Although some nations appear to be slowly formalizing, such as Canada and Norway, countries including Denmark, Finland, France, the UK and the USA have all witnessed a process of informalization, not formalization, over the past half a century or so. This is not due to a growth in the time spent on unpaid work. It is because the time spent on paid work has decreased quicker than the time spent on unpaid work (Gershuny, 2000). Different advanced economies are therefore witnessing divergent development paths.

Consequently, there is no natural and inevitable trajectory of formalization and neither is the formal economy hegemonic. Even in so-called advanced economies, not only is the informal economy about the same size as the formal economy, measured in terms of the amount of working time spent in each sphere, but no evidence exists of any universal trajectory towards formalization.

Although there are few, if any, longitudinal studies of the trajectory of urban economies in terms of their formal/informal balance, various snapshot surveys of individual cities display that the informal economy is not some minor residue (e.g. Caldwell, 2004; Pavlovskya, 2004; Williams and Round, 2007, 2008; Shevchenko,

Table 7.1 Unpaid work as a % of total work time, 1960–present day

Country	1960–73	1974–84	1985–present day	Trend
Canada	56.9	55.4	54.2	Formalization
Denmark	41.4	–	43.3	Informalization
France	52.0	55.5	57.5	Informalization
Netherlands	–	55.9	57.9	Informalization
Norway	57.1	55.4	–	Formalization
UK	52.1	49.7	53.9	Informalization
USA	56.9	57.6	58.4	Informalization
Finland	–	51.8	54.5	Informalization
20 Countries	43.4	42.7	44.7	Informalization

Source: Williams (2007: Table 3.2)

2009). The two boxed features below provide case studies of how the informal economy is a substantial feature of contemporary cities by respectively examining the post-socialist global city of Moscow followed by the Western cities of Sheffield and Southampton in England. Examining the sources of labour used to get 44 common everyday tasks completed in these cities, the finding is that in Moscow, just 7% of these tasks were last conducted in the formal economy whilst in the English cities, it was only slightly higher at 15%. In major part, this variation is probably because in Moscow, tasks when monetized are more usually conducted in the paid informal economy with 19% of all tasks being conducted using paid informal work in Moscow compared with just 4% in English cities where a greater share of tasks when monetized are conducted in the formal economy. The share undertaken on an unpaid basis, meanwhile, is remarkably similar (75% in Moscow and 79% in English cities), although in English cities a greater proportion of tasks are conducted using self-provisioning (76% compared with 68%) whilst in Moscow a greater share is carried out using unpaid community exchanges (7% compared with 3%).

The Informal Economy in the Post-Socialist World: The Case of Moscow

In 2005/06, Williams and Round (2008) conducted 313 face-to-face interviews in an affluent, a mixed and a deprived district of Moscow to evaluate the prevalence and nature of the informal economy. Examining the sources of labour last used by households to undertake 44 common domestic services, Table 7.2 portrays the limited degree to which the formal economy has permeated the household services sector in this supposedly global (and globalized) city.

These results also display the unevenness of the formalization process. Dwellers living in the affluent district pursued more formalized work practices than those in the deprived or mixed areas. It might be therefore argued that the reason for the shallow

Table 7.2   Type of labour last used to conduct 44 domestic tasks in Moscow: By district

	% of all tasks done	Self-provisioning		Unpaid exchange		Paid informal work		Formal employment	
		No. of tasks done	%	No. of tasks done	%	No. of tasks done	%	No. of tasks done	%
All	51	9.0	68	0.9	7	2.5	19	0.9	7
District									
Affluent	58	9.0	62	0.9	6	3.2	22	1.5	10
Deprived	51	8.8	67	1.1	9	2.7	20	0.6	4
Mixed	49	9.5	78	0.9	7	1.4	11	0.5	4

Source: Derived from Williams and Round (2008: Table 3)

penetration of the formal economy in Moscow is because a large proportion of the population are excluded from the formal sphere and use the informal economy out of necessity as a survival practice. Williams and Round (2008) find that this is indeed a generally accurate depiction of those living in the deprived district surveyed but does not explain why those living in the affluent area continue to use informal work which is often used as a matter of choice rather than due to a lack of choice.

The Informal Economy in the Western World: The Case of Two English Cities

Examining two English cities, namely Southampton in the south of England, and Sheffield in the north, Table 7.3 displays that formalization is again far from complete. Less than one in seven (15%) of the 44 everyday domestic services surveyed were conducted using formal labour in these English cities. Contrary to the rhetoric that Western urban economies are formalized commodified spaces saturated by market relations (see Williams, 2005), this study suggests that they are less formalized than often assumed. Of course, examining the realm of everyday domestic services perhaps underplays the penetration of the formal economy since this is probably a sphere that is less formalized than other spheres. Nevertheless, it still clearly portrays that urban populations in the Western world continue to pursue a plurality of work practices and are far from totally reliant on the formal economy to secure their livelihood.

Table 7.3 Type of labour last used to conduct 44 domestic tasks in English cities: By neighbourhood type

	Tasks done	Self-provisioning		Unpaid exchange		Paid informal work		Formal economy	
	%	Av. No.	%	Av. No.	%	Av. No.	%	Av. No.	%
Southampton:									
Deprived inner city	43	14.2	75	0.6	3	0.8	4	3.3	17
Deprived council estate	47	15.5	75	0.8	4	0.9	5	3.6	17
Both deprived areas	45	14.9	75	0.7	4	0.9	4	3.4	17
Affluent suburb	57	18.0	71	0.5	2	1.6	6	5.1	20
Sheffield:									
Deprived inner city	50	16.6	76	0.9	4	1.4	6	3.0	14
Deprived council estate	48	16.8	79	0.8	4	0.9	4	2.7	13
Both deprived areas	49	16.7	77	0.9	4	1.2	5	2.9	13
Affluent suburb	53	17.1	73	0.4	2	2.6	11	3.3	14
All	47	15.8	76	0.8	4	1.0	5	3.2	15

Source: Derived from Williams (2004b: Table 3)

(Continued)

(Continued)

The extent of formalization, nevertheless, is highly uneven. Those living in the affluent suburbs of these cities are more formalized and money-orientated in their work practices. However, the number of tasks they conduct through self-provisioning is also greater than in deprived neighbourhoods, suggesting that informal work is not always conducted as a last resort by marginalized groups. There are also differences between the two cities. Households in the affluent southern city more heavily use formal labour, akin to affluent neighbourhoods. The difference, however, is that those in the more affluent southern city do not also engage in a wider range of informal work. The tentative intimation, therefore, is that differences in 'work cultures' might exist between these cities with more of a 'self-reliance ethic' in the northern English city than its southern counterpart (Williams, 2004b).

The Informal Economy in India: The Case of Ahmedabad

In India, 93% of the total workforce and 83% of the non-agricultural workforce is in the informal economy (ILO, 2002). In this country, therefore, the informal economy is very much the 'mainstream' and the formal economy a minor peripheral 'backwater'. Evaluating its extensiveness across sectors, informal work accounts for virtually all employment in agriculture and in trade (99% for both industries), the vast bulk of employment in construction (94%) and the majority of workers in transport and storage (79%) and in social and personal services as well as financial services (66% in

Table 7.4 Formal and informal employment and income in Ahmedabad city, 1997–98

	Employment		Income	
	Total	Informal*	Total	Informal*
Agriculture	2.3	59.4	0.6	84.8
Manufacturing	35.4	67.4	36.4	43.1
Electricity	0.8	–	2.3	–
Construction	9.3	100	3.6	100
Transport	12.7	91.5	11.7	80.5
Storage	0.1	–	0.2	–
Trade, hotels and restaurants	19.0	90.5	18.9	63.1
Communications banking & insurance	3.9	–	12.5	–
Services	16.4	81.5	11.6	48.9
Rentals	–	–	2.2	–
Total	100	76.7	100	46.8
Estimates	1.504,033	–	60,130**	–

Notes: * Share of the informal sector in each industry group; ** In Rs million

Source: Rani and Unni (2003: Table 2.5)

both industries). The National Accounts Statistics of India estimate the contribution of the formal and informal sectors to Net Domestic Product (NDP) that is, the GDP minus depreciation. In 1997–98, the contribution of the informal sector was 60% of total NDP. Excluding agriculture, the informal sector contributed 45% of non-agricultural NDP (see ILO, 2002).

Similar findings are identified in urban India. Unni and Rani (2003) calculate the employment, income and labour productivity in the formal and informal sectors of Ahmedabad city (see Table 7.4). Of the 1.5 million employed in this city, some 1.1 million (76.7%) were employed in the informal economy and of the Rs 60 billion income generated, some Rs 28.1 billion (46.8%) was generated by the informal economy. The bulk of this informal income derived from manufacturing, trade, hotels and restaurants. More income was generated in the informal economy in industry groups such as agriculture, transport and trade, while the formal economy did better in the rest.

In consequence, when this is combined with other literature on South-East Asia (McGee, 1991; Leaf, 1996, 2005; Rigg, 1997), the strong intimation is that the urban informal economy is totalizing, extensive and near hegemonic in urban areas in India and elsewhere in South East Asia, whilst the formal economy is a minor realm existing in a few small pockets of the urban economic landscape.

In sum, there is now an emergent body of evidence that the urban informal economy is not a residue. It is a persistent and substantial component of contemporary urban livelihood practices. How, therefore, can this persistence of informal work be explained?

EXPLAINING THE PERSISTENCE OF THE URBAN INFORMAL ECONOMY: COMPETING PERSPECTIVES

Until now, the persistence and growth of informal work in urban economies has been explained in three contrasting ways. Each perspective is here considered in turn.

The Urban Informal Economy as a By-Product of the Urban Formal Economy

A first perspective depicts the urban informal economy as expanding due to the emergence of a de-regulated open world economy, which is encouraging a race-to-the-bottom in terms of labour standards (Castells and Portes, 1989; Portes, 1994; Sassen, 1997a; Gallin, 2001; Hudson, 2005). On the one hand, therefore, the growth of the urban informal economy, particularly paid informal work, is a direct by-product of employers seeking to reduce costs by adopting informal work arrangements, reflected in the growth of sub-contracting to off-the-books workers employed under degrading, low-paid and exploitative 'sweatshop-like' conditions (e.g. Bender, 2004; Ross, 2004). As Davis (2006: 186) puts it, what is re-emerging in contemporary capitalism are 'primitive forms of exploitation that have been given new life by postmodern globalization'.

On the other hand, the expansion of the urban informal economy more broadly defined to include unpaid work is resulting from the demise of the full-employment/comprehensive formal welfare state regime characteristic of the Fordist and/or socialist era (Hudson, 2005). In the new post-Fordist and/or post-socialist era, those of little use to capitalism are no longer maintained as a reserve army of labour and socially reproduced by the formal welfare state but, instead, are off-loaded, resulting in their increasing reliance on the urban informal sphere as a survival strategy. Informal work is therefore extensive in marginalized populations where the formal economy is weak since it acts as a substitute for formal work in its absence, and is undertaken by those involuntarily decanted into this sphere and conducted out of necessity in order to survive (Castells and Portes, 1989; Sassen, 1997b).

In this by-product thesis, the informal economy is thus a core and integral component of contemporary urban capitalism. As Fernandez-Kelly (2006: 18) puts it, 'the informal economy is far from a vestige of earlier stages in economic development. Instead, informality is part and parcel of the processes of modernization'. Although rejecting the temporal sequencing of the residue thesis, its normative hierarchical reading is nevertheless perpetuated. The urban informal economy is depicted as possessing largely negative attributes and formalization as the route to progress, albeit more as a prescription for urban economic development rather than as inevitable. An example is the ILO (2002) which recognizes that informal work is growing and inextricably inter-twinned with formal work and its 'decent work' campaign prescribes formalization as the path to progress.

The Urban Informal Economy as an Alternative to the Urban Formal Economy

A second perspective inverts the above hierarchical ordering that privileges the formal economy as the path to progress, instead viewing informalization as the route to advancement. Akin to the residue discourse, informal and formal work are here often seen as separate spheres but unlike both the residue and by-product approaches, participation in informal work is depicted as possessing positive attributes and impacts and as conducted as a matter of choice rather than due to a lack of choice (Cross, 2000; Gerxhani, 2004; Maloney, 2004; Snyder, 2004). As Gerxhani (2004: 274) argues for example, workers 'choose to participate in the informal economy because they find more autonomy, flexibility and freedom in this sector than in the formal one'.

Conventionally, this is most commonly argued by neoliberals who portray informal workers as heroes casting off the shackles of an over-burdensome state (e.g. Sauvy, 1984; de Soto, 1989). However, they are joined by radical green commentators who positively view informal work as resonating with their desire for localization and self-reliance (e.g. Robertson, 1991; Henderson, 1999) and more recently, an array of post-development, critical and post-structuralist scholars seeking to imagine and enact alternative futures for economic development beyond formalization and commodification (e.g. Escobar, 1995; Gibson-Graham, 1996, 2006; Leyshon et al., 2003; Williams, 2005). This perspective thus counters the conventional normative portrayal of urban economic development as a process of formalization with an alternative inverted view of progress as a process of informalization.

The Urban Informal Economy as a Complement to the Urban Formal Economy

A third and final perspective again depicts the urban informal economy as substantial, and as possessing largely positive attributes and impacts, but views the formal and informal economies as inter-woven rather than discrete, and as growing or declining in tandem, rather than one contracting when the other expands (Beck, 2000; Williams and Windebank, 2003; Williams, 2005). Relatively affluent populations and households, who are the major beneficiaries of formal work, are thus seen as the major beneficiaries of informal work, conducting not only more self-provisioning, unpaid community exchange and undeclared work than households excluded from the formal economy but also more rewarding forms of informal work (e.g. Pahl, 1984; Fortin et al., 1996; Williams, 2004a, 2005).

Consequently, uneven urban economic development is characterized not as a polarization between those pursuing formalized work strategies and those consigned to informal work practices. Instead, uneven development is represented as a rift between 'work busy' or 'fully engaged' populations and/or areas with multiple formal jobs and high levels of engagement in self-provisioning, unpaid community exchange and undeclared work, and 'work deprived' or 'dis-engaged' populations and/or areas excluded not only from the formal economy but also engagement in informal work due to their lack of resources, skills and networks (Pahl, 1984; Fortin et al., 1996; Williams and Windebank, 2002; Williams, 2004a, 2006). Here, therefore, 'development' is not formalization. Rather, it is the ability of populations to engage in both formal and informal work to secure a livelihood (Williams, 2004b).

EVALUATING THE COMPETING EXPLANATIONS FOR THE PERSISTENCE OF INFORMAL WORK

Given that informal work remains a persistent and substantial feature of contemporary urban economies, which explanation is most valid? Has a large segment of the urban population been involuntarily decanted into the informal economy to eke out their livelihood as intimated in the by-product thesis? Are urban dwellers pursuing such work as a chosen alternative to the formal economy? Or is the urban informal economy operating in a manner that complements the urban formal economy? Drawing upon evidence from urban economies around the world, and taking each form of informal work in turn, it will be here shown that no one representation accurately captures the diverse nature and the multiple meanings of urban informal economies and that each of the three competing explanations are applicable to different populations engaged in different forms of informal work in various places.

Self-Provisioning in Urban Economies

Nearly every urban household throughout the world engages in self-provisioning. To differentiate the multifarious forms of self-provisioning, firstly, subsistence-oriented households that primarily rely on self-provisioning to secure their livelihood are analyzed, and secondly, we look at the routine and non-routine types of self-provisioning conducted by households as part of their overall portfolio of work practices.

Starting with subsistence-oriented households that rely on self-provisioning for their livelihood, although their numbers might be dwindling, such households continue to exist. In Western cities, they are mostly 'downshifters' seeking to voluntarily reduce their dependence on the urban formal economy by both consuming less and pursuing more subsistence-oriented self-reliant practices (Brown et al., 1998; Jacob, 2003). In many majority (third) world cities, however, such subsistence production by urban dwellers is not always a voluntary choice but more an economic necessity due to their exclusion from the urban formal economy (Davis, 2006). Similarly, in many post-socialist cities, as Williams and Round (2008) found in Kiev, a significant minority (8%) of urban households rely chiefly on subsistence work to secure their livelihood, and do so out of necessity.

Those households in Western cities voluntarily choosing to pursue subsistence-oriented lifestyles, therefore, provide some support for the depiction of informal work as a chosen alternative. The subsistence-oriented households doing so out of necessity found in cities in the majority and post-socialist world, meanwhile, lend some credence to the by-product perspective, and where their numbers are smaller, the residue perspective.

Examining routine and non-routine forms of self-provisioning more generally, it is similarly the case that evidence can be found in various types of self-provisioning and amongst different populations to support contrasting representations of informal work. Analysing routine self-provisioning, especially in lower-income populations, one finds support for the by-product thesis (Williams, 2004b, 2005; Biles, 2008). This form of informal work is extensive in marginalized populations where the formal economy is weak and primarily conducted out of necessity as a survival practice. Where the formal economy is stronger, such non-routine self-provisioning is more commonly out-sourced to the formal economy.

Analyzing non-routine self-provisioning such as do-it-yourself activity, however, the finding is that affluent urban populations not only do more than deprived populations, but also engage in more creative and rewarding forms of DIY out of choice whilst deprived populations do DIY out of economic necessity and engage more in repair and maintenance (rather than home improvement) tasks (Watson and Shove, 2005; Williams, 2008). Comparing non-routine self-provisioning across affluent and deprived populations thus provides evidence to support the depiction of informal work as a complement of formal work, and as reinforcing, rather than reducing, the disparities produced by the formal economy.

Unpaid Community Exchange in Urban Economies

Unpaid community exchange ranges from kinship exchange through neighbourly exchanges and unpaid exchanges with acquaintances to unpaid work conducted by and for voluntary and community organizations. The finding, as revealed in the first two case studies above, is that despite the purported demise of social capital in contemporary urban economies, such exchanges persist. On the whole, and as Tables 7.2 and 7.3 above displayed, unpaid community exchanges are relied on more in deprived than affluent urban populations as a means of securing a livelihood.

Although the overall prevalence and intensity of unpaid community exchange, akin to self-provisioning, is greater in relatively deprived populations, again, these populations are also more likely to do this work out of necessity and in the absence of alternatives whilst affluent populations are more likely to engage in such an endeavour out of choice. Indeed, comparing people living in the affluent and deprived districts of Kiev, Williams and Round (2007) find that the former were two times more likely to assert that receiving work on this basis was a choice compared with those living in the deprived district. While unpaid community exchange in deprived populations thus provides support for the by-product thesis, in relatively affluent populations it provides more support for the discourse that depicts informal work as a chosen alternative.

Undeclared Work in Urban Economies

In recent years, a diverse array of types of undeclared work have been identified ranging from endeavour conducted on a one-to-one basis for friends, neighbours and kin as paid favours (displaying the monetization of reciprocity), through various forms of self-employment to an array of types of informal waged employment (Williams, 2004a, 2006; Pfau-Effinger, 2009).

Examining waged informal employment, one finds considerable support for the by-product representation of the urban informal economy. Not only are many undeclared employees throughout the world's urban areas working under 'sweatshop-like' conditions (Castells and Portes, 1989; Cremers and Janssen, 2006; Meléndez et al., 2009), but in post-socialist cities, a widespread practice is that formal employees are forced by their formal employers to accept a portion of their wage on a cash-in-hand basis (Williams, 2009). This again reinforces the by-product depiction of informal work as becoming an inherent part of employment practices in late capitalism, possessing largely negative attributes and impacts, and as conducted out of necessity rather than choice.

Turning to informal self-employment, meanwhile, one finds considerable support for the representation of informal work as a positive alternative to the formal economy and resistance practice. In both Western cities (Snyder, 2004; Williams,

2006; Marcelli et al., 2009), post-socialist cities (Williams and Round, 2007) and third world urban areas (de Soto, 1989; Cross and Morales, 2007; Osirim, 2009), many self-employed have been found to choose to operate informally. For many, the formal economy is often seen as possessing largely negative attributes and impacts due to the existence of corrupt state officials and their lack of belief that taxes would be used for the social good, while the informal economy is perceived as a positive alternative that gives them free reign and is largely entered out of choice rather than necessity. This group of informal workers and type of work thus strongly supports the representation of the informal economy as an alternative to the formal economy and sphere of resistance.

Analyzing the realm of paid favours, however, one finds support for yet another representation. For suppliers, paid favours are conducted to make a little money 'on the side' but at the same time to provide some service to people they know who would otherwise be unable to get the job undertaken. For consumers, meanwhile, people they know are often paid for undertaking some task in order to redistribute money to them in a way that does not appear to be 'charity' and also to develop or cement social ties (Williams, 2004a, 2006; Williams and Round, 2008). To seek to eradicate such paid favours in urban economies, moreover, would eliminate around a half of all acts of one-to-one reciprocity and lead to a diminution of community self-help and thus social cohesion (Ledeneva, 2006; Williams and Round, 2007). This informal work therefore provides some support for attributing more positive characteristics to the informal economy, particularly the representation of the informal economy as a 'complement' to the formal economy. This is because when this has been studied in Western and post-socialist cities, higher-income populations are found to give and receive more paid favours than the average household, whilst the lowest-income households receive and provide just one half of the paid favours as the average household, displaying how this informal work reinforces the socio-spatial disparities of the formal economy (Williams, 2006; Williams and Round, 2007).

EVALUATING REPRESENTATIONS OF THE URBAN INFORMAL ECONOMY

Depending on the types of informal work and populations studied, different representations of the informal economy are appropriate. When considering the limited number of households pursuing subsistence modes of production, for example, and how very few households remain untouched by the formal economy, the residue perspective appears valid.

When considering other types of informal work, however, it is the representation of the informal economy as a by-product of a new emergent form of capitalism that is using informal working arrangements to compete and off-loading onto the informal sector those no longer of use to it which is valid. Support for this comes not only when examining forms of informal waged employment such as 'envelope wages' and sweatshop-like work, as well as routine self-provisioning, but also when wider trends are recognized such as that participation in the informal economy is more important as a coping practice amongst lower-income populations. However, not all types of informal work and populations can be depicted in this manner.

As the evidence in support of the representation of the informal economy as a complement to the formal economy clearly displays, some varieties of informal work are not conducted by the marginalized, but rather, reinforce, rather than reduce, the socio-spatial disparities in the formal economy. This is exemplified in the realm of do-it-yourself activity for example, as well as the sphere of paid favours. There are also types of informal work and populations who engage in such endeavours as a chosen alternative to the formal economy. Not only is there a culture of resistance to immersion in the formal economy, at least amongst some engaged in subsistence production as their primary work strategy, especially in the Western world, but the extensive 'hidden enterprise culture' of off-the-books enterprise and entrepreneur-ship being pursued as a widespread resistance practice to the (in their eyes) over-excessive regulation and state corruption, provides solid support for the depiction of informal work as a chosen alternative.

However, although varying representations are appropriate for different types of informal work and various populations, no one articulation fully captures the diverse nature and multiple meanings of the informal economy in contemporary urban economies. If the view that they are competing views is transcended and each is recognized as a representation of particular populations and types of informal work, as Chen (2006) suggests, then a finer-grained understanding of the complex and diverse meanings of the informal economy could be achieved. How, therefore, might this occur? Superficially, it does not appear achievable.

On the one hand, in the representations of the urban informal economy as a resi-due and an alternative, formal and informal work are discrete, while in discourses of the informal economy as a complement to, and by-product of, the formal econ-omy, they are viewed as inextricably inter-related and there is vehement opposition to any notion of separateness (e.g. Smith, 2004; Smith and Stenning, 2006). In lived practice, however, some forms of informal work are entangled in the formal econ-omy and others relatively separate. 'Envelope wages' where formal employees are paid a portion of their wages on a cash-in-hand basis, for example, provides solid support for the depiction of formal and informal work as inextricably inter-related. Yet this intimate entanglement is not apparent when examining subsistence-oriented households who are only loosely and marginally engaged with the formal economy, or when analyzing those operating wholly off-the-books businesses on a self-employed basis. There is a case to be made, therefore, for recognizing a spectrum of informal work ranging from varieties that are relatively separate from the formal sphere (e.g., subsistence-oriented households) to those that are relatively inter-twined with the formal economy (e.g. 'envelope wages', do-it-yourself activity).

On the other hand, while the residue and by-product perspectives universally attribute informal work with negative attributes and impacts, the complementary and alternative approaches do the inverse. However, it is again wholly feasible to conceptualize a continuum of types of informal work ranging from those with mostly positive attributes and impacts (e.g. paid favours, unpaid community exchange, informal entrepreneurship) to those with largely negative attributes (e.g. exploitative 'sweatshop'-like informal waged employment).

These discourses, therefore, can be read as valid depictions of particular types of informal work and populations which need to be integrated to achieve a finer-grained fuller understanding of the diverse nature of the informal economy. Indeed, this is now starting to be recognized (e.g. Chen, 2006; Williams and Round, 2007, 2008). Figure 7.1 provides a graphic representation of how this might be accomplished. The four contrasting discourses are here used to depict particular types of informal work and populations firstly, on a spectrum that ranges from forms of informal work that are relatively separate from the formal economy to types that are heavily embedded in the formal economy, and secondly, on a spectrum of types of informal work ranging from those with largely negative attributes to those with largely positive attributes and impacts.

Adopting this conceptual framework has important implications for understanding informal work and urban economic development. On the one hand, adopting this more integrative conceptual framework might start to result in more nuanced public policy approaches towards the urban informal economy. At present, a largely negative approach predominates, reflecting the dominance of the residue and by-product perspectives. This is particularly the case when considering what needs to be done about undeclared work where the dominant approach is to eradicate such work by increasing the probability of detection and the penalties if caught (Williams, 2004a, 2006). It is similarly the case when considering other forms of informal work. Few, if any, governments move beyond an employment-centred discourse when discussing urban economic development. If the above conceptual framework were adopted, however, then this would help identify those forms of informal work that

Formal and informal economy
relatively intertwined

BY-PRODUCT	COMPLEMENTARY
Examples: - Informal envelope wages - 'Sweatshop'-like informal employment	Examples: - Paid favours - Do-it-yourself activity
Negative	Positive
Attributes	Attributes

Examples:
- Enforced subsistence-oriented
  households
	Examples:
	- Informal entrepreneurs
	- Voluntarily subsistence-oriented
	  households

RESIDUE	ALTERNATIVE

Formal and informal economy
relatively separate

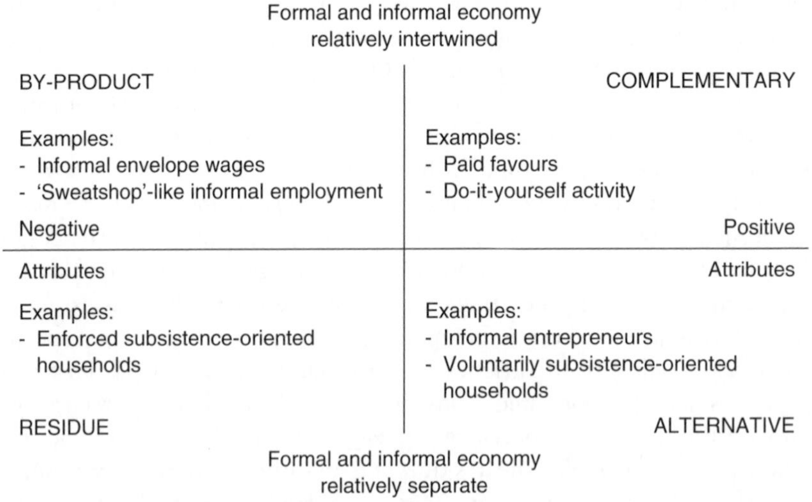

Figure 7.1   The relationships between formal and informal work

Source: Williams and Round (2007: Figure 1)

need to be eradicated and those that need to be either transformed into formal employment or tacitly condoned rather than adopting a 'one size fits all' urban economic policy approach which treats all types the same.

On the other hand, this conceptual framework also helps commentators to move beyond the long-standing simplistic arguments about whether formalization or informalization is the path to urban economic development. Rather than an 'on-off' decision about whether formalization or informalization is the way forward for urban economies, more nuanced and finer-grained debates about urban economic development could emerge adopting a more 'pick and mix' approach so far as various types of informal (and formal) work are concerned.

CONCLUSIONS

This paper has transcended the residue thesis by displaying how the informal economy is a persistent and substantial feature in many urban economies. Evaluating critically the competing explanations for the persistence of the informal economy that variously view this sphere as a by-product, complement or alternative to the formal economy, this paper has revealed that universal generalizations about the informal economy are not possible. Although evidence can be found to support all of these representations by examining specific types of informal work and particular populations, no one representation accurately depicts the urban informal economy as a whole in all places.

To more fully capture the diverse nature and the multiple meanings of the urban informal economy, this paper has therefore transcended the notion that these are competing representations and instead shown that each applies to particular types of informal work and specific populations. To achieve a finer-grained and more comprehensive understanding of the complex and multiple meanings of the informal economy, this paper has recognized firstly a spectrum of informal work ranging from varieties that are relatively separate from the formal sphere (e.g. subsistence-oriented households) to those that are relatively intertwined with formal work (e.g. 'envelope wages', do-it-yourself activity) and secondly, a continuum of types of informal work ranging from those with mostly positive features (e.g. paid favours, unpaid community exchange, informal entrepreneurship) to those with largely negative attributes (e.g. exploitative 'sweatshop'-like informal waged employment).

By adopting this more multi-layered and finer-grained articulation of the urban informal economy, the contention has been that a more comprehensive understanding of such work can start to be achieved along with a more refined and nuanced discussion about the way forward for urban economic development. Instead of debating whether either formalization or informalization is the way forward, finer-grained both/and approaches towards urban economic development can perhaps begin to emerge that adopt a more 'pick and mix' approach. If this chapter encourages greater discussion of this fresh approach to urban economic development, then it will have achieved its objective.

Useful Websites

Film on 'India's Informal Economy: the tailors of Dharavi' (http://www.youtube.com/watch?v=0U0iCe9ZFH8)

Film on 'Build Rights Build Unions – The Informal Economy (Part 1 of 3)' (http://www.youtube.com/watch?v=Hl9Ybdiyn9A)

Measures used to tackle undeclared work in 27 countries (http://www.eurofound.europa.eu/areas/labourmarket/tackling/search.php)

Self-employed Women's Association (http://www.sewa.org/)

SECTION 2

STEERING THE URBAN
ECONOMY

8

Boosterism, Brokerage and Uneasy Bedfellows: Networked Urban Governance and the Emergence of Post-Political Orthodoxy

Iain Deas and Nicola Headlam

BACKGROUND

This chapter explores recent experiences of city governance, focusing in particular on the emergence of entrepreneurial governance strategies and considering whether this represents a new orthodoxy in urban policy. Drawing upon its application in different contexts, the chapter attempts to identify the different elements of entrepreneurialism in urban governance, arguing that the evolution of governance in cities is more complex and multi-faceted than is sometimes appreciated. The chapter concludes by considering the degree to which urban governance can be considered 'post-political' and speculating on the scope for a future deepening in the extent of neoliberal governance strategies.

City policy elites in different international settings have over several decades tried to develop governance structures and policy initiatives that place the pursuit of economic growth as their principal objective. This has applied to established cities grappling with the collapse of their manufacturing bases and the resultant social and environmental consequences, where the challenge is to develop new economic potentials and possibilities that might eventually form part of a future *raison d'être*. It has also applied to apparently more successful cities, where the retention of competitive advantage becomes ever more of a challenge in an international context in which capital and labour are perceived to be highly mobile, and in which economic performance is measured relative to rival cities.

Yet identifying effective ways in which to govern these different types of city is far from straightforward. Policy-makers have long sought effective mechanisms through which to govern urban areas in ways that reconcile social and environmental objectives with economic development goals, while simultaneously representing citizen interests in the decision-making process. More recently, added to this historic purpose of urban government has been a different set of challenges. One has been the daunting task of managing the loose and sometimes disparate network of agencies and actors involved in different ways in devising and delivering urban policies. This is reflected in a relentless search for appropriate institutional vehicles through which to govern the reticulated terrain of the city. Bolstering institutional capacity and developing 'thick' governance structures have become important elements of a policy doctrine which suggests that stable, cohesive political relations can help to advance urban economic growth. Alongside these structural challenges, another goal relates to the practice of governance. Some proponents of the modernization of urban governance have posited that behavioural norms amongst urban policy-makers need to be radically reoriented, instilling amongst elite actors a more entrepreneurial, business-friendly mindset that contrasts with the kinds of bureaucratic culture held to have hampered urban economic growth in the past.

These kinds of principle have helped induce a sometimes radical transformation in the ways in which cities are governed. From the late twentieth century, there has been widespread recognition that public policy formulation and delivery is no longer the exclusive preserve of local government, but is instead developed and implemented through an array of institutions and processes, both formal and informal, which form governance networks that sometimes look quite different to municipal governments of the past (Pierre and Peters, 2000). Previously, responsibility for inducing urban economic and social revival rested largely with the state, through a sometimes uneasy combination of central and local government. More recently, however, the delivery of urban policy has undergone significant change, as the governance of cities has fragmented across a complex assortment of unelected non-departmental public bodies, in harness with a variety of private and voluntary sector actors.

This shift from government to governance has been extensively documented, in part because of the complexity and disparateness of the institutional structures and policy initiatives that have emerged. The emergence of multi-actor, cross-sectoral coalitions and partnerships, the growing significance of elite actor networks as a discrete and specific modality for urban governance, and the emergence of hybrid forms of governance have disrupted the binary relationships between state and market which once underpinned social, economic and political relations in cities. International experience is one in which monolithic local government has been in decline, with power and responsibility dispersed across networks of institutional actors. In part, this has been driven by a consensus around the notion that economic development in cities and regions is best pursued on a multi-sector 'partnership' basis. This view holds that it is through cross-sector, inclusive partnership working that policy coherence can best be maximized and resources most effectively marshalled in the context of otherwise highly fragmented institutional environments. Building capacity across networks and encouraging stable political relations, often linked to consensual ideas about what is appropriate in policy terms, is thus often viewed as a key ingredient of successful urban economic development.

The result is that alongside the fundamental shift in urban governance structures and policy actor views, there has also been an equally far-reaching transformation in the substantive content of urban policy efforts. In particular, there is wide-ranging evidence that urban policies have begun to move beyond their historical focus on 'problem' urban areas and towards a concern with promoting economic growth regardless of urban socio-economic context. Two factors have helped prompt this shift. The first is the emergence of the view that the economic vitality of cities is a critical component of broader national economic competitiveness, and that concerted effort is therefore needed to help maintain and enhance the performance of already successful places (for example, by accommodating growth pressures and facilitating further development), as well as to manage, slow or reverse the decline in lagging areas. A second factor underlying the reorientation of urban policy relates to hegemonic discourses of global urban economic competition and urban entrepreneurialism, and the contested view that the way in which cities, regions and other sub-national territories are governed has become more important in the context of an internationally more integrated economy over which nation-states have limited and diminishing influence (see, for example, Brenner, 1999; Jessop, 2000; Scott, 2001b). This in turn has helped fuel a growing sensitivity amongst urban policy actors to the performance of their cities when benchmarked against international peers, and a related desire to bolster their standing by focusing policy more exclusively on the promotion of economic growth.

In the remainder of this chapter, we explore in more detail the politics associated with this networked, entrepreneurial governance of cities. The chapter reviews a variety of attempts to interpret the emergence of urban governance arrangements characterized by a series of complex, often nebulous urban networks of elite actors which can transcend formal institutions and around which policy for economic development, inward investment activity, and the branding, marketing and promotional activities of cities can cohere. Firstly, we look briefly at shifts in the substance of urban economic development *policies*, arguing that boosterist strategies, once viewed as novel, are now central to economic development strategies. Secondly, we highlight some of the research efforts to describe and decode the changing *structures* of governance, noting in particular the characteristics of the shift from first to second generation governance. And third, we devote the bulk of the chapter to a review of *concepts*, exploring critical efforts to interpret shifts in urban governance, and arguing that while there is evidence of the emergence of a post-political orthodoxy, its contours are more complex than is sometimes appreciated.

BOOSTERISM AS THE NEW IMPERATIVE FOR MUNICIPAL LEADERSHIP?

Boosterism has become central to the policy-making agenda for cities. Alongside efforts, *inter alia*, to create flexible local labour markets, stimulate property-led commercial and residential redevelopment, enhance business competitiveness through light-touch regulation, subsidy and non-punitive and non-redistributive taxation, and maintain a physical environment conducive to internal and external business investment, boosterist strategies are at the core of urban economic development policy in many cities (Brenner and Theodore, 2002). They infuse a number of related attempts employed by cities to promote economic growth. Attempts to attract foreign direct investment, for example, have often worked in tandem with place promotion. Similarly, knowledge-based economic development – a prominent element of the strategy employed by many cities – is seen as critically dependant on a city's ability to promote itself to skilled workers, lured by the promise of 'liveable' neighbourhoods, in which affordable housing is situated in secure, well-designed residential areas with good access to employment opportunities and a range of public and private services. In some cases, place promotion has also emphasized the existence of a vibrant cultural life, a social climate of tolerance and liberalism and a sense of enterprising creativity amongst its residents as further ingredients in the mix of attractions that help entice skilled, 'creative' professionals, drawing upon what is held by some to be the exemplary experience of places like Austin, Texas. Ideas such as this, propounded by policy entrepreneurs like Richard Florida (2002), have proved extremely alluring to urban policy actors. This is despite claims that a focus on liveability and creativity in stimulating economic development can lead to profoundly unjust socio-economic outcomes (Peck, 2005; McCann, 2007), especially when applied inappropriately in the context of low-growth or no-growth industrial cities in a range of different international settings (see, for example, Zimmerman (2008) on Milwaukee, or Sasaki (2010) on Osaka). Under this critique, the fixation with boosterism is said to have concealed the regressive consequences of urban policies which no longer seek to resolve intractable social problems in cities (Paddison, 2009).

The emphasis on boosterist forms of urban economic development relates in part to a world-view amongst policy elites which views cities as competing at a global scale: for events, mobile labour and capital, publicity and so on. A feature of the rise of neoliberal governance of urban economies is the receptiveness of local policy actors to discourses of international urban competition. This particular form of entrepreneurial behaviour amongst urban policy actors has been acknowledged for many years (see, for example, Harvey, 1989a). Yet as Lovering (2001) has argued, it is based on a perception that in important respects is divorced from an empirical reality in which many cities, at least those outwith the major global cities, are weakly integrated with the international economy. This has prompted critics like Lovering to argue that policy-makers are unrealistically preoccupied with consolidating or improving cities' international standing, at the expense of the more mundane but under-appreciated issues, for example, of building skills amongst the labour force, ensuring an adequate supply of developable land, providing efficient infrastructure, or maintaining and enhancing readily accessible and equitably allocated consumption services.

Alongside competition to attract and retain labour, entice business investment, or lure tourists and prestige events, boosterist strategies employed by urban policy actors have also been geared towards the procurement of public funding. Some cities, as a result, have received regular injections of finance, capitalizing on the adroitness of their urban elites in constructing what Cochrane et al. (1996: 1331) refer to as 'grant coalitions' that can pinpoint opportunities for funding and articulate their case to external funders in central government or supra-national bodies like the European Union. There are, however, losers in this process, as some cities have proved less successful in attracting discretionary grant funding – even in cases where there were ostensibly strong objective arguments for resourcing on the basis of socio-economic circumstances (Southern, 2002; Davies, 2004). In some instances, this has reflected concern from national or supra-national government about inter-institutional friction at the local level, a history of overt local authority hostility to higher levels of government, the supposed marginalization of the private sector or a continued weddedness to what have been seen as outmoded and non-entrepreneurial distributional concerns (see, for example, Boddy, 2003).

This form of 'challenge funding' has nevertheless remained a feature of urban policy. In Britain, it has existed intermittently over several decades, from the City Challenge initiative launched in 1992 to the Regional Growth Fund introduced in 2010 and the competition for the award of Enterprise Zone status in 2011. But even during periods in which central government opted to allocate regeneration resources on a more objective and non-competitive basis (principally through the use of statistical indices of deprivation), the embeddedness of the idea of inter-city competition amongst local policy actors remained apparent in the continued interest in securing flagship cultural and sporting events. For example, the competition amongst British cities to be awarded European Capital of Culture status for 2008 involved bids, *inter alia*, from Birmingham, Bristol and Newcastle, as well as Liverpool, the eventual winner (O'Brien, 2011). That the competition attracted media interest on a scale entirely disproportionate to the modest funding on offer to the successful city was partly reflective of the degree to which this form of entrepreneurial urbanism had impregnated the outlook and behaviour of policy actors. This, in turn, reflected the policy-maker consensus, following the experience of several other cities, notably Glasgow in 1990 as European City of Culture, which held that substantial spin-off benefits could be generated directly as a result of the award of Capital of Culture status and the resultant growth in tourist and visitor numbers, and indirectly as a result of the fillip to the winning city's international status and visibility (Mooney, 2004; Garcia, 2005).

Boosterism, place marketing and inter-city competition have evolved over several decades to become accepted features of the urban policy landscape in many countries. This has generated extensive academic interest. But while the development of these areas of activity amongst city policy actors confirms that local economic strategies have been driven by an underlying desire to become more entrepreneurial, other types of activity pursued by urban institutions have changed in sometimes more subtle and complex ways. Even in the many instances in which the local state has ceded its role as direct deliverer of services to private and voluntary providers, it has often managed to continue to play an important, if indirect, role as commissioner, planner or regulator ('steering' instead of 'rowing', in Osborne and Gaebler's (1993) widely employed metaphor). This reoriented role, in several European countries, is now susceptible to further change. 'Austerity' measures introduced in the

wake of the international financial crises of 2007–08, in the form of radical programmes of public expenditure cuts, potentially preface a further, more fundamental
redistribution of power away from the local state and towards a range of civil society actors and business interests amongst whom an underlying market logic often
underpins decision-making (Peck, 2012; Meegan et al., 2014). The need for local
actors in many countries to find new ways of delivering services in the face of dwindling resources increases the possibility of further diversification in the range of
institutions operating alongside elected local government, thereby rendering still
more complex the often elaborate networks through which cities are governed – as
the next section of the chapter goes on to explore.

BROKERAGE, NETWORKS AND THE SHIFT TOWARDS SECOND GENERATION URBAN GOVERNANCE

A unifying theme across cities in different contexts is that contemporary urban governance has often evolved in ways that have left it more complex and less transpar-
ent than before. Unsurprisingly, the complexity of urban governance arrangements
has presented some difficulty for the many attempts to conceptualize local institutional and policy networks, resulting in a 'cacophony of heterogeneous concepts,
theories and research results' (Oliver and Ebers, 1998: 549). What is clear amidst
this variability and complexity, however, is that contemporary governance is characterized increasingly by its network character (Powell, 1991). In place of rigid, hierarchical government dominated by clear lines of accountability and bureaucratic
modes of decision-making, contemporary network-based urban governance is held
by proponents to offer a leaner and more flexible means of promoting economic
development and social well-being (Parker, 2007: 116). To adherents, the rigidity of
old-style hierarchical 'big government' ought ultimately to be supplanted by more
inclusive and elemental forms of partnership-based governance:

> Hierarchy, generally, is losing its legitimacy while partnership is in the
> ascendant as different interest groups flex their muscles and individuals start
> to take back control of their lives from organizations and governments.
> (Handy, 2004: 98)

For many European cities, the embrace of looser network-based forms of governance has therefore been accompanied by a rejection of formal hierarchical government (Parker, 2007). This has involved a transition to forms of governance based
on privatization, contracting and marketization. The result has been an upsurge in
the array of quangos, cross-sector partnerships, sub-contracted service providers
and voluntary sector bodies upon which the local state has become ever more reliant for the delivery of public services (Goss, 2007). Authors such as Kjaer (2009)
have argued that this represents a fundamental transition to a new, network-based

form of governance, succeeding an earlier post-war settlement in the form of the development of big government, and a second 'new public management' market-facing phase from the 1970s.

A different perspective is provided by Hooghe and Marks (2003), who distinguish between formal and informal governance mechanisms as drivers of different types of multi-level governance (Table 8.1). Under this interpretation, Type I governance is based on 'stacked' or 'nested' institutions, in hierarchical form, whereas Type II institutions are characterized by their flexibility, their connectivity within and between other jurisdictional levels, and their ability to focus on specific policy issues. As a result, they are said by proponents to be more fleet-of-foot and flexible – but also less likely, sometimes by design, to be lasting. They may also be less likely to be democratically accountable or subject to direct or indirect citizen scrutiny, in contrast to formal Type I institutions. The upsurge of 'government by task force', of concordats, agreements and of institutional and organizational hybrids of varying shapes, sizes and complexity provides evidence of the rise of this type of second generation governance.

Table 8.1 Type I and II governance

Type I	Type II
General-purpose jurisdictions	Task-specific jurisdictions
Non-intersecting membership	Intersecting memberships
Jurisdictions organized on a limited number of levels	No limit to the number of jurisdictional levels
System-wide architecture	Flexible design

Source: Hooghe and Marks (2003)

Table 8.2 Democratic alignment of Type I and II entities

	Type I entity	Type II entities		
		Club	Agency	Polity-forming
Features	Established through constitution building or legislation by higher level of government	Self-generated to deliver benefits to members	Created by government to deliver policies through flexible management under arm's-length political supervision	Established to engage well-defined constituency of users/residents in formulation and delivery of specific public policy
Legitimacy	Electoral system and civic support	On basis of benefits accruing to members	On basis of central government mandate	On basis of popular participation
Consent	Elected representatives	Self-interested assessment	Appointment or nomination by government	Deliberative processes between board and constituency
Accountability (TO)	Legislative body of elected representatives and to citizens	Organizational stakeholders in terms of cost-benefit ratio	Government at higher level on basis of policy performance	Constituency on basis of democratic process and policy achievement

Source: Skelcher (2005: 98)

The existence of second generation entities is part of the wider emergence of networked forms of urban governance. This is evident in the UK, for example, where efforts in the period 1997–2010 to develop coherent sub-national governance and economic development policy remained restricted largely to Type II form, as attempts to develop more permanent and democratically accountable institutions ultimately foundered because of the combination of lukewarm support from central government, a wholesale lack of popular endorsement, and a reticence amongst local policy elites to sanction the creation of more formal and powerful institutions. That Type II entities are not susceptible to the vicissitudes of democratic scrutiny may itself have been important in informing the unwillingness of these elites to move beyond the complex but impermanent network of governing institutions in cities and their regions.

The evolution of urban governance, and its network form, rests in part upon an optimistic stance which views it as best able to promote urban economic development. However, this is not a view that has gone uncontested. The black box nature of many of the second generation networked governance mechanisms has attracted the critical attention of many scholars. Skelcher (2005), for example, argues that Type II governance entities break down into three distinct sub-categories (club, agency and polity-forming), on the basis of their variable legitimacy, and the form and extent of democratic consent and accountability (Table 8.2).

Clearly the three different types of Type II entity can vary in character. In focusing on distributed public governance and the specific differences between Type I and II governance mechanisms, Skelcher's perspective is more critical than those propounded by advocates of looser, network-based governance as a normative means of promoting economic growth. It is to the critique of 'governance enthusiasm' that the chapter now turns.

UNEASY BEDFELLOWS: THE 'DEMOCRATIC DEFICIT', POST-POLITICS AND THE GOVERNANCE OF THE NEOLIBERAL CITY

Other, more radical critiques have tended to view the emergence of networked urban governance in quite different terms. For critical geographers, in particular, fragmentation in city governance and the changing nature of the vertical relationships across scales of governance reflect wider political and economic changes in the form of concerted efforts to neoliberalize public policy, linked in part to the reorganization of politico-institutional space in response to the internationalization of economic activity. For Jessop (2002) and others, change in governance arrangements is driven by the crisis of the Fordist regime and the associated decline in the ability of the state to employ Keynesian demand management policies. The response involves the increased importance of local state power, expressed not through local government but via new sets of institutions espousing an entrepreneurial urbanism aimed at strengthening place competitiveness (Brenner, 2004). Building on this, Ward (2006) and many others present the argument that the proliferation of governance actors and agencies within cities and regions is symptomatic of a wider process of rescaling: a restructuring of the territorial basis on which the state is organized. Driving this process is said to be economic internationalization, the response to which involves the 'roll-out' of a variety of policies influenced, to varying extents and in different ways, by neoliberal thinking. Reflecting this, the restructuring of the state has been guided by a desire to promote economic growth and reassert the dominance of capital over labour, through new governance arrangements and policy initiatives that are super-imposed in complex fashion on residual, inherited government structures (Peck and Tickell, 2002). This leads to a diversity of institutional and policy outcomes in cities, as neoliberal reforms encounter widely differing inherited economic, social and political landscapes, reflecting the uneven outcomes engendered by economic restructuring over several decades. The super-imposition of neoliberal forms of urban governance on quite different inherited political landscapes – perhaps especially beyond the particular circumstances of Europe and North America – can result in the emergence of hybridized policy, driven by local contestation: the existence of multiple 'local neoliberalisms' (Geddes, 2010: 163).

The argument here is that urban governance structures and policies have been informed by a pervasive neoliberal consensus, manifested in variable, 'variegated' and path-dependent ways in different places at different times, adapted to suit local circumstances and modified (but rarely fundamentally challenged) in the face of criticism (Sites, 2007; Brenner et al., 2010; Haughton and McManus, 2011). Reflecting this view that the precise expression of neoliberalism in urban governance arrangements varies locally but adheres to a common core of ideas, Guarneros-Meza and Geddes (2010: 116) argue that 'neo-liberalism is complex, diverse and contested…[but involves] a deep, taken-for-granted belief in neoclassical economics, [and] consequent normative principles favouring free market solutions to economic problems, …a lean welfare state, low taxation and flexible labour markets'.

The extent and depth of the apparent agreement amongst urban policy actors around these core aspects of neoliberalism has led some authors, drawing upon Mouffe (2005) and others, to argue that the governance of cities is increasingly 'post-political' or post-democratic in form. Policy debate, it is argued, is increasingly narrow in scope, restricted to largely technical matters and eschewing more fundamental questions about the nature and form of policy intervention. The entrepreneurial market logic that underpins urban governance is therefore left unchallenged, and alternatives implicitly or explicitly deemed not to merit discussion (Swyngedouw, 2009). This explains in part why the scope for meaningful political involvement in urban governance via formal channels is increasingly restricted: citizen participation and in-depth discussion are seen almost as inimical to the kind of expeditious, business-like, evidence-based decision-making that adherents of growth-focused city government are keen to promote (Peck, 2011). For some authors, the apparently diminishing scope for choice about urban development strategies, and the ubiquity of purportedly ideology-free objective scrutiny of policy efficacy, means that policy is much more mobile than before, undergoing international export as 'best practice' is sought by conference-attending and video-conferencing local elites seeking '"hot" policy ideas' as an 'evidence-based' justification for their actions (McCann, 2011: 109). The obvious danger, however, is that policies devised in different political, economic and social contexts may be applied inappropriately on an off-the-shelf basis, without recognition of the need for adaptation to suit local circumstances (Hutton, 2011).

Such a risk may be especially marked if there is restricted room for dissent and debate about policy choices. Post-political urban governance, it is argued, allows only for informal self-scrutiny by a narrow range of policy actors, as an alternative to more broadly-based and formalized oversight in which fundamental debate about the nature of policy is permitted (or even actively encouraged). Post-political modes of decision-making purport to be apolitical, technocratic and able to bring to urban governance a focused business-like mindset that stands in contrast to the unwieldiness of old-style city government.

The result of this highly restricted form of decision-making is that policy rarely departs from a core of neo-liberal ideas which emphasise the pursuit of urban economic growth as the paramount objective. Though dressed in appealingly neologistic language, these ideas about the need for lean and efficient decision-making are not new; urban economic development agencies in the United States and Britain under the Reagan and Thatcher administrations of the 1980s imported working methods from the private sector and consciously positioned themselves as business friendly alternatives to the bureaucratic sclerosis of elected local government (Barnekov et al., 1989). But as Allmendinger and Haughton (2009) argue, what is noteworthy here is the persistence and pervasiveness amongst policy actors of the notion that democratic debate – protracted and messy as it often is – is an unnecessary impediment to the pursuit of urban economic growth.

The basic critique offered here is that 'governance enthusiasts' have tended to view state restructuring simply as a process of pragmatic policy adjustment rather than a fundamental shift connected to broader social, economic and political processes that affect the local state (see, for example, MacLeod and Goodwin, 1999; Geddes, 2006). Part of this critique holds that hyperbole about new forms of urban governance masks the erosion – or even dismantling – of local democracy, as post-political forms of governance begin to emerge. In contrast to past urban government, new networks of governing institutions and policy actors in cities tend often to reject democratic involvement in, and scrutiny of, the policy-making process on the grounds that it is too unwieldy, unresponsive and a hindrance to the kind of flexible, fast-moving market-oriented governance they favour (see Imrie and Raco, 1999; and Table 8.3).

Spaces of post-political governance, some have argued, are inhabited by policy actors whose backgrounds look quite different to those historically charged with governing cities. This is important because connectivity within and between actors and agencies is likely to be critically important in an environment in which network-based forms of governance predominate (Mulgan, 2010). Stephenson (2004) argues that 'whether the jungles are green and leafy or concrete, they are brimming with intricate webs of relationships, which when viewed from afar reveal elementary

Table 8.3   Characterizing local government and local governance

Local Government	Local Governance
Bureaucratic	Flexible and responsive
Democratic	Post-democratic
Centralized	Decentralized
Collectivized	Privatized
Municipal	Entrepreneurial
Pursuit of social/welfare goals	Pursuit of market goals

Source: Imrie and Raco (1999: 46)

structures'. For cities, this means that the nature and form of governance and policy reflects the actions not just of politicians and their urban bureaucrats, officials of mandated (Type I) government entities who exercise agency through hierarchical and formal means. Alongside them is a disparate assortment of 'policy entrepreneurs' (Mintrom and Norman, 2009) who deploy technocratic rationales for a governance project which emphasizes flexibility and engagement with the business community. They are accompanied by a wider set of 'imagineers': influencers who help contribute to policy agendas through 'spectacle', and cultural and artistic endeavours (Short, 1999).

There is an abundance of empirical evidence, then, to show that urban governance has become more entrepreneurial, the outlook of policy elites more growth-fixated and the emphasis of public policy influenced to an increasing degree by neoliberal thinking. However, this is not to deny the existence of alternative governance strategies. The extensively documented Brazilian cases of Porto Alegre (on neighbourhood-based participatory budgeting and deliberative democracy) or Curitiba (in relation to sustainable development), for example, illustrate the degree to which there is scope for socially, politically and environmentally progressive and innovative forms of policy-making even in an international context in which, as we have seen, growth-oriented approaches to governance abound (see, amongst numerous examples, Baiocchi, 2001; Irazábal, 2005; Novy and Leubolt, 2005). Despite the seeming globalization of the neoliberalization of urban governance, the unevenness of its specific application, both in form and intensity, means that scope for progressive politics remains. In Bolivian cities, neoliberal-influenced attempts to encourage citizen participation as a means of bolstering legitimacy had the unintended side effect of creating space in which progressive politics could develop, and around which oppositional social movements could cohere (Geddes, 2010). Likewise, chronicling the experiences of Mexico City and Buenos Aires, Kanai and Ortega-Alcazár (2009) note the variable ways in which local circumstances mediate the processes of economic globalization and the neoliberalization of governance, creating possibilities for the emergence of policy (in this case related to culture-led urban regeneration) in which grassroots interests have significant voice. As the boxed text below demonstrates, the import of neoliberal perspectives on urban policy has sometimes created complex amalgams of different styles of governance.

Policy Mobility and the Emergence of Hybridized Urban Governance in Mexico

Networked forms of urban governance, exported beyond their European and North American heartlands, have been applied in a variety of ways in different international cities. Established local political cultures, pre-existing administrative structures and inherited economic histories can affect the ways in which new, imported governance innovations are applied, resulting in uneven institutional and policy outcomes. As McCann and Ward (2011: xv) argue, local polices evolve both relationally and territorially in that their shape is influenced by a process of international import and export of 'mobile' policies across 'global circuits of policy knowledge', but is also simultaneously affected by the spatially-rooted legacy of economic, political and social phenomena which vary from city to city. The former are said to promote conformity and similarity in that local policy actors looks to emulate perceived best practice elsewhere; the latter militates against uniformity by imprinting a specific local stamp on the shape and form of local governance arrangements.

The development of networked urban governance in Mexican cities illustrates the degree to which the precise application of imported policy orthodoxies is contingent upon local specificities. In the context of historically authoritarian, corporatist politics and bureaucratized and hierarchical institutional structures, Guarneros-Meza (2009) explores the interplay between the processes of neoliberal reform of governance and policy-making, consolidation of democracy, and political, administrative and fiscal decentralization from the national-state. Although the roots of these three processes differ, their combination has meant the evolution of locally particular politico-institutional forms in which a variety of styles of governance coexist within a wider network-based framework which involves a much broader range of non-state actors than before. This means, on the one hand, a familiar, neoliberal-influenced landscape of urban governance, populated by public-private regeneration partnerships and cross-sector local economic development agencies. On the other hand, it also means that more progressive forms of governance have been able to persist – and in some cases to grow. Urban social movements, in particular, have played a key role in Mexican cities in delivering services and encouraging citizen participation. Their efforts have in some instances been co-opted by strengthened urban governments in developing other forms of participative democracy.

There is evidence, however, that despite this broadening of the participative base for decision-making, marginalized groups remain excluded. In the cities of Querétaro and San Luis Potosí, for example, Guarneros-Meza chronicles the limited levels of participation by neighbourhood-based citizen groups and street traders in new public-private regeneration partnerships, whose focus has been directed predominantly at enhancing the external image of the historic urban cores, rather than allocating housing or delivering services more equitably. This provides a compelling illustration of the complex and variable ways in which internationally-sanctioned received wisdom about urban governance and policy-making is interpreted and applied locally in light of specific local political and economic circumstances.

Source: Guarneros-Meza (2009)

Experience of recent innovation beyond Latin American cities also illustrates the complex and varied ways in which neoliberal perspectives on urban governance have been interpreted and applied outside the North American and European heartlands in which they developed over the last quarter of the twentieth century. Sorensen (2011), in an assessment of Japanese cities, concludes that although overall experience of the governance of urban development is one in which the national state has tried increasingly to promote deregulation, local political and environmental pressures for the reinforcement of land-use planning and environmental management continue to play an important role, as part of a complex, multi-scalar process in which interplay between centre and locality contributes to a sometimes uncertain trajectory of change. This reinforces the conclusion of Tsukamoto (2012), who argues that economic development policy in Japan has followed a paradoxical path, with the longstanding commitment to national growth (latterly, increasingly neoliberal in its emphasis) juxtaposed against efforts to promote socio-spatial equality, with uneven results for different cities and regions as local actors respond with varying degrees of enthusiasm or opposition to the import of Western neoliberalism.

Bold, oppositional political leadership has sometimes been important in challenging the ubiquitous neoliberal tenets at the heart of entrepreneurial city governance strategies and developing alternative policy approaches. Indeed, on the basis of experience in cities like Los Angeles, some authors have argued that the shift towards network-based urban governance has had the unexpected effect of enabling pioneering and progressive cross-sector and pan-ethnic coalitions to respond to intensifying socio-spatial disparity and environmental degradation by challenging neoliberal hegemony in urban governance and promoting an equity-based politics of 'spatial justice' as a viable alternative (Pastor, 2001; Pastor et al., 2009; Soja, 2010; Nicholls, 2011). Such experiences, though, have not been the norm, and much of the recent discourse around leadership and political capacity in cities has been pitched in terms of wider policy debate informed by market-oriented pro-growth thinking. This applies to attempts to develop more potent forms of city governance, sometimes involving the creation of leadership structures – what Stone (2008: 150) refers to as 'miniature presidencies' – that might eventually help to attract the kinds of charismatic, risk-taking mayors who are said to have effected the revitalization of some US urban economies, but who have been notably absent in other contexts like the UK (Hambleton and Sweeting, 2004).

Attempts to develop more expansive city-regional or metropolitan spaces of governance also illustrate the decreasing extent to which equity concerns feature in debates about urban governance. Over recent years the impetus for metropolitan institution-building has tended to relate overwhelmingly to a desire to advance economic development and allow cities to compete with international rivals. For a time, this related to the idea that powerful city-regional institutions were beginning in a few celebrated cases to acquire a global significance, and perhaps starting to supplant the role of some nation-states in creating conditions in which capital accumulation could best occur (Scott, 2001a). As we have seen, some authors extended this thesis, arguing that sub-national governance appeared to be undergoing a profound transformation, as the geographical organization of the state began to alter fundamentally in complex multi-scalar ways in response to the internationalization of capital and the associated rise of the politics of neoliberalism (see, for example, Brenner, 2004). The result in some cases was an attempt by local (and sometimes national) policy actors to return to the long-standing goal of creating more powerful – and therefore more competitive – metropolitan territories. Historically, the stimulus for metropolitan regionalism has tended to derive from the combination of fiscal consolidation for poorly resourced under-bounded local government units, and enhanced strategic planning of services linked to the creation of more meaningful jurisdictions that reflected functional labour market geographies, commute sheds and service spheres-of-influence. More recently, the impetus for efforts to modify local political and administrative geographies has come from quite different sets of factors: from a wish to consolidate governance struc-tures and address institutional proliferation, and to build local political and institu-tional capacity, 'thickness' and reputational capital. This, in turn, has been viewed as a means of providing a firmer base on which to procure extra-local private and public resources and, ultimately, promote growth in order to maintain or enhance a city's national and international standing.

These kinds of reform of metropolitan governance, it is clear, have been informed by a growth-oriented entrepreneurial outlook which has neoliberal politics at its heart. There have, of course, been some interesting and important attempts to chal-lenge this. The influential social movement regionalism documented by Pastor et al. (2009) illustrates how community interests can challenge established policy ortho-doxy by mobilizing on a regional basis and – as in the San Francisco Bay Area – latching onto established structures initiated originally to promote private sector growth. Clark and Christopherson (2009), likewise, draw on examples from Rochester, Atlanta and Los Angeles to highlight the possibility of an equity-led 'distributive regionalism' of endogenous development as an alternative to the growth-led 'invest-ment regionalism' that has predominated in contemporary governance strategies. And some cities in the United States have made progress in developing city-regional structures through which to promote environmentally-focused growth management policies, as the celebrated experience of Portland, Oregon, outlined in the box below shows. However, such efforts are substantially outweighed by the battery of govern-ance reforms inspired by the kinds of neoliberal ideas which the chapter has tried to document. In the final part of this chapter, we consider whether this process of neo-liberalization is intensifying, and whether it is reasonable to characterize the consen-sus underlying contemporary urban governance as post-political.

Regionalism and Growth Management in Portland, Oregon

It is tempting, so potent is the thesis that urban governance has become ever more entrepreneurial, to identify neoliberal influences in institutional and policy reform where none exist. Institutional innovations that elsewhere have been interpreted – correctly – as symptoms of wider efforts to make governance more entrepreneurial and market-focused can, in some cities, have a less clear-cut rationale.

This is illustrated by the experience of governance reform and policy innovation in Portland, Oregon. Over several decades, the city has garnered sustained international interest from academics and policy-makers drawn to what is seen by many as a compellingly far-sighted effort to build metropolitan regional strategy and manage urban growth. With the establishment of Metro in 1979, Greater Portland gained the first elected regional government in the United States, building on an already established history of metropolitan-scale policy-making over the previous two decades. Alongside the advantages conferred by formal regional government, Portland's approach to growth management is said also to have benefitted from a high degree of consensus and tradition of pragmatism in local political affairs, popular buy-in from residents linked to concerns about environmental issues, and the existence of a well developed and inclusive partnership that extends across a range of private and voluntary sector stakeholders (Seltzer, 2004).

This has provided a strong institutional base on which to develop growth management policy, and the region has been widely lauded by proponents of the development of a normative, planning-led metropolitan 'new regionalism' in North America (see, for example, Calthorpe and Fulton, 2001; Wheeler, 2002). Beginning with a series of ground-breaking efforts to develop regional public transport infrastructure, Greater Portland has subsequently been at the forefront of attempts to manage the distribution of land-use, combat sprawl and promote smart, environmentally sustainable growth as a viable alternative to low-density suburban and ex-urban development. Portland, according to Downs (2004: 10), has become 'the poster child of smart growth'.

Some have argued, however, that Portland has been unjustifiably lionized, and that its exemplary status ignores frustration and failure in relation to some aspects of regional policy-making. As Calthorpe and Fulton (2001) note, some critics, notably house-builders' lobby groups, have bemoaned the perceived constraints that urban containment and densification policies have posed for economic growth, arguing (contentiously, and in the face of considerable evidence to the contrary) that the city's urban growth boundary has led to an increase in house prices and shortfall of developable land. Others, from quite different political standpoints, have noted the failure to ensure an adequate supply of affordable housing in a wider context of economic growth and increasing demand for land (Provo, 2009).

These debates notwithstanding, Portland is widely seen as a pioneer in its attempts to develop cohesive city-regional structures in the often fragmented context of local government in urban America. But what is especially interesting is that the structures and policies through which growth management strategy has been pursued look on first inspection to be similar, superficially at least, to some of the governance innovations developed elsewhere, not least in English cities. This emphasizes the importance of looking beyond structures, and considering content when reviewing the degree to which, and the ways in which, urban governance has become genuinely more entrepreneurial. Whereas spasmodic and often faltering efforts to develop city-regional governance in England have been driven almost entirely by a desire to promote economic growth (Harrison, 2007), the impetus for structural change and policy development in cities like Portland lies in a more multi-faceted and nuanced desire to regulate growth, for social and environmental as well as economic reasons. This is not to say that economic development goals have not formed part of the impetus for governance reform in Portland, but that the city and its regional institutions have embarked on a more broadly-based strategy that is less preoccupied with growth than is the case for some of the neoliberal informed policies catalogued elsewhere in this chapter.

CONCLUSION: FUTURE DIRECTIONS – MORE ENTREPRENEURIAL STILL?

The notion that entrepreneurial styles of urban governance have become the norm is not new. Its roots lie in Harvey's (1989a) observations about the ways in which cities began to respond to related sets of political and economic pressure, in the form of the apparent disintegration of the post-war Fordist-Keynesian consensus, the intensification of economic globalization, and the accompanying restructuring of urban economies. The upshot was significant change in the ways in which cities were governed, putting in train a process over the next two decades and beyond that saw the role of urban governance move decisively from its roots in allocating services, mediating conflict and representing citizen interests. This has subsequently developed for many cities into a powerful, deeply ingrained conventionality in which policy actors feel compelled to compete – and to do so by employing a neoliberal approach to urban economic development which emphasizes the pursuit of private sector growth, the value of self-regulating markets, the desirability of privatized provision of public goods and the importance of governing cities in a business-like, non-bureaucratic way.

As we have seen, some authors have argued that the effect of a two decade long process of neoliberalization of the governance of cities has been the creation of a post-political or post-democratic form of urban politics (Crouch, 2004; Mouffe, 2005). What this does not imply is that urban political relations have ceased to be important; even cursory examination of the way in which cities are governed reveals an abundance of conflict – particularly since network-based forms of governance can mean friction related to rival institutional affiliations within, as well as between, cities. Instead, urban governance can be viewed as post-political in the sense that there is significantly reduced scope for departing from core neoliberal assumptions as a result of the depth and breadth of consensus about of the nature and purpose of urban economic development policy (Deas, 2013). Cities can be viewed as post-political in the sense that traditional representative forms of democracy have become less important, as voter disenchantment and disengagement has grown and as governance, decision-making and policy formulation have come to be seen as essentially technical, managerial exercises, off-limits to voter scrutiny or serious debate.

One consequence of the seeming preponderance of this form of urban politics, and of neoliberal or entrepreneurial forms of city governance, is to reduce the level of heterogeneity in local economic development policy. Despite a welter of high-profile rhetoric about the importance of tailoring policy to local circumstances, the salience of the neoliberal accord – and the extent to which debate is curtailed in a post-political environment – means that policy often takes on a one-size-fits-all uniformity, regardless of uneven development and inter-city disparities in economic health and social well-being. This is perhaps again a reflection of the removal of genuine choice about the direction of policy in a post-political world dominated by a consensual, conventional wisdom which, as some authors see it, amounts to a neoliberal hegemony in the governance of urban areas. The point here (notwithstanding some notable exceptions documented earlier in the chapter) is not only that social equity goals are subordinated to economic development objectives, but that the latter are interpreted narrowly: to mean growth rather than redistribution.

The marked degree to which local actor autonomy is restricted by central government might also explain why there is a degree of uniformity in the economic development strategies employed by cities. On the one hand, their scope for rejecting consensus and embarking on more progressive approaches is limited because the national state plays the key role in setting the context for local policy, in terms of allocations of resource, the setting of objectives for policy and the inception of new policy initiatives. On the other hand, the potential for embarking on more radical variants of neoliberal economic development is also reduced: the adoption of, say, flatter, less redistributive local taxation would be a practical impossibility for cities in the many national contexts in which local fiscal autonomy is weakly developed and reliance on the centre for funding acute.

This chapter has argued, then, that urban governance has undergone radical change, driven by a desire to neoliberalize policy, perhaps resulting in what might be described, somewhat tautologically, as a post-political urban politics. It has attempted to chart the emergence of the consensus around the notion that urban governance ought to be entrepreneurial, as evidenced by attitude and behaviour amongst elite actors, the rhetoric underpinning policy, and the actual shape of economic development policy and the institutional structures through which it is pursued. Although it is important to acknowledge that change in urban governance is complex and sometimes contradictory, the overall direction of travel is clear in that evidence of the neoliberalization of policy abounds. Moreover, there is the prospect of a quickening in the pace of the neoliberalization in urban governance, as retrenchment in public finances, in the aftermath of international financial crisis, compels state actors to operate more creatively, to engage capital, work alongside civil society actors and so on. The extent of any such redistribution of power within urban governance networks may be limited because of the absence of any obvious sources of funding for non-state actors, especially for European cities lacking a US-style tradition of corporate social responsibility and activism. However, the prospect of further contraction in funding for local government means that, several decades in, the process of reform of urban governance is not yet exhausted.

Useful Websites

European Urban Knowledge Network (http://www.eukn.org/): This provides information about the activities of the EU, where they impact upon cities and city-regions.

OECD's Public Governance and Territorial Development Directorate (http://www.oecd.org/gov): This is a repository for advice and guidance, statistics and policy research, intended to inform efforts to reform public sector governance at national and sub-national scales.

UN Habitat Agenda (http://ww2.unhabitat.org/campaigns/governance/): Information linked to the UN Habitat Agenda goal of promoting 'sustainable human settlements development in an urbanizing world' through the reform of governance.

World Bank (http://web.worldbank.org/WBSITE/EXTERNAL/COUNTRIES/LACEXT/EXTLACREGTOPURBDEV/0,,menuPK:841079~pagePK:34004175~piPK:34004435~theSitePK:841043,00.html): World Bank projects on urban governance and management in Latin America.

9

The Resilient City: On the Determinants of Successful Urban Economies

Mario Polèse

'...long run urban success does not mean perpetual growth. Long run urban success means successfully responding to challenges.'

Edward L. Glaeser (2005b: 121)

'There are no absolute rules in this game; chance happens to great cities too.'

Sir Peter Hall (2000: 649)

INTRODUCTION

In this chapter, we propose a critical look at the determinants of successful urban economies; that is; cities that consistently generate high levels of income and employment. The focus is on factors that allow cities to successfully overcome outside shocks. Cities are continually subject to shocks, be they technological, political or other. Change is in the very nature of modern society, not to mention growing environmental risks. Some cities have been more successful in responding to outside challenges than others. Successful cities are necessarily 'resilient' cities; were they not, outside shocks would have permanently arrested (or diminished) their ability to generate wealth, hence the title of this chapter.

A growing literature has sprung up around the concept of resilience as applied to cities and regions[1]. And, as with all concepts of this nature no consensus exists on a

---

1 The *Cambridge Journal of Regions, Economy and Society* recently devoted an entire issue to the subject (Cambridge, 2010).

precise definition. As Christopherson et al. (2010: 2) readily admit, it can mean different things to different people. The origins of the term lie in environmental studies, describing the biological capacity of organisms to adapt and thrive under changing (often adverse) conditions, which in part explains the penchant of some authors for an evolutionary perspective (Simmie and Martin, 2010). We shall argue that for cities 'resilience' comes in at least two shapes. Resilience can refer to the ability to *survive* shocks (which we call **a**-Resilience) or, alternatively, the ability to *change* in the face of outside shocks, which we shall call **b**-Resilience. The first, we argue, is an almost universal trait of cities, while the second is less common.

Cities are amazingly resilient. No example exists in modern times of a large city that has actually succumbed – disappeared – due to an outside shock, although some have ceased to grow or have declined. In this chapter, by 'city' is meant an urban or metropolitan area; that is, an urban agglomeration which functions as an integrated economy and labour market. A particular municipality, township or borough may disappear, administratively speaking, but it is highly unlikely that the urban area to which it belongs will cease to exist. The 'City of London' (which covers a minuscule area) might conceivably be abolished, but London – the agglomeration – will in all likelihood continue to be Britain's economic powerhouse. London has survived numerous shocks in modern times – the Great Depression, the Blitz, the loss of empire, several financial meltdowns – yet has never been wealthier or more dominant within Britain (within Europe, some might even say); raising the question not only of its continuing success, but also of the sources of such dogged resilience.

Yet resilience is by no means a given, nor is it an attribute easy to acquire. We shall argue that the determinants of resilience are most often rooted in a city's history, geography, and other inherited traits, and as such not easily amenable to local policy intervention. Outside shocks that undermine the city's ability to provide a competitive environment can cause it to permanently diverge from its previously established growth path. Although examples are few in recent times among large cities, they are not non-existent (Polèse and Denis-Jacob, 2010). The difference, we shall see, between shocks that cause temporary and permanent damage is essential. Although inherited traits (industrial structure, location, size, institutions…) will strongly influence how a city responds, they rarely constitute the sole explanation. In the vocabulary of economic geographers, the forces driving path dependency are strong, but no path is ever irretrievably 'locked-in' to use the term coined by Martin (2010). Indeed, in some cases, successful adaption may mean deviating from historically established paths of growth.

A-RESILIENCE: WHY CITIES DON'T DIE

In October 2005, in the wake of Hurricane Katrina which devastated the City of New Orleans, a panel of experts came together to consider the question: 'Is New Orleans a Resilient City?' (Lang and Danielson, 2006). Most of the panellists had collaborated on an earlier book on the subject of resilient cities (Vale and

Campanula, 2005). One of the editors of that book commented on the fact that almost no large city in the last two hundred years failed to rebuild no matter how dramatic the destruction. More to the point, the panel failed to come to an agreement on whether or not New Orleans was a resilient city (Lang and Danielson, 2006: 246). This should come as no surprise. New Orleans did rebuild, and thus meets the definition of what I have called a-Resilience. It survived. However, visibly, New Orleans did not break out of its long-term decline: once the American South's largest city, it is now overshadowed by Atlanta, Houston and Dallas. Thus, New Orleans does not meet the criteria of b-Resilience. The city did not, it would appear, turnaround and reinvent itself following Hurricane Katrina. The shock did not alter the underlying (social and economic) conditions that accounted for the city's slow growth.

Only rarely do 'temporary' shocks of this nature alter existing urban growth paths. It is difficult to imagine a more brutal shock than the atomic bomb. Davis and Weinstein (2002) show how both Hiroshima and Nagasaki resumed their historical growth paths after only a 20 year interval. Visibly, Hiroshima and Nagasaki meet the criteria for a-Resilient cities. In accounting for this remarkable resilience and path consistency, Davis and Weinstein (2002) come down squarely on the side of locational fundamentals and increasing returns explanations. Locational fundamentals (natural harbours; climate; soil fertility; water; etc.) are often put forward as an explanation of why urban hierarchies and city size distribution are so surprisingly stable over time (Krugman, 1996; Eaton and Eckstein, 1997; Gabaix and Ioannides, 2004). Such 'fundamentals' largely determine where major cities will first emerge, whose initial advantages are then further entrenched by the accumulated weight – increasing returns – of decades (centuries, even) of investments in physical and in human capital (Romer, 1986; Krugman, 1991). It is difficult to imagine an outside shock that would dislodge Paris, London or New York from their dominant positions within their respective nations. Their 'resilience' is, in sum, a product of geography and history, a fact on the ground that in turn affects the growth potential of other cities.

Germany presents an arguably even more dramatic example of brutal outside shocks: not only the sustained bombing of its major cities (1940–1945), but also loss of territory, and political and economic partition (1947–1990), which reoriented trade and cut off cities from their natural hinterlands. Despite all this, Brakman et al. (2004) note the overall stability of West Germany's city size distribution with, however, a shift down the hierarchy (the largest cities were explicitly targeted by Allied bombers); while Bosker et al. (2008) in turn show that the basic stability of Germany's city-size distribution does not necessarily mean that cities exhibit parallel growth paths, which is not surprising considering the disruptive effects of both the war and its divisive aftermath. More surprising, in a sense, is the fact that all German cities sprung back (although with differing growth paths) despite being reduced to rubble in many cases. What greater proof can one ask for of the built-in resilience of major cities, although resilience in this case often meant deviating from previously established growth paths.

A Hinterland Lost

Vienna presents a particularly dramatic example of a city forced to adjust to a major outside shock that permanently altered its fortunes. As the imperial capital of Austria-Hungary, the city grew rapidly in the years preceding World War I (Nitsch, 2003). Around 1919, the city's growth stopped abruptly, the direct result of the loss of some 85% (in population and in territory) of its traditional hinterland, following the dismantling of Austria-Hungary. The Iron Curtain (1947–1990) further shrunk trade and interaction with Vienna's former eastern hinterland. Central place theory predicts that cities adjust to the size of their hinterlands. Vienna is eminent proof of that principle; its population in 2010 is still below that of 1910, the last census before the first war. Yet, today Vienna is one of Europe's wealthiest cities, with a GDP per capita some 70% above the EU average, in the same league as Stockholm (Eurostat, 2009). If wealth is the criterion for economic success, Vienna is certainly a success story, but one which required that the city live through many difficult years of (relative) stagnation and accept its new role as a smaller, non-imperial, European city.

Vienna's story, however, begs the question of the determinants of its economic rebound. Is the source to be found *in* Vienna, in actions taken by city fathers and other local players, or in the (inherited) fact that Vienna is the capital and central place of the Austrian Republic, albeit (now) a small nation, but also one of Europe's wealthiest, now located in the heart of an enlarged European Union?

Staying within the central part of Europe most touched by the upheavals of the twentieth century, Wroclaw – Poland's fourth largest city – presents an interesting case. Formerly called Breslau when it was part of Germany, its entire (ethnically German) population either fled or was evicted in 1945, to be replaced by ethnic Poles. By some accounts 70% of the city was destroyed during the war. Today, Wroclaw is a prosperous city by Polish standards with a population above that of former Breslau. How should one view this case of resilience? Rebirth might perhaps be a more appropriate term. Explanations founded on accumulated human capital do not hold, since all pre-1945 human capital vanished. As such, the increasing returns argument, arguably one of the most powerful theories in urban economics, cannot be invoked. On human capital, the city started afresh. Where then should one look for the sources of the city's rebirth? The most obvious answer is political will: the decision by the new Polish state to rebuild and to resettle the city as a Polish city (which it once was, many centuries earlier), as much a symbolic as a political statement.

This brings us back to the intrinsic, inherited, value – economically and symbolically – of cities once they have emerged. Cities, certainly major cities, do not close down or go bankrupt like firms, once their economic prime is passed. Nor do they die out like species that were unable to adapt to changing conditions. The evolutionary biological analogy should not be carried too far. Venice may no longer be a great merchant city, but it has gone on to become something else. Visibly, some part of what we may call 'resilience' is built-in to cities. Locational fundamentals are a major factor, but so are the accumulated physical infrastructures – roads, canals, railways, etc. – which add value and the symbolic, historical, and emotional significance that cities acquire over time. As one of the participants of the

New Orleans panel noted, the Germans (or the Allies) could have chosen to decommission Berlin following its almost complete destruction in 1945, but they did not (Lang and Danielson, 2006: 249).

Capital Cities Lost

In the course of the last century, several cities lost their status as capital, a not insignificant shock. Examples (by date) are: Calcutta (1911); Fès (1912); Istanbul (1923); Rio de Janeiro (1960); Dar es Salaam (1974); Abidjan (1983); Lagos (1991).

The historical evidence suggests that the loss or gain of capital city status is of less economic consequence than sometimes believed. In the first two cases cited, the nation's new political capital, respectively New Delhi and Rabat, did not emerge as the nation's economic capital. In the other cases, save one (Rio), the loss of capital status did not diminish the city's economic dominance. True, in Calcutta, Fès, and Rio, the loss of capital city is 'a' factor in the decline of the city's relative economic weight, compared to others, but not the only factor (Polèse and Denis-Jacob, 2010).

Indeed, an argument can be made that being a capital constitutes an economic disadvantage, especially in market economies. The bureaucratic (and high cost) culture of capitals is not necessarily conducive to innovation and enterprise. Shanghai, Bombay, and São Paulo spring to mind as examples of emerging economic (but not political) capitals. In North America, the case against capitals is even more stronger. None of the three major metropolises (New York, Los Angeles, Chicago) is a capital of anything, not even a US state. Nor are the two high-tech hubs of the West Coast (San Francisco Bay, and Seattle). But then, Austin and Boston are.

B-RESILIENCE: TURNING AROUND IN THE FACE OF CHANGE

The cities mentioned above survived often traumatic shocks – proof of their intrinsic resilience. However, survival is not the same as change. Nor are all shocks the same. Some shocks – bombs, earthquakes, hurricanes, etc. – are essentially temporary in nature, no matter how devastating their impact. Such calamities do not, as a rule, alter the city's locational fundamentals or the city's economic base; that is, the industries in which the city specialized at the moment the shock occurred. Once the city is physically rebuilt, its social and economic structure will, in most cases, mirror that which existed prior to the shock. Thus, it is entirely normal that cities should resume their historical growth paths once the effects of the shock have worn off. However, this does not necessarily tell us anything about the city's resilience in the face of shocks that demand fundamental changes in the city's economic base and way of doing things.

To illustrate this point, let us return to Nagasaki, which 20 years after the event did, as noted, resume its growth path at its previously historical rate (Davis and Weinstein, 2002). But, like New Orleans, that historical rate mirrors a long-term decline, which in both cases began in the last half of the nineteenth century. Nagasaki has been systemically slipping down the Japanese urban hierarchy from 6th place in 1900 to 24th place in the year 2000 (Polèse and Denis-Jacob, 2010). A major reason for that decline was an outside shock of an entirely different nature, less lethal than the atom bomb but with much more durable economic consequences. Up until the opening-up of Japan following the Meiji Restoration (1868), Nagasaki held a near-monopoly as port of contact with the outside world, a monopoly it subsequently lost. Visibly, that shock irremediably altered its growth path. One cannot say that Nagasaki was not (is not) resilient, for it continued to grow, albeit at a slower pace than other Japanese cities, and is today a prosperous place by any standard. But, it was not able to reverse the effects of that more fundamental shock on its long-term growth prospects.

A city's ability to overcome shocks like that of the opening-up of Japan (for Nagasaki) provides a much tougher test of resilience. The change brought by the shock is irreversible; it cannot be undone or rebuilt. Shocks of this nature are most often political or technological. An example of the former is the redrawing of national boundaries, which may open up or, alternatively, close off markets (hinterlands). Vienna is a case in point (see box headed 'A Hinterland Lost'). Free trade agreements, including those leading to the European Union (EU), are of a similar nature. Technological change can fundamentally alter the economic value of competing locations. In the US, the invention of air-conditioning together with improvements in medicine, sanitation, and nutrition 'suddenly' made southern cities attractive locations for industry and people, upsetting the former competitive balance between colder northern and warmer southern cities. Along the same lines, changes in preferences and demographics can alter the comparative attractiveness of competing places. In all advanced economies, not only in nations with a US-type Sunbelt/Snowbelt split, the attraction of sun, surf, and other natural amenities has become a primary driver of urban growth, challenging cities that are less blessed by nature (Rappaport and Sachs, 2003; Cheshire and Magrini, 2006; Rappaport, 2007, 2009; Davezies, 2008).

In the face of such fundamental changes, how should one evaluate 'resilience'? There is not much city fathers or the local business community can do about national boundaries or the weather. It is self-evident that factors of this nature will cause some cities to grow faster and, alternatively, cause others to grow less rapidly and generate less wealth. Slower growth in such cases should not necessarily be interpreted as a sign of a lack of resilience. One should *expect*, on average, cities with less inviting climates to grow more slowly than others. By the same token, asking post-1919 Vienna to grow at its pre-1914 pace would have been an unreasonable expectation. In modern parlance, one might say that Vienna was required to downsize, but not necessarily to change its vocation as essentially a service and administrative city. It did not, to my knowledge, shed its economic base to replace it with another.

A truer test of resilience is the ability of local economies to transform themselves in the face of technological shocks that undermine their economic base, in essence asking them to reinvent their economies. Current technology largely determines what constitutes a growth industry at any moment in time. High-tech is a fleeting reality. If an informed observer were asked in 1890 which were the most technologically advanced and innovative cities at the time, he (or she) would most probably have mentioned Manchester in England and perhaps Pittsburgh in the US and Essen in the German Ruhr. Half a century later, Detroit would perhaps be the first place to spring to mind. The automobile industry was the principal driver of the US economy for a good part of the twentieth century. Today, nobody thinks of automobile manufacturing, and even less textiles and steel making, as high-tech industries. Not so long ago, clothing was New York's largest export industry; today it is finance and business services (Glaeser, 2005a). Why have some cities been continually more successful than others in replacing declining industries with growth industries?

Two Very Different Examples of **b**-Resilience

In search of answers, let us turn to Boston. Rappaport (2003) cites Boston as an example of a city which, like New York, overcame a period of decline. In both cases, municipal and metropolitan populations declined between 1970 and 1980, only to start growing again in the 1990s. The long-run vitality of Boston, Glaeser (2005b) suggests, rests on that city's success in continually reinventing itself in the face of technological change; first, in the nineteenth century faced with the arrival of steam powered ships, which undermined its maritime trading and fishing empire founded on sailing ships, and then in the twentieth century in the face of the collapse of its manufacturing base founded on immigrant (largely Irish) labour. Indeed, during a good part of the twentieth century, the Boston area was characterized by slow growth and a deindustrialization process reminiscent of today's Rustbelt cities, a far cry from the Boston of 2010 with its concentration of high-tech and other knowledge-intensive industries. Why did Boston not go the way of Detroit or Pittsburgh?

Let us begin with the distinction between 'extractive' economies, on the one hand, where cities arose to exploit a particular resource (be it cotton, coal or something else) and, on the other hand, settlements that arose because people *wanted* to live there with the goal (ideal) of building a community in tune with their beliefs and values. New England, unlike the Southern States (and unlike, later, the coal and iron-ore based economies of the Midwest) had no major cash crop or resource (Glaeser, 2005b). From the beginning, the Boston area economy was based on ingenuity and on commerce, not primarily on the exploitation of a nearby resource, fish notwithstanding. Managing a far-flung trading empire and fleets of sailing ships required diversified skills, which set the tone early-on. The early skill-based focus was further reinforced by the work ethic and egalitarian principles of the Calvinist settlers (a remarkably well-educated group who put a high premium on education for all). Harvard College was founded in 1636.

Boston's first turnaround in the mid-nineteenth century to become a successful manufacturing centre was, Glaeser (2005b) argues, in part the result of a technologically-led historical accident. Before the arrival of steam ships, the Liverpool-Boston run was the least expensive crossing, resulting in the massive arrival of Irish immigrants, fleeing the potato famine of the 1840s, in turn providing an abundant industrial labour pool, which combined with Yankee capital and ingenuity, allowed Boston to rapidly industrialize. Glaeser stresses the difference with specialized manufacturing cities such as Detroit and Pittsburgh. Boston's success was not the result of one industry. Combined with inherited skills in maritime services and in ancillary sectors such as insurance, Boston developed a diversified economic base in which iron-bashing industries were only a minor element. As in other cities, that manufacturing base was destined to decline in the mid-twentieth century. When manufacturing employment did begin to fall, Boston began a period of relative decline. By 1980, Boston was no longer a particularly well-off city. Bostonians earned somewhat less than the residents of Atlanta (Glaeser, 2005b: 147). Twenty years later the Greater Boston Area registered the fourth highest per capita income among US metropolitan areas. Boston was able to *replace* its lost manufacturing base with high-paying, knowledge-rich, jobs in both high-tech manufacturing and services, a true example of **b**-Resilience.

Glaeser places special emphasis on Boston's initial existence as a city where people choose to settle for reasons other than purely economic; Bostonians 'responded to crisis by innovating, not by fleeing' (Glaeser, 2005b: 151). This begs the question of how cities succeed in preventing their residents from fleeing – or investing elsewhere – during periods when things are not doing well and when better opportunities are emerging elsewhere. Urban economies are, by definition, open economies. In the US context, a highly mobile society, Boston's success is all the more remarkable in that it is a northern city with a generally cold climate, although blessed with an attractive shoreline. Among US cities, once (good) weather is accounted for, a city's initial endowment in human capital (average educational and skill levels) is the most powerful predictor of long-term growth (Glaeser and Saiz, 2004). In the battle for human capital – holding and attracting it – Boston has done remarkably well. The Boston example illustrates that climate can be overcome; which is good news. On the other hand, the attributes that make Boston attractive are not easy to replicate. **b**-Resilient cities ('adhesive' might be a more appropriate word) are not created overnight. Boston's success rests on a legacy of education, skills, and values, whose roots go back decades, even centuries.

Let us now turn to a second example of change in the face of decline: my home city, Montreal. In this case, the shock to be overcome was political in origin, not technological. Until the mid-1960s, Montreal was Canada's largest city, its chief corporate and business centre. Then the trend-line broke: Montreal's growth slowed to be suddenly over-taken by Toronto (Polèse and Shearmur, 2004). Thirty years later, Toronto has emerged as the undisputed corporate, business, and financial centre of Canada, with a metropolitan population some 50% above that of Montreal. During much of the 1970s and 1980s the unemployment rate in Montreal was in the double digits, almost twice that of Toronto. The city was clearly in decline. Corporate headquarters fled to Toronto. However, starting in the latter half of the 1990s, various indicators turned positive, without necessarily indicating a complete turnaround: unemployment fell and employment grew, although still at a somewhat slower rate. More importantly, the city spawned an impressive array of home-grown companies in a variety of areas (aerospace; engineering; computer gaming; entertainment; etc.), some of which have gone on to become multinationals, the embryo of a new corporate headquarter economy.

What happened and what were the roots of the revival? Montreal's abrupt inter-
ruption of growth was the result of the rise of Quebecois nationalism in the 1960s
with the accompanying (now waning) threat of Quebec's separation from Canada.
That threat plus the introduction of measures to promote the French language triggered a flight of much of the old Anglo-Scots business elite together with their capital, networks, and head offices. The resurgence of French also made Montreal a less
competitive place to do business for firms that wished to or needed to function in
English. As a corporate service centre, Montreal in essence lost its traditional Canadian hinterland (beyond the province of Quebec) to Toronto. An analogy with
Vienna is not unwarranted: in the first instance, the city saw its hinterland shrunk
by an international boundary; in the second, by a language boundary. In both cases,
the city was forced to downsize. Montreal is still a metropolis and a central place,
but for a smaller space, essentially the province of Quebec with a population of some
eight million.

The reversal, if it may be called that, occurred because Montreal remained a
metropolis and a central place for a population that looks to it as its focal point.
Much (fortunately not all) of the old Anglo-Scots business elite did flee, but the
Francophone population did not. A young, newly educated, Francophone elite
gradually stepped in to replace the former elite. For aspiring young Francophone
Canadian entrepreneurs, entertainers or otherwise ambitious individuals, Montreal
is the natural magnet, the equivalent of New York or Paris. A Francophone-
controlled firm would no more think of moving its head office to Toronto than a
German Hamburg-based firm would think of moving its head office to Paris. We
thus come back to Glaeser's point of 'responded to crisis by innovating, not by fleeing'. In Montreal, as in Boston, the turnaround took time to come to fruition; but in
both cases its roots lay in the past and in the particular culture (and loyalty, one
might add) that the city had succeeded in developing over time.

Another similarity with Boston (and also New York and, possibly, London) is
worthy of note: the city's merchant background. Montreal, like the other two, was
initially a trading city and financial centre rather than primarily an industrial city.
The industries that did emerge were, as in New Work and in Boston, most often
founded on cheap labour, immigrant labour in the former two cases, and rural
French-Canadian in-migrants in the second. Until very recently, clothing was Montreal's chief source of manufacturing employment. Montreal, like its two sisters, had
the good fortune of not having nearby coal and iron ore deposits. Why I say 'good
fortune' will become clearer as we now consider the obstacles to b-Resilience.

BARRIERS TO RESILIENCE: WHY SOME CITIES FIND IT MORE DIFFICULT TO CHANGE

Resilience means constantly shedding declining industries and replacing them with
new ones. The vast majority of cities do this surprisingly well, without it even being
noticed. Indeed, were this not so, most cities would have gone under long ago. It is

in the very nature of cities to constantly transform their economic base. However, the ease with which a city is able to move from one industrial specialization to another is not the same for all. I shall argue that the city's industrial legacy – the industries that shaped its work and business culture – is the most common impediment to b-Resilience.

Some industrial legacies are more difficult to overcome than others. Both in Europe and in North America, cities that have found it difficult to renew their economic base often have similar histories. This is no accident. Almost all have a legacy of heavy industry, mining or other industries dominated by large plants and factories. The five US urban areas that exhibited the slowest growth during the latter half of the twentieth century (St. Louis, Pittsburgh, Buffalo, Detroit, and Cleveland) were all typical Northern Rustbelt cities (Rappaport, 2003), trapped in what McDonald (2008) calls a vicious circle of decline. Among the rare Southern cities that declined continuously is (aptly named) Birmingham, Alabama, whose economy, like its English twin, was built on steel. In England, continuously under-performing cities remain concentrated in the old industrial heartlands of the North: Liverpool, Manchester, Newcastle... (Simmie et al., 2006). In continental Europe, the stubbornly most problematic cities tell the same story: Lille in northern France; the coal-mining cities of Charleroi and Mons in Belgium; and the steel towns of Asturias in Spain.

The Intrusive Rentier Syndrome

Why do such cities find it so difficult to shed their past? One possible answer lies in what my colleagues and I have dubbed the Intrusive Rentier Syndrome (Polèse and Shearmur, 2006; Polèse, 2009), initially formulated to explain the lack of diversification of Canada's resource-dependant regional economies. The explanation is as much sociological as economic. Every industry or occupation – farming, fishing, mining, steel making, automobile assembly, computer programming, banking, etc. – produces its own culture, work ethic, pattern of industrial relations, and outlook. Some will be more conducive to change than others. Industrial cultures will have little effect on economic performance in cities where no single industry dominates the local landscape. But, where one industry is dominant, its culture will become the local norm with either a positive or a negative effect.

Why intrusive 'rentier'? The notion of economic 'rent' pertains to income earned for reasons other than greater personal effort or higher productivity. The most common sources of such rents are natural resources. In the late nineteenth and early twentieth centuries, given then-current technologies, the combined presence of coal and iron deposits created a potential economic rent. Who captures this rent? Owners and shareholders of course, otherwise why invest? Governments will take a share via taxes. But, so might workers, by way of higher wages; that is, if they can seize their share. Industries associated with this epoch (steel mills, mines, textile mills, shipyards...) were typically large. Size facilitates unionization. The cities concerned often became – and have often remained – among the most heavily unionized within their respective nations. The outcome is a local work culture in which perceptions are in large part moulded by the practices (and past histories) of large firms and labour unions, producing a mindset that does not necessarily facilitate change. On a personal note, I remember being in England in the early 1970s during the miners strike and watching Arthur Scargill on television, leader of the National Union of Miners. His message was straightforward: my father worked in the mines and my grandfather before him, and my sons and grandsons should be able to do so – hardly a recipe for **b**-Resilience.

We have identified the 'rentiers': large plants and large unions. But, why are they 'intrusive'? Firstly, they discourage young workers from looking elsewhere; specifi-cally, from starting up their own business. It's simply not part of the mindset: 'busi-ness' is for others. By the same token, they discourage new manufacturing firms, especially small firms, from locating there. The local workforce has expectations that, often, are beyond the means of small businesses and other start-ups. In many cases the legacy is also visual and social. The debris left behind by coal mines and abandoned brown-fields hardly make for attractive urban landscapes. The image problem is further compounded if the cities are located in the colder less attractive parts of the nation, as is often the case in the US, UK and France. The Midwest, the Midlands, and the Lorraine, respectively, do not conjure up positive images for most persons, their undoubted qualities notwithstanding.

The social impacts do not end there. Large plants will often have attracted immi-grant and, in the US case, Afro-American labour, creating ethnically and racially divided cities. McDonald (2008) points to such divisions as a major ingredient in the vicious circle of decline in which many old US industrial cities are seemingly trapped. The City (municipality) of Detroit is over 80% Black (2000 census), while the suburbs are white in similar proportion, hardly a recipe for metropolitan har-mony and inter-municipal cooperation. Racial tensions are also a common feature in many of the old industrial cities of France and England. At another level – more common in Europe – large plants will often have nurtured a culture of social mili-tancy, legacy of the horrendous working conditions and labour disputes of earlier periods, culminating in a local political environment dominated by left-wing parties (socialist or communist), with little sympathy for big businesses, hardly a recipe for attracting outside investors.

Summing up, the mix of these assorted ingredients – social, climatic, industrial, visual, and political – has in all too many instances produced a particularly toxic cocktail, difficult to unscramble. Each city is of course a unique case. However, the fact that so many Rustbelt and other old manufacturing cities are *still* under-performing, half a century after coal and steel began their decline, suggests that the legacy left by their industrial past runs very deep. The changes called for may be more in the nature of a cultural than a technological revolution.

Troublesome Manchester and the Limits of Culture-focused Strategies

A particularly troublesome case, at least for an outsider looking in, is Manchester, England, the very symbol of the Industrial Revolution, the city where it all began.

Troublesome, because the history of Manchester stands fashionable theories (with Florida, 2002, certainly the most well-publicized proponent) extolling the healing virtues of the arts, culture, and a Bohemian lifestyle on their head. Manchester emerged as the largest industrial agglomeration in the world in the nineteenth century, as well as one of Europe's leading intellectual and corporate centres, a position it still held at the beginning of the twentieth century. In 1900, Manchester boasted more large manufacturing headquarters than any British city (Peck and Ward, 2002). Benjamin Disraeli is reputed to have said that 'Manchester is as great a human exploit as Athens.'[2]. Such economic dominance was reflected in an extraordinary vibrant cultural life, much of it underpinned by migrant entrepreneurs, scientists, and professionals from continental Europe (Dicken, 2002). The Hallé Orchestra, founded by such a migrant in 1858, remains the oldest professional symphony orchestra in Britain. It was no coincidence that it was able to attract the then most famous conductor in the world, Hans Richter, to lead it in the 1890s. In short, late-nineteenth century Manchester was a highly successful economy, a cultural magnet, and clearly attractive to what Florida (2002) calls the creative class.

The picture at the outset of the twenty-first century is very different. From a driving global city then, writes Dicken (2002: 19), Manchester has become something of a second-class passenger, being led rather than leading. Almost all large manufacturing headquarters have since moved to London. Peck and Ward (2002) lament that most economic trend lines continue to track steadily in the wrong direction, adding that, compared to other UK cities, only Liverpool has fared worse in terms of overall labour-market performance. Simmie et al. (2006) paint a similar picture. Two symbolic events in recent times illustrate the decline of Manchester, first as a corporate centre then as a cultural centre. The Royal Exchange (founded by Manchester cotton traders) closed its doors in 1968. The *Manchester Guardian*, Britain's famed 'radical' newspaper, dropped the 'Manchester' from its title in 1959 and, adding insult to injury, moved its editorial offices to London in 1970[3].

I do not have sufficient knowledge of Manchester to adequately analyse the roots of its decline. Nonetheless, I cannot help but speculate that Manchester is an example – perhaps, *the* leading historical example – of what I have called the Intrusive Rentier Syndrome. As late as 1959, half of the labour force was employed in manufacturing – jobs which then began to disappear. As Peck and Ward (2002: 12) note, many of those jobs were dirty, but they were better paid than those that (sometimes) followed, going

---

2 The quote is in fact that of a character in one of Disraeli's novels: *Coningsby, or The New Generation*: Book IV, Chapter 1, third paragraph, digitalized version, Harvard College Library (Publishers: Carey & Hart, Philadelphia, 1844). Available at: http://www.gutenberg.org/etext/7412.

3 In an attempt at regional outreach, the BBC moved its BBC North studios to Salford, part of Greater Manchester, in 2011. However, the move remains controversial, in part because of the high travel costs incurred (ferrying guests and staff between Salford and London). It is too early to judge whether the move will have a lasting impact on the Manchester economy.

on to observe: 'For the working-class men of the city, in particular, the factory and the football ground were the fundamental coordinates of an uncompromising lifestyle'. I can think of no better illustration of the difficult-to-erase impacts of industrial histories on local lifestyles, perceptions, and expectations.

But, what of the role human capital and, indirectly, cultural activities in shaping successful urban economies? Having a skilled and educated population is an indisputable asset. The problem lies in the mobile nature of that asset and in the difficulty of sorting out causes and consequences. Florida (2002) argues that certain urban lifestyles – cafés, the arts, cosmopolitanism, and so on – are attractive to highly educated young professionals. In this he may be right. From this follows the recipe that a rich cultural scene, by attracting the so-called creative class, will produce successful local economies. The question however is this: Are culturally-rich environments the *outcome* of cities that have grown and become wealthy or the source of that growth? I do not believe that a clear answer is possible. Atlanta, one of the fastest growing metropolitan areas in the US, does not owe its rapid growth to an initial above-average endowment of educated workers, world-class universities, museums, and cafés. Growth attracts talent. If Atlanta keeps on growing, we may reasonably predict that it will in time house a highly educated population and also spawn top-notch universities and cultural institutions, and perhaps even trendy neighbourhoods where the bohemian classes can hang out. But will these assets, in turn, ensure further growth? Perhaps, but then again perhaps not, since they were not necessary in the first place. Manchester's strength as a cultural magnet in the nineteenth century did not, we saw, ensure its future growth in the twentieth century.

The surest recipe for attracting talent, skills, and money is to be a growing city with plentiful job opportunities and high wages. This is not terribly helpful, for essentially circular. All one can do is repeat that an educated population is a positive asset. But, as Manchester's story attests, it is also an asset that can be lost. I do not know how many Mancunians have left for London, a reminder of the porous nature of urban economies. Perhaps the question that one should be asking is why so many (talented) Mancunians seemingly felt no compunction about leaving Manchester and why, by the same token, the young and ambitious of Detroit and Pittsburgh probably consider it entirely normal to move to San Francisco or to New York. We thus come back, full circle, to Glaeser's (2005b) 'responded to crisis by innovating, not by fleeing'. Visibly, neither Lancashire nor the industrial Midwest developed a sufficiently 'adhesive' identity to make its young and ambitious want to stay and fight rather than flee. In this respect, Montreal's good fortune was the language border, which initially caused its shrinkage, but also created a protective barrier holding its 'creative' class in. However, such cultural barriers within nations are the exception.

Creativity, Centrality and Chance

Why then do some cities succeed – weather and natural amenities aside – where others fail? My very imperfect answer is 'centrality'. The most successful 'b-Resilient' cities are often the *centre* of a regional empire – a hinterland – to which its inhabitants look as

their metropolis. Many such cities initially evolved as central places before the industrial era, often hubs for converging transport networks. Chicago, whose resurgence
since the 1990s is documented by Rappaport (2003) and McDonald (2008), largely
owes its success to its position as the metropolis of the Midwest, notwithstanding the
fact that the region as a whole continues to lag. Chicago's centrality is in part the
'natural' outcome of its central location; but, reinforced over time by a net of transportation links of which it is the hub, first canals and rail, and air today. The story of
Atlanta is similar, the transport hub and dominant corporate and financial centre of
the American South (Odell and Weiman, 1998). It is no coincidence that Atlanta and
Chicago house, respectively, the two busiest airports on the continent.

The problem however, in terms of devising useful policy recipes, is two-fold.
Firstly, a region can have so many central places and, by definition, only one dominant centre. Those wonderfully creative people who flock to London, New York or
Chicago come from other places. All cannot win in this game. Boston is unrivalled
in New England. True, smaller central places can also emerge, but they will be necessarily limited in number. And, it is no accident that the North-eastern and Midwest
US cities that sprung back in the 1990s (besides New York, Boston, and Chicago)
were all either State capitals or regional service centres with little or no history of
heavy industry (McDonald, 2008) – Columbus; Indianapolis; Kansas City; Minne-
apolis-St. Paul – an indication, yet again, of the negative after-effects of (dirty)
manufacturing and the positive influence of service-based legacies. One might call
this Christtaller's revenge. As manufacturing recedes as a driver of (large) urban
economies, so central place theory again comes into its own as the dominant organizing principle for economic activity. The resurgence in recent times of Edinburgh in
Scotland, compared with the much less glorious performance of Glasgow, points in
the same direction. Edinburgh also has the good fortune, like Montreal, of having
an institutionally (though not linguistically) defined hinterland.

A second problem is that centrality is most often an inherited trait. Central places
will, simply *because* they are central, have developed urban economies and lifestyles
that are conducive today to high-order services and knowledge-rich industries. Add in
the workings of increasing returns (especially, to human capital) and the process
becomes circular and essentially irreversible. London is London because it *was* London.
Fortunately, at least from a policy perspective, reality is not totally linear or 'locked-in',
borrowing Martin's (2010) term. Chicago demonstrates that a legacy of heavy industry
is not an insurmountable obstacle. Chicago was able to overcome its blue-collar heritage because of its parallel role as the corporate centre of the Midwest. But, then again,
its position as the metropolis of the Midwest was an inherited trait. This sends us back
to the 'troublesome' case of Manchester. Why did Manchester not evolve along the lines
of Chicago to become – or rather to remain – the corporate and cultural capital of
northern England? Manchester not only seemingly invalidates the culture-as-an-urban-
economic-driver argument, but also strict path dependency and increasing returns
interpretations. With a population of about 1.3 million in 1900, greater Manchester
was the largest urban centre in northern England, the second city in Britain, three times
the size of Leeds. A hundred years later Leeds was poised to overtake it on both counts, and
has emerged as the banking and business service centre of the North, a historical reversal.

I have no satisfactory answer of why Leeds replaced Manchester. Nor do I really have a satisfactory explanation of why Atlanta replaced New Orleans as the centre of the American South. I began this essay in New Orleans, and shall end there. Its evolution provides an additional reminder of the difficulty of formulating universal, path-predictable, explanations of urban growth. New Orleans was about four times the size of Atlanta in 1900. Today, the proportions are reversed. New Orleans, like Manchester at the time, was a cultural magnet. What is arguably the South's greatest cultural export – jazz – was born in New Orleans. Few cities were as open and, at least outwardly, tolerant to socially divergent behaviour. Few would argue that New Orleans continues, despite Katrina, to house one of America's most attractive historical centres. But, something in its social dynamics caused its economy to stall. Most attempts at explanation point to the legacy left by slavery and the cotton trade, producing a stilted social structure and closed business elite (Odell and Weiman, 1998; Lang and Danielson, 2006; Polèse, 2009), another example of the weight of history, but also of chance, recalling Hall's (2000) quote, cited at the outset of this chapter. Sir Peter Hall's call for prudence is sobering; following as it does what is arguably the most exhaustive recent study of the roots of urban greatness. There is still much we do not understand. Hall's (2000: 649) quote was preceded by the following words: 'On reflection, I am far from sure I have a satisfactory answer', a useful reminder that the roots of urban success (or failure) rarely lend themselves to simple answers.

CONCLUSION

The recipe for successful urban economies is fairly easy to enunciate. A city will grow and prosper if it: a) is home to a highly skilled and educated population; b) is centrally located, at the heart of a rich market, and/or well positioned for trade with expanding markets; c) has a diversified economy with a significant proportion of high-order services, largely untainted by a legacy of Rustbelt-type industries; and d) boasts a climate and/or natural setting superior to most other cities in the nation. If a city is fortunate enough to score well on all four, its long-term growth is assured, its 'resilience' a foregone conclusion. Within Britain, Greater London would undoubtedly score well on all four, compared to other UK cities. It should thus come as no surprise that wages and income in London have remained systematically – and significantly – above that of other British cities.

In urban economics, all advantages are relative. It is difficult to argue that London has a marvellous climate, but it is marginally better (or at least no worse) than in other British cities. In any case, there is little a city – or anyone – can do about the weather. The trouble with the other three positive attributes is that they are most often inherited, and as such also difficult to alter through local policy. In addition, such positive traits tend, as a rule, to be closely related and correlated with size. A centrally-located regional service centre (b) will, almost by definition, be a large city with a higher proportion of information-rich business services (c) and a proportionately better-educated labour force (a). But, on what button does one push first to promote growth? In recent times, city economic development strategies have tended to emphasize (a), which is not necessarily a bad thing. Yet, if *all* cities push on button (a) then those cities that are *relatively* most attractive to highly-educated workers will win out in the end. We have seen that asset (a) can be won and lost. Urban economies are porous by definition. The surest way to attract skilled and educated populations is to be a growing city with plentiful job opportunities and high wages; which is not terribly helpful.

National Context

The national context is all too often the main constraint on the ability of cities to respond to outside shocks. Buenos Aires and Port au Prince – cities the author knows well – are cases in point.

In the 1920s, Buenos Aires had a standard of living comparable to that of London and other great cities of the industrialized world. Today, its income per capita (adjusted for living costs) is barely a third that of London. The initial shock to the local economy was the Great Crash of 1929, which put an abrupt end to Argentina's wheat (and meat) export boom. Buenos Aires never fully recovered, beginning a long slide down in (relative) incomes. Much of the blame must go to successive national governments (democratically elected or not) with an almost unbroken record of economic mismanagement. But then, much of the nation's political elite stems from Buenos Aires.

Port au Prince was never a First World city. But, its elegant French colonial architecture, much now deteriorated or destroyed, is a reminder of past glories. Real incomes have steadily declined since the 1950s, making Port au Prince the poorest (1 million plus) city in the Americas. Decades of dysfunctional national governments not only undermined the local economy but also the city's ability to respond to the devastating 2010 earthquake, in which some 250,000 people perished. At the time of writing, some four years after the quake, little has been rebuilt. The people of Port au Prince are certainly resilient, remarkably so, but it is a resilience of survival.

I have argued that attribute (b) – centrality – is often a key factor in success and that, alternatively, a legacy of heavy industry (the inverse of c) is often the principal obstacle to success. Both the US and UK experiences suggest that the negative after-effects of a Rustbelt legacy are extremely difficult to overcome. Chicago is an exception: a rare example of a city that has succeeded in overcoming its blue-collar past, but precisely because of its strength on criterion (b), the corporate and cultural centre of the US Midwest. Manchester, on the other hand, has not been so fortunate. Here, the negative social after-effects of its (glorious) industrial past have, seemingly, over-powered the advantages of its former dominant position as the central place of the North, today overtaken by Leeds. Manchester's former position as a European cultural and intellectual magnet was not, apparently, sufficient to halt its decline. Centrality, in sum, is also an attribute that can be won and lost. In the end, policies that reinforce a city's role as a transport hub, distribution centre, and regional focal point may be as essential as those aimed at attracting human capital.

A closing caveat is in order. Most of the literature on urban economic development implicitly assumes, as we have done so far, the existence of a reasonably well-functioning state that provides the essential preconditions for development: a stable macro-economic environment; the rule of law; a reasonably efficient and honest bureaucracy; basics infrastructures; etc... Unfortunately, this assumption does not hold in many parts of the world (see 'National Context' box above). In such cases, even basic a-Resiliency takes on a different meaning. New Orleans, the ineptitude of the initial Federal government response notwithstanding, could count on the institutional and financial resources of the nation to help it rebuild after Katrina. Not so Port au Prince. The terrible 2010 quake could not be prevented. But, much of the devastation and far too many deaths were a direct result of the absence of a functioning state and social order: unenforced (non-existent!) building codes; poorly planned and maintained infrastructures; deficient public health services; the list goes on. By the same token, the rebuilding process has been severely hampered, among other things, by the absence of clear property rights and functioning land management systems. In the end, successful urban economies, able to rebound and to create wealth for their citizens, are the reflection of policy choices over many decades at all levels of government. The most important policy levers are not necessarily local.

10

Imagineering the City

Marguerite van den Berg

URBAN COMPETITION IN AN AGE OF MEDIATIZATION

Commodifying the Urban Spirit

Cities today are products. The urban experience is commodified into marketable items by urban entrepreneurs. Urban administrations, city marketers, politicians, local businesses and other actors all over the world are developing entrepreneurial strategies to sell their city. From 'I ♥ New York' to 'The Fairest Cape of them All' to 'I AMsterdam', cities compete for investment and tourists in the globalized economy and the age of mediatization.

Many cities in the West developed entrepreneurial strategies in the 1980s and thereafter. Especially former industrial cities met severe economic challenges in the 1970s, as manufacturing, steel and other industries rationalized and moved their production across the world. Pittsburgh (Hollcomb, 1996), New York (Greenberg, 2008) and Glasgow (Ward, 1998) are early examples of cities where governors saw themselves forced to attract new investors and compete with other urban areas for new economic opportunities. Although deindustrialization hit urban regions in Britain, France, and elsewhere hard as well, US cities were the first to develop place-marketing because they were more dependent on their local tax base and, thus, on their local economies. In the words of Stephen Ward: 'the USA has been the principal source of place-marketing ideas' (Ward, 1998: 46). The 'I ♥ New York' campaign is the first famous example of city boosting (Greenberg, 2008) and Boston and Baltimore led the way in developing strategies to change their cities into consumption places. These formulas have been highly influential in the development of entrepreneurial strategies in the 1980s elsewhere (Ward, 1998).

Many accounts of city marketing, urban entrepreneurialism and connected phenomena focus primarily on the Anglo-Saxon world (see, for example, Kearns and Philo, 1993; Hall and Hubbard, 1998; Tallon, 2010). This can thus in part be explained by the history of urban entrepreneurialism, because entrepreneurial strategies were first designed there. Today, however, cities across the globe are behaving like entrepreneurs and branding their cities in highly competitive fields. Urban entrepreneurialism is omnipresent in the West *and* the Rest. In fact, it has been said that the effects of entrepreneurialism and city marketing in the global south have been even more far-reaching than in the West (Broudehoux, 2000; Davis, 2005; Freeman, 2008). This chapter therefore aims to move beyond the Anglo-Saxon or Western focus and incorporate an investigation of the shape of place-marketing in Africa, Latin-America and Asia as well.

IMAGINEERING

Image is everything[1], or so the slogan goes. The ability to capture the imagination of (future) inhabitants, investors or other publics has fast become one of the most important assets of cities. That is why city administrations, city marketers and other actors are consciously sculpting image, images and urban narratives. The city is a primary place of image production and consumption. This chapter is about the way in which cities engineer the social, political and spatial through the production of imagery. In the words of Disney: it is about *imagineering*.

Walt Disney Imagineering is the arm of the Disney Company that develops theme parks, resorts and real estate. The most well-known example of Disney Imagineering is Celebration, the utopian village in Florida. Celebration, and other themed environments of Disney, are famous for their synergy between different products: hotels, resorts, parks, merchandising and film. Celebration was meant as a fantasy to live in, a fantasy of community spirit and social control (Zukin, 1991; Kargon and Molella, 2008). Today, the term imagineering is also used as a verb. To imagineer (again in the terms of Disney) is 'combining imagination with engineering to create the reality of dreams' (Paul in Yeoh, 2005: 42). In this chapter, imagineering is incorporated in a critical perspective on place marketing. Here, the term imagineering is defined as the *rewriting* of meaning that is attached to urban environments and the social and economic effects this produces.

Attracting Visitors, Investment and Inhabitants

Imagineering and 'selling places' (Kearns and Philo, 1993) in today's globalizing markets is about the attraction of a) visitors, b) investment, and c) inhabitants (Paddison, 1993; Hall and Hubbard, 1998; Broudehoux, 2000). Urban tourism has become a key sector in global tourism today. Cities thus market themselves as 'visitable' (cf. Dicks, 2003) to attract the tourist's dollar, euro or yen. Marketing urban areas by presenting culturally existing images and coherent historic narratives proves to be successful to attract certain groups of inhabitants and investments, as well as visitors.

One of the things the urban entrepreneurs are after is what Markusen and Schrock (2006) have termed 'the artistic dividend'. The 'creative class' (cf. Florida, 2002),

---

1 The slogan was used by Canon in the early 1990s. See Short and Kim, 1998.

including artists, but also bankers, accountants and architects, is the most desired group of inhabitants today and in today's thinking about urban governing, creativity is most important in attracting investors as well. After all, if the 'creative classes' reside in your city, Florida (2002) would argue, chances are that interesting investors and companies will follow. Economic restructuring has resulted in more or less foot-loose businesses. Service sector companies are far less tied to place than industrial businesses were in the past. In the past decades, this resulted in a market inversion (Hernes and Selvik, 1981 in Burgers, 2006): businesses are not competing for locations anymore. Instead, locations are competing for business.

A dominant idea in place marketing today is thus that the attraction of a creative class will lead to an interesting cultural climate that will attract investors, and will thus lead to job growth and revenue throughout the economy (Burgers, 2006; Hubbard, 2006; Marlet and van Woerkens, 2007). Richard Florida's book (2002) on the creative classes has proven to be immensely influential in making this argument. Cities thus sell themselves as culturally exciting places, cosmopolitan centres and playgrounds of (sexual) diversity. Images that communicate such messages have become immensely important in entrepreneurial strategies to regenerate cities and the 'creative frame' today is the most prevalent in 'place marketing' in the West. In the following paragraph, the global and regional city is theorized as a product, entrepreneur and event. The remainder of this chapter is dedicated to the analysis of the use of identity politics in the production of uniqueness in the international city marketing game.

THE CITY AS PRODUCT AND EVENT

The City as Product: Engineering by Imagineering

The city increasingly behaves like an entrepreneur that is promoting itself as a (cultural) product (Harvey, 1989a; Paddison, 1993; Hall and Hubbard, 1998; Gimeno Martinez, 2007; Tallon, 2010). The public sector has, in the words of Hubbard, taken 'over characteristics once distinctive to the private sector: risk-taking, inventiveness, promotion and profit motivation' (1996: 1141). The selling of images of the urban is thus motivated by an economic rationale (Paddison, 1993; Hall and Hubbard, 1998; Broudehoux, 2000; Kipfer and Keil, 2002). Urban mythologies, or narratives that are told to reflect the image, spirit or soul of the city are remarkably durable (Blom Hansen and Verkaaik, 2009). Remaking, engineering or even rewriting (Hubbard, 2006: 86) mythologies and images is thus a challenging task for urban administrations and many are unsuccessful.

The City as Brand

The amount of cities that engage in the marketing game has increased tremendously since the 1970s, when New York's emblematic 'I ♥ New York' boosterist campaign hit off (Jessop, 1998; Short and Kim, 1998; Greenberg, 2008). Many other cities' campaigns copied the strategy. It still serves as an important inspiration to many contemporary city marketers (Ward, 1998). Cities indeed copy strategies that worked someplace else and develop remarkably similar slogans and brands. This is why the marketing of cities tends to homogenize: all highlight their infrastructure, population, exciting urban life and strategic location. Many cities call themselves 'gateway' or present themselves as entertainment centres (Short and Kim, 1998). Most cities organize cultural festivals, participate in bids for sporting events or international summits and develop landmarks. Cosmopolitanism is another characteristic or, rather, empty signifier, that is enthusiastically sold in slogans that include the words 'world city' (Hemelryk Donald et al., 2009). Cities sometimes almost desperately look for image in a striking 'me-tooist way' (Jessop, 1998: 86). Such homogenizing tendencies reveal that much place marketing is what Harvey termed the production of a 'carnival mask' (1989: 35) that is to cover up underlying economical problems and that reflects ambitions of urban marketers, elites and administrators rather than urban dynamics, city characteristics or urban social problems (see the box on Rio de Janeiro for an example).

Slogans such as 'I ♥ New York' and 'Glasgow (s)miles better' are part of one-dimensional brands (Ward, 1998). City *branding* reduces the urban in a single trademark (Hubbard, 2006). According to Kavaratzis (2005), branding originates from regular marketing theories and practices and frees city marketers from the physical of the product (which in this case is the city). In branding, for example, a single aspect product of a city can become the basis of the city's brand. Cities can brand themselves according to their location alone, or focus on a single famous historical figure that connotes a selling message or meaning (Kavaratzis, 2005; Hubbard, 2006) or become projected around an iconic building as is famously the case in the city of Bilbao (Gomez, 1998). The above-mentioned slogan 'I AMsterdam', for example, has no meaning in itself, or no direct connection to meaning that is given to the city of Amsterdam. Instead, it is an empty brand, which can be given meaning in a branding campaign. Like 'I ♥ New York', the brand is designed to stimulate positive feelings that consumers have for the brand that is being sold, rather than the product, even though the consumption of the product is of course the ultimate goal. City brands need constant updating. Most often, brands do however relate to the city or meanings that are attached to it. Imagery of landscapes is particularly apt to communicate a city image that goes beyond the one-dimensional brand alone.

The Landscape as Image

As Hall asserted: 'There is probably no greater advert for cities than their own landscape' (1998: 29). To name one of many possible examples: the Eiffel tower is not only a landmark for Paris, but also its brand and logo. Urban entrepreneurial strategies employ architecture as one of its crucial strategies while at the same time reducing it to the two-dimensional visual image (Broudehoux, 2000). Landmark buildings appear on promotional material and in the visitor's gaze that wants to consume the city as a whole. Major urban restructuring is thus part of the making of imagery for the city as much as it is part of other entrepreneurial strategies. The demolition of squatter neighbourhoods, the beautification of sidewalks and the sanitization of touristy public places all serve the two-dimensional image of the city. These transformations of the material make-up of the city, of the built environment and spatial structures are thus important consequences and forms of imagineering.

Failing city marketing can have detrimental material effects for cities. Governors and administrators fear that in the event that businesses decide to locate elsewhere and local economies have to do without revenue from tourism, this can result in joblessness, and an overall downward spiral of disinvestment. Therefore, urban 'make-overs' or 'carnival masks' most often are designed to relate to the durable narratives of identity, or charisma (Blom Hansen and Verkaaik, 2009) of cities. Public culture and urban image are, after all, first and foremost socially constructed at the micro level, even though the image construction by marketers is definitely influential (Iwata and del Rio, 2004, see the box on Rio de Janeiro). Imagineering always runs the risk of not sufficiently connecting to these everyday constructions. Branding may be freed of the actual city, imagineering and city marketing as a whole is not. In the end, '(t)he question of who can occupy public space, and so define an image of the city, is open-ended' (Zukin, 1995: 11).

Cidade Maravilhosa: Rio de Janeiro

The 'marvelous' city of Rio de Janeiro (as it likes to call itself) presents itself today as a leisurely waterfront. The beachfront is the city's most important symbol in the twenty-first century global competition for tourism and in the construction of the local identity (Iwata and del Rio, 2004; Freeman, 2008). However, the city also struggles with the persistent image of one of the most divided and violent cities in the world. In the nineteenth century, Rio's waterfront first emerged as a therapeutic bathing resort, developing into the recreational sea resort of the twentieth century. In the 1920s, new ideas about sun, sea and air popularized, and living near the southern shores and in the city centre became the modern symbol of social status it still is today.

Between the 1960s and the 1990s, the image of Rio de Janeiro as a tropical paradise was compromised by the Military regime and the transfer of the federal government to the newly built Brasilia. The economic crisis and the disinvestment resulting from the move of the government left Rio de Janeiro struggling. A steep increase in street crime, drug traffic and violence dominated the image of the city in the 1980s and 1990s, to the disappointment of many carioca (Rio inhabitants). As del Rio (1992) showed, US coverage of the carnival usually showed only a short segment on the samba schools and the parade, and then moved to a story on violence, street children and poverty. As a result, and like other sectors, tourism suffered.

In the 1990s, the administration of the city embarked on a massive regeneration strategy and image campaign. The start of this 'renaissance' was marked by the 1992 United Nations Conference on the Environment and Development for which the city was 'beautified' and 'cleaned up' (Broudehoux, 2000). These efforts were, again, focused on the city's beachfront areas and mainly were to enhance the aesthetics of the city, leaving many of the underlying social problems untouched and serving mainly the elite that can afford to live there. The city's poor were, as a result, excluded from the city's image and actual public space (Broudehoux, 2000; Freeman, 2008). They were denied their 'right to the city', as authorities prioritized the security of the rich and the tourists. However, as Broudehoux (2000) showed, a romanticized image of the favelas remained part of the international tourists' imagination. And soon, even poverty and violence were commodified into exotic tours of favelas.

The case of Rio de Janeiro shows how a lack of fit between the marketing image of the city and the historic and social reality can produce an unsuspected *inclusion* of the imagery that was supposed to be excluded and overwritten. Moreover, it shows the real social consequences that marketing can have for local populations: in a divided city like Rio de Janeiro, funds were used in cosmetic attempts of beautification rather than in social investments for the city's poor.

In 2014, Rio will be hosting the World Cup and in 2016 the Olympic Summer Games. For these events, the city is now being given an 'extreme makeover' (Whitefield, 2010); slums are being 'cleared', airports enlarged, infrastructure further developed and, of course, stadiums built.

It remains to be seen how the two sporting events will impact the city socially and economically in the long term. Rio de Janeiro has been 'beautifying' the city by violently expelling residents from favelas (Broudehoux, 2000; Davis, 2005) and commentators are by no means certain of the economic outcomes. In the months before the 2014 World Cup, carioca took to the streets in protest of the World Cup investments. In recent history, other Olympic cities often only reached a break-even point in revenue (see below for further discussion on these economic effects).

The City as Event

Festivals and other events, such as the Olympic Games or large international summits are effective instruments of 'place marketing' (Holcomb, 1993; Kearns and Philo, 1993; Hannigan, 1998; Richards and Wilson, 2004; Gold and Gold, 2008). Spectacular events project desired images (Ossman, 1994) and usually have a wide audience. The usage of events for the promotion of places is not a recent phenomenon. When French guests visited the colony of Morocco in the 1920s, the Moroccan lord of the South sent all his tribes a message that they were all required to line a route 'with your horses, your rifles and your women (...) the women will wear their finest clothes, they will line the roadside and will sing with their finest voices' (Maxwell in Ossman, 1994: 80). This creation of a display of 'the Moroccan people' is just one example of early place promotion and still, in 1988, Casablancans were obliged to assemble to welcome the French president Mitterand when he visited the country. Later, 'the entire population watched these images of Morocco played back on television screens and captured by photographers' (Ossman, 1994: 84). In other words: the event was used for the people *to consume themselves* as a people.

These narratives of Moroccan place promotion before the era of city marketing reveal that festivals can be employed to uphold the 'dominant political system' (Belghazi, 2006: 99) and to form an *urban habitus* that is larger than the inhabitants themselves (cf. Blom Hansen and Verkaaik, 2009). In a sense, festivals are used to create cohesion in otherwise often fragmented cities (compare Burgers, 2002). Events still fulfill this role today, but, in addition are used as an instrument for economic growth and for the development of cultural industries (Hannigan, 1998; Belghazi, 2006; Gold and Gold, 2008). The narratives that are promoted in festivals are designed, on the one hand, to unite inhabitants in a shared idea of the city, and on the other hand to enhance the attractiveness of the city to outsiders (compare Richards and Wilson, 2004).

The economic rationale for organizing mega-events such as the Olympic games is contested. One of the 'best practices' of the past was Barcelona in 1992. The city was successfully promoted as a tourist destination and has in fact seen increased tourist revenue over the past two decades. Barcelona's success was in large part the result of urban improvements, such as the Metro, that were paid for with 83% of the total expenditure (Gold and Gold, 2008). Barcelona's strategy of spending much more of the budget on urban investments than on the sports event itself has become a model for future Olympic cities, such as Rio de Janeiro. In a way, Barcelona is the ideal type of 'Games-related urban regeneration' (Gold and Gold, 2008: 307). However, many examples exist of cost over-runs and marketing fiasco's that harmed rather than enhanced a city's image. Beijing, for example, only marginally benefited economically (*New York Times*, 2 October 2009), although it is still too early to say anything about the long-term effect of the 2008 games.

Presenting an attractive city to the world usually necessitates very large investments, and returns are at best uncertain. However, 'the most eagerly sought and most elusive benefits arise less from the financial balance sheet than from opportunities for place promotion (...) the prestige of the Olympics and the sustained attention that they attract provides unparalleled opportunities to make a statement on the world stage (Gold and Gold, 2008: 301).

URBAN MYTHS: FORMS OF IMAGINEERING

Imagineering is a form of myth-making. The function of urban imagineering is to transform images of the city into ideologically laden and potent narratives (compare Selwyn, 1996). Perspectives in anthropology and semiology on mythologies lead to better understandings of the way in which cities promote themselves, their people, economies and places through imagery. Theories of myth-making are helpful in analysing imagineering because they: 1) provide better understandings of discursive strategies in which contemporary narratives make use of history; 2) provide analytic tools to explain the specific *forms* imagineering takes; and 3) provide ways to move away from the vocabulary that is used by the city marketers themselves by deploying 'mythology' as a concept.

Barthes' perspectives on mythologies are especially instructive (1972 [1957]). For Barthes, a myth is a meta-language – a way in which a sign becomes a signifier, or, rather, a way in which extra meaning is given (and imposed) to what is seen and interpreted. Myth makes first-order images into second-order meanings. In this sense, myth does not mean 'unreal' or 'fake' as it often does in everyday use. Myths, rather, distort meaning instead of letting meanings disappear, although they are often 'vehicles of forgetfulness' (Selwyn, 1996: 3). This distortion is to 'simultaneously reveal and conceal, undercommunicate and overcommunicate' (Selwyn, 1996: 3). In Barthes' terms, this is a process of *inflexion*. Myth functions to *naturalize* certain narratives of history and meaning. In this perspective, imagineering is about influencing particular inflexions. It serves to present a certain shallow narrative of history as matter-of-fact, not to be questioned: 'Myth has the task of giving a historical intention a natural justification and making contingency appear eternal.' (1972 [1957]: 142). For Malinowski, myth is not defined by its subject, but by the way it is used in present day societies as a legitimizing or mobilizing 'cultural force' (1948 [1926]: 97). In addition, Vermander presses us to consider myths as tales that give identity to territories and to trace 'out mythical stories and their connections (as a) way for understanding not only representations but also social strategies' (2007: 9).

Modern cities in the global marketplace need to produce *uniqueness* and, for that purpose, produce such 'social strategies' (Vermander) and 'cultural forces' (Malinowski). After all, as we have seen above, much city marketing leads to converging images. To stand out from other cities, they produce unique selling points: they highlight their unique vistas, scenery, historic treasures or specific food culture. Today, urban governors often find uniqueness in the form of a mythology of an ethnic, gendered, sexual, aged or classed identity. These categories of identities are distinctly modern and very useful to produce the *difference* that cities are looking for, because they are the emancipating identities that were and are used by much of the New Social Movements of the twentieth century (Calhoun, 1995). Identity politics thus becomes an instrument in the hands of city marketers. Urban myth-making always excludes certain narratives. However, with the use of collective identities of groups of inhabitants as signifiers in myth-making, exclusion of 'the Other' on the basis of precisely such categories becomes a new risk and likely product of imagineering. On the other hand, such myth-making may also enable certain groups and emancipate them further. At any rate, social conflict is mirrored in urban myth-making and the selling of places.

IMAGERY, HISTORY AND IDENTITY POLITICS

Three modern categories of identity are highlighted in this chapter with concrete examples of global and regional cities. Firstly, the ethnic city is often located in the global south and finds itself under the 'tourist gaze' (Urry, 2002), which leads to articulations of specifically 'ethnic' characteristics; secondly, the gendered city tries to influence mythology by focusing on specific gendered characteristics; and thirdly, the sexed city uses ideas about sexuality and sexual identity to promote specific places.

The Ethnic City

Urban areas that are part of what was formerly known as the Third World are major tourist destinations. Rio de Janeiro is one of Brazil's most popular tourist sites while in India backpackers often visit the country's metropolitan areas. These cities find themselves under a Western 'tourist gaze' (Urry, 2002) which leads to specific articulations of ethnic identities, or ethnicized mythologies. Ethnic diversity is also a stake in the place marketing of cities in the West, where, for instance, China Towns are urban assets (Aytar and Rath, 2012). Tourists are myth-seekers 'par excellence', seeking for imagery of the city as a whole (Selwyn, 1996). Today, many tourists seek to purchase ethnic myths.

Ethnicity moves into the marketplace (Comaroff and Comaroff, 2009: 5). The Western thirst for 'authenticity' not only moves Americans and Europeans to travel to previously remote areas in search for true native tribes and untouched sceneries. Ethnic identity also becomes a major asset in the global market of *urban* tourism. And most global tourism, is, in fact, urban tourism today (Broudehoux, 2000). In their quest for uniqueness, cities highlight specific representations of ethnicity. They claim uniqueness because of their people, history, spirit and customs. Tradition, culture, and people are then put forward as unique selling points. Many of these representations suggest a high level of homogeneity and abstraction and oftentimes, ethnic identities are in such instances actively produced by commerce (Comaroff and Comaroff, 2009). Moreover, the production of such identities is often not only meant to enhance cities' visitability, but also to 'rally potentially alienated populations to a common cause' (Belghazi, 2006: 99) and to sublimate social conflict.

Bickford-Smith (2009) analyzed the marketing of Cape Town (South Africa) and asked why this contemporary place promotion did not incorporate new 'Africanist' visions more extensively. In fact, the city's histories are packaged in a distinctively White and European tourism myth. Cape Town still presents itself to some extent as the 'mother city' of the White South African Nation (as opposed to, for example Durban, which has a much more racialized mythology). Nineteenth-century grand narratives of South African history are to this date very important in the selling of Cape Town. This excludes newer interpretations of the identity of Cape Town from the myth. Of course, as South Africa's most popular tourist destination, Cape Town also highlights recent history in its marketing. However, some critiqued the lack of 'African-ness' in the city's myth-making, deeming it too 'White' and welcoming only to 'White' visitors (Bickford-Smith, 2009). Cape Town's marketing, in this sense, resembles the 'caricature' (Ward, 1998: 289) of the post-industrial city of the North (Bickford-Smith, 2009). Many entrepreneurial cities construct a distinct White myth. The desired visitors, inhabitants and investors are most likely to be White and entrepreneurial strategies often '(mirror) the material polarization of populations' (Hall and Hubbard, 1998: 26).

In the city of Fez, Morocco, governors use cultural festivals to reproduce such dominant power structures (Belghazi, 2006). Belghazi's case-study on the 'Fez festival of World Sacred Music' reveals how the cultural and ethnic construction in the marketing of Fez becomes a stake in social conflict as local Islamists protest the commercial use of the city's traditions for tourism. The essentializing of Fez's history and cultural repertoire into festive activities portrays the city as heir to an Andalusian, sanitized history of ethnic diversity and tolerance. The use of religious symbols in this myth-making was what spurred the Islamists' protest.

Ethnic myth-making for commercial use thus often underlines existing power structures. In the case of Cape Town, the historic dominance of White, or even European groups limited possibilities for other interpretations of Cape Town's identity to be incorporated. In Selwyn's (1996) terms, Cape Town's myth under-communicates 'African' interpretations and over-communicates White histories. Fez's contemporary power struggles surface in the conflict about a festival of sacred music. The festival enables an inclusive ethnic message, but, in doing so, insults religious inhabitants. In the words of Comaroff and Comaroff, the selling of ethnicity carries 'a host of costs and contradictions: (...) the power both to animate and to annihilate' (2009: 139).

The Gendered City

Another modern social category that is a source of inspiration for city marketers is gender. In fact, many cities are thought of as gendered entities. The people of Karachi think of their city as a girl (Blom Hansen and Verkaaik, 2009) and Frank Sinatra sang 'L.A. is my Lady'. Cities make use of such feminine or masculine mythologies. The city of Rotterdam, the Netherlands, for example, highlights certain aspects of its masculine mythology while gender-bending it to fit a more feminine imagined future (see box below).

One of the models for these changes in Rotterdam is Vancouver, in Canada. Vancouver is often considered an international emblem for urban 'liveability'. The city was successful in attracting desired inhabitants to its urban core. Vancouver developed a gendered strategy to attract these groups: it built family-friendly housing in inner city neighbourhoods (Hutton, 2004). Imagineering Vancouver thus included a gendered message of family-life in the city. This narrative consisted of the necessity for many middle-class groups to combine work and care-duties. The gender equal ideals that underlie this, directed the spatial strategy to enhance the attractiveness of Vancouver for new inhabitants.

Paris is the quintessential feminine city. The eroticized mythology of nineteenth-century Paris is still highly visible. Paris was the city of revolution and pleasure and often symbolized by the figure of the prostitute or queen (Wilson, 1991). Despite Haussmann's and Napoleon's macho demolition of narrow streets in favour of the grand and uniform boulevards, Paris still uses its feminine mythology in today's city marketing. Paris' contemporary mythology consists of playful and theatrical images and of narratives of shopping and fashion. On the other hand, though, Paris (as New York and London) employs distinctly masculinist neoliberal techniques to enhance the cities' 'liveability'. In fact, Hubbard (2004) argues that neoliberal strategies such as urban revanchism and gentrification are always inherently masculine, often executed by 'city fathers', such as New York mayor Giulliani.

Rotterdam: From Muscleman to Pink Stilettos

Rotterdam is the second largest city of the Netherlands. Its economy was dependent on the large harbour and related industries for the better part of the nineteenth and twentieth century. Rotterdam now attempts to introduce a new economy: one that is service-based and post-industrial. For this purpose, it imagineers a distinct *feminine* mythology. According to the city marketing bureau, Rotterdam suffers from a *masculine*, industrial image that needs adjustment in order to become the 'creative city' it aspires to be. The working-class mythology of Rotterdam has many 'masculine' features, such as the figure of the muscleman.

This was the main reason that the festival 'La City' was organized in 2008. 'La City' was a month-long chain of events in fashion, music, dancing, arts, sports and dining. But, importantly, it was a national marketing endeavour to highlight the 'feminine side' of Rotterdam. This 'feminine side' was symbolized in narratives of Rotterdam as temptress, pictures of stiletto shoes, cocktails and pink promotional material. This hyper-feminine imagery was used to balance the hyper-masculine mythology of the Rotterdam muscled worker.

The festival was designed to cleanse the city of this *working-class* mythology that was thought to mitigate innovations. The aspired new economy is to replace the lost jobs for men in the harbour and industry by new jobs for men and women in tourism, healthcare and creative industries. Blue collars are to be replaced by pink collars; masculine 'work' by, slightly exaggerated, feminine 'professions'. The old myth of the 'working ethos' of the city is adjusted to fit a new mythology of doing and daring and is adjusted to fit new strategies. Myths that were once compatible parts of the masculine mythology are now rearranged and juxtaposed: the 'working city' is a 'daring city' that moves 'beyond the harbour' and can ultimately even change its gender.

Source: van den Berg, 2012

The Sexed City

Sex sells. City marketers know how to use sexual images to sell places like any other product. A sexualized mythology communicates excitement and the fulfilment of desire. For Amsterdam, in the Netherlands, the sex industry of the Red Light District is an important asset in attracting tourists. As Wonders and Michalowski (2001) showed, city officials do not support the marketing of sex tourism in any open way. Nevertheless, the commodification of bodies in sex tourism plays an important part in the city's libertine youthful mythology and thereby creates revenue for the city. Another example of the sexualized selling of places is the marketing of Iceland that today uses a myth of the promiscuous Icelandic Supermodel in addition to the more traditional marketing of natural attractions. Reykjavik, in this new sexualized mythology, appears as the 'erotic party city' (Alessio and Jóhannsdóttir, 2011).

Arguably the most influential scholar in the field of urban economies today is Richard Florida. His analyses of successful cities have focused on creativity and diversity. According to Florida (2002), for cities to attract the much desired creative classes, they need diversity, and the way in which Florida measures diversity in his empirical studies is by measuring the amount of inhabitants that identify themselves as being gay or lesbian. Notwithstanding much critique on these measurements and fundamental problems with equating diversity with sexual orientation (for an overview see Hubbard, 2006), these analyses have led to cities aiming to attract gay inhabitants and gearing their city marketing towards this goal. It seems that what cities are after when seducing gays (and mostly gay men) is in reality a group of inhabitants that is interested in conspicuous consumption (Bell and Binnie, 2004; Hubbard, 2006).

Binnie and Skeggs (2004) showed how in Manchester (UK), 'gay space' came to be marketed as a cosmopolitan spectacle. With cosmopolitanism as a heavily classed concept, the gay cosmopolitan figure was used to make space in Manchester appear less threatening and more desirable for a wider and straight audience. In general, the more overtly sexual aspects of the gay communities of Manchester were under-communicated, and what was considered 'cosmopolitan' over-communicated. Difference could therefore be consumed in a safe imaged cosmopolitan experience. However, only a certain 'respectable' amount of difference was considered cosmopolitan and desirable (Binnie and Skeggs, 2004).

Amongst the many cities that have sought to include gay communities, San Francisco sees itself as the 'gay capital of the world'. In many ways, San Francisco was the frontier of non-conformist sexual lifestyles, at least since the 1950s and 1960s (Duyvendak, 2011). As the destination for many young gay men and women leaving home in the past decades, San Francisco is and was home to many gays seeking refuge from homophobic societies. This sexed identity is incorporated in the city's marketing and strategies to enhance tourism. As Duyvendak (2011) noted: 'tourism to San Francisco in large part depended on the city's libertine image'. In local protests against mainstream society's influences in the gay neighbourhood the Castro, this imagery is even given the language of mythology: 'The Castro has a kind of "mythic regard" overseas, and we are the "guardians" of this place for future generations' ('Save the Castro', quoted in Duyvendak, 2011).

Both Manchester and San Francisco are examples of how gay communities are used in the image of a city. The imagineering of gay space in both cities reflects social conflict about sexuality. In Manchester, the cosmopolitan gay that is interested in conspicuous consumption is embraced by the straight visitor, and in San Francisco, the Castro-dwellers struggle to prevent their neighbourhood from being swallowed by 'mainstream' society. The inclusion of homosexuality in the image of the city produces space for gays and empowerment on the one hand, while on the other mainstreaming and commodifying it. Presenting a city as cosmopolitan because of a highly visible gay community can thus produce highly exclusionary effects when the aspects that appear threatening to the mainstream audience are still seen as social problems.

THE CITY MOVES

Images freeze movement, demonstrating choice. Once sights are set in pictures, fleeting experience is stilled. Movement is not banished; rather, it appears residual, a memory of the process of fashioning the image, a reference to potentially disturbing spaces beyond the edges of pictures.

Susan Ossman (1994: 19)

The city moves. A mythology of the essence of a city is always a simplified package without multiple meanings. Of course, the inhabitants of cities do experience these 'under-communicated' (Selwyn, 1996) urban aspects. And urban dwellers live and work in the 'potentially disturbing spaces beyond the edges of pictures' (Ossman, 1994: 19). These urban inhabitants have lost the game of capturing the imagination of the ones making the choices, the battle to be seen. Sometimes they have been actively excommunicated for the abstract homogenous image that is to engineer the mythology of their city. As the examples of contemporary cities around the world in this chapter have shown, existing inequalities are almost always mirrored and reproduced through the rewriting of urban myths for place promotion. Imagineering produces places to play, but also puts 'places *in* play' (Sheller and Urry, 2004). Mythologies are ideologically potent narratives (Selwyn, 1996) and serve to legitimate practices of place-making and restructuring. Imagineering has very real effects. Choices are made to revitalize certain neighbourhoods while neglecting others, to build football stadiums instead of children's playgrounds, to invest in a marketing campaign while leaving inequalities intact.

The relationship between the production of imagery and the dynamics of the city is a balancing act with winners and losers. Cities can win or lose, as can inhabitants. For some cities, imagineering is an especially difficult task because of persistent narratives of violence, and dystopian urban images. Neill (2001) has shown the challenge of producing a narrative against the odds of being the most violent city in a country, resulting in the incorporation and aestheticization of at least some aspects of violence. The examples above have shown how imagineering can turn out to be unsuccessful because of a lack of fit between the experienced urban reality of inhabitants and visitors and the presented mythology. Urban mythologies prove to be durable. Berlin may want to present itself as a cultural hub of diversity today, but it cannot escape its heavy history altogether (Weiss-Sussex, 2006).

Inhabitants of cities can win or lose in imagineering too, for example when they are displaced to make room for a theme park in China (Ren, 2007) or are not deemed 'creative' enough in the West. In this chapter, special attention was given to the inclusion of identity politics in the production of difference and of unique selling points for cities. Sexuality, gender and ethnicity prove to be reservoirs of meaning for urban marketers. Sometimes, these strategies can be empowering for certain groups of inhabitants, as the example of the gay villages has shown (see above). Inhabitants whose identity resembles aspects of the new urban myth can experience new opportunities, just as it excludes others. In any case, city marketing is often the result of a struggle for meaning as much as it mirrors existing power (im)balances. The in- and exclusions that imagineering produces should be at the centre of attention in the investigation of imagineering practices. Moreover, more research should be conducted on the relationship between urban identities and the way in which inhabitants understand themselves.

Cities are charismatic entities (Blom Hansen and Verkaaik, 2009). The soul of the city is incorporated by its people. A mythology that is larger than all individuals and all campaigns is fed by imagineering practices just as it is by the everyday social construction of reality in the urban streets and squares. Changing the mythology of the city changes how its inhabitants understand themselves.

11

Inclusivity

Edgar Pieterse

Today, about 85% of all new employment opportunities around the world occur in the informal economy and young people in slums are more likely to work in the informal sector than their non-slum peers. Despite some advantages, informal employment ends up trapping slum-dwelling and other low-income young people in perpetual poverty. Unfortunately, slum areas remain a 'blind spot' when it comes to policy interventions, job creation and youth support. (UN-Habitat, 2010a: xiv)

The World Urban Forum convened in Rio de Janeiro in March 2010, drawing together over 18,000 urbanists from across the globe to discuss 'the right to the city – bridging the urban divide'. It is noteworthy that this event convened two weeks after the international media's attention was drawn to the Forbes World Billionaire list, a publicity gimmick that is nonetheless very revealing about the grotesque nature of inequality.[1] Forbes proclaimed that '... the World's Billionaires have an average net worth of $3.5 billion, up $500 million in 12 months. The world has 1,011 10-figure titans, up from 793 a year ago [...] Of those billionaires on last year's list, only 12% saw their fortunes decline' (Miller and Kroll, 2010). This exclusive club accounts for a larger share of the global GDP than all the low-income economies combined, where one third (2.6 billion) of the global population resides – a fact conveniently omitted from the Billionaire list announcement. Furthermore, the Forbes list ignores the reality that economic exclusion is a structural feature of the global economy – the same economy that can generate a US$500 million net worth increase in the midst of the worst economic recession in a hundred years. This effectively means that inequality and economic exclusion is likely to persist.

It is intriguing that against this backdrop, the dominant policy discourse at the World Urban Forum was one of rights and over-coming urban divides. Furthermore, the *State of the World Cities 2010/2011* report of UN-Habitat more specifically foregrounds urban inequality as the primary source of poverty and exclusion from 'the benefits of urban advantage' (UN-Habitat, 2010a: 15). The focus on urban inequality

---

1 Miller, M. and L. Kroll (2010) World's Billionaires 2010, Forbes.com, p. 1. http://finance.yahoo.com; accessed 11 March 2010.

is a significant shift away from a 'poverty alleviation' discourse that was more prominent in earlier mainstream policy statements on advancing urban inclusion (UNDP, 1991; World Bank, 1991, 2000). Furthermore, given that the 'right to the city' discourse stems from the Marxist oeuvre of Henri Lefebvre (Merrifield, 2002; Gilbert and Dikeç, 2008), it is particularly interesting to explore whether the ground has been prepared for radical interventions to advance inclusion versus the traditional focus on ameliorative urban public policy. In this chapter, I will explore fascinating policy trajectories in the South and North pertaining to agendas about how best urban inclusion can be advanced at the urban scale. I will tell a story of very different contexts and policy responses but also one that suggests a greater degree of convergence in thinking and practice, especially in middle-income countries in the South. An interesting question to then pose is whether this convergence stems from a shared understanding of the drivers of urban poverty and inequality, which are increasingly beyond local administrative boundaries as economic fortunes are tied to globalized value chains and systems of production and consumption. I will restrict my focus to OECD and middle-income countries, given the vast field of consideration.

The next part of the chapter provides a brief sketch of urban poverty and inequality trends in different regions of the world, drawing on the latest sources of UN-Habitat and the OECD. The trends discussion is followed by an exploration of why urban inclusion is important and how different scholars and diverse constituencies understand it. This leads into sections that draw together the contemporary mainstream public policy agenda in the South and the North before teasing out similarities and differences across cities to understand whether there is a convergence or divergence in responses across cities.

URBAN POVERTY AND INEQUALITY

A World Bank report was released in 2007 that provides a more accurate picture of the prevalence of urban and rural poverty between 1993 and 2002, based on data for 90 countries (Ravallion et al., 2007). According to this study, in terms of $1-a-day income poverty measure, the urban share increased more rapidly than the level of urbanization between 1993 and 2002. However, in terms of the $2-a-day poverty measure, this was not the case. One conclusion to draw is that it is erroneous to

Table 11.1 Urban and rural income poverty, 1993 and 2002

		Number of poor (millions)			% of developing world's population below each poverty line			Urban share of the poor (%)
		Urban	Rural	Total	Urban	Rural	Total	
$1 a day	1993	236	1,036	1,272	13.5	36.6	27.8	18.5
	2002	283	883	1,165	12.8	29.3	22.3	24.2
$2 a day	1993	683	2,215	2,898	39.1	78.2	63.3	23.6
	2002	746	2,097	2,843	33.7	69.7	54.4	26.2

Source: Ravallion et al. (2007: 16)

talk about a generalized urbanization of poverty (DESA, 2008). Nevertheless, the $1-a-day trend line is of course cause for grave concern, especially if one considers the absolute numbers of people implicated.

However, there is general recognition that an income-based measure of poverty is wholly inadequate to get a rounded understanding of the experience of poverty and, more importantly, how households may move in and out of poverty over time (Beall, 2004; Moser, 2008). As signalled at the outset, in the last few years the question of intra-urban inequality has come to the fore to understand the ways in which it drives structural poverty. The focus on inequality leads to a consideration of the broader urban opportunity structure, in addition to income, to understand the possible pathways out of exclusion. The recent data on patterns of income inequality using the Gini coefficient measure is telling.

Urban inequality is the central concern of the UN-Habitat *State of the World's Cities Report*, published in 2010, which is useful for my purposes here. I will draw heavily on its findings because it represents the most comprehensive overview of urban inequality trends. The report admits that data on urban inequality is tricky because most countries collect inequality data at a national level and often researchers have to extrapolate urban dynamics. This can be problematic because inequality in rural areas tends to be lower than in urban areas. To respond to the problem of a lack of inequality data at the city scale, UN-Habitat undertook its own primary research to measure income and consumption inequality in a select number of cities in each of the major regions of the world. The following quote from its report summarizes the findings for these regions and references the number of cities that formed its sample:

> African cities appear to be the most unequal in the world (sample of 37 cities with an average Gini coefficient of 0.58). Next come Latin American cities (24 cities, with a Gini average of 0.52). Asian cities (30) feature a comparatively low degree of income inequality, as measured by a Gini coefficient of 0.384. Eastern Europe (8) and CIS cities (10) feature the lowest average Gini values and, presumably, the greatest degrees of equality, at 0.298 and 0.322, respectively. (UN-Habitat, 2010a: xiii)

The report continues to discuss the trends in the North as well. Interestingly, data is available for most American cities but not European ones. Overall, the report finds that inequality has worsened in the developed world between the mid-1980s and 2005, although not as dramatic as some commentators may suggest. A report by UNRISD (2010) confirms that in some developed countries inequality has in fact declined over this period. However, the United States is a different story. There, significant discrepancies exist between rural areas. 'The most surprising variations between national and city-specific Gini coefficients of income or consumption disparities are found in the United States of America, where around 2005 the national coefficient stood at 0.38, but exceeded 0.5 in many major metropolitan areas including Washington, D.C.; New York City; Miami; and others' (UN-Habitat, 2010a: xii). This puts urban inequality in the same league as some Latin American cities, which is significant.

A really important and useful argument made by the *State of the World's Cities Report* pertains to spatial inequality. Spatial inequality refers to the differential access that different groups in the city have to a range of urban opportunities and resources. UN-Habitat suggests that the dynamics of land markets and various barriers between the rich and the poor in the city often compound urban poverty. Thus: 'Combined, the physical and social distance between poor and rich neighbourhoods represents a spatial poverty trap marked by six distinct challenges: (a) severe job restrictions; (b) high rates of gender disparities; (c) deteriorated living conditions; (d) social exclusion and marginalization; (e) lack of social interaction, and (f) high incidence of crime' (UN-Habitat, 2010a: xiii). Unsurprisingly then, the report finds that in cities with very high levels of slum prevalence (discussed below), the prospects of new entrants into the labour market landing a formal job is very slim indeed. This is related to the fact that 'about 85 per cent of all new employment opportunities around the world occur in the informal economy and young people in slums are more likely to work in the informal sector than their non-slum peers' (UN-Habitat, 2010a: xiv). This is a good point at which to consider the final aspect of this context-setting section: the prevalence of slums.

The critical indicator of urban poverty in the South is slum living and the depth of deprivation as measured against the five-fold criteria of slum living. According to UN-Habitat, a slum household is defined as a group of individuals living under the same roof lacking one or more of the following conditions: access to improved water; access to improved sanitation facilities; sufficient living area (not more than three people sharing the same room); structural quality and durability of dwellings; and security of tenure. The first four aspects all measure physical expressions of slum conditions. The fifth indicator – security of tenure – has to do with legality, which is not as easy to measure or monitor, as the tenure status of slum dwellers often depends on *de facto* or *de jure* rights – or lack of them (UN-Habitat, 2008: 92). The key issue here is that slum prevalence indicates the scale of basic deprivation, which is an important aspect that drives how urban inclusion is facilitated. Within that, the role and function of land tenure security is a particularly important indicator.

Table 11.2 Proportion of the urban population living in slums (%)

	1990	2000	2007	2010
Developing regions	46.1	39.3	34.3	32.7
North Africa	34.4	20.3	13.4	13.3
Sub-Saharan Africa	70	65	62.4	61.7
Latin America and the Caribbean	33.7	29.2	24.7	23.5
Eastern Asia	43.7	37.4	31.1	28.2
Southern Asia	57.2	45.8	38	35
Western Asia	22.5	20.6	25.2	24.6
Oceania	24.1	24.1	24.1	24.1

Source: UN-Habitat (2010a: 9)

This section clarified that urban poverty and inequality – two critical drivers of urban exclusion – remain pervasive, especially in the global south. Urban poverty is most starkly reflected in the widespread prevalence of informal shelter conditions or slums, in the parlance of UN-Habitat. The stubborn persistence of slums has much to do with the spatial enactment of inequality, which makes it very difficult for the urban poor to access urban opportunities that may lead to an improvement in living conditions. However, the more important issue is what lies beneath these trends. I will now explore this theme through a focus on the terms of urban exclusion/inclusion before a more in-depth exploration of various agendas to advance greater urban inclusion.

THE TERMS OF URBAN INCLUSION

There seems to be almost universal agreement in the literature (across paradigmatic and disciplinary lines) that the dramatic changes in the global economy stemming from the information and telecommunications revolution of the 1970s have produced more pronounced lines of segregation, exclusion and inequality between classes. These effects are manifested most viscerally in spatial terms in the contemporary dynamics of urban development. At the core of these trends is the intense valourization of high-end knowledge economy or service jobs against the devalourization of low-end, low-skill employment categories (Sassen, 1997a). With the growth of the contribution of new forms of economic activity (related to financial markets and services) that are delinked from material economic output and consumption, the locus of economic aspiration and comparative advantage has shifted, with profound implications for public policy. With the continuous rise in the share of financial-related services, enabled by a 24/7 electronic trading system across time zones, it has become possible to grow economic output without necessarily increasing the level of labour market participation. In fact, some economists point to a phenomenon of 'jobless growth', which represents a disconnect between economic growth and employment generation.

There are critical consequences to these processes for the broader dynamic of urban exclusion. The first is that the significant growth of disposable income for the middle and elite classes has fuelled significant processes of re-spatialization of both residential areas and retail centres. From the 1980s onwards, we therefore witnessed, in both high-income and middle-income cities, the tendency for more elite and gated residential property stock, often further away from the traditional city centre and typically on the opposite geographical locations to where the poor reside. The consumption aspirations of the new middle-classes have generally fuelled suburban sprawl, combined with greater segregation between classes and more intensified efforts to securitize such settlements, linked in turn to all kinds of ecologies of fear (Caldeira, 2000; Marcuse, 2000). This has also been tied to speculative financial products, as evidenced in the sub-prime mortgage crises in the US that triggered the global recession of 2009 (Turok, 2011). These tendencies are in evidence in both cities of the North and South. It is significant to note how international consultancy firms see this emerging class of urban consumers as the most important growth market for multinational corporations seeking to grow their business (BCG, 2010b). Figure 11.1 illustrates how this burgeoning middle-class is quantified; it is obvious that the intense spatial divides bemoaned by UN-Habitat are only likely to intensify as these consumers enter the market.

The second consequence to these processes for the broader dynamic of urban exclusion is the intensification of cumulative disadvantage among individuals and communities who are cut off from the new economic activities or the redefined traditional industrial, manufacturing or low-end service jobs. It is particularly new entrants into the labour market from these areas that experience structural exclusion from urban economic and political processes. Their marginality was intensified by various forms of state withdrawal from daily life and social reproductive processes as neoliberal policy reforms became hegemonic and widespread during the 1980s and well into the 1990s, with a severe hangover in evidence in many cities across the world – even though crude neoliberalism has been roundly critiqued and exposed.

In high-income countries with well established welfare regimes, rising levels of urban exclusion was defined as a policy issue to be dealt with through revised forms of social protection and an adaptation of traditional welfare regimes to discourage 'dependency' and encourage re-entry into the labour market (Turok, 2011). In middle-income countries, the prism of informality and the imperatives of regularizing informal settlements and facilitating pathways from informal to formal labour markets framed the challenge of urban inclusion. The question of social protection and targeted welfare regimes have only really come onto the

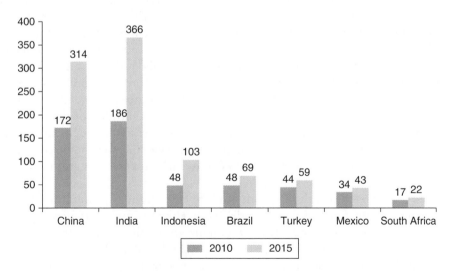

Figure 11.1   Middle-class populations of emerging cities' market growth, 2010–2015 (millions)

Source: adapted from BCG (2010b: 13)

agenda in the 1990s but even then framed by the imperatives of integrating people into regularized settlements (Tannerfeldt and Ljung, 2006). This chapter fore-grounds and emphasizes the inclusion debates in the context of cities in the global south before briefly rehearsing how some parallel debates have emerged in the north. The final section of the chapter concludes with a consideration of possible convergences between debates and issues on inclusion inbetween the two stylized geographies.

URBAN INCLUSION IN THE SOUTH

Empowerment, a synthetic work by John Friedmann, was published in 1992 and remains one of the most eloquent elaborations on various strands in development studies, planning and urban development literatures on how to understand the systemic processes of large-scale poverty and economic exclusion in cities of the South. This work draws together the vital ideas of Brazilian theorist Paulo Freire, who elaborated the field of critical pedagogy to capture the imperative of a psy-cho-social transition in which poor people come to terms with how their own cultures and values, shaped by dominant ideologies, reinforce their marginal status in society. Friedmann extends the insight about individual psychic transitions into a broader social transition (i.e. collective subjectivity) as manifested in the rise of social movements in the virulent 1960s and 1970s, to recover a radical sense of critical agency that has to be at the core of empowerment (Giroux, 1994). Cru-cially, in Friedmann's approach he actively seeks to critique and dispel the populist and anarchist claims of radical development theorists who regard the state as inherently anti-poor and exploitative. And premised on such assumptions, he argues that movements of the poor need to focus on retaining their autonomy and elide the state as much as possible. In this move, he identified a paradoxical conflu-ence in attitude towards the state among pro-market neoliberal advocates of state withdrawal and minimalism and radical exponents of autonomous movements. Instead, Friedmann (1992, 1996) insists that the only viable poverty reduction approach must place the state at the centre of urban reform measures. This line of argument about the 'developmental' role of the state has been extended and refined most recently by Peter Evans (2008). The focus on the centrality of the state pro-vides a fascinating precursor to recent efforts by mainstream development agencies such as the World Bank (2007, 2009) and other development economists (Stiglitz, 2008) to foreground the importance of effective and responsive states to poverty reduction efforts.

At the same time, Friedmann's work also pre-empted the vast literature that has accumulated around the idea of sustainable livelihoods and asset-based poverty reduction measures that arguably have dominated the urban development litera-ture over the past 15 years (Mitlin, 2000; Rakodi, 2002; Beall, 2004; Moser, 2008). In the extensive discussion on the economic realities of the urban poor in *Empowerment*, Friedmann also manages to pull together and extend the parallel literatures on informality in cities of the South. The 'whole economy' model that is presented by Friedmann prefigures the post-structural elaboration by Gibson-Graham (1996) and the more recent forays into social economies (Amin, 2010) in literatures focused on economic inclusion pertaining to both northern and southern economies.

In these senses, *Empowerment* represents an important milestone in a large and diverse literature on the drivers of urban exclusion and poverty and possible ways of thinking about how to respond not only to ameliorate poverty but to strive to transcend it. Three critical themes can be identified to crystallize the various strands in the debates on urban exclusion and inclusion: moving from a narrow to an expanded conception of urban poverty; appreciating the centrality of the political voice in advancing the interests of the poor while also consolidating it in routine decision-making and execution practices of the state; and recognizing the constitutive nature of informality in the lives and daily practices of the urban poor.

From Income-Poverty to Livelihoods

Mainstream urban development policy, until the late 1980s, was attached to an income-based understanding of poverty proliferated by the World Bank's $1- and $2-a-day benchmarks. These measures remain profoundly influential but, after a sustained critique throughout the 1970s and 1980s, have lost their intellectual currency. This critique received impetus in the wake of the 1982 debt crises and the subsequent social consequences that stemmed from the raft of indiscriminate structural adjustment policies that were implemented across the world in both northern and southern contexts, but with much more severe impacts in the South because of limited or non-existent social safety nets (Mitlin, 2000). Thus, in a critique of income-based poverty measures, Rakodi argued for poverty policies to be '... informed by an understanding of the ways in which households cope, adapt and manage in deteriorating economic situations, in circumstances of personal adversity and in response to opportunities to improve their well-being so that it supports rather than damages the efforts of the poor to help themselves' (2004: 100). It was against this imperative for a more rounded understanding of the living conditions and coping mechanisms of the urban poor that the 'livelihoods' literature emerged, adapted from rural development contexts and reworked to better define and understand practices of the urban poor (Wratten, 1995; Moser, 2008).

At the core of the livelihoods and asset-based models of understanding poverty is the idea that all poor households have a portfolio of assets – physical, financial, human, social and natural capital – that they continuously manage to simultaneously mitigate risks (to reduce vulnerability) and improve or enlarge their assets. Furthermore, these frameworks locate the relative capacity of poor households to access and deploy their asset endowments within a larger set of structural and institutional factors, e.g. exposure to unforeseen shocks and disasters, the nature and functioning of various levels of government, the impacts of laws, policies, cultural norms and institutions (Beall, 2004). The argument thus follows that until poverty is understood in all of these dimensions, it fails to engage with the structural and subjective dimensions of the problem (Rakodi, 2002; Satterthwaite et al., 2003; Pieterse, 2008a).

This approach was broadly reinforced with the rise of the social capital literature and policy movements in the 1990s because it provided a more in-depth elaboration of the social dimension of the asset portfolio (Wilson, 1995; Storper, 2005). Social assets were also seen as the critical element that required poor households to cooperate with other actors to achieve more effective power in engaging the various institutions and systems that circumscribe livelihoods. In this sense, many of the livelihood advocates saw an easy and obvious alignment between the ideas of civil society empowerment that were on the ascendency in the 1980s (culminating in the collapse of the Berlin wall in 1989) and the concept of social capital. This alignment could offer an explanatory framework for why and when households may aggregate into social formations and how they can be effective. The social capital literature foregrounded concepts like trust, reciprocity and mutuality (Putnam, 1993). But it was precisely on the question of 'the social' and its relations to broader power dynamics that served as the basis for criticisms of this bottom-up, pro-civil society package of concepts and approaches to dealing with urban poverty.

A number of radical scholars who draw on Marxist and/or Foucauldian deconstructive techniques to understand new forms of governmentality[2] (often inflected by Gramscian readings of hegemony) suggested that the growing emphasis on the 'empowerment' of civil society and withdrawal of the state from the domains of social and economic reproduction was simply too convenient to be unrelated (Miraftab, 2004). At the core of these criticisms was a suggestion that the growing emphasis on civil society autonomy slides too easily into a self-help and 'self-responsibilization' discourse that allowed a contracting neoliberal state to get off the hook in terms of its basic obligations to provide a decent quality of life for all citizens (Cornwall and Brock, 2005). For these scholars, the financialization of everyday social and cultural domains through the 'capitals' framework of the livelihoods literature is further vindication that these discourses seek to extend an economic rationale to all domains of life, which at its most fundamental level, reinforces a market and commoditized outlook on life (Fine, 1999). This particular debate has been almost equally prevalent in both the North and the South during the past decade (Geddes, 2005; Harrison, 2006).

Through a reworking of advances in political theory building on the work of Foucault, the concept of neoliberal governmentality has become fashionable as an approach to deconstruct and critique 'buzz words' such as participation and empowerment (Cornwall and Brock, 2005). In a provocatively entitled essay, 'Making Neoliberal Governance: The Disempowering Work of Empowerment', Miraftab (2004)

---

2 Governmentality is a Foucauldian concept, which refers 'to the complex array of techniques – programs, procedures, strategies and tactics – employed by both non-state administrative agencies and state institutions to shape conduct of individuals and populations' (Gabardi, 2001: 82).

makes an important argument for my purposes here. She asserts that for all the reference to, and promotion of, participatory democracy and empowerment in post-apartheid South Africa, one should be cautious to take the formal discourses and attendant policy frameworks at face value. According to Miraftab, a set of radical and transformative discourses such as community participation, empowerment and social capital have been turned into depoliticizing 'tools of the trade for governments [and] establishments such as the World Bank' (Miraftab, 2004: 239). The key challenge in the contemporary moment is to understand how this (re)appropriation has taken place. This requires an appreciation of how neoliberal reforms have involved economic liberalization along with public sector reforms to bring market forces and dynamics to the challenges of service delivery. As a consequence of these reform processes, state budgets for social wage expenditures are reduced and private sector actors are brought into the realm of public services through privatization. As a consequence, public services have been thoroughly commoditized and all those who use a service must pay the full market value for that service irrespective of economic position. In societies with already high levels of inequality and exclusion, this essentially means that those who cannot afford to pay are cut off from public support. To soften this hard and unforgiving core of the neoliberal agenda, it is necessary, ideologically, to make this problem of exclusion an individual one as opposed to a collective or societal one. Following this line of critique, Miraftab suggests that her case studies reveal how:

> Participation and empowerment are treated as independent of the structures of oppression, and simply processes by which programs foster individuals' sense of worth and esteem. This individualization inherently depoliticizes the notion of empowerment, often reducing it to individual economic gain and access to resources, and leaving the status quo unchallenged. (Miraftab, 2004: 242)

Predictably, Miraftab argues that we must look beyond the rhetoric in its own terms but rather start 'paying attention to the post-apartheid government's efforts to *tame* community participation and *control* the claims of citizens on the state' (2004: 253, emphasis added). This seam of analysis appears in her other studies and in a growing body of literature that explores community-level protests against municipal authorities across South Africa but always cross-referenced with similar dynamics in both the North and the South (e.g. McDonald and Pape, 2002; Bond, 2003). I have offered a critique of this reading elsewhere (Pieterse, 2008b) but for now want to simply draw attention to the fact that South Africa has demonstrated contradictory tendencies. On the one hand, there has been an intensified managerialism in the organization and functioning of the state, which includes a number of new public management reforms; on the other hand, the state has also introduced and expanded a range of social welfare and basic service subsidies to effect greater urban inclusion (see box below). Many of the scholars that work with the governmentality analytical frame often fail to account for these contradictory dynamics.

Social Security and Other Redistributive Instruments in South Africa[3]

South Africa does not have comprehensive social security for the unemployed but it does provide a number of other social security benefits, tabulated here by category and number of beneficiaries in 2009:

Table 11.3   Types and number of social grant beneficiaries, 2009

Grant	Number of Beneficiaries (2009)
State old-age pension	2,343,995
Disability grant	1,371,712
Child support grant	8,765,354
Foster care grant	476,394
Care dependency grant	107,065
War veterans grant	1,599
Total	**13,066,119**

In addition to these social security grants, the government has an extensive programme to facilitate access to basic services for the poor. Thus each municipality is required to have an indigents register to administer the following subsidies:

- Free basic water: 6kl (6,000 litres) per month per household;

- Free electricity: 50kWh per month per household for a grid energy system;

- Free sanitation: 100% of rate/charge if household income is below a certain level;

- Housing subsidies: since 1994, more than 2.3 million housing units have been made available for almost 11 million people. The value of these subsidies has increased in recent years after it failed to keep pace with inflation between 1996 and 2002. The subsidy translates into a transfer of a serviced house and title to the beneficiaries. Due to the cost of the programme, there remains a considerable waiting list but on average approximately 300,000 of these subsidies are disbursed per annum;

- Transport subsidies are made available for people who use the bus and rail public transport modes.

POLITICAL ENROLMENT AND VOICE

At the centre of the disputed academic appreciation of the significance of a growing emphasis on the role of civil society in urban governance, are divergent conceptions of the nature of the state, politics, political power and institutionalization. It is well beyond the scope of this chapter to tease through all of these differences but it is

---

3 Drawn from Bosch et al. (2010).

relevant to briefly touch on competing views on the institutional enrolment of the urban poor to address more effective urban inclusion.

The past decade has been marked by a definite optimism about the proliferation of democratic reforms, including mechanisms to enrol urban majorities into urban planning, management and political processes (Pieterse, 2008a). The emblematic case is Brazil where, through the introduction in 2001 of the City Statute, a raft of institutional mechanisms has been introduced to consolidate and expand a grass-roots-driven urban democratization process. Certain progressive cities in Brazil were known for their experiments with participatory budgeting instruments in the 1990s (Abers, 2000). These experiments, along with planning reform and the establishment of participatory sectoral councils in cities, came together in the provisions of the Statute of Cities in 2001 (Menegat, 2002; Fernandes, 2010). Since then, there has been concerted effort to experiment with practical institutional mechanisms to expand the opportunity structure for the urban poor in many Brazilian cities. Provisional assessments of these experiments in a more participatory democracy that can potentially influence the power over decision-making about scarce urban resources such as infrastructure investment priorities and land are mixed. Fernandes (2010) suggests that a number of interesting and challenging dynamics have emerged.

Firstly, it is clear that a tension develops over time between scales of planning and deliberation. The participatory budgeting system often allows community groups to deliberate over competing priorities at the local level but without reference to how this impacts at the city-wide scale. This is exacerbated by the absence of metropolitan government in Brazil. Most importantly, local investments could have a detrimental overall impact at the city-wide level over time. Secondly, new institutional mechanisms had to be created to address the fact that people in one local area did not understand or appreciate the importance and significance of the needs of another community in a different part of the city, which then led to the establishment in some areas of a so-called 'Caravan of Priorities'. These caravans involved people from one community travelling to another to learn first-hand about their issues and challenges in order to moderate their own claims. Thirdly, there has been a reluctance to clarify what is considered optimal outcomes of these processes, which made it difficult to explore impacts of the mechanisms and priorities in terms of mundane general aspects that enable effective urban management, e.g. 'economic efficiency, fiscal balance and administrative rationality' (Fernandes, 2010: 293). Finally, and most importantly, Fernandes (2010: 298) regards the biggest shortcoming of the participatory democratic experiment lies in the fact that 'they have not called into question the exclusionary nature of the overall land and urban development model, especially in that they have not significantly supported the strengthening of a more inclusive framework for land governance'. Participatory budgeting and associated instruments in Brazil, and increasingly a number of other countries, is probably the most visible frontier of democratic reform to enrol the urban poor in a meaningful way into urban governance and management processes but it is by no means the only mechanism. For a comprehensive and critical review of other experiments in democratic engagement, consult the works of Pieterse (2000), Fung and Wright (2003), Manor (2004), Williams (2004), G. Gaventa (2006) and de Souza Briggs (2009).

In a review of a range of urban democratization and participatory instruments – devolution of powers to local councils, the creation of 'user committees' in development programmes, direct engagement by government of enlightened civil society actors, inducing more competition among elites for support by poor groups – James Manor (2004) underscores how difficult it is in practical terms to overcome the systemic political weakness of the least well off. The learning from Brazil, the insights of Manor and the theorization by Cornwall (2004) and G. Williams (2004), all suggest we need to think in more differentiated and relational terms about the effective empowerment of the urban poor. This means going beyond the simplistic pitting of enrolment in development projects (seen as reactionary and a form of co-option), versus direct action by social movements of the poor (seen as transformative and radical). The relative power of the urban poor depends on the active articulation of diverse political moments and strategies to continuously enlarge their claims on urban resources and autonomy over the deployment of such resources (Pieterse, 2005). A fine-grained understanding of scale, symbolic economies and coalition-building should underpin such an approach, as cogently argued by Garth Myers (2011).

ATTENUATING INFORMALITY

Given that the majority of employment and shelter opportunities for urban citizens are in the informal domain, it is fair to assume that the most vital dimension of inclusivity in cities of the South is to focus on various means to attenuate informality. A substantial part of the scholarship on cities in the South focuses on informal settlements and their gradual formalization or consolidation. This is a vast and often technocratic literature. Another body of work focuses on informal employment and enterprise. I will now briefly distil the key dimensions of these literatures because they go to the heart of how inclusion is envisaged in cities of the global south.

The fundamental feature of most of these cities is large-scale informalization in terms of shelter conditions as evidenced in the UN-Habitat data on slums presented above. One strand in the literature adopts a very practical and often technocratic approach and explores the most efficacious ways to upgrade the dwellings and the settlements in which slums are embedded so that a gradual process of formalization and consolidation can occur. At the heart of this literature is a focus on tenure security and various financial instruments to support the efforts of the poor to gradually improve and securitize their dwellings (Tannerfeldt and Ljung, 2006). However, it is recognized that insecurity of tenure presents an insurmountable obstacle to investment and formalization. Critical scholars take a different tack. They argue that the over-emphasis on the practical procedures of gradual reform to persuade urban elites to grant or extend tenure security and housing support detracts from the underlying structural drivers that produce the prevalence of slums in the first place. These drivers are highly unequal access to capital, reinforced by an urban land market and accumulation dynamic that rewards the investments of those with capital and assets, further skewing wealth distributions and making it impossible to unlock the resources and land that can be transferred to the urban poor. In this reading, it serves the interests of the elites to keep land markets highly concentrated and out of reach of the urban poor and it is of course these very same elites who control political processes that determine subsidies, investments and regulation of land markets (Marcuse, 2000). Thus, for these scholars, it is more important to understand how the urban poor and marginalized can aggregate their potential political power and claim more entitlements, rights and control over public resources and private actions.

More recently, scholars such as Garth Myers (2011), are arguing for a synthesis of these polar approaches. Myers suggests it is important to acknowledge and recognize the pervasive nature of informal land and housing practices and markets with an eye on developing a much more fine-grained appreciation for diversity and specificity across informal or slum settlements. Furthermore, it is vital to bring the agency and efforts of ordinary people in their routine and banal activities into the analytical frame in order to decipher possible connecting points for more systemic interventions that work with the grain of improvized lives and livelihoods. A third move is then to explore how informal logics can best be articulated with formal systems in order to evolve, through democratic experimentation, new systems that can simultaneously address structural deprivations but also build onto the makeshift inventions of ordinary people (Myers, 2011).

On the economic front, the scholarly and policy interventions of Marty Chen provides the clearest articulation of how best informality can be understood, disaggregated and responded to positively. Chen (2008: 6) reminds us that 'Informal employment broadly defined, including self-employment in informal enterprises and wage employment in informal jobs, comprises two-quarters of total employment in development countries; three-quarters or more in South Asia and Sub-Saharan Africa; and around 60 per cent in the Middle East, North Africa, and Latin America.' However, in discussions on the informal sector, a lot of conflation occurs. Chen (2008) urges scholars and policy-makers to adopt a more rigorous differentiation

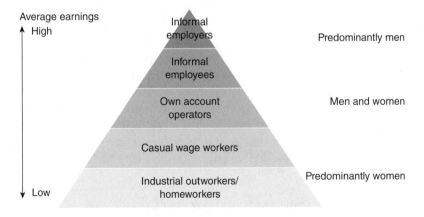

Figure 11.2 Segmentation of informal employment by average earnings and sex

Source: WIEGO in Chen (2008: 6)

Table 11.4   Integrated policy responses to informality

Segmentation of informal economy	Regulation	Protection	Promotion
Self-employment: micro enterprises, own account operations	Registration; licensing; corporate taxes	Commercial law; property rights; social protection	Price policies; procurement; sector policies; infrastructure and services
Wage employment: informal employees and casual day labourers	Labour regulations; payroll taxes; social security contributions	Minimum wages; non-wage benefits; social protection	Skills training; job matching

Source: WIEGO in Chen (2008: 7)

between various positions within the informal economy in terms of average earnings per employment category (see Figure 11.2). From this typology it is clear that we can expect significant gaps in earnings between informal employers and their employees, let alone home-workers. It would therefore be obvious that an effective policy response would need to be mindful of these economic and gendered differences.

Building on this differentiated analysis, Chen proceeds to develop a useful framework for how best to respond to informality (see Table 11.4). The one dimension allows recognition of the two main categories of informal employment – self-employment and wage-employment – read against the three main policy responses: regulation, protection and promotion. Regulation is typically where official government responses often end (Lindell, 2010) and then takes on the form of punitive regulation to discourage or eliminate informal economic activity. More benign regulation sees the informal economy as a stepping stone to formal economic life and, with the appropriate forms of regulation, maturation can gradually occur. The view of Chen and WIEGO [Women in Informal Employment: Globalizing and Organizing] is that this is a very narrow approach and unless regulation is treated in relation to policies that advance protection and promotion, it will be ineffective or retrogressive in terms of urban inclusion. Protection denotes the acknowledgement and protection of 'business, labour, and property rights of the working poor', with an eye on embedding it in a broader social protection agenda (UNRISD, 2010). Promotion includes a variety of measures to enhance the productivity of informal enterprises and the skills base of informal workers. Critically, however, all of these policy measures fundamentally depend on the level of organization and mobilization of the working poor so they can project a representative voice into the policy domain and continuously expand the bounds of official recognition and visibility (Chen, 2008; Lindell, 2010). A good example of an organized movement of the working poor is StreetNet, which represents hundreds of local and national informal workers' organizations in many African cities.

URBAN INCLUSION IN THE NORTH

The terms of urban inclusion and exclusion are very different in industrialized countries that form part of the OECD because of the prevalence of a relatively widely distributed set of social policies that are implemented by the welfare state, combined with a fundamentally different labour market structure. As opposed to the high levels of informal employment in the global south, most of the labour force is in formal jobs even though unemployment can spike during times of financial crisis (Adema and Ladaique, 2009). To be sure, the nature and scope of the welfare state across the OECD territories is by no means uniform or consistent but it still represents a much more generous and wide-ranging scope of social support mechanisms compared to what is available in most medium-income countries, let alone low-income contexts (ILO, 2010).

The literature identifies three categories of welfare state: 'the "institutional-redistributive" model [which] covers the principal risks of the entire population on the basis of the recognition of social rights'; 'the "residual" welfare model [in which] public protection is directed towards covering only those social groups in conditions of poverty and dire need'; and 'the "industrial-achievement performance" model [in which] insurance against principal risk is not based on a citizenship right but on occupational status' (Trigilia, 2002: 170). The first of these models is most clearly in evidence in the Scandinavian countries – Norway, Sweden and Denmark – that had a long-term confluence of powerful labour movements and left-wing government, at least until the late 1990s. The second model is most evident in the United States where public social protection is addressed at the poor and those in need with an assumption that private, contributory systems will take care of those in formal employment. The massive shortfall in healthcare coverage that animated public debate in recent times is a direct consequence of this approach. The third model typifies most of Western Europe with important national specificities (Trigilia, 2002).

Given that social policies cover a great diversity of 'cash benefits (e.g. pensions, income support during maternity leave and social assistance payments), social services (e.g. childcare, care for the elderly and disabled) and tax breaks with a social purpose (e.g. tax expenditures towards families with children or favourable tax treatment of contributions to private health plans)', it is dangerous to over-generalize (Adema and Ladaique, 2009: 9). What is clear across contexts is that the public welfare state and associated benefits have been under severe ideological and institutional stress since the 1980s. However, interestingly, in real terms there has actually been an increase in the share of social expenditure to GDP ratios across the OECD. This has been driven largely by pensions and public health expenditures that can be related to the ageing population in these societies. 'Gross public social expenditure on average across the OECD increased from 16% of GDP in the 1980s to 21% in 2005, of which public pensions (7% of GDP) and public health expenditure (6% of GDP) are the largest items' (Adema and Ladaique, 2009: 3).

The general thrust to reduce the role of the state in the provision of an ever-expanding social welfare bill found expression in the public policy shift away from universal welfare entitlements to a 'welfare-to-work' or 'workfare' approach. At the core of the welfare-to-work standpoint is the assumption that universal or targeted social security benefits creates dependency on state grants and over time this becomes unaffordable and creates a class of long-term unemployed people. In the 1990s, the welfare-to-work agenda was couched in an elaborate humanist

discourse of self-help and empowerment, which was interpreted by radical scholars as another expression of the governmentality efforts of neoliberal states that
sought to promote and entrench a 'self-responsibilization' discourse in society
(Peck, 1998; Convery, 2009). However, as Turok (2011) points out, there are
some justifiable issues to be addressed in the potential of welfare measures to sup-
press proactive job-seeking and other measures to transition, particularly unemployed people into various forms of active engagement, whether in formal jobs or
various categories of social economy work. Turok argues that the core issue is
whether the broader economy can be more inclusive, i.e. enhance job opportunity,
stronger workplace regulation and a higher minimum wage in order to reduce the
growing income gap. The latter matters because in a context of very low minimum wages, a lot of job seekers find it more convenient and preferable to draw
benefits than enter those occupations.

The shifts in the nature of the welfare state and the ideological framework about
the entitlement of citizens has given rise to a number of urban-centred social programmes that seek to address the spatial manifestation of exclusionary dynamics.
Thus, in the UK and various European cities, there has been a long-standing practice of area-based policies to facilitate access to particular public services, labour
market intelligence and community-based or driven social development processes
to facilitate integration into mainstream society (Moulaert, 2000). Area-based
approaches to address poverty and social exclusion stem from a policy analysis
that defines the problem of urban exclusion as rooted in institutional fragmentation between various government departments and agencies that seek to provide
services in these areas. Thus, area-based approaches promote and emphasize better
co-ordination and the institutional model of partnerships (Cochrane, 2000). This
involves partnerships between various public entities but also between state bodies
and the private sector and community organizations. Conservative political programmes employ these discourses to transfer public responsibilities back onto
society whereas more liberal ones seek to find a 'happy medium' between market-
based solutions, community responsibility and responsive government. However,
regulation theorists such as Frank Moulaert (2000) view these trends and discourses as an opportunity to advance a more radical agenda of civil society
empowerment, autonomy and partial control over local resources to promote
more endogenous approaches to integrated local development. They see 'integrated
area development' as the only viable way in which urban inclusion can be achieved
(Moulaert, 2000). This reverts us back to earlier debates regarding the various
dimensions that shape and inform the agenda of urban inclusion in both the North
and the South.

CONCEPTUAL AND POLICY CONVERGENCE?

The suggestion by UN-Habitat that the right to the city can be universally applied
in both the North and the South signals an important conceptual convergence
about how inclusion should be defined and promoted. In truth, the welfare state

model of social inclusion remains the preserve of northern countries but it is equally clear that a very significant debate about social protection measures is now firmly on the agenda of middle-income countries such as Brazil, Chile, Mexico, South Africa, India and Thailand (Barrientos, 2010; UNRISD, 2010). Social protection should be 'Protecting individuals and households during periods when they cannot engage in gainful employment or obtain enough income to secure their livelihoods' (UNRISD, 2010: 16). In least developing countries, the focus of inclusionary efforts remains centred on a basic needs agenda, i.e. providing access to essential services for the urban poor. This agenda is typically hinged onto a slum-improvement programme. It is interesting that middle-income countries, my main focus in this chapter, are exploring combinations of social protection measures, informal settlement upgrading and economic policies that seek to support and enhance informal economic activities. But across these diverse approaches, a number of shared research and policy themes are emerging.

Firstly, there is clearly an ascendency of institutional theory in planning (Healey, 2007), development theory (Evans, 2008) and debates in geography on 'recapturing democracy' (Purcell, 2008), as ways of thinking in more nuanced terms about civil society empowerment and engagement with the local state. Institutional theory has been central in development studies to demonstrate the centrality of the state to more endogenously based and driven development, especially if efforts are more interventionist. This marks a critical reversal of neoliberal ideas about the role of the state. In a related move, the role of urban planning and soft or differentiated regulatory practices has also emerged as a critical area of focus to substantiate how public interest objectives can be advanced along with socio-economic imperatives (UN-Habitat, 2009). Moreover, there is also a stronger recognition that the cultural and political fabric of public, private and civil society institutions matter a great deal for their capacity to collaborate and contest, work in an integrative fashion and address systemic exclusionary challenges that require long-term strategies that are broken into short-term actions (Lowndes, 2001; Hamann et al., 2009). This more nuanced reading of the institutional glue that holds multi-actor and multi-dimensional coalitions together in the interest of higher-order development goals is also forcing a reconsideration of the binary discourse on urban politics that has been overly dominant over the past two decades. Conceptual frames on relational politics and institutional embedding are clearly on the ascendency in both the South and the North (Pieterse, 2005; Storper, 2005).

Secondly, there is a clear convergence in the foregrounding of a rights-based normative framework for recalibrating the interactions between organized formations of the urban poor, the local state and other players in the local public sphere, especially organized private capital (Purcell, 2008; Parnell and Pieterse, 2010). As a result, for example, social movements in São Paulo have been able to combine participation in institutionalized participatory forums – housing councils – without foregoing their autonomous actions to occupy vacant buildings on the basis of asserting their 'right to the city centre' (Earle, 2009). In this way, they insist on greater inclusion by exploiting both participatory democratic institutions and extra-governmental symbolic spaces for claim-making. In thinking through the concrete procedural aspects of realizing particularly socio-economic rights and the right to the city, it becomes possible to consolidate and extend the advances in thought and policy of the past two decades in both the North and the South.

Thirdly, in the wake of the global financial crisis of 2008–2009 and the overwhelming informalization of labour markets in developing countries, there is a major discussion emerging around recasting the conceptual terms of urban economic life. On the one hand, competitiveness and productive robustness of city-regions are being recast to take account of climate change adaptation imperatives, increasingly being referenced under the banner of the green economy (Kamal-Chaoui and Roberts, 2009). On the other hand, calls are being made to recognize the growing centrality of the social economy (Amin, 2010). Long-standing research and advocacy on decriminalizing the informal sector is finding its way into new public discourses on recognizing and enhancing informal economic life, interestingly in both the North and the South (Jütting and de Laiglesia, 2009). Research and policy attention will turn increasingly to fundamentally broadened conceptualizations of more inclusive urban economic systems as the broader debates gain momentum on internalizing social and environmental costs into the life-cycle costing of privately produced goods and services. Ultimately, most scholars agree, urban inclusion is best secured through full employment and the prospect of decent work but in a world where very large proportions of the working age population can be discarded from the so-called formal economy, the challenge for establishing broad-based employment is severe.

Finally, there seems to be a convergence around the idea of needing to bring together and articulate diverse bodies of knowledge that includes the practices and affective sensibilities of ordinary people excluded from urban opportunities. This view is premised on the idea that without access to lived experiences of the city, which categories of excluded people have, it is impossible to conceive, let alone implement, effective inclusionary programmes. This suggests a profound methodological adaptation to understand how best to triangulate and nuance both quantitative, qualitative and participatory knowledge production approaches within a recognition that the co-production of intelligence for urban interventions are vital for successful application of urban inclusionary measures (Parnell et al., 2009).

IN CONCLUSION

This chapter has provided a high-level overview of poverty, inequality and slum conditions in cities across the world with an eye on understanding how structural urban exclusion is reproduced. The empirical entry point was set against a conceptual discussion about the socio-spatial effects of profound economic changes that have been sweeping most countries since the 1970s as globalized financial markets and a new international division of labour impacted on national and regional territories. These framing moves were used to explore how urban inclusion has been translated into policy discourses to address urban poverty, first in medium-income cities of the South and then with reference to cities of the North. The chapter closed with an exploration of critical convergences between the South and the North, which also points to a vital research agenda for better understanding how urban inclusion can be advanced. All in all, it remains to be seen whether the recent ascendency of the 'right to the city' discourse will accelerate transformative urban policies and practices or simply serve as a foil for the reproduction of the status quo.

12

Urban Economic Development and Environmental Sustainability

Mark Whitehead

INTRODUCTION: ON URBAN BINARIES AND ACTUALLY EXISTING URBAN SUSTAINABILITIES

As many chapters in this volume attest, in the contemporary era of neoliberal globalization, cities constitute key command-and-control-centres for economic activity of various kinds (Sassen, 2002, 2001; Brenner and Keil, 2006). While the centrality of cities to global economic life has been recognized for some time, their role in the disruption, regulation and maintenance of variously scaled environmental systems is only now starting to be discussed in a systematic way (see Girardet, 2006; Heynen et al., 2006; Marcotullio and McGranahan, 2007). This chapter is concerned with the opportunities and tensions that derive from the role of cities as hubs of economic development and environmental management. At the centre of the argument developed here is a realization that while the meeting of key economic and environmental imperatives within twenty-first century urban space provides opportunities for the development of innovative and inventive approaches to eco-developments of different kinds, it also exposes key, and often irreconcilable, contradictions between the priorities of different metropolitan constituencies. Consequently, by moving within and beyond the celebratory practices and rhetoric associated with accounts of green towns, eco-metropolises, urban ecological modernization, and sustainable urban development, analysis exposes the highly uneven compromises that are made between economic and environmental priorities within the decision-making architectures of different cities.

While introducing key theoretical and empirical perspectives on sustainable urban economic development, this chapter excavates an analytical binary that tends to characterize much work in the field. This binary serves to mask the contingent and complex nature of the relations that exist between urban economies and the environments within which they are embedded. On one side of this binary is a vision of urban economic and environmental policies as isolated *solitudes*: with diametrically opposed economic and ecological goals being pursued in isolation from each other within urban communities. On the other side of the binary are accounts of the seamless meshing of compatible economic imperatives and environmental visions around technologically infused visions of sustainable urbanism and eco-development. While both accounts of the nature of urban environmental politics are seductive in their simplicity (and even suggestive of radical action: namely the construction of anticapitalist urban environmentalisms that oppose the obdurate logics of metropolitan economic elites (Binary 1); and the forging of antagonistic ecological movements to challenge the stale consensus of corporate environmentalism (Binary 2)), neither capture the contingent complexity of *actually existing urban sustainabilities*[1] in specific cities. Although the emergence of this unhelpful binary perspective is in part related to the normative positions adopted by those studying sustainable urbanism (with those most suspicious of urban eco-development found in first binary category, and those more sympathetic to the potential success of sustainable urban development in second binary community (although the reverse is also sometimes the case)), it is also clear that this division is based upon the analytical problems presented by the terms *economy* and *environment*. While the simplifying effects of these two categories on urban studies are clear, this chapter claims that the aggregating of varied metropolitan processes under the ontological categories of *environmental* and *economic* also actively supports the binary classification of sustainable urbanism described above. It is important not to conceive of either urban economic development or urban environmental sustainabilities as thematic singularities with easily defined, and thus easily divided, metropolitan agendas. The processes that we collectively refer to as the urban economy include, inter alia and in varied combinations, financial investments, property markets, production facilities, service industries, energy production systems, labour markets, and public sector economies. Environmental sustainability can be deconstructed in similarly complex ways so as to include, the provision of urban green spaces, quality of life considerations, air quality calculations, water course pollution abatement, urban habitat restoration, carbon emissions, and housing quality assessments. Disaggregating questions of urban economic development and sustainability not only serves to illustrate the vectors of potential contradiction and compatibility

---

1 I use the term 'actually-existing-sustainabilities' here in a slightly different context to the way it has been deployed by Krueger and Aygeman (2005). For Aygeman and Krueger 'actually-existing-sustainabilities' refer to the processes of sustainable development that constantly occur in cities but do not get officially labelled as acts of sustainability. I use the term here, and elsewhere in the chapter, to refer to the division between the ideals and visions of sustainable urban development and the realities that are being delivered within metropolitan centres throughout the world (to this end my use of the term is derived from the more widely known notion of 'actually-existing socialisms').

that inform attempts to create more environmentally benign brands of urbanism, it also illustrates the varied scales where metropolitan sustainability is contested and from time-to-time achieved (see Chapter 3 in this volume). As later sections of this chapter illustrate, it is only in certain instances that questions of urban economic and environmental need are discussed, and (in)effectively addressed, at a pan-urban scale. At other times such negotiations are critically framed by issues and processes that are either particular to sub-urban locales and turfs, or decision-making regimes that transcend metropolitan jurisdictions.

This chapter begins by exploring the nature of this binary perspective within urban sustainable development studies through a review of the historical emergence of policy regimes that have sought to re-position urban economic growth within an environmental frame of reference. The following section charts key conceptual developments and empirical studies within the field which have both supported and confounded a binary mindset within urban sustainability studies. Drawing on innovative theoretical and methodological approaches to studying the sustainable city, which collectively stress the complex, and geographically specific, nature of regimes of sustainable urban development, this section ultimately sets out a framework of analysis that offers a more diverse and empirically-grounded interpretation of the relationships between urban economic development and environmental sustainability. The final section mobilizes this framework to explore the emergence of a particular model of pragmatic urban sustainability in the city of Birmingham, which transcends any neat binary classification.

URBAN HABITATS AND THE RISE OF THE SUSTAINABLE CITY

There is one iconic curve that has come to symbolize the nature of urban economic and environmental relations at the turn of the twenty-first century. The Kuznets Curve is a visual expression of Simon Kuznets (the Nobel Award Winning Economist) hypothesis. First developed to express the relationship between economic inequality and economic development, the hypothesis/curve has provided an increasingly popular analytical framework for explaining the evolving environmental relations of the developing metropolis (see Marcotullio and McGranahan, 2007). The adapted version of Kuznets Curve deployed by urban theorists depicts a gradual increase of localized forms of environmental degradation as the economic basis of industrializing cities expands. These emerging forms of degradation are the environmental externalities produced by unregulated industrial activities and include particulate air pollution, the contamination of local water courses, and the unsafe disposal of solid waste (McGranahan et al., 2001). At a certain threshold of urban wealth creation the environmental Kuznets Curve suggests that the local environmental impacts of urban development start to decline. There have been a series of critiques of the applicability of the Kuznets Curve to urban-environmental relations. Some of these concerns have focused on whether such a model of economic-environmental relations can be effectively applied

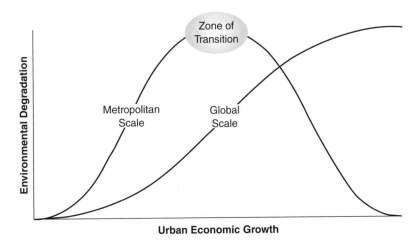

Figure 12.1 The urban environmental Kuznets Curve (drawn by Ian Gully; adapted from Marcotullio, 2007).

to the rapidly industrializing cities of the global south in the same ways as it has been used to analyze the longer-term economic development of Western metropolises (Marcotullio, 2007).[2] Other critiques have exposed the fact that while local environmental degradation may decrease in severity as a city's wealth increases, its contribution to large-scale, global environmental problems (particularly in the form of global warming and *virtual water* use) may actually increase (see McGranahan et al., 2001). Perhaps the most ambiguous aspect of the environmental Kuznets Curve is the issue of precisely what triggers the gradual improvement of environmental conditions (middle-class sensibilities towards quality of life issues; political mobilizations; improved industrial efficiencies; increased state regulation), and whether these activated forces can be relied upon to instigate ecological transitions in the same way in all cities (I will return to these questions in the following section).

The Environmental Kuznets Curve can be utilized within studies of sustainable urban development in three ways. Firstly, it can act as an analytical heuristic against which to test evolving economic-environmental relations within different cities (essentially exploring the extent to which such relations follow similar patterns in different geographical locations). Secondly, it can be interpreted as a theory of how all urban economies develop in relation to their environmental hinterlands. Thirdly,

2 A statistical analysis of the relevance of the Environmental Kuznets Curve to Chinese urbanization is provided by Hayward (2005). Looking at a range of environmental indicators across different Chinese cities during the 1990s (including ambient SO_2 levels, Total Suspended Particulates, and ambient NO_x levels), Hayward identifies *unappreciated* signs of environmental improvement paralleling urban economic growth. There is little sense in this analysis, however, of how these average levels of exposure are differentially experienced among geographical communities within Chinese cities, or whether they are part of the broader statistical trending you would expect from the K-Curve.

the Environmental Kuznets Curve can be used to gain insight into the policy men-talities that have informed attempts to construct more sustainable relations between urban economies and metropolitan environments. In this section I utilize the Environmental Kuznets Curve in this third modality (I reflect upon the theoretical import of the curve in the following section). To these ends I argue that the relationship that is forged between urban economic development and environmental relations – with continued wealth creation leading unerringly to an eventual improvement in environmental systems of various kinds – by the curve of Kuznets hypothesis has been a central assumption of sustainable urban development policy regimes.

The political architectures that have given rise to the sustainable city agenda are both complex, multi-scalar, and, at times, historically discontinuous. Frameworks for devising sustainable forms of urban development consequently exist at a global level (under the auspices of the United Nations, World Bank, and World Health Organiza-tion); supranational scales (European Union; TACIS[3], ASEAN); under the auspices of national governments; and are at times implemented by complex alliances of municipal authorities (Cities for Climate Protection; International Centre for Local Environmental Initiatives [Now ICLEI – Local Governments for Sustainability]; E-Polis) and NGOs (European Environmental Bureau; Ecopolis). While these differ-ent policy frameworks and organizations focus on different aspects of sustainable urban development, in more or less holistic ways, most can be clearly linked back to the discussion of urban environmental improvement that emerged at an interna-tional level immediately following the United Nations Conference on the Human Environment in 1972. In 1976 the United Nations Centre for Human Settlements (UNCHS) was established in order to organize the delivery of key UN agendas on environmental protection and social justice in urban and rural settlements that were agreed in 1972. What is interesting about the early work and intentions of the UNCHS was that it sought to pre-empt the key tipping-point in urban-environment relations depicted in the Environmental Kuznets Curve. Consequently, rather than trusting that environmental improvements would come as a 'natural' part of enhanced economic development, the UNCHS sought to re-envision the economic and political bases of metropolitan life as a way of directly delivering varied socio-environmental improvement. The *Vancouver Declaration*, which laid the operative foundations for the early work of the UNCHS, consequently asserted two key pri-orities. Firstly, it asserted the importance of increasing the opportunities of urban residents to become involved in actively shaping the urbanization process through various forms of participatory and representative metropolitan political systems. Secondly, and perhaps most significantly, the Vancouver Declaration called for an end to *uncontrolled urbanism*, driven by the dictates of economic expansionism; to be replaced by an *orderly process of urban development* (UNCHS, 1976). It is, per-haps, important, as we now stand 25 years on from the Vancouver Declaration, to

---

3 TACIS is an acronym for *Technical Aid to the Commonwealth of Independent States*. It is a European Commission aid programme that supports development programmes in the states of the former Soviet Union, and Mongolia.

note how few cities have actually been able to attain its vision of controlled urban-ism (largely small, slow-growth European cities, and politically and geographically constrained cities such as Singapore). Moreover, it is important to ask how relevant such a blueprint of urban constraint and popular empowerment is to the rapidly growing cities of Asia, Africa and Latin America.

The UNCHS established an approach to urban environmental sustainability that sought to directly challenge the neoliberal orthodoxies of urban deregulation and avaricious commercialization. To these ends it is clear that sustainable urban develop-ment is in many ways a successor planning concept to the urban growth management and containment policies, which became particularly prominent in European cities in the post World War II reconstruction period.[4] The challenge to prevailing laissez faire logics of post-war urban economic development presented by the UNCHS has been continued by its predecessor UN-Habitat (Girard et al., 2003: 11–12). But just as different organizations have been responsible for promoting diverse species of urban sustainability, it is possible to discern a very different brand of sustainable urban development emerging from another armature of the UN's own bureaucracy. Follow-ing the 1992 United Nations Conference on Environment and Development, the United Nations Environment Programme (UNEP) has been pursuing sustainable urban development goals through its Local Agenda 21 framework. LA21 requires all metropolitan authorities (from signatory states) to form pan-urban strategies for sustainable urban development[5]. What is significant about the LA21 process, and the broader discourses of sustainable development it supports, is that they have actually emerged out of a very different epistemic community than the visions of eco-development promoted at Stockholm and subsequently pursued by the UNCHS.

Countering arguments that contemporary forms of sustainable development find their origins in certain scientific epistemologies (specifically the notion of sustainable yield), Bernstein (2000) argues that officially sanctioned understanding of sustainability

---

4 It is also important to recognize that sustainable urban development has much in com-mon with more recent planning paradigms, including New and Smart Urbanism. While sustainable urban development shares a concern with the balancing of urban social, economic and environmental priorities exhibited by these planning movements, it has key defining characteristics. Firstly, sustainable urban development places much greater emphasis on the democratic inclusion of urban communities within the decision-making processes that shape cities (public consent and involvement is seen in this context as vital to fostering the lasting sustainability of any initiative). It also has a much stronger com-mitment to questions of social and environmental justice in present and future urban generations.

5 Prominent urban examples of Local Agenda 21 operate within Dar es Salaam (United Republic of Tanzania), Durban (South Africa), Santos (Brazil), Troyan (Bulgaria), and The Community of Greenpoint-Williamsburgh, New York City (USA). For details of these and other LA21 schemes, go to the *International Council for Local Environmental Initiatives* (now ICLEI, Local Governments for Sustainability) available at: http://www.iclei.org/index.php?id=1613.

actually find their genesis in the economic rationales pursued by the OECD during the 1970s and 1980s (pp. 495–7). Working through the World Commission on Environment and Development, neoliberal *policy entrepreneurs* were able to discredit the protectionist environmental norm-complex that characterized Stockholm (and the UNCHS) and replace it with a distinctly *liberal environmentalism* (ibid: 497). According to Bernstein, the liberal environmentalism that is typical of the LA21 process is characterized by the prioritization of market-mechanisms for dealing within environmental protection (de-regulation) and involves the creation of economic incentives for various forms of environmental improvements (ecological modernization). Liberal environmentalism consequently not only suggests that economic growth is compatible with environmental enhancements (a common mantra of sustainability), but that only the efficient distribution of both resources and incentives associated with the free market can deliver long-term sustainability. In essence this is a vision of urban sustainability, which rather than utilizing the environmental Kuznets Curve as a rationale for early intervention into urban-environmental relations, suggests that the curve should be allowed to follow its inexorable path of (unimpeded) economic growth towards the eventual promise of environmental improvements.

I introduce the competing strategies of liberal environmentalism and the more regulatory visions of urban sustainability promoted by the UNCHS not only to illustrate the diversity that exists within contemporary approaches, but to make two important points. The first point is that despite having a much longer history, the approaches to urban sustainability first enunciated by the UNCHS in the mid 1970s are far less prevalent than the liberal environmental rationalities that now permeate various metropolitan authorities' approaches to developing more sustainable cities (the mandated institution of LA21 strategies into the operational logics of local authority work has secured the effective geographical spread of liberal environmentalism). The second point is to reflect on the fact that it could, in part at least, be the presence of two such contradictory approaches to sustainable urban development that has fostered the binary interpretations of the sustainable city outlined in the introduction to this chapter. On the one side it is possible to see the desire of the UNCHS to develop a more radical approach to sustainable urban development as form of urban-eco-development that simply operates outside of the hegemonic economic functioning of the city. On the other side of the spectrum, the liberal environmentalisms associated with the LA21 clearly promote the idea that the fusing of unimpeded economic growth imperatives and environmental improvements is a relatively unproblematic goal[6].

---

6 I note here that at times these two contradictory perspectives on sustainable urban development come together in the same programme. We can see this in the example of the UN's Sustainable Cities Programme, which is jointly run by UN-Habitat and UNEP. While potentially straddling the divided approaches to the sustainable city, it appears that the model of *Environmental Planning and Management* and the prioritization of pro-poor governance mean that the Sustainable City Programme has maintained a strong regulatory and progressive edge.

THEORIZING SUSTAINABLE URBANISM

In this section I move beyond a concern with the emergence of sustainable urbanism as a diverse field of policy to consider prominent approaches to analyzing and theorizing the relationship between urban economic development and environmental sustainability. The first subsection excavates the emerging binary division that has characterized much work within sustainable urban development studies. The second subsection introduces a series of geographically-grounded accounts of sustainable urbanism that appear to promise a more diverse sense of what the sustainable city can be, and reveal how the political and economic infrastructures of cities contribute to this differentiation process.

Excavating an Analytical Binary: Between the Smart and Stupid City

In Girard et al.'s recent book, *The Human Sustainable City* (2003), we find the binary framework for thinking about urban economic and environmental relations embodied within the work of two of the leading writers on contemporary urban affairs. Firstly, we have the renowned planning theorist, and key advisor to the British government, Peter Hall. Building on previous work (Hall, 1998; Hall and Pfeiffer, 2000), Hall argues for the unique and privileged role of the urban economic form in delivering environment sustainability. Focusing on the future of European cities, Hall argues that urban centres are now confronted with two major challenges: maintaining high levels of economic competitiveness (particularly in the context of highly globalized economic sectors); and transforming themselves into 'models of high quality life' (Hall, 2003: 55). (Hall's deployment of 'quality of life' as a broad reference to a range of issues concerning environmental sustainability is significant, and we will return to its implications shortly.) Hall argues that these twin challenges can be met simultaneously through a mixed 'portfolio approach' of urban reforms, which essentially utilize a set of positive feedback loops between urban socio-economic restructuring and environmental enhancements as a basis for urban redevelopment (ibid: 65). The portfolio approach to urban reform envisaged by Hall attempts to move beyond attempts at urban restructuring which place unyielding faith in the virtues of urban-cramming and mixed use developments. Hall's portfolio approach involves a flexible strategy of urban sustainable development, which at different times, and in varying geographical locations, involves the creation of linear clusters of mixed residential and work environments, of medium densities, on interconnected green and brownfield sites, which all exploit excellent public transport infrastructures (ibid: 65).

Hall's vision is essentially of a polycentric form of urbanism, meshing urban villages (brownfield) and garden cities (greenfield), which are both self-contained, but inter-connected (ibid). What is perhaps of most significance about Hall's portfolio approach to urban sustainable development is the evident faith it places both in the power of re-organized urban space to recalibrate urban economic and environmental relations, and in the capacity for capitalist economic relations to provide a supportive context for the sustainable city. In the first instance, it is clear that Hall believes that the selective application of urban policies for concentration and decentralization can simultaneously aid an urban economy to make greater savings in efficiency and resource use (by balancing the need for proximity with anti-congestion measures) and thus reducing a city's ecological footprint, while also preserving a city's reputation as a pleasant place to live and work (by balancing vibrant mixed-spaces with the need of separating out homes from polluting activities). In the second instance, Hall's account of the sustainable city is ultimately based upon a belief that the contours of urban space can be used to ensure that urban capitalism maximizes the financial gains and competitive advantages that reconstituted environmental relations promise (ibid: 56).

Opposing the views of Hall we have the ecological economist Joan Martinez-Alier. Drawing on the work of environmental urbanologists, such as Lewis Mumford, and the physical chemist Alfred J. Lotka, Martinez-Alier challenges Hall's belief in the ability of cities to evolve into ecologically efficient spatial systems (Martinez-Alier, 2003: 98–9). Martinez-Alier's argument is predicted upon the assertion that *the struggle for life is the struggle for available energy* (after Boltzmann), and that the socio-economic evolution of cities embodies a competitive struggle for energy and a subsequent survival of the fittest metropolis (after Lotka) (ibid: 98). The availability and use of energy is, of course, vital to the expansion of commercial opportunities for cities. Consequently, whether it be about the use of energy within the production complexities of the city (see Harvey, 1989a), or the spatial expansion of real estate (and the transportation energies this necessitates) (see Molotch, 1976), Martinez-Alier argues that so long as cities depend on non-renewable energy sources, urban development can never really be about sustainability. While cities depend on the effective utilization of limited resources for their economic advantage, urban development will be dominated by a desire to maximize energy use (and the commercial gains in output and commercial land this enables) regardless of the ultimate environmental costs (ibid). Ultimately, Martinez-Alier's work leads us to the conclusion that urban sustainability is merely an environmental veneer, which serves to obfuscate the enduring *ecological distribution conflicts* that derive from the logics of urban development (ibid: 88). For Martinez-Alier, the clearest indicator of this form of urban development is found in the fact that many cities in the global north with stable or decreasing populations continue to increase their energy requirements and occupy ever increasing swathes of peri-urban ecological space. The cities that achieve the highest levels of sustainability are thus often not those with the greatest commitment to environmental justice of *ecophilia*, but are, to paraphrase Martinez-Alier, metropolises whose accrued wealth has enabled them to resolve the internal environmental tensions of the city, while displacing other ecological externalities to other spaces and scales (ibid: 104) (one, perhaps controversial reading of the environmental Kuznets Curve).

Despite embodying clear figureheads for the binary interpretative framework that structures much urban sustainability framework, it would be wrong to see either Hall or Martinez-Alier as the instigators of this divided logic. The

Hall/Martinez-Alier debate is best conceived as a single manifestation of a much deeper analytical logic within urban studies. This divide is between those who conceive of cities as potentially benevolent spatial forms, which can be marshalled and regulated to secure social and environmental justice (see Peter Hall, Ebenezer Howard, Herbert Girardet), and those who argue that cities ultimately reflect the spatial logic of industrial-military complexes, and are thus hard-wired into a logic of economic avarice, environmental exploitation, and creative destruction (Joan Martinez-Alier, David Harvey, Lewis Mumford, Harvey Molotch). This divided analytical logic is also under-girded by a more-or-less explicit pro-and anti-capitalist creed: with the pro-capitalist lobby arguing that as an economic system it offers the best hope for ecological innovation and the efficient allocation of environmental resources at all human scales (see Porritt, 2007); and the anti-capitalist coterie asserting that it is urban capitalism that is the very cause of the contemporary ecological crisis (Harvey, 1996: 366–402). It is interesting to note that a key inspiration behind the pro-capitalist visions of an environmentally efficient city has been the ecological records associated with socialist cities (see here Whitehead, 2005). Research has consistently shown that the levels of environmental pollution associated with socialist urbanization regularly outstripped even the most ecologically damaging capitalist cities (see Pavlinek and Pickles, 2000). At one level, it is clear that the environmental legacies of socialist cities were directly connected to the political and economic practises of communism (and in particular the removal of the economic incentives that at times exist within market economies to improve industrial efficiencies; and the lack of political opportunities that existed for the consolidation of green movement – producing in both instances a late onset environmental Kuznets Curve). At the same time, however, it is also apparent that the expansionist economic logics of socialist urban systems (which often embodied distinctly state monopoly capitalist tendencies) had much in common with their capitalist counterparts (Whitehead, 2005).

At times both sides of this powerful binary logic can co-exist within existing theories and analysis. While proffered by some as a useful heuristic to test the complex nature of urban sustainable development projects in different geographical contexts, it is possible to see the environmental Kuznets Curve as a mathematical articulation of dualistic thought. Although the environmental Kuznets Curve taken as a whole appears to reflect a pro-capitalist economic rationality (with continued economic growth and expansion leading ultimately to environmental improvements) it is also possible to see either half of the curve as symptomatic of prevailing ideologies of capitalism. Consequently, the upward portion of the curve can be interpreted as the inevitable environmental harm that unregulated capitalist expansion must cause to the environment (and may continue to do so subject to an uncertain set of mechanisms of transition to a more environmental benign growth regime), while the downward section of the curve can be read as proof positive of the ultimate aggregate compatibility of urban environmental improvement and wealth creation. If we look more specifically at the work of Jonas and While (2007) on *Greening the Entrepreneurial City* we can find traces of this twin argument in one chapter. Jonas and While thus observe that:

There is even some evidence that urban managers and political leaders in certain privileged 'global cities' are devising socially and environmentally effective and inclusive planning, decision-making, and governance structures [...] there is much more going on in cities than a narrow economic reading of the literature on urban entrepreneurial might allow. (2007: 128 29)

Later, however, they reflect:

[i]t appears that urban managers are being steered towards at best a rather selective vision of urban sustainability in which 'light green' policies aimed at making cities more liveable can substitute for more radical actions on the environment that could by implication threaten the competitive approach to urban economic growth. (Jonas and While, 2007: 130)

While it is perfectly valid to argue, as Jonas and While do, that these two patterns of urban sustainable development can co-exist in different urban locations, the existence of these two quotes reflects the binary trending that characterizes much work on the contemporary sustainable city. The challenge, which Jonas and While among others actually take-up, is to move beyond these broad stereotypes in order to explore the varied options and trajectories taken in urban economic and environmental development.

Excavating Actually Existing Urban Sustainabilities: On the Empirical Turn in Sustainable City Studies

Recent attempts to circumvent binary analysis of the relations between urban economic development and environmental sustainability have involved a distinctly empirical turn in studies of the city. In order to understand the nature of this empirical turn it is necessary to understand the phases that have characterized sustainable urban development studies over the last 20 years. Much early work on sustainable urbanism (particularly in the wake of the Brundtland Report and the UNCED) focuses on the practical steps that needed to be taken to implement sustainability in an urban context. Following on from these more applied and normative accounts of sustainability came a body of work that sort to theoretically interrogate the very premise of the sustainable city (see Martinez-Alier, 2003; Whitehead, 2003). Although this shift into theory provided a much needed critical political and economic perspective on the sustainable city project, its abstract tendencies, as we have seen, lend themselves to the forms of binary categorization we have previously discussed. It is within this broad context that more recent work on sustainable urbanism has sought to explore the apparent opportunities and contradictions of the urban sustainability agenda within the context of specific urban experiences (see Lake, 2000; Portney, 2003; While et al.,

2004; McManus, 2004; Raco, 2005; Whitehead, 2006; Krueger and Gibbs, 2007; Jonas and While, 2007). Raco effectively explains the shift into this theoretically informed, but empirically grounded phase of sustainable city studies when he observes that, 'the extent to which SD agendas and frameworks take on neoliberal forms becomes an empirical question to be interrogated in and through specific case studies' (2005: 330).

A clear example of this form of 'third wave' urban sustainable development studies is provide by While et al.'s (2004) analysis of the tensions between the environmental and entrepreneurial imperatives currently facing British cities. Although While et al.'s focus on the simultaneous pressures that currently exist to form entrepreneurial and unregulated patterns of urban development alongside more environmentally benign urbanisms could easily lead into a system of dualistic thinking, they utilize this context to develop a highly differentiated account of the nature of different urban sustainable development strategies. Rather than accepting that urban economic and environmental relations are either an entirely positive-sum, or zero-sum game, While et al. deploy the notion of sustainability fix to reveal the contingent, and geographically specific compromises that are made over eco-developments of various kinds in different cities. Focusing on emerging patterns of sustainable development in the English cities of Manchester and Leeds, While et al. describe how transformations in their urban economic fabric (largely from primary goods production and manufacturing, to retail, leisure and professional services sectors) have facilitated the prioritization of certain environmental agendas and the marginalization of others. Despite mobilizing their own sustainable urban development fixes, what we see in Manchester and Leeds is the prioritization of environmental strategies that are commensurate with their emerging post-industrial economies (namely those that promote the quality of life in the city – particularly in relation to clean air programmes, green space provision, and the cleaning-up of prominent water ways), and the suppression of ecological programmes that compromise emerging regimes of economic accumulation (particularly those restricting airport expansion and associated strategies prioritizing climate change abatement) (ibid: 559)[7].

At the heart of While et al.'s analysis is an implicit assumption that both the economy and environment may be analytical category mistakes when it comes to the assessment of urban sustainability. The notion of sustainability fix suggests that sustainable urban development is not about the aggregate reconciliation of urban economic and environmental imperatives, but the geographically specific prioritization of those environmental goals that support emerging urban growth regimes. Although While et al.'s focus on Manchester and Leeds developed a broad concern with the environmental priorities associated with post-industrial

---

7 For more on the emerging tensions between regimes of urban development that prioritize tourism, consumption and leisure and attempts to address a city's contribution to climate change, see While and Jonas's (2007) analysis of sustainable urban development in Barcelona.

economies, more recent work has sought to open-up the post-industrial urban economy to a more forensic form of analysis. The work of Gibbs and Krueger (2005, 2007), for example, has sought to move beyond broad analyses of urban entrepreneurialism in order to consider the connections between a specific urban economic sector and the pursuit of environmental sustainability[8]. To these ends Gibbs and Krueger have analyzed the rise of the so-called *new economy* in cities such as Austin (Texas) and Boston (Massachusetts) and the ways in which these novel urban economies are meshing within sustainable development practices.

Gibbs and Krueger define the new urban economies as those focused primarily upon knowledge production industries (including communication technologies, software development and bio-technology) and the FIRE sector (Finance, Insurance, and Real Estate) (2007: 95). The recent economic and environmental transformations experienced by new urban economies in Austin and Boston reveal the complex trade-offs associated with the contemporary urban sustainability agenda. At one level, both Austin and Boston have been keen to embrace the broad principles of environmental sustainability. To these ends urban authorities and developers in Austin and Boston have found that the promotion of certain environmental protection orders and improvements have complemented the desire to promote a high quality of life for those living and working in the cities (see reference to Hall's analysis above). This so-called *liveability agenda* prioritizes the clean air, open spaces, and congestion-free streets desired by the highly mobile and aspirational creative class of workers who tend to service the new economy sector. Yet in the case of both Austin and Boston, Gibbs and Krueger reveal how the new economy's dependence upon open space, low living densities, and large properties has contributed to significant amounts of sprawl, long commuting journeys, traffic congestion, air pollution and threats to ground water ecology (2007: 101–16). Drawing on studies conducted by Segal, Quince and Wicksteed (2000), Gibbs and Krueger reflect upon the fact that in certain circumstances for every hectare of land used to house high-tech enterprises an additional 15 hectares have to be used to provide housing, open space and transport facilities (2007: 102). What we can clearly conclude from Gibbs and Krueger's analysis is that new urban economic spaces are neither able to ignore, nor fully reconcile their economic and environmental goals. A good quality environment is clearly a prerequisite for a successful new economy: yet the environmental aspirations of the creative class appear to undermine the broader ecological sustainability of a city. What results, according to Gibbs and Krueger, is a situation where the environment remains a real and pressing consideration for urban authorities and developers alike, but one that tends to operate at the level of the preservation of certain aesthetic lifestyle visions and less at the level of aggregate environmental sustainability gain.

---

8 For more information on Gibbs and Krueger's project, 'The New Economy, Regional Development and Sustainability' go to: http://www.wpi.edu/Academics/Research/Sustainability/Home.html

---

FIRE, Smart Urbanism and the Boston Metro Region

The US city of Boston (Massachusetts) provides an interesting example of the tensions that surround attempts to develop sustainable urban development in relatively prosperous new urban economies. The Boston city-region has expanded enormously in the post-war era on the basis of the development of a significant Defence Contracts industry and a dynamic FIRE sector (Finance, Insurance and Real Estate). Its success as a new urban economy has seen Boston become a key destination for skilled workers. The work of Krueger and Gibbs (2007) reveals that the economic success of Boston has resulted in significant levels of sprawl in the broader region, with the urban economy becoming dependent on 300,000 daily commuters. The rapid growth of the real estate sector in and around Boston has had serious socio-economic consequences: including increasing commuting times, elevated house prices, and development threats to surrounding wetlands (ibid). As the governor of Massachusetts, Mitt Romney attempted to implement a system of smart urban planning and development control in the Boston city-region. This initiative was designed to reconcile some of the emerging tensions between the social, economic and environmental sustainability of the city. It involved funding support for more compact exurban development, support for the development of affordable housing, and the promotion of public transport oriented development. The basic premise behind such smart urbanist initiatives is the belief that through the careful management of urban sprawl it is possible to address local and transnational environmental concerns, create a more socially inclusive city, and continue to support urban economic growth and development. In their analysis of smart urbanism in and around Boston, however, Krueger and Gibbs claim that it has been more about creating a politically acceptable basis for sustaining urban economic growth than addressing issues of social justice, the creation of more liveable neighbourhoods, or the protection of the environment.

Key Reading

Krueger, R. and Gibbs, D. (2008) 'Third wave sustainability: Smart growth and regional development in USA', *Regional Studies*, 49: 1263–74.

Taken together, this chapter asserts that work on the contingent, contested, and highly variable articulation of economic development and environmental sustainability in entrepreneurial and new urban economies can provide a framework for moving beyond the binary classification of sustainable urban development tropes. Table 12.1 indicates the varied landscapes of urban sustainability that an empirically grounded, third wave approach to studying the articulations of urban economic form and environmental policy regimes may start to reveal. As a typology of urban environmental priorities supported and contested in different urban economic regimes, Table 12.1 is neither meant to be a definitive or indicative of the complex articulations of economy and environment that exist in the different cities listed. Rather, Table 12.1 serves to indicate that different urban economic trajectories (including oil-production economies, global financial centres, and boomburbs) do not lead inevitably to either the mobilization or marginalization of environmental

Table 12.1 A typology of urban environmental policy regimes and economic development patterns

Urban economy trajectory	Example cities	Environmental priorities supported	Environmental priorities contested
Oil-based urban economies	Lagos, Khartoum Caracas	Local environmental improvements, urban greening.	Polluter-pays initiatives, carbon reduction imperatives, energy descent strategies.
Rapidly expanding mega-cities (global south)	Shanghai, Delhi, Sao Paulo, Kuala Lumpur, Jakarta, Beijing	Slum improvement, environmental beautification, eco-town developments.	Air pollution abatement, urban hinterland protection and growth boundaries, workplace environmental reform, improved water quality standards.
Declining, heavy industrial urban economy	Katowice, Sofia	Environmental clean-up of contaminated land, enforcement of tougher air and water quality standards.	Improving workplace environments, pollution taxation.
High-tech, knowledge-based urban economies	Boston (USA), Cambridge (UK), San Francisco	Investment in environmental services connected to improved quality of life (green open spaces, improved air quality).	Reduced dependence on air transport and airport expansion.
Centres for consumption-based services and entertainment	Las Vegas, Dubai (United Arab Emirates)	Innovative eco-architectures, quality of life infrastructure, water conservation.	Compact-living and anti-sprawl measures, reduce, re-use and recycle philosophies, energy efficiency.
Global financial centres	London (UK), Frankfurt (Germany), Sydney (Australia), Tokyo (Japan), New York (USA)	Climate change initiatives and carbon rationing.	Restrictions on environmentally harmful international investments.
Boomburbs and property-based urban economies	Austin (USA), Mesa (USA)	Quality of life infrastructure.	Compact-living and anti-sprawl measures, congestion-charges and anti-road traffic measures.

sustainability, but to the highly differentiated support and contestation of varied ecological priorities, quality of life targets, and environmental enhancements.

A final, important contribution to this collection of third wave urban sustainability studies is provided by Kundu's (2007) study of urban development in Delhi. Kundu's study of Delhi indicates that not only is the city marked by a specific set of compromises between economic development patterns and environmental policy priorities, but how these compromises are spatially differentiated within the city itself. The Delhi urban agglomeration has been characterized in recent years by rapid urban expansion and annual population growth of 4% per annum since 1931 (Kundu, 2007: 157). Delhi's rapid economic growth has supported the formation of an elite metropolitan class who have lobbied and campaigned for a cleaner and less congested city. At one and the same time, however, while Delhi's rapid demographic expansion has actively contributed to the characteristic congestion of the city, it has also provided a vital source of cheap and willing labour for its primary industrial sector. According to Kundu (2007), the long-term solution to Delhi's competing economic and environmental imperatives appears to have involved a form of spatio-environmental segmentation. At one level, this process of segmentation has seen the gradual improvement of the environment within the core of the city: with the clearance of slums, tighter enforcement of environmental standards, and provision of better quality public spaces (ibid). This spatially focused strategy of environmental improvement has, however, been made possible by the relocation of migrant worker accommodation and polluting industries to the expanding peripheral areas of the metropolis (ibid: 163). While this is, of course, not a novel form of urban development (having been practised by many urban authorities throughout the world), it serves to remind us that one way of making urban economic development compatible with environmental sustainability, is simply to insulate the worst environmental effects of urban development from those with the greatest power and influence within the urban economy.

Urban Rapid Transport Systems and the Case of Bogotá's *Transmilenio*

Having established the diverse, and geographically contingent, compromises and contestations that are forged between urban economic development and environmental sustainability, it is important to reflect upon the policy implications of this perspective on the sustainable city. At perhaps the most obvious of levels, recognizing the uneven geographical development of the sustainable city ideal signals the need to develop strategies for sustainable urban development that mirror local circumstances and priorities. But the localizing of the sustainable development agenda has been a guiding principle of sustainable city programmes since at least the 1980s and the proclamations of the World Commission on Environment and Development. The real lesson of contemporary work on actually existing urban sustainability is that the political, economic and infrastructural fabric of different cities mean that only certain sustainability options are feasible in different metropolises.

(Continued)

(Continued)

A good example of the varying geographical potentials of different urban sustainability policies is provided by the case of mass rapid transport systems. Congested roads are bad for the economic competitiveness, quality of life, and broader environmental footprints of large cities. The construction of mass, rapid transport systems appears to offer one of the best ways for urban economies to reconcile their need for economic growth and broader responsibilities towards the global climate. But the construction of expensive subway systems, mono-rail, or tram systems (favoured in many European and North American cities) would make the costs of public transport prohibitive in many developing cities. In response to such limitations, the city of Bogotá (Columbia) has developed an innovative Bus Rapid Transport System. Best thought of as a surface subway, *Transmilenio* uses segregated bus lanes, raised and covered stations, and a complex system of inter-modal transport connection (including free feeder buses and cycle lanes) to provide a popular and cheap ($0.55 per trip) alternative to private transport. While popular, and appropriate in Bogotá (the BRT system actually carries 1.3 million passengers a day on average), it has proved less successful in more affluent cities (such as Los Angeles) where the cost of travel is less constraining, or in India where there are strong cultural attachments to scooters and tuk-tuks as inexpensive means of transport (*New York Times*, 19 July 2009).

See StreetFilm's (2008) 'Bus Rapid Transport: Bogotá' film at: http://www.street-films.org/archives/bus-rapid-transit-bogota/. Also visit the *Bus Rapid Transport Policy Center* at: http://www.gobrt.org/Transmilenio.html

EXPLORING THE SUSTAINABLE CITY IN PRACTICE: BIRMINGHAM – 'THE FIRST SUSTAINABLE GLOBAL CITY IN BRITAIN'?

In this final section I turn to recent research I have been carrying out on sustainable urban development in the British city of Birmingham. I draw on this research in order to illustrate the value of a more complex and spatially segmented interpretation of the relations between urban economic development and environmental sustainability. To these ends, my turn to this case study is not an attempt to try and empirically prove some of the theoretical trajectories and ideas I have previously outlined, but to illustrate the methodological potential of an approach to urban sustainability analysis that moves beyond binary categorization.

Birmingham is a large industrial city in the heart of the English Midlands. With a resident population in excess of one million people, Birmingham also provides the economic and administrative hub for the broader West Midlands City Region (the city is home to an estimated 42,000 businesses, and is ranked in the top 80 global cities in the world (Birmingham City Council, 2008)). As the 'cradle of the industrial revolution' during the nineteenth century, Birmingham was synonymous with heavy industries including mining, metallurgy and chemical production. During the mid-twentieth century, Birmingham became the hub of the British car manufacturing industry with Rover, Jaguar, Peugeot, Austin, and LDV all having production plants there. While the traditional economic fabric of Birmingham is typical of an unsustainable city, the decline of car manufacturing in the region over the last 20 years, and the recent closure of the Rover Plant at Longbridge, has provided impetus for the search for a more environmentally sustainable urban future.

Birmingham's first official engagement with the sustainable urban development agenda began in 1993 with the formation of the City's Sustainability Forum. Comprised of a range of stakeholders from across the city, the Sustainability Forum was established in order to develop a Local Agenda 21 strategy for the city. This Forum ultimately led to the creation of Birmingham's *Sustainable Communities Strategy*, which establishes the economic and environmental goals the city wishes to achieve by 2026 (Birmingham City Council, 2008). While early attempts to support environmental sustainability within the city were over-shadowed by the local desire to save manufacturing jobs and remnants of the metropolis's Fordist economy, more recent economic changes have generated new opportunities for the pursuit of urban sustainability. In 1976 the National Exhibition Centre was opened on the southeast edge of the conurbation. As a key hub for international conferences, concerts, and conventions, the opening of the NEC was to herald the gradual emergence of a post-industrial visitor economy in the region, which, it was hoped, would supplement the contracting manufacturing industry of the region. With the subsequent development of the International Convention Centre (and Symphony Hall), National Indoor Arena, and Bull Ring Retail Complex, Birmingham has sought to bolster its visitor economy. Such developments mean that Birmingham is now second only to London in the UK in terms of available retail space, and now boasts a visitor economy that was worth £2.5 billion in 2006 (up from £740 million in 1996) (Birmingham City Council, 2008). The desire to make Birmingham a 'meeting venue for Britain' has added economic weight to the desire of local environmental groups to conserve Birmingham's 3,200 acres of parks and 140 nature conservation sites: such sites are now seen as crucial in supporting the image of Birmingham as a desirable place to travel to. In addition to its new visitor economy, the City authorities in Birmingham have also been keen to support the development of a new *Science City* infrastructure. The Science City vision has been under-girded by the development of Birmingham's flagship Millennium Point (housing the city's science museum – *Think Tank*, the Technology Innovation Centre) as a hub for technological training, development and interfacing within the city. The Science City vision is, however, primarily focused on the economic opportunities and spin-offs that surround the city's university and research hospital. As with the development of a visitor economy, Birmingham's move into the digital and bio-technology arenas has leant support to programmes dedicated to the preservation and enhancement of the living environment in the area. As noted above, a high quality living environment is a key prerequisite for attracting the elite workers associated with high-technology economies.

The new economies currently being pursued in Birmingham have also posed some significant threats to the environmental profile of the city. As Birmingham's population has expanded (in part because of its new found desirability as a place to live and work) and house ownership patterns have changed (with much more single occupancy purchases among an increasingly young population), the pressure for house building has increased significantly. According to the latest estimates of the West Midland Regional Assembly, the city-region will need an additional 50,000 new homes to be built over the next 20 years in order to keep up with current demand (West Midlands Regional Assembly, 2007). The demand for more housing is placing what is arguably Birmingham's main environmental asset in jeopardy. As the pressures for more housing and urban sprawl grow, Birmingham's 923 square miles of green belt is coming under increasing threat (the green belt has long been under threat from expansion around the city's airport and National Exhibition Centre). While historically protected from new forms of urban development, recent reviews of the British planning system have suggested that certain parts of the green belt should be opened up for development. In addition to inhibiting urban economic expansion, many claim that the necessary leapfrog development that characterizes green belts adds unnecessarily to commuting times and increases the metropolis's carbon footprint.[9] In response to these threats, the Campaign to Protect Rural England – West Midlands composed an eloquent defence of the West Midland Green Belt. The CPRE-WM report, *What Price West Midlands Green Belts?* (2007), emphasized the role of the green belts as a key recreational asset to the city; important spatial habitat for a range of animal species and ancient woodlands; and provider of eco-systems services to the city (particularly in relation to flood buffering) (CPRE-WM, 2007: 3).

It is not difficult to equate the story of Birmingham's economic and environmental policy agendas with the types of binary thinking I have outlined in this chapter: with the new economic visions of the city initially seeing the seamless incorporation of sustainability objectives, only to see environmental objectives marginalized when they threatened the economic logic of the city's property-led expansion. However, through interviews with key planning officials within the West Midland Regional Assembly, and representatives from CPRE-WM, my own research has actually revealed a complex set of spatially specific compromises emerging around sustainability objectives in the city. In order to try and balance the needs of urban expansion and environmental conservation, a complex set of compromises are being mooted among planning officials and environmental campaigners. Following detailed discussions within planning officials, CPRE-WM are showing signs that they may support new developments in the green belt in exchange for the protection of sites of nature in the hub of the metropolis. CPRE-WM's potential support for this policy direction is based upon recognition that many areas of the green belt are not of particular ecological importance or diversity (particularly after decades of agricultural exploitation). By ceding certain portions of the green belt (particularly in the Meriden Gap, which separates Birmingham and Coventry, and in and around the National Exhibition Centre and International Airport site), the CPRE-WM hope to protect and enhance much more significant and accessible environmental spaces in the heart of the city. The kinds of pragmatic compromises that are being forged between economic development and environmental sustainability do not

_____

9 Birmingham's carbon footprint stood at 6,3245 kg of CO^2 per person in 2005: that is three times what would be deemed as a 'fair share' at an international level (Birmingham City Council, 2008).

fall into the generic win-win or win-lose scenarios of many accounts of sustainable urban development. What appears to be emerging in Birmingham is a form of negotiated policy-making within which economic gains and environmental losses in one part of the city are being offset by environmental gains and economic regulations in others. This spatially differentiated system of win-lose/lose-win compromises appears to be becoming an increasingly important characteristic of actually existing urban sustainabilities. Empirically studying the uneven impact of such compromises on different urban communities appears to be a central goal of much future research in this field.

CONCLUSION: ON DIVIDED URBANISM AND FLEXIBLE THINKING

This chapter has explored the complex relations that characterize the urban quest for economic development and environmental sustainability. At the heart of this chapter has been a desire to expose an unhelpful binary framework for thinking about urban sustainability and economic growth: within which the sustainable city is defined as either an impossible or unproblematic goal. At one level, this binary has been supported by a divided polity, with more radical (and often marginalized) visions of the sustainable city (supported by the UNCHS) coming in to competition with the liberal environmentalisms that typify the Local Agenda 21 programme. At another level, this binary is under-girded by competing philosophies of the urban form: with some claiming it offers the greatest hope for a sustainable future, and others arguing that, as a capitalist spatial form, it can only ever be the harbinger of unsustainability. While offering an important context for critical debate over the potential of the sustainable city agenda to improve the social and ecological footprints of cities, we have seen that the binary categorization of such programmes has masked the complexities that characterize *actually existing urban sustainabilities*. Actually existing urban sustainabilities problematize the unquestioning faith that some policy-makers, urban planners, and academics place in the emergence of a reliable (Kuznets) curve of economic development and enhanced environmental protections emerging in all cities. To this end, the recent work of McGranahan (2007) has claimed that we need to develop multiple curves to depict very different modes of urban environmental transition. To these ends, McGranahan claims that particular attention should be given to the mechanics of environmental transition in rapidly developing cities of the late twentieth and early twenty-first centuries. In these cities the rapid pace of urban industrialization, and the associated escalation of pollution levels, may well mean that there is not time for the gradual evolution of environmental governance (based upon an evolving middle-class ecological consciousness), if serious public health crises are to be avoided (McGranahan, 2007: 24–30).

The second half of this chapter introduced a new wave of sustainable urban scholarship that has sought to develop more empirically grounded and geographically specific accounts of the relations between urban economies and environmental sustainability. This, so called, 'third wave' of urban sustainable development study has sought to expose the ways in which cities with different economic profiles (including new economies, property-based urbanisms, manufacturing hubs, primary resource extraction, or visitor-based economies) have very different opportunities to pursue environmental sustainability on varied fronts. More recent, spatially informed analysis has also sought to reveal not only how urban economic and environmental imperatives are negotiated at a pan-urban, aggregate scale, but how economic gains/losses in one of part a city may be offset against environmental gains/losses in another district. Beyond the specific economic trajectory of a city, analysis has also revealed how different economic factors, such as average household incomes, may have a significant impact on the success of different environmental initiatives (particularly in relation to the relative success of mass rapid transport systems in different urban economies). The emphasis that this chapter has placed upon the contingent spatial coupling of economic development priorities and environmental goals should not be interpreted simply as a call to recognize that all cities are different. Instead, it is meant to emphasize the importance of allowing analytical room to study the subtle interplay of economic and environmental goals in urban decision-making before assessing the efficacy of a particular urban development strategy. At a more normative level, the analytical perspective developed in this chapter also serves as an important framework for thinking through and developing the forms of non-ideologically driven and flexible policy frameworks that are clearly needed if cities are going to meet their varied economic and environmental responsibilities in the future.

Web Resources

Birmingham City Council (http://www.birmingham.gov.uk/birmingham2026.bcc): Provides more details on the Sustainable Communities Strategies and related attempts to manage economic development and environmental protection in the city.

Bus Rapid Transport Policy Center (http://www.gobrt.org/): Provides more information on the implementation of Bus Rapid Transport initiatives throughout the world.

Property and Environment Research Centre (http://www.perc.org/articles/article688. php): Provides a good introduction to the principles of the Environmental Kuznets Curve.

StreetFilm (http://www.streetfilms.org/archives/bus-rapid-transit-bogota/): An excellent documentary film on the *Transmilenio* Rapid Public Transport System in Bogotá, Columbia.

United Nations Habitat (http://www.unhabitat.org/): This site provides a detailed description of key UN agreements and strategies for the development of more sustainable cities throughout the world.

SECTION 3

REFLECTIONS

13

Theories of Place and a Place for Theories

K. C. Ho

THEORIES OF PLACE

Does place matter in understanding the dynamics of production? For the Chicago School, the concept of the 'natural area' was the product of theorizing that people and activities were sorted by the competitive pressures exerted by land-use in the city allowing for a mapping out of these areas. While the Chicago School perspective was not explicitly focused on economic activities (Swedberg, 1991: 265), it can incorporate these as part of the general social terrain of the city. This is especially when later efforts responded to criticisms of the Chicago School's biological reasoning by introducing a social dynamic in the form of sentiments and symbolism and how these variables worked to attract and retain similar people and activities while resisting incompatible ones (Firey, 1945). This perspective can lay claim to being a comprehensive attempt to link macro processes (competition and the city) to its micro outcomes (natural areas).

Zukin's (1980: 579) celebration of the 'new urban sociology' arising in the mid-1970s observed that 'by tying together urbanization, the quest for profit and accumulation, the state's attempts to moderate domestic conflict between social classes, the new urban sociology achieved a coherence the field had lacked since Weber typified the 'city'. This may well be true but in the process, new urban sociology lost place and its critical dynamics because of the new attention given to structural forces moderating the development of the city. Two decades later, Sassen's (2000b) reflective essay highlighted the Chicago School's emphasis on place (and ethnography) as a way of understanding global-local interactions at the level of the city. Abbot's (1997: 1153) retrospective review of the Chicago School legacy makes a similar point when he says this perspective demanded a view that 'social facts are located facts'.

To apply place or 'locatedness' to understanding economic change in cities requires that we put context as a key element. It is, as Abbot (1997: 1171ff) explains, not just about detail but rather the specific elements in the place context which shapes or relates to the object of inquiry in question. Doreen Massey (1984: 117, 120) once said that 'no two places are alike ... the layers of history which are sedimented over time are not just economic; there are also cultural, political and ideological strata, layers which also have their local specificities'. This statement is at once insightful in drawing on a geological image to highlight how society features are locked in place, and at the same time makes it incumbent on us to unpack what this means in terms of economic change and the city.

I propose to do this through three broad sweeps through the literature, not a systematic review, but a selective set in order to see how a theory of place can be understood. The section on governance recognizes the agents involved in the shaping of the city. The key actor is what Lewis and Neiman call the 'custodians of place' (2009) – city officials whose jobs and careers involve the management of the city. Lewis and Newman make three points which are important in understanding how city governments behave. Firstly, following Petersen (1981) they suggest that city officials share a similar interest with residents which are tied to the general welfare of the city (2009: 11). It is therefore possible to talk about the interest of the city. Secondly, in opposition to Peterson (1981) Lewis and Neiman suggest, city officials do not always favour developmental policies as other types of policies and expenditures are also important in increasing the legitimacy of city governments. Thirdly, Lewis and Neiman (2009: 5–6) also steer away from perspectives which see officials as being captives of big business, city politics or higher governments and argue that there is room for city officials to manoeuvre. How they respond depends in part on the city's economic history, the nature of the urban economy and the composition of the urban community (ibid: 5). A theory of place from the perspective of governance allows for an understanding of how the urban actors interact in shaping the development path of the city.

The section on industry and work styles draws on the work of economists and geographers and recognizes that while a governance system goes some way in shaping the path of economic change, the urban economy is constituted by a diverse set of activities which have industry logics as well as inter-sector relationships. Here the work in urban economics as well as industrial geography complement each other and go some way in understanding the relationships within industry and the connections between sectors in the shaping of the urban economy. This research tradition has been significant in accounting for the growth of city-regions, regions of innovation, and new sources of growth in the city.

A focus on production in the theory of place should be balanced by a treatment of lifestyles and consumption. If production deals with livelihoods and shapes the economic foundation of the city, then lifestyles and consumption in turn determines the city's complexion. The two are by no means unrelated. Sassen (1991) in her famous treatise on the rise of producer and financial services, also mentions the development of a glamour zone which caters to the taste and lifestyles of this class of service workers.

GOVERNANCE STYLES

Place is both an enabler and a constraint on the urban economy. Nowhere is this clearer than with the institutional facilitators of economic change. The logic driving urban economic policy suggested by Petersen (1981) is that if urban economic growth results in benefits which lock in the interests of stakeholders, then municipal governments will act rationally and devote their last dollar to developmental expenditures and leave redistributive activities to the federal government. While this reasoning is certainly appealing, the actual public policy conditions and institutional features on the ground become important in shaping the operation of such logic. Wading through the data for US cities, Clarke and Gaile (1998) found that it is those cities which pushed market-based strategies who were rewarded with job growth, new firm formation and faster growing firms for less well-off communities (1998: 105). Their two case studies show contrasting private-public partnerships (loosely versus tightly-coupled partnerships) but in both cities, the key lies in how critical organizations (the chamber of commerce, organizations with private-public partnerships) have been able to get the economic work of the city done and shield the city from some of the more disastrous effects of deindustrialization.

It is important to move beyond the narrow questions of successful city economic development to consider broader issues of participation and the outcomes associated with such involvements. Savitch and Kantor (1995: 498) suggest that socially progressive strategies are preferred to growth centred approaches because they link development projects to larger public goals and non-market considerations, for example by incorporating preservation, parks and public amenities. And since socially progressive are tied to mass support, developmental projects are more likely to involve greater public participation and scrutiny. Their analysis of eight case studies suggest that those cities with a combination of strong economic position (versus weaker economies), supported (as opposed to fractionalized) by different levels of government, along with strong neighbourhood representation, create an environment which facilitates the identification of good quality projects which add to the vitality of the city and at the same time satisfy the expectations of the city's constituents.

By introducing the notion of socially progressive development strategies, Savitch and Kantor (1995) have shifted our attention to a larger, broader-based institutional structure. This is significant on three counts. Their distinction between socially progressive and growth centred orientations require us to think about how development goals are influenced by centrists versus participative regimes of governance. We need therefore to not just look at the ways in which projects are shaped but also whether these networks which influence the shaping of projects are fractionalized and as a result create highly divergent development approaches.

Secondly, the consideration of inter-governmental relations focus require us to think 'vertically' in determining the role metropolitan governments play in determining its economic futures. We need to consider the myriad of networks not just for the United States but in cities from other parts of the world. In the East Asian and South-East Asian case, the strength of central governments and the weakness of local governments mean that cities are usually implicated in national development and infrastructural plans, often with the capital city taking a much larger share of the development budget. On this note, the East Asian case has provided examples of national state-driven initiatives in terms of the development of science

parks and the building of industrial clusters. But more broadly, national state initiatives have been directed at shaping a competitive national technological and
industrial infrastructure, even to the extent of creating artificial assemblages where
none existed or where without state intervention, localized clusters are under-
developed or fail to rejuvenate. The ideology of national state intervention has
been shaped increasingly by the logic of globalized production, where intervention
is needed to rejuvenate ailing industry, create new layers of activities and retrain
the local labour force made obsolete or rendered uncompetitive by new sites of
production in distant shores.

Thirdly, Savitch and Kantor's paper is also significant for its highlight on the role
of local communities in the development process. Abers (2000) studied the Brazilian
regional development forums which allow neighbourhood associations to participate in developing local initiatives that compete for funding at the regional development forum. Her study not only demonstrated the ability of local communities to
organize in order to tap into a resource pool, but also highlighted the tendencies of
communities to build alliances with other communities.

This last point indicates how the insertion of local community organizations into
the wider institutional structure of decision-making and funding creates a closer
match between community visions and state projects. The focus of these studies has
been typically top-down. There is also value in beginning our query from bottom-up
and seeing how these connect to other sectors. Albert Magnaghi's (2000) *The Urban
Village* represents an intellectual break with mainstream urban studies and economic
geography because it raises the question of local self-sustainable development with
local communities as self-organizing units. Based on self-employment, craft, micro
firms and fair trading companies (including cooperatives), Magnaghi insists that
such forms of production are possible when a new alliance between the producer
and resident is established (see Chapter 5). The framework requires a rescaling of the
economic sphere to local ecological units and a reconsideration of the size of the city
in relation to the wellbeing of its citizens (Magnaghi, 2000: 139). Many of
Magnaghi's arguments may work if we subscribe to a sustainability framework.
Whether we are sceptics or believers, it is worth thinking about the conditions which
need to be in place for local self-sustaining community clusters to work. At the level
of production activities, such a shift to localized production will favour smaller-scale
types of activities such as crafts, some types of more labour intensive manufacturing,
urban farming and some services activities. An obvious conclusion may be that this
will be a better fit for 'ordinary cities' where traditional kin and community structures operate to organize local production. However, if we consider a mixed urban
economy situation, it is highly possible for example that cities with a significant
tourism economy can develop a successful integration to such 'traditional' segments
in ways which can support the 'modern' sector (the conventions industry for example) and local community life.

If Magnaghi's self-sustaining communities of production represent ecological
units bound by tradition and shared work practices, Lloyd's (2006) neo-bohemian
communities are accidental collections of members of society's fringes. If there is a
connection, it is because the reputation of the place keep the prices of housing

affordable and therefore the result is a mix of struggling artists and students, along with the 'down and outs' who call the neighbourhood home. A local economy of music and design created by this mix allows for experimentation and learning and Lloyd's case studies show how the local talent nurtured by this economy has the ability to transfer skills learnt to new economy firms in the rest of the city. Lloyd's study shows an interesting variation to community-based models in a number of ways. Firstly, the accidental nature of such collectivities suggests the difficulty in planning for such communities or even in supporting them. In most instances, such assemblies operate under the radar of metropolitan governments mainly because the crime and poverty in such neighbourhoods trigger redistributive rather than developmental policy responses. Moreover, given their very nature, such places are fluid. Places with interesting architecture stock and proximity to the city core face threats of gentrification and therefore its residents are likely to move to other lower-cost neighbourhoods. Thirdly, unlike the type of communities described by Magnaghi, there is little by way of local community organization as the types of economic activities and skill transfers are more likely to be based on loose inter-personal networks. Lastly, Lloyd demonstrates an essential connection between the unconventional and the mainstream. In the area of design where new ideas come from the unexpected, the subcultural roots of creativity are being demonstrated in the migration of ideas and practices from the marginal to the mainstream. The exchange of ideas is as much to be understood by the nature of industry and work organization as from the community nature of production.

As an acknowledgment of the sign of the times, a section on governance and eco-nomic change cannot ignore the tide of neoliberal ideas on regulatory practices for the economy and government. As suggested by Leitner et al. (2007: 4), the neoliberal city is the entrepreneurial city, where the dominant strategies are economic ones, dedicated to improving the city's competitiveness, where services are increasingly privatized and management is by clear targets, and where city residents are expected to be in charge of their own livelihoods and are seen to contribute positively to the economic success of the city. Thus to the extent that neoliberalism takes root, developmental policies and expenditures win over welfare types of spending, inter-government linkages and government community linkages are being compromised in favour of accountability and self-responsibility and in a climate of competition for funds (instead of sharing them).

Leitner et al. (2007: 8) however, caution against over-generalizing the neoliberal impact on cities and governance, suggesting instead an examination of the oppor-tunities in which neoliberal ideas and practices can take root, an understanding of the different institutional histories and roles, as well as the resistance to neoliberal-ism. It is also important to see, as Lewis and Neiman (2009) do, that city officials have resources and the capacity to intervene despite the pressures placed on city governments. This is even more so for the cities of East Asia. While there is some retreat from the developmental state apparatus responsible for the spectacular industrialization in East Asia some 30 years ago, governments in East Asia have been active in supporting a range of development programmes, especially in the face of an enlarged civil society in Korea and Taiwan. In these two countries, a well developed bureaucratic system, healthy state revenues, coupled with a vibrant civil society has produced a state-society relationship which balances development with a range of societal welfare needs.

Aside from political and economic context, it is also important to lay neoliberal tendencies alongside other logics. Scott (2008: 142–7) in particular argues that the agglomeration tendencies creating city-regions, and the importance of such functional units as engines of growth, imply that governments are likely to continue intervention through the provision of large-scale infrastructure projects necessary to support this scale of organization in the face of competitive economic pressures and such need for collective action works against neoliberal tendencies.

INDUSTRY AND WORK STYLES

The very large literature on agglomeration has enabled us an understanding on why cities matter in economic development. Central to this tradition of research is the idea of a set of shared resources external to the firms but internal to the sub-region. Termed localization economies and seen as the basis for the concentration of an industry, the driving forces include the advantage enjoyed from the sharing of information and the pooling of labour (Fujita and Thisse, 2000; Maskell and Kebir, 2006). The process of concentration and growth of an industry involves a number of localized spillovers (Maskell and Kebir, 2006: 34) and snowball effects (Fujita and Thisse, 2000: 10). Urbanization economies shift the focus on to the advantages enjoyed by the diversity of economic activities in the city and by implication a multi-industry context. Duranton and Puga's (2004: 2110) conclusions, after a lengthy review of the foundations of urbanization economies, is that the heterogeneity of workers and firms account for most of the mechanisms (sharing, matching and learning) they discussed. Henderson et al. (1995: 1068) suggest certain types of industrial activities (high-end fashion, business services) thrive on urbanization economies, while smaller and mid-sized firms in textiles, apparels, and food-processing benefit more directly from locationalization economies.

As research approaches, the predominately econometric studies informing this tradition sit uncomfortably alongside ethnography case studies. Firstly, the variable centric nature of econometric analysis means that places have been reduced to the status of a variable or attribute (e.g. size) or a variable set (income, ethnicity, etc.). Secondly, the dependence of econometric analysis on existing large datasets means that the researcher's analysis is limited by the scope of the dataset. Census tracts, county, city level data define the imprecise boundaries of actual places (Glaeser, 2000: 88–9). The contrast then is between the thick description (including historical analysis as well as moving between several geographic scales) provided by case studies versus the breath provided by econometric analysis, between the case study's emphasis on discovery versus the measurement, validation and extension of existing models favoured by urban economics. One useful way of considering the contributions of both perspectives is to use the case study to drill deeper into the many pathways developed by urban economics.

The urban economics research finds more in common with the industrial geography perspective. Both are concerned with the economic base of the city, city-region linkages as well as the dynamics of agglomeration. Industrial geography, however, is characterized by 'the geographical constitution of institutions; that institutions are ... constructed in particular places and spaces, and therefore are quite different from one another, producing varied effects' (Barnes, 1999: 14). This sensitivity to location leads geographers to examine site-specific dynamics, the organization of various economic actors, and the types of effects (virtuous and otherwise) which are self-reinforcing of the emergent system, as well as path dependency changes. As Scott (2000: 17) suggests, these systems should not be seen merely as 'simple physical inputs and outputs, but also of business information, know-how, and technological expertise'. Barnes (1999: 16) also attributes to Storper, the development of conventions and norms which are tied to places, resulting in 'different worlds of production'. While economists depend on existing datasets, industrial geographers concerned with an emerging ecology which is tied to specific districts, cities and regions are more likely to assemble data at this particular scale in order to uncover the relationships and dynamics that represent the mainsprings of urban economic performance[1].

There is value in combining the insights derived from macro-city models of relationships developed by the economists, with the place-specific efforts from geographers and the ethnographic approaches favoured by sociologists and anthropologists. One example is the cluster typology developed by Paniccia (2006) which is useful in its attempts to specify and incorporate socio-economic institutional settings, locational as well as urbanization economies, size of the urban area, and the types of industries (from craft to science-based industries) and the variety of industries. The six ideal types identified allow the researcher to develop a strong place-base explanation within each type. For example, the 'canonical type' represents a low diversity, small spatial scale, and small firm structure. In terms of governance structure, such a configuration is likely to create a community-based production pattern discussed in the earlier section representing a specific type of locational economy where knowledge and skill is shared among the tight network of family-run firms enabled by community institutions within the context of towns as well as cities.

Another type is a 'science-based industry' cluster which combines universities, research centres as well as firms of different sizes. Clusters of this nature can be an outcome of several dynamics. The role of a large research university can give rise to different types of knowledge spillovers which link firms to the research resources of the university (Walcott, 2001: 523–4; Audretsch et al., 2005). Other types of science-based clusters are outcomes of more deliberate policies initiated by governments which provide funding to universities (in contrast to funds raised by venture capital) that link up research capacities with industry applications (see for example

---

1 Borrowing the phrase from the Chapter 2 title of Scott's (2000) *The Cultural Economy of Cities*.

the triple-helix studies initiated by Etzkowitz and Leydesdorff, 2000). Whether it is an evolved or planned outcome, science-based industry clusters represent a form of organized creativity where innovations reside within the capacities of the organization, where teamwork is more rigid and formal contracts bridge the relationships between firms and agencies.

At the opposite end of the innovation spectrum is what Drake (2003: 511) terms as 'individualized creativity'. This is similar to Shorthose and Stranges' (2004: 47) description of artistic work as 'an expression of one's creative capacity through self-determined labour', both describing a type of work style which stems from an individual control of creative labour. Grabher (2002a, 2002b) extends the notion of an individualized workstyle through the concept of a self-organized project. In advertising, the specific tailoring to client needs – personalized loyalties built from past projects – produce repeated opportunities for collaboration thereby building personal networks within the industry (Grabher, 2002a). In new media companies, the fast pace of change requires intense client involvement, where solutions are derived in an iterative and interactive process, thereby giving rise to what Grabher (2002b) terms fluid project ecologies, where different skills are pulled together in a specific project. Two important implications arise from considering this particular research. The first is the need to consider how the particular environments (rapid changing technology, client-based services, individualized creativity) require us to shift our focus from the firm-to-loose personalized networks that are configured by projects. The second more important implication is that the association with the growth of business services as an outcome of the urbanization economies enjoyed in large diversified cities. Grabher (2002b: 1918) attributes the advantages enjoyed by new media firms as arising from locationalization economies (labour supply, pool of specialized supplier firms, and knowledge spillovers). A parallel argument can be made about the role of urbanization economies in the diversity created by inter-industry concentrations in creating successful matches among very diverse and specialized skill sets as well as the collaboration and learning opportunities which Grabher's respondents mentioned in both new media firms and advertising firms.

While not quite discussed within the scope of urbanization economies, there are a number of ways in which the social diversity of urban life influences the nature of economic change. Thus, Lloyd's (2006) *Neo-Bohemia* links place, subcultural forms, and new expressions in design which make their way into the new economy through links between creative labour, small enterprises and larger corporations (2006: 211–19). Based on interviews with creative workers in digital design and craft metal work, Drake's (2003: 518) sketched out four ways in which place and creativity is linked. Firstly, as locality-specific communities of creative workers, in ways described by Lloyd (2006) but also more generally as live and work places of production-based groups. Over time, locality-specific communities may develop into a second form of place-based production defined a strong reputation and tradition. This fits closer to the canonical type described by Paniccia (2006), where the reputation of place is prevalent among craft traditions. Drake's respondents talk about how this reputation ensures a certain quality as well as a design tradition. Grabher's (2002a, 2002b) description of project ecologies which are based on networks fit with Drake's third form, suggestive of more elastic and fluid linkages which are more easily established within the context of a large city.

Drake's fourth link of how place can be a resource of visual raw materials and stimuli is perhaps most easy to verbalize but really difficult to pin down in analysis. In discussing inspiration, Curtis (2002: 104) pointed to a following episode:

> walking home one day after work, I passed the Yohji Yamamoto store on the corner of Mercer and Grand in Soho and noticed these great posters featuring their clothes. I stopped and studied them for a while and everyday after that when I passed the store I looked at them again. They were photos cropped at odd angles with blocks of black and bold white lettering. The effect was arresting and suggested excitement and youthful vigor. At about the same time I was trying to figure out how to design and treat a new video featuring the band Sum 41. The visual inspiration I got from the Yamamoto posters was the answer.

Curtis (2002: 107) goes on to say 'it became clear that we, as creatives, are walking a shared path, strewn with the ideas of those who have walked it before us. We felt that once on the path, we couldn't help but pick up some of those ideas on our way'. If we imagine that creativity and inspiration has many sources, being in the city with its size, density and heterogeneity may actually intensify the likelihood of such influences in the lives of creative workers.

CONSUMPTION AND LIFESTYLES

Examining US data on real wages by city sizes over two time periods – 1970 and 2000 – Glaeser and Gottlieb (2006: 1283) found that in the 1970s, real wages had a strong positive relationship with city size, while in 2000, it was an inverse relationship. They suggest that the decline in real wages in big cities in 2000 suggests that people are valuing urban social amenities and are therefore willing to accept lower wages to live in larger cities.

Pinning down what this non-wage component which people implicitly give up in order to enjoy urban social amenities associated with large cities requires that we understand a number of inter-related processes defining consumption and the city. On the production side of things, a significant proportion of the city's business (producer services, the creative economy) is associated with the lives producers and workers live. Currid's (2007) research into the lives of producers in New York's arts and culture economy indicates the numerous ways in which proximity and socializing is important to the work process, thereby blending lifestyles and workstyles. Advanced service professionals are also more likely to have, as Warde (1994: 893) suggests, 'sharing style, have considerable access to relevant knowledge, or a clear sense of rules and a source of belonging'. A clear example of the link between the work and consumption comes from a comment made by a creative director from a Hong Kong advertising firm:

Of course, it is important to dress decently for my job, because what I sell
are ideas, my brains ... It is not the same as selling a fax machine or a
microwave oven, where the consumer can check out the product, and hold
it in his hands and look at it before deciding to buy it. For advertising, if
you cannot show the client you have good taste, how can they trust you
enough to put their products into your hands? (Field material from Chan,
2000: 121–2)

Lash and Urry (1994: 164) also point out that 'this core of upper professionals possess highly valued intellectual resources, is employed in powerful organizations, and
gets involved in the cosmopolitan side of economic and cultural life in the city'.

The deeper change is the way consumption has come to signify one's identity and
the role cities play in the shaping of taste. Two key processes reinforce this process.
In an age where middle class is expanding and class boundaries are blurring, consumption has emerged to shape lifestyles and define status (Featherstone, 1991).
Thus, the growth of services in the city, along with the expanding urban middle
class, are reinforcing tendencies creating distinct spaces of consumption in the city.
In late modernity, the growth of education has in turn led to an extended transition
to adulthood. This process, coupled with the decline in religion and family as institutions responsible for the shaping of identities, plus the expansion of the market
to capture youth interests, has strengthened the relationship between consumption
and youth identity (Cote, 2000). In the transition to adulthood, consumption
emerges as a flexible malleable resource, within which young people can assert a
sense of who they are and establish a sense of stability, however temporary in
nature (Miles, 2003).

This process is most importantly a social one. In this regard, Seabrook's comment
regarding consumption and style is quite insightful: 'Fanship, brandship and relationships are all a part of what the statement "I like this" really means. Your judgement joins a pool of other judgements, a small relationship economy, becoming one
of millions that continually coalesce and dissolve and reform around culture products –
movies, sneakers, jeans, pop songs. Your identity is your investment in these relationship
economies ... The reward is attention and self-expression' (Seabrook, 1999: 109,
quoted in Lury, 2002: 219). Large cities are where young people want to be. To the
extent that audience is required for style, then the youthful lifestyle spaces of the city
operate to provide a clearer form to what is initially a vague expression.

Cities are therefore beachheads of consumption. This role is not new, as cities in
the past have always been important markets and conduits for the introduction of
new products and therefore the shapes of taste. What is new is the increased importance of consumption, the accelerated process of change, and an increased desire to
experience the city.

Tourism has introduced visitors to the city as new groups of consumers. In this
regard, the city, with its diverse cultures, lifestyles and markets, is the natural site for
the expansion of tourism. Increasing consideration for the tourist dollar in municipal
planning has led to mega projects (stadia, malls, theme parks) and mega events, and
these have come to define the rhythm and image of the city. Fordist cities are

ordered; cities of consumption arrest attention by design and diversity. Industrial cities are ruled by the workday; cities of the cultural economy are sustained by play and night-time activities. To the extent that the services and cultural economies take root and flourish, new landscapes are created based on a desire to project affluence, lifestyle, and creativity.

Policy-makers who think that urban amenities and quality of life issues may be the magic pill-pulling in firms and talented individuals may be disappointed to know that for both types of decisions, a combination of economic (especially for firms – see Rogerson, 1999) and social (especially for individuals – see Brown and Męczyński, 2009) are uppermost in location decisions. Quality of life may be relevant, but it is, as Brown and Męczyński (2009: 249) suggests, a steering factor, not a trigger factor.

A PLACE FOR THEORIES (IN RESEARCH AND PRACTICE)

The way this article has stated and discussed the theory of place makes it clear what the place of theory ought to be. In my view, theory has a specific contribution in a research strategy which requires a combination of an inductive (discovery function) and deductive (guiding function) approaches. Forms of economic globalization may work on a similar logic but as Smith (2001) argues in his debate with Harvey, the key is in understanding agency on the ground, the nature of representative power and how the global and the local come together in particular urban formations. And so it is if we want to understand how economic activities flourish and take root in the city. Taking the local setting as the starting point of research requires the researcher to consider the multiple linkages that are embedded within each study site.

In this search, the grounded approach to let theory and concepts emerge from fieldwork research seems one likely avenue. However, the idea (as originally espoused by Glaser and Strauss 1967) to enter the field relatively uninformed by the distorting effects of theories and concepts seems rather untenable. By Snow et al.'s (2003) reckoning, this version of ethnographic approach has sacrificed theoretical insights in the search for understanding local subjectivities. The idea of going into the field relatively uninformed seems naïve as it ignores a potentially helpful literature which is available to the researcher. Instead, the approach suggested by Snow et al. (2003) puts theory back into the driver's seat as the existing literature is used as a guide to further research. Summarized, the focus in analytic ethnography is 'to explore the possibility of transferring concepts and theory representing social forms or types across diverse contexts' (ibid: 190). This position is also in keeping with Walton's (1992: 121) point that 'cases are "made" by invoking theory'. By suggesting that theory guides the selection of cases, Walton (1992) is in favour of putting theory before the data and that cases only have a structure that is illuminated by an existing theoretical lens. This position is clear when Walton (1992: 124) remarks that 'case studies … drift without anchor unless they are incorporated into some typology of general processes, made causally explicit within the case, and ultimately referred back to the universe which the case represents'.

Thus, if we take these suggestions, then a place of theory is in its contribution as the navigation points in any research endeavour, illuminating the path which the researcher is to take. It is, as Curtis (2002) suggests (in a different context), a path strewn with ideas of others who have walked before us. *However*, once we are on the path, the boundaries of that path are sufficiently blurred by everyday complexities, contingencies suggested by different place sites, and the new social and economic formations that the inductive function and discovery possibilities will rear its head at each turn. The theories of place represent critical ways of seeing the city and its economy, from the way its institutional features and politics are configured, the different industry dynamics and workstyles and a changing lifestyle and what this means for the metropolitan economy. Such ways of seeing the city draws from a rich bedrock of existing ideas, but the creative student always approaches the field with an eye towards expanded accounts, alternative concepts and new ways of seeing which is guided by discoveries which lay at place specific sites of research.

Many relationships are implicated by development projects (Healey, 2000: 520). Theories of place inform practice by highlighting the key relationships; the political (in governance), the economic (industry and workstyles) and the social (consumption and lifestyles). But theories of place can only go so far as to highlight critical relationships. John Friedmann (2002) reminds us that city builders need not only blue prints for their work but guiding normative images. The good city can only exist when an enlightened process of intervention: considers the relationships which are necessary to build healthy and sustaining economic clusters; is cognizant of the livelihoods which may be affected by economic change; and above all, must have in place a consultative system of stakeholders.

14

Epilogue: Economic Change, Globalizing Cities, and the New Urban Order

Tom Hutton

INTRODUCTION: INDUSTRIAL RESTRUCTURING AND THE TRANSFORMATION OF THE CITY

In this volume we have been concerned with an interrogation of the complex relationships between cities and the economy, broadly conceived, in an era of insistent globalization, industrial restructuring, and policy experimentation. For this concluding chapter I intend to draw upon the rich scholarship embodied in this book to offer some conjecture on the configurations of urbanization and urbanism, informed in large measure by an appreciation of the economy and its multi-faceted intersections with cities.

As a first task in this essay I sketch the lineaments of urbanization in a global context, emphasizing the multi-level rescaling of cities and the urban order configured by the imperatives of capital and the state.

Secondly, and continuing a narrative of urban rescaling driven by insistent economic change, I address the dynamics of industrial restructuring and their impacts on urban growth and change, which collectively shape what Stefan Krätke has described as an emergent 'industrial urbanism on a global scale' (Chapter 4, this volume). The manufacturing landscape has clearly been transformed, but production is still a propulsive sector among both advanced and developing economies, however much celebrated urbanists may proclaim the ascendancy of the 'consumer city'.

Next up on the agenda is a commentary on relations between processes of economic change and employment, occupations and labour markets in cities both of the global south and the global north. Here we acknowledge the emergence of a transnational capital class, buttressed by legions of managers and professionals who comprise an affluent new middle class in the global cities, under-pinning what some see as a redefining upgrading of urban economies, and the professionalization of the labour force (Hamnett, 1994; Ho, 2005). But informality persists both among 'advanced' and 'transitional' societies, as well as inequality which contributes to poverty and marginalization.

I then turn to a consideration of the critical issue of space in the evolution of the metropolis and contemporary economy. Here one prominent example takes the form of a revitalization of obsolescent districts of the city, areas which can accommodate both the structures and systems of the new cultural economy as well as upscale housing. This reconstruction of space might seem to follow earlier models of finer-grained reterritorialization, notably Edward Soja's concept of 'postmetropolis' (2000). But there are more complex processes of the reconfiguration of space in the city than can be accommodated in a single model.

Finally, I conclude this essay with a foray into the realm of urban re-theorization, a parlous enterprise perhaps in the midst of innovation and restructuring, but still an essential task of scholarship on the city: both for framing the larger meanings of urbanization, as well as for parsing the quotidian experiences of city life.

GLOBALIZATION, TRANSNATIONALISM, AND RESCALING THE METROPOLIS

The world city has antecedents in the rise of Venice and Genoa in the sixteenth century and the imperial aspirations of Castilian Spain in the reign of Phillip II, situated for the most part in the Mediterranean world (Braudel, 1973),[1] then more expansively in the centres of empire in the seventeenth and eighteenth centuries, underscored by the ascendancy of London and Amsterdam, with the reach of these cities extending ever-further from the national territory. A new era of colonialism and expanding commodity trade in the nineteenth century, together with advances in transportation and communications technologies, and the waxing power of industrialization, shaped a roster of globalizing cities which included New York, Paris and Berlin, a process continuing over the belle époque, but truncated by the catastrophe of the Great War. Defeat saw the end of four dynastic empires – Hohenzollern, Romanoff, Habsburg and Ottoman – while even the world cities of the victors, notably London and Paris, suffered the trauma and psychic fatigue of the Great War.

Following World War II, new outbreaks of conflict and mostly regional wars, some quite devastating in their impacts among combatant states and societies, have in respects impeded development and trade, but overall have only temporarily slowed the unprecedented diffusion of industrial innovation throughout the

---

1 As a marker of the expanding scope of empire over successive colonial eras, in his magisterial treatment of the history and geography of the Mediterranean World of Phillip II, Fernand Braudel observed that 'Venice's possessions at the end of the sixteenth century would be the equivalent of the British Empire stripped of its holdings east of Suez' (1973, Vol. II: 846).

world, and an attendant growth of trade and exchange of all kinds. As a corollary development, certain cities have emerged as the control centres of this era of economic development and the expansion of trade and investment, prefiguring first the 'world city' of Peter Hall (1966), within which urban scale, specialization, and corporate projection were critical signifiers of primacy, and then the global city variants proposed by John Friedmann, Saskia Sassen, and other contributors, for whom finance, corporate control and specialized intermediate services are key to global city formation.

The more narrowly economistic expressions of what globalization means for cities have been vigorously contested, not least in Michael Peter Smith's concept of *transnational urbanism* (2001), within which diasporic social relations in the service of progressive activism are accorded a more central influence in the operation of world cities; and by P.J. Taylor, John Beaverstock and their colleagues at the Global and World City (GaWC) centre at Loughborough, UK – a contingent of scholars whose contributions include a demonstration of the need to acknowledge social, cultural and political functions as important elements of global city taxonomies.

Economic Change as Driver of Urban Rescaling

As John Harrison (Chapter 3, this volume) has persuasively argued, economic change has in diverse ways contributed to a complex rescaling of cities at the supra- and sub-national levels, a tendency seen by some as marginalizing the traditional Westphalian nation-state, but in Harrison's analysis still involving state agencies and actors in the inscribing of new scripts of urbanization. Certainly, global processes have in many ways subverted the integrity of nationally-specific production systems in all but a few examples (Germany as the best case), supplanted by recombination of localized industrial districts and regional innovation zones. These include supra-state configurations such as the constellation of conurbations extending from London to Milan; and, at the regional scale, by the advanced industrial northern arc of Italy, extending from the Ligurian Sea to the Adriatic. As Harrison observes, the state in most cases has promoted these emergent forms of economic development, notionally at least in the national interest.

At the centre of power projection lies the rarefied domain of intermediate finance, and more particularly the animating agencies of capital, which in Harrison's view are always engaged in a search for 'favourable conditions' for accumulation, the effects of which include a destabilizing 'reterritorialization of capital' among (and within) global cities. Capital accumulation underpins the emergence of a new constellation of global cities in the Asian realm, including Tokyo, Seoul and Shanghai, as well as Hong Kong and Singapore. In this latter connection, Ackbar Abbas has observed that it is 'imperialism that produces by definition the colonial city, but the colonial city can also prefigure the global city' (1997: 3), in turn suggesting that the imposition of entrepôt roles on cities by imperial powers and agencies can facilitate globalization in the post-colonial city: a form of competitive advantage in terms of the legacy effects of colonialism.[2] At the very least there is now manifest a multi-polar global city reality in Asia: the leading growth theatre of the twenty-first century.

Opening up the Global City Discourse

Other regions and narratives have come to the fore within the urban studies discourse. These include metropolitan centres of what Edgar Pieterse (Chapter 11, this volume) characterizes as 'middle income' societies where global processes (including capital flows, international immigration, and cultural fusion as well as conflict) are increasingly prominent, including the principal metropoles of Latin America, South Asia, and sub-Saharan Africa, and which incorporate (to illustrate) São Paulo, Rio de Janeiro, Johannesburg, Istanbul, Mexico City, Mumbai, Delhi, Chennai and Bangalore.

The complex economic geographies of these cities comprise both high-powered multi-nationals as well as very large informal sectors, as Pieterse acknowledges; but as he also observes, dualism is very much a condition of cities in advanced societies as well. In this regard, Björn Surborg has written about the dualistic structure of Johannesburg, South Africa's candidate global city (Surborg, 2011), while others have highlighted the co-presence of the first and third worlds within principal metropolitan cities of the North, such as New York and Los Angeles (Abu-Lughod, 1999). The ascendant cities of the South must now be incorporated in any serious discourse of the global city.

The impress of globalization reflects Sassen's well-known dictum concerning the socially polarizing consequences of globalizing cities ([1991]2001). At the upper social echelon of major cities in both the global north and south is the transnational financial élite, following the expansion of new forms and instruments of capitalism worldwide, and including a large and expanding contingent of the super-wealthy in China and India, as well as among the petro-economies of the Middle East and Russia. This nascent financial power is expressed in various ways, including within the upper echelons of residential markets within globalizing cities.[3]

---

2 The colonial city was a site of exploitation, dislocation and cruelty. But positive legacies for some cities in a globalizing age include early investments by imperial powers in the infrastructures, institutions and systems of trade, together with network formation – contributing in part to the accumulated competitive advantage of the post-colonial city.

3 The examples of residences selling for upwards of £50 million in districts such as Mayfair and Knightsbridge in London are well known as expressions of the financial power of global élites in cities at the peak of the urban hierarchy, but there may be similar effects in smaller, transnational cities. In Vancouver, for example, housing prices are by some distance the highest in Canada, but wages exceed the national average by only a little, suggesting the inflationary impacts of immigration and capital inflows within the local housing market. See in this regard David Ley's (2011), *Transpacific Lifelines: Millionaire Migrants* (Wiley-Blackwell).

But as Niall Ferguson has observed recently, another blunt fact of global capitalism is the sharply reduced returns to unskilled labour – both in 'developing' and 'advanced' cities (Ferguson, in Posner, 2011). As Pieterse (Chapter 11, this volume) makes clear, income inequality is highest in African cities, while the evidence from advanced economies such as the United States and Canada points to widening divides in incomes and earnings (Bourne et al., 2011).

Governance and Governmentality in the Global City Project

The defining political feature of globalizing cities is the commitment to building competitive advantage as a means of attracting capital and skilled professional labour. In this regard Ian Deas and Nicola Headlam (Chapter 8, this volume) have observed that 'boosterism is the new imperative', underscored by their reference to Eric Swyngedouw's remark that entrepreneurial governance is 'so potent a credo that it forecloses the political' (2009: 11).

But there are also points of resistance to the globalization narrative. These include movements as diverse in their ideologies and practices as the jihadist campaign against what Islamists see as the Western mission to impose a form of capitalism inflected with Judeo-Christian values among Muslim states and societies, in opposition to their own fervent hopes for a renewal of the Caliphate, as a particularly zealous and apparently unappeasable force; as well as 'indigenous' or informal resisters such as the 'Occupy [name a city]' tendency of 2011, and innumerable other examples *ad hoc*.

Deas and Headlam acknowledge that the formation of 'multi-actor, cross-sectoral coalitions and partnerships', the influence of 'élite actor networks' as governance modality, and the emergence of 'hybrid forms of governance' have in the aggregate 'disrupted the binary relationships between state and market which once underpinned social, economic and political relations in cities'.

Complex arrangements of state and quasi-state agencies in the pursuit of urban-regional development are of course endemic to the European Union (Moulaert, 2000); but tendencies in this direction can also be found in middle-income states of the global south. To the example of Brazil, where as Pieterse acknowledges the state has enabled institutional mechanisms in an effort to expand 'grass-roots driven urban democratization' (Chapter 11, this volume), Deas and Headlam add the case of Mexico, where hybridization is now a significant mechanism of urban-regional development. Here the authors note that in Mexico the familiar landscape of neoliberal governance (exemplified by private-public partnerships) coexists and in some cases constructively interacts with more progressive movements and social forces to achieve public benefit from economic growth. There is no suggestion of course that even in the best of cases these emergent forms of governance are likely to succeed in elevating community needs over business interests within coalitions of social forces, but meaningful amelioration of the human impress of capital within cities is apparently possible.[4]

BEYOND THE POST-INDUSTRIAL CITY: CULTURE, INNOVATION AND DUALISM

The onset of the classic industrial city of the nineteenth century generated ensembles of production and dense congeries of worker housing, and distinctive forms of social interchange and consumption, engendering a new kind of city in Europe and North America, although this defining industrial vocation coexisted with important commercial and other service functions of the city.

The collapse of Fordism and a shift of production capacity and labour to the growth economies of Asia combined to shape a New Industrial Division of Labour (NIDL) (Fröbel et al., 1980), and a trajectory of post-industrialism in the cities of the Atlantic realm. Defining processes included (firstly) an attenuation of the old urban working class and its residential, social and landscape correlates; and, secondly, the emergence of a post-industrial city, the leading features of which were: (1) an emergent intermediate services economy; (2) the rise of a modernist high-rise central corporate complex, together with a segmented and hierarchical office labour force; and (3) a 'new middle class' of professionals and managers, anticipated by Daniel Bell in his prescient volume on the coming of post-industrial society in the United States (1973), a cohort projecting cultural, social and political significance. Marxist scholars rejected both the terminology and the political message of post-industrialism, in favour of *post-Fordism,* which more narrowly described a manufacturing landscape in the West largely stripped of its unionized, mass-production sectors, supplanted by *flexible specialization* as redefining production modality.[5]

The Persistence of Developmental Informalism and Inequality

Developmental dualism shapes in large part the thematic features of a vast literature on transitional states, societies and cities, including innumerable studies of

---

4 In this regard, a key finding of a five-year collaborative project on 'Multilevel Governance in Canada' directed by Robert Young and Andrew Sancton of the University of Western Ontario concluded that in the many studies of social forces coalitions undertaken in the project, business interests prevailed over community organizations in setting agendas, managing processes, and achieving benefits in the large majority of cases.

5 In a cogent review of the post-industrial thesis and its contested meanings and discourses, David Ley (2005) concludes that in the most important respects Daniel Bell's forecast of an emergent information- and knowledge-based society projecting cultural and political as well as social signifiers was correct, citing David Harvey's observation that Bell's reading of the seminal 1970s period of transformational change was 'probably more accurate than many of the left attempts to grasp what was happening' (1989b: 353).

informality in South-East Asia (see, for example, Leaf, 1996), as well as in Latin America, the latter exemplified by Janice Perlman's longitudinal study (2010) of the Rio *favelas* over four decades.

But as the contributors to this volume attest, informality is increasingly also a feature of advanced economies, shaped both by the market and by the neoliberal state in capitalism. In this regard Colin Williams observes (Chapter 7, this volume) that informal economic activity and forms of work, far from constituting 'left-overs' of pre-capitalist economies, are 'part and parcel of the processes of modernization' within cities and developmental regimes: a 'persistent and substantial feature of many urban economies' throughout the world urban system.

Precarious employment – labour cohorts subject to deskilling, marginalization, and downward pressure on salaries and income, mostly in the non-unionized (or de-unionized) sectors – has been seen largely as characteristic of occupations embedded within the lowest rungs of the urban economy, such as janitorial work, cleaning, repair, taxi drivers, private security staff and some forms of clerical, sales and personal services. But precarity is making inroads in the higher echelons of the urban economy and labour market, including the legal and financial sectors, as the idea of the 'sovereign consumer' (Glaeser et al., 2001) is extended from its traditional milieu of the retail market and other final demand services to the hitherto privileged professions.

This point can be illustrated by reference to the fortunes of office labour force, the lead employment growth sector of late-twentieth-century urban economies among advanced societies. Employment in the office economy comprised a complex strata of workers, comprising holders of capital, senior executives, middle managers, sales staff, supervisors, technical support, secretaries, junior clerical workers and receptionists, temporary staff, security personnel, and cleaners. Staff were mostly salaried, and enjoyed at least a modest benefit package. It was in many cases possible to transition upward, at least within broad occupational categories.

But there has been pervasive job-shedding and deskilling in some of the major occupational cohorts. Corporate mergers, down-sizing and global competition have substantially thinned the ranks of middle managers, while capital substitution and de-skilling have shredded the clerical ranks. Office occupations have also been impacted by out-sourcing, including IT staff. The New International Division of Labour first postulated to explain the shift of manufacturing labour from the old Atlantic industrial economies to the lower-cost jurisdictions of the growth economies in the East increasingly involves service workers, a point acknowledged by Danny MacKinnon (Chapter 6, this volume). In consequence the office workforce has become more sharply polarized, as 'employment processes and work practices for different groups of people become increasingly '"unbundled" and fragmented' (MacKinnon, Chapter 6, this volume), and is therefore not quite the mainstay of the middle class it once was. At the same time, senior managers have overall done well throughout the vagaries of deep restructuring, especially those in the financial sector, as Alan Walks has shown (2011).

Urban economies and labour markets incorporate a large share of low-paid, often dirty and even dangerous jobs. Formerly, there was a tacit belief that with diligence and accumulated experience workers could in many cases progress within the urban labour market – the fabled storyline of the city of opportunity and upward mobility writ large. But the experience of economic change in advanced cities over the past two decades suggests that workers on the lower rungs of the occupational ladder are finding it more difficult to transition upwards, while even many in the middle and upper-middle echelons of the labour market are vulnerable to down-sizing, capital substitution and job-shedding, and to housing market pressures.

From 'Creative Class' to 'Cognitive-Cultural Economy' – Post-Industrialism *Redux*?

The urban studies literature, including urban and economic geography, sociology, cultural studies, and planning, offers a proliferation of readings and interpretations of the new cultural economy of the city (or, alternatively, the *creative economy of the city*, a term endorsed in a report published in 2010 by UNCTAD). Andy Pratt and the author (Pratt and Hutton, 2013) have generated a synthesis of the analytic fields of the creative economy of the city, within which the following genres are acknowledged: (1) *global cities and the cultural economy*, which recognizes that creative industries, institutions and labour now comprise part of the deep specialization and power projection of global cities, along with finance and head offices; (2) *the cultural-historic city*, exemplified by the unique centres of cultural production, imagery and spectacle, such as Rome, Florence, Siena, Paris, and Beijing, including cultural tourism; (3) *culture as hook for Foreign Direct Investment*, an arena in which cultural amenity is ostensibly designed to attract talented professionals and leading-edge enterprises; (4) *culture as social regeneration*, a stream which incorporates local policies and programmes which combine aspects of social inclusion and humanistic cultural enhancement; and (5) *culture as industrial policy*, in which the cultural sector is treated essentially as a mainstream industry of the urban-regional economy, and is subject to inducements which include investment, infrastructure provision, and labour market programmes.

The new cultural economy of the city has for many scholars now taken centre stage in the larger arena of urban studies discourse and debates. Its positionality within urban studies parallels to a degree the long-running contestation concerning the meanings, experiences and policy conflicts of post-industrialism. Stringent criticisms of post-industrialism as ideology, and more specifically the positioning of services as successor to manufacturing industry in Western societies, a school of critique exemplified by Doreen Massey and Richard Meegan in the UK (1981), and Barry Bluestone and Bennett Harrison (1982) in the US, can be seen as antecedents of contemporary disparagements of creative industries as panacea of urban regeneration, as asserted by Jamie Peck, Stefan Krätke, Roger Keil and others.

One of the sharp divides which characterize the field of urban studies concerns the role of the artist within certain communities of the city, and more particularly within the post-industrial terrains of the inner city, with some social geographers identifying the artist as (in essence) the villain in the piece, the almost inevitable precursor to more comprehensive social upgrading and dislocation, while others, notably economic geographers such as Ann Markusen, recognize the artist as the lead actors in urban regeneration (see Markusen and Schrock, 2004).

Similarly, while some celebrate the extraordinary vibrancy and creative energies characteristic of the contemporary cultural quarter, and the rich employment and social realization possibilities of these areas for (especially) younger workers, others just as fervently point to the deep inequalities of the creative economy labour market (Peck, 2005), while others extend their analytic gaze beyond the (apparently) cozy confines of these cultural sites to proximate industrial communities, acknowledging property inflation tendencies and dislocative outcomes of creative industry formation (Catungal et al., 2009).

THE IMPRESS OF ECONOMIC CHANGE IN THE CITY: FROM THE REPRODUCTION OF SPACE TO THE RECONSTRUCTION OF PLACE

Space in the city has been conventionally constructed in terms of social aggregates, notably in the form of neighbourhoods and communities, on the part of urban and social geographers and urban sociologists, and in terms of the industrial district (which traditionally formed prominent features of the urban-regional space-economy), by practitioners of industrial urbanism. These constructions of space in the city were integral to the development of theory; to the situation of evocative case studies which have animated the urban studies discourse for over a century; and to the full range of policy and programme initiatives conducted by the local state and its partners – from an extended lineage of housing and welfare initiatives, to the area-based regeneration programmes of the contemporary city.

The theoretical utility of these social and economic territories was based to a degree on the perception of their durability and resilience, preconditions for advancing new concepts which might have some empirical and explanatory purchase over time. But the comprehensive restructuring experience of the late twentieth century subverted many of the assumptions of urban theory, producing a new literature which attempted to explain the reconfiguration of space and its underlying logics.

Economic Change and the Urban-Regional Space-Economy

The influence of seminal ideas explaining the relationship between the economy and urban space continue to filter down to the present age, following the effects of industrial innovation, restructuring and crises. Thus, the *industrial district* which played such a prominent role in the foundational economic theory of Alfred Marshall, and in the formation of the classic industrial city (see Lewis, 2008 for the evocative Chicago case), was picked up and recast in the literature on the 'new industrial district' which had its heyday in the 1980s (Harrison, 1992), and included influential work on interdependency between technological innovation, production practices and social relations in iconic regions such as Emilia-Romagna, and Baden Württemberg, in Europe, and Silicon Valley and Route 128, in the US. Here the emphasis was on the extended 'regional' dimension of the urban-regional economy (including Jean Gottmann's original model of the *megalopolis* which under-scored the importance of Manhattan's corporate office complex, while encompassing the economy of the much larger US north-eastern seaboard; Gottmann, 1961).

Traditional industrial districts based on manufacturing have experienced sharp declines and in some cases collapse. Here we can reference the famous mosaic of specialized production, engineering and warehousing districts in the London's inner north-east quadrant which positioned the British capital as a 'world-scale' centre of light manufacturing over the span of much of the nineteenth and twentieth centuries, but which suffered a precipitous decline over the 1970s and 1980s. A more recent example is that of Manhattan's storied fashion and garment district, identified by Norma Rantisi as late as 2002 as the largest and densest industrial district in the United States, but a complex which has been described as in 'freefall' owing to a mix of exogenous (offshore competition) and local (property market tendencies) factors.

The collapse of traditional industrial districts in the late twentieth century created theoretical disjuncture and conceptual experimentation. These efforts included Michael Dear and Stephen Flusty's whimsical interpretation of 'postmodern urbanism' (1998) based loosely on the geography of Los Angeles, within which the received logics of location (centrality, agglomeration, clustering and networks) were ostensibly suspended in favour of an apparently random positioning of activities within the urban landscape – an outcome, it was alleged, of the workings of 'Keno Capitalism'.

More penetrating analyses have produced a series of propositions that incorporate templates of urban morphology shaped by economic change, including Allen Scott's influential sketch of the role of industry and new divisions of labour in the structure of the late twentieth-century metropolis (1988b). Peter Hall's structural model (2006) of the global city makes room for cultural, retail and experiential industries and activities, in addition to the conventional 'power sectors' of international banking and multi-national headquarters, a formulation exactly 40 years on from his original model of the 'world city' (Hall, 1966). In a similar vein Stefan Krätke (Chapter 4, this volume) offers a finer-grained portrayal of urban zonal structure informed by the emergence of new economic spaces, a model which incorporates (1) 'extended edge cities' (such as Heathrow in Outer London); (2) 'outermost edge city complexes', exemplified here by Reading in the London-South-East Region; (3) 'internal edge cities', such as La Défense (Paris) or London's Docklands; and (4) 'specialized subcentres' within the city, a category which comprises the plethora of convention centres, exhibition and entertainment complexes which increasingly shape the urban landscape in large- and medium-size metropolitan cities.

Commingling of the Social and the Industrial in the City: The Revival of Place

'Place' occupies a rich and prominent niche within the ethnographic tradition of urban studies, including an extended stream of case studies of communities and neighbourhoods within cities, often emphasizing the distinctive quality and more universalist aspects of class, occupations, household formation, institutional affiliation, and social values and practices. This tradition includes some of the famous studies of class and community in the industrial city, exemplified by Michael Young's influential study of the working-class populations and community in Bethnal Green, in East London (Young and Willmott, 1957), as well as numerous monographs and papers featuring 'thick description' on aspects of continuity and change in communities (Geertz, 1973).

With the late-twentieth-century collapse of traditional manufacturing, this particular genre of urban studies lapsed for a time, as scholars sought to elucidate the empirical dimensions and theoretical import of the new service cohorts, including their incursion into traditional working-class communities. Thus, the ascendancy of a 'new middle class' of managers and professionals, their behavioural signifiers, and more particularly their lead role in social upgrading and dislocation, evolved as one of the most powerful study areas of urban geographers and sociologists (Ley, 1996). But since the 1990s new trajectories of urban growth and change have reinserted an industrial narrative in studies of community development. In this regard K.C. Ho (Chapter 13, this volume) has posed the question: Does place matter in the dynamics of production?

What Ivan Turok (Chapter 5, this volume) calls 'redundant spaces' produced as residuals of protracted industrial decline have been key to the urban regeneration storyline of the past two decades or so. As Turok observes, much of the economic malaise of cities in the post-industrial era is associated not with conditions of overall urban decline – and here he cites the fact that only 13 European cities have experienced demographic or 'systemic' contraction over a quarter-century – but rather selective processes of disinvestment and restructuring internalized within the city.[6] The primary motive force for the regeneration of place, including both residential and commercial areas as well as the perhaps better-known cases of obsolescent industrial districts, has been *production* of various kinds, including, initially, artistic production, then higher-value design, and professional services, including, famously, the complex of new media industries and labour that has played such a central role in urban redevelopment in cities such as London, Berlin, San Francisco, and New York.

Local-regional contingency also shapes the specific processes and outcomes of place-based urban regeneration (Evans, 2004; Hutton, 2008/2010). To illustrate: Michael Indergaard's evocative account (2004) of the rise (and fall) of a world-scale

---

6 These include three cities in the UK (Greater Liverpool, Newcastle, and Glasgow) and seven in Germany, including cities in the Ruhr, Saarbrucken and Leipzig (Turok, Chapter 5, this volume).

new media economy in South Manhattan in the 1990s reflects general processes, but was shaped by a distinctive (and in some regards unique) mélange of forces, including New York's financial, property, advertizing, media and fine arts industries, animated in turn by a *dramatis personae* including individuals and groups drawn from the ranks of professionals, managers, entrepreneurs, publicists, politicians and speculators. In contrast, K. C. Ho (Chapter 13, this volume) recalls the cast of influential characters brought to life in Richard Lloyd's resonant account (2006) of Wicker Park's 'neo-Bohemia' (Chicago), a diverse community comprised of 'accidental collections of members of society's fringes', including struggling artists, students and down-and-outs, each contributing to a new blend of 'art and commerce in the post-industrial city'.

CULTURES OF CONSUMPTION AND THE NEO-INDUSTRIAL CITY: EXCURSIONS IN PLACE-MARKETING

As Marguerite van den Berg (Chapter 10, this volume) observes, the increasingly sophisticated and aggressive place-marketing of the current century had its modern origins in the deindustrialization of the late twentieth century, especially in the United States. Here she writes 'US cities were the first to develop place-marketing because they were more dependent on their local tax base and, thus, on their local economies'.

While the revival of evocative (if in many cases obsolescent or 'redundant') urban places can be attributed to a reassertion of specialized production of one form or another, the storyline has included a more eclectic mix of factors and actors, including gentrifiers. To this familiar social form of displacement we must now add what Andy Pratt describe as 'industrial gentrification' (2009), entailing a succession process privileging élite creatives and professional design enterprises, including 'starchitects', film-makers, music business moguls, and others, adding momentum to the pervasive upgrading tendency of certain districts of the city, and dislocating start-up and low-margin creatives.

The remaking and reimaging of place as elements of city marketing programmes represents not simply a logic of entrepreneurship and a natural desire to underscore the distinctive attributes of cities and communities in a globalizing world, but rather a highly contested and regressive ideology of urbanism. Here, van den Berg asserts that the city 'is a primary place of image production and consumption' across a range of (often divergent) perspectives and motivations, including the state, market actors, and citizens, with the latter involving individuals as well as 'communities' – both place-based collectives, and communities of identity. Image-making has become part and parcel of the function of the local state, for which '[t]he ability to capture the imagination of (future) inhabitants, investors or other publics has fast become one of the most important assets of cities' (van den Berg, Chapter 10, this volume).

As van den Berg attests, the more pervasive tendency in place-marketing takes the form of myth-making – the rewriting of meaning attached to cities, their environments and their constituent communities and districts, as well as the social and economic effects they produce. Cities are (re)branded as international gateways, and as sites of entertainment and cosmopolitan living, as inducements to foreign capital and talent. Here, van den Berg cites David Harvey's pithy observation from almost a quarter-century ago (1989b) that place-marketing often presents a 'carnival mask' to visitors, designed to cover underlying economic and social problems in the city. She offers as a particularly evocative example of high-stakes place-marketing in the case of Rio de Janeiro, host to both the 2014 football World Cup, and also the 2016 Summer Olympic Games. Certainly the magnitude of financial risks associated with these two enormously costly ventures, to be staged only two years apart, are clear enough, with the state (and thereby the public) on the hook for what are likely to be massive over-runs and debts.

But there are other costs to consider in social accounts, not least in the attempts to produce scripts attractive to prospective foreign attendees and visitors. Here, van den Berg observes that the place re-branding for Rio has produced highly romanticized imaginaries of two of the city's most evocative environmental features: the beaches, especially Ipanema and Copacabana, and the *favelas*, portrayed at least subliminally as contrast to the resolutely commercial and industrial tonality of São Paulo, and deflecting the visitor's gaze from the chronic conditions of deprivation and marginality which form the essence of socio-economic reality in two of Rio's iconic 'places'.

POSTSCRIPT: ECONOMIC CHANGE AND THE EMERGENT URBAN LANDSCAPE

In this essay I have explored some ideas concerning the development of cities of the twenty-first century, viewed through the lens of economic change, while acknowledging the extent to which social, cultural and environmental factors permeate the workings of advanced economies. What follows is a summary of some key observations.

Economic Change and Multi-scalar Urbanization

The global cities landscape continues to evolve, reflecting important changes in patterns of control, in the practices and diffusive effects of capitalism, in the role of technology in urban growth and change (Corey et al., Chapter 2, this volume), and changes in relations between the state and the economy. An earlier global cities discourse privileging London, New York and Tokyo has been supplanted by a multi-polar landscape of primacy and specialization which takes into account the emergent metropoles of the new growth regions, especially – but not exclusively – in the East Asian economic realm. Here Shanghai, Beijing, Seoul, Hong Kong and Singapore already possess significant projection capacity, perhaps threatening Tokyo's primacy in the region (Campanella, 2008); while the next phase of global city formation is likely to include important niches for Mumbai, Jakarta, Mexico City, São Paulo, Johannesburg, and Istanbul.

As K. C. Ho (Chapter 13, this volume) has observed, primacy is still a potent force in Asia, in part owing to the extraordinarily high concentration of political, economic and cultural power in the capitals. In the US the rise of the cities of the Sunbelt over the past quarter-century has reconfigured inter-regional growth dynamics, although the post-2008 recession has hit several of these very hard, underscoring the importance of economic resiliency to the welfare of the city (Polèse, Chapter 9, this volume). Seattle, too, is an interesting economic story, with no fewer than six world-scale multinationals of global power projection and cultural influence encompassed within its metropolitan territory in the Pacific North-West. But the established American world cities of New York, Chicago and Los Angeles still retain much of their traditional strength, and indeed have added some important sectors, notably in the cultural economy. In Germany, Berlin and Hamburg and the cities of the Ruhr project economic power and urban vitality, but there has been something of a shift in dynamism to the cities of the *Süddeutsche*, notably Frankfurt, Stuttgart and Munich, based on strengths in finance, knowledge industries, and advanced-technology and high-design manufacturing, notably in the automotive and electronic industries.

Linking the global and the local in a multi-scalar urbanizing world are the strategic shifts in the economic structures and systems of the metropolitan space-economy. The growth and development of suburban (and exurban) areas of the city-region is of great significance, a fact recognized in a major international collaboration on 'Global Suburbanisms' directed by Roger Keil of York University, Toronto. These include not only the huge suburban industrial and employment clusters in North American cities, but also the expansion of regional centres and labour in Chinese city-regions distant from the urban core, shaped in part by the relaxation of controls from the Maoist era and the rise of the local developmental state, and now producing dispersion in Guangzhou, among other cities (see Wu and Yeh, 1999). At the same time, though, the post-industrial core has been revitalized as a critical zone of new enterprise formation, innovation and experimentation over a sequence of restructuring processes from the 1990s, not only in Western cities such as London, Milan, Barcelona, and New York, but also in the 'new economic spaces' of East Asian cities, such as Tokyo, Seoul, Shanghai and Singapore (Daniels et al., 2011).

Revisiting the Production-Consumption Debate

Scholars such as Terry Nichols Clark and Edward Glaeser (2008) have suggested (firstly) that the urban production function among advanced cities has been undermined, and (secondly) that these cities are now better positioned to perform as sites of consumption. Cities such as Chicago and London have been largely stripped of manufacturing, and have very large consumption sectors which cater both to domestic markets and to visitors of all kinds.

But this viewpoint seems too narrowly wedded to the traditional view of the classic industrial city. Aside from the continuing importance of the *producer services* sector, a major feature of advanced urban economies, and still an important measure of global city specialization, we can assert that the 'knowledge-based economy' includes a critical *(knowledge) production* platform (universities and colleges, think-tanks and institutes of various kinds, R&D agencies and so on); the new cultural economy of the city is likewise characterized by a diverse array of *production industries* and activities, from fine arts and graphic design to video games and internet services; and the 'livable' or 'convivial city' which has entered the discourses of urbanism as a kind of exemplar is also dependent on 'production' – from the *reproduction* of space and place, to the *production* of imageries and imaginaries. Then there are the contemporary storylines of *reindustrialization* to acknowledge, shaped in part by the green economy agenda, a selective phenomenon, certainly, but indicative of a significant trajectory of urban redevelopment among some advanced cities. The production function is still a critical sector for most cities.

Economic Change and the Urban Economy: Re-inserting the Environment

In the classic industrial era there was a tacit consciousness of the interdependency between cities and the environment, as seen in the inflows of material resources required for production – iron, coal, timber, water, sand and gravel, for example – and the equally tangible quality of manufactured outputs. And indeed social effects of environmental externalities formed part of the Marxist critique of the nineteenth-century industrial city.

But as a series of benchmark conferences highlighting the role of cities in the global sustainability problématique attests (the Rio summit 1992; Habitat II), cities have in important ways a more intimate connection with both the regional ecology and the larger bio-sphere, measured in part by the alarmingly expanding human consumption dimensions of the 'urban ecological footprint', as developed by William Rees. As Mark Whitehead (Chapter 12, this volume) observes, the 'role of cities in the disruption, regulation and maintenance of variously-scaled environmental systems is only now starting to be discussed'. Whitehead is critical of the false binary projected by the two solitudes of urban economic and environmental policy, acknowledging the 'forging of antagonistic ecological movements to challenge the stale consensus of corporate environmentalism'. Where the urban economy comes in is suggested in the transition from narrowly-conceived 'industrial ecology' systems of the late-twentieth-century to the more holistic ideas of 'eco-localization' (see for example, Unsworth, 2011).

Economic Change in the City: Theoretical Conjecture

We cannot conclude without some mention of where all this might lead in terms of the ongoing theoretical enterprise. Certainly the profile of twenty-first century cities shaped by our contributing authors suggests important departures from the contours of the post-industrial city and post-Fordist urban economy, while the intensifying relations between cities and global circuits of capital, culture, knowledge and trade have produced new narratives of globalizing cities. I tried to make a point earlier in the paper concerning the striking parallels between the nature of the debates around post-industrialism and post-Fordism in the late-twentieth-century, and the contrasting ideas of Richard Florida's 'creative class' (2002) and Allen Scott's concept of the 'cognitive-cultural economy'. In each case there are ideological issues at stake, as well as conflict over taxonomies and empirics, and concerning policy choices and consequences. The theoretical outcomes, however, are framed somewhat differently. Those who fought the political values of post-industrialism in the 1980s, though in most cases unsuccessful in reversing policies, remain largely unreconciled; but the weight of scholarship has largely endorsed the predictions of Daniel Bell concerning the social outcomes of a knowledge-based economy (Ley, 2005).

In the contestation over the new cultural economy, the weight of scholarship is sharply – sometimes viscerally – critical of Florida's more ebullient view of the creative class and its social hegemony in the contemporary city (Krätke, 2011). Overall the judgement must be that his class taxonomies are somewhat promiscuous, inclusive of occupational groups better positioned within the larger intermediate services sector and the 'new middle class'; the benefits over-sold and social costs under-accounted; and the policy prescriptions overly universalist and boosterish. Here, Allen Scott's proposal for a 'cognitive-cultural economy' has more purchase, with the 'cognitive' signifier at least gesturing to the long-run value appreciation of knowledge as the critical underpinning of urban economies, both in the developed urban world and increasingly in transitional cities, and therefore of more conceptual utility. It has the flavour, though, of a 'transient taxonomy', rather than a durable theory of urban-economic change. Might this be the best we can do, for now?

References

Abbas, A. (1997) *Hong Kong and the Politics of Disappearance*. Minneapolis, MN: University of Minnesota Press.

Abbot, A. (1997) 'Of time and space: The contemporary relevance of the Chicago School', *Social Forces*, 75(4): 1149–82.

Abers, R. (2000) *Inventing Local Democracy: Grassroots Politics in Brazil*. Boulder, CO & London: Lynne Reiner Publishers.

Abu-Lughod, J. (1999) *New York, Chicago, Los Angeles: America's World Cities*. Minneapolis, MN: University of Minnesota Press.

Adams, D. and Watkins, C. (2002) *Greenfields, Brownfields and Housing Development*. Oxford: Blackwell.

Adams, D., Disberry, A., Hutchinson, N. and Munjoma, T. (2001) 'Ownership constraints to brownfield redevelopment', *Environment and Planning A*, 33: 453–77.

Adema, W. and Ladaique, M. (2009) 'How expensive is the Welfare State?: Gross and Net Indicators in the OECD Social Expenditure Database (SOCX)', *OECD Social, Employment and Migration Working Papers*, No. 92, Paris: OECD Publishing.

Alessio, D. and Jóhannsdóttir, A.L. (2011) 'Geysers and "girls": Gender, power and colonialism in Icelandic tourist imagery', *European Journal of Women's Studies*, 18(1): 35–50.

Allen, J., Massey, D. and Cochrane, A. (1998) *Rethinking the Region: Spaces of Neoliberalism*. London: Routledge.

Allmendinger, P. and Haughton, G. (2009) 'Soft spaces, fuzzy boundaries, and metagovernance: The new spatial planning in the Thames Gateway', *Environment and Planning A*, 41(3): 617–33.

Amin, A. (ed.) (2010) *The Social Economy. International Perspectives on Economic Solidarity*. London and New York: Zed Books.

Amin, A. and Thrift, N. (1995) 'Globalization, Institutional "Thickness" and the Local Economy', in P. Healey, D. Cameron, S. Davoudi and A. Madani-Pour (eds) *Managing Cities – The New Urban Context*. Chichester: Wiley. pp. 91–108.

Amsden, A. and Chu, W.W. (2003) *Beyond Late Development: Taiwan's Upgrading Policies*. Cambridge, MA: MIT Press.

Anttiroiko, A.V. (2009) 'Making of an Asia-Pacific high-technology hub: Reflections on the large-scale business site development projects of the Osaka City and the Osaka Prefecture', *Regional Studies*. 43(5): 759–69.

Arauzo-Carod, J.-M. and Viladecans-Marsal, E. (2009) 'Industrial location at the intra-metropolitan level: The role of agglomeration economies', *Regional Studies*, 43(4): 545–58.

Atkinson, R. (2004) 'The evidence on the impact of gentrification: New lessons for the urban renaissance?' *European Journal of Housing Policy*, 4(1): 107–31.

Audit Commission (2008) *A Mine of Opportunities: Local Authorities and the Regeneration of the English Coalfields*. London: Audit Commission.

Audretsch, D.B. and Feldman, M.P. (1996) 'Innovative clusters and the industry life cycle', *Review of Industrial Organization*, 11: 253–73.

Audretsch, D.B., Lehmann, E.E. and Warning, S. (2005) 'University spillovers and new firm location', *Research Policy*, 34: 1113–22.

Aytar, V. and Rath, J. (2012) *Selling Ethnic Neighborhoods: The Rise of the Neighborhood as Places of Leisure and Consumption*. New York: Routledge.

Bailey, N. and Manzi, T. (2008) *Developing and Sustaining Mixed Tenure Housing Developments*. York: Joseph Rowntree Foundation.

Baiocchi, G. (2001) 'Participation, activism and politics: The Porto Alegre experiment and deliberative democratic theory', *Politics and Society*, 29(1): 43–72.

Baldwin, R.E. and Martin, P. (2004) 'Agglomeration and regional growth', in J.V. Henderson and J.-F. Thise (eds) *Handbook of Regional and Urban Economics*. Amsterdam: Elsevier. Volume 4. pp. 2670–788.

Barnes, T.J. (1999) 'Industrial Geography, Institutional Economics, and Innis', in T.G. Barnes and S. Gettler (eds) *The New Industrial Geography: Regions, Regulations and Institutions*. London: Routledge. pp. 1–20.

Barrientos, A. (2010) 'Social Protection and Poverty', *Social Policy and Development Programme Paper*, No. 42. Geneva: United Nations Research Institute for Social Development.

Barthes, R. (1972 [1957]) *Mythologies*. New York: Hill and Wang.

Bartik, T.J. (2009) 'The revitalization of older industrial cities: A review essay of *Retooling for Growth*', *Growth and Change*, 40(1): 1–29.

Barnekov, T., Boyle, R. and Rich, D. (1989) *Privatism and Urban Policy in Britain and the United States*. Oxford: Oxford University Press.

Bathelt, H., Malmberg, A. and Maskell, P. (2002) 'Clusters and knowledge: Local buzz, global pipelines and the process of knowledge creation', *Danish Research Unit for Industrial Dynamics*. Druid Working Paper No. 02–12. Aalborg: Aalborg University.

BCG [The Boston Consulting Group] (2010a) *Winning in Emerging Markets. A Guide to the World's Largest Growth Opportunity*. Boston: BCG.

BCG [Boston Consulting Group] (2010b) *The Global Infrastructure Challenge. Top Priorities for Public and Private Sectors*. Boston: Boston Consulting Group.

Beall, J. (2004) 'Surviving the City: Livelihoods and Linkages of the Urban Poor', in N. Devas (ed.) *Urban Governance, Voice and Poverty in the Developing World*. London: Earthscan. pp. 53–67.

Beatty, T., Fothergill, S. and Powell, R. (2007) 'Twenty years on: Has the economy of the UK coalfields recovered?', *Environment and Planning A*, 39(7): 1654–75.

Beauregard, R.A. (2003) *Voices of Decline: The Postwar Fate of US Cities*. 2nd edition. New York: Routledge.

Beauregard, R.A. (2009) 'Urban population loss in historical perspective: United States, 1820–2000', *Environment and Planning A*, 41: 514–28.

Beaverstock, J.V., Smith, R.G. and Taylor, P.J. (1999) 'A roster of world cities', *Cities*, 16: 445–58.

Beaverstock, J.V., Faulconbridge, J.R. and Hoyler, M. (2011) 'Globalization and the City', in A. Leyshon, R. Lee, L. McDowell and P. Sunley (eds) *The SAGE Handbook of Economic Geography*. London: Sage. pp. 189–201.

Beck, U. (2000) *The Brave New World of Work*. Cambridge: Polity.

Belghazi, T. (2006) 'Festivalization of urban space in Morocco', *Middle East Critique*, 15(1): 97–107.

Bell, D. (1973) *The Coming of Post-Industrial Society: A Venture in Social Forecasting*. New York: Basic Books.

Bell, D. (1974) *The Coming of Post-Industrial Society: A Venture in Social Forecasting*. London: Heinemann.

Bell, D. and Binnie, J. (2004) 'Authenticating queer space: Citizenship, urbanism and governance', *Urban Studies*, 41: 1807–20.

Bell, D. and Jayne, M. (eds) (2004) *City of Quarters: Urban Villages in the Contemporary City*. Aldershot: Ashgate.

Bender, D.E. (2004) *Sweated Work, Weak Bodies: Anti-Sweatshop Campaigns and Languages of Labor*. New Brunswick, NJ: Rutgers University Press.

Bernstein, S. (2000) 'Ideas, social structure and the compromise of liberal environmentalism', *European Journal of International Relations*, 6: 464–512.

Bertaud, A. (2013) 'Introduction: Urban Planning and Housing Affordability', in 10th Annual Demographia International Housing Affordability Survey 2014, Ratings for Metropolitan Markets. Available at http://www.demographia.com (accessed March 2014).

Beyers, W. (2002) 'Services and the new economy: Elements of a research agenda', *Journal of Economic Geography*, 2: 1–29.

Beyers, W. (2008) 'Revisiting the geography of the new economy', Western Regional Science Association 47th Annual Meeting, Waikoloa, Hawaii, February. pp. 1–34.

Bickford-Smith, V. (2009) 'Creating a city of the tourist imagination: The case of Cape Town, "The Fairest Cape of Them All"', *Urban Studies*, 46(9): 1763–85.

Biles, J. (2008) 'Informal work and livelihoods in Mexico: Getting by or getting ahead?', *Professional Geographer*, 60(4); 541–55.

Binnie, J. and Skeggs, B. (2004) 'Cosmopolitan knowledge and the production and consumption of sexualized space: Manchester's gay village', *The Sociological Review*, 52(1): 39–61.

Birmingham City Council (2008) *Birmingham 2026 – Our Vision for the Future: Sustainable Community Strategy*. Birmingham: Birmingham City Council.

Biswas, R.R. (2004) 'Making a technopolis in Hyderabad, India: The role of government IT policy', *Technological Forecasting and Social Change*, 71: 823–35.

Blake, D.P. and Mayhew, G.D. (2006) 'On the sustainability of the UK state pension system in the light of population ageing and declining fertility', *Economic Journal*, 116: F286–F305.

Block, F. (1990) *Postindustrial Possibilities*. Berkeley, CA: University of California Press.

Blom Hansen, T. and Verkaaik, O. (2009) 'Introduction – Urban charisma. On everyday mythologies in the city', *Critique of Anthropology*, 29(1): 5–26.

Bluestone, B. and Harrison, B. (1982) *The Deindustrialization of America: Plant Closing, Community Abandonment, and the Dismantling of Basic Industry*. New York: Basic Books.

BmBau (Bundesministerium für Raumordnung, Bauwesen und Städtebau) (1995) Raumordnungspolitischer Handlungsrahmen – Beschluss der Ministerkonferenz für Raumordnung in Düsseldorf am 8 März. Bonn: BmBau.

Boddy, M. (2003) 'Competitiveness and Cohesion in a Prosperous City-Region: The Case of Bristol', in M. Boddy and M. Parkinson (eds) *Changing Cities*. Bristol: The Policy Press.

Boeke, J.H. (1942) *Economies and Economic Policy in Dual Societies*. Haarlem: Tjeenk Willnik.

Bond, P. (2003) 'The Degeneration of South African Urban Policy After Apartheid', in P. Harrison, M. Huchzermeyer and M. Mayekiso (eds) *Confronting Fragmentation: Housing and Urban Development in a Democratising Society*. Cape Town: UCT Press.

Boonyabancha, S. (2008) 'Upgrading Thailand's Urban Settlements: A Community-Driven Process of Social Development', in *Assets, Livelihoods and Social Policy*. Washington, DC: World Bank. pp. 195–214.

Bosch, A., Rossouw, J., Claasen, T. and du Plessis, B. (2010) 'A Second look at measuring inequality in South Africa: The Gini co-efficient revisited'. Unpublished paper. Pretoria: Reserve Bank of South Africa.

Bosker, M., Brakman, S. Garretsen, H. and Schramm, M. (2008) 'A century of shocks: The evolution of the German city size distribution 1925–1999', *Regional Science and Urban Economics*, 38: 330–47.

Bourne, L.S., Hutton, T.A., Shearmur, R. and Simmons, J. (eds) (2011) *Canadian Urban Regions: Trajectories of Growth and Change*. Toronto: Oxford University Press.

Brakman, S., Garretsen, H. and Schramm, M. (2004) 'The strategic bombing of German cities during World War II and its impact on city growth', *Journal of Economic Geography*, 4(2): 201–18.

Braudel, F. (1973) (translated by Siân Reynolds) *The Mediterranean and the Mediterranean World of Phillip II*. Volumes I and II. Bungay: Fontana/Collins.

Brenner, N. (1998) 'Global cities, global states: Global city formation and state territorial restructuring in contemporary Europe', *Review of International Political Economy*, 5: 1–37.

Brenner, N. (1999) 'Globalization as reterritorialisation: The re-scaling of urban governance in the European Union', *Urban Studies*, 36(3): 431–51.

Brenner, N. (2004) *New State Spaces: Urban Governance and the Rescaling of Statehood*. Oxford: Oxford University Press.

Brenner, N. (2009a) 'Open question on state rescaling', *Cambridge Journal of Regions, Economy and Society*, 2: 123–39.

Brenner, N. (2009b) 'Cities and Territorial Competitiveness', in C. Rumford (ed.) *The SAGE Handbook of European Studies*. London: Sage. pp. 442–63.

Brenner, N. and Keil, R. (2006) *The Global Cities Reader*. Abingdon: Routledge.

Brenner, N., Peck, J. and Theodore, N. (2010) 'After neoliberalization?', *Globalizations*, 7(3): 327–35.

Brenner, N. and Theodore, N. (2002) 'Cities and the geographies of "actually existing neoliberalism"', *Antipode*, 34(3): 349–79.

Brockman, J. (1996) *Digerati: Encounters with the Cyber Elite*. San Francisco: HardWired.

Broudehoux, A. (2000) 'Image Making, City Marketing, and the Aesthetization of Social Inequality in Rio de Janeiro', in N. AlSayyad (ed.) *Consuming Tradition, Manufacturing Heritage: Global Norms and Urban Forms in the Age of Tourism*. London: Routledge.

Broudehoux, A. (2004) *The Making and Selling of Post-Mao Beijing*. New York: Routledge.

Brown, A. (2006) *Contested Space: Street Trading, Public Space and Livelihoods in Developing Cities*. London: ITDG Publishing.

Brown, J. and Męczyński, M. (2009) '"Complexcities": Locational choices of creative knowledge workers', *Built Environment*, 35(2): 238–52.

Brown, R.B., Xu, X. and Toth, J.F. (1998) 'Lifestyle options and economic strategies: Subsistence activities in the Mississippi Delta', *Rural Sociology*, 63(4): 599–623.

Bryceson, D. and Potts, D. (2006) *African Urban Economies*. Basingstoke: Palgrave Macmillan.

Bryson, J.R. (2007) 'The "second" global shift: The offshoring or global sourcing of corporate services and the rise of distanciated emotional labour', *Geografiska Annaler B*, (S1): 31–43.

Bryson, J.R. (2008) 'Service Economies, Spatial Divisions of Expertise and the Second Global Shift', in P.W. Daniels, M. Bradshaw, D. Shaw and J. Sidaway (eds) *Human Geography: Issues for the 21st Century*. Harlow: Pearson. pp. 339–57.

Bryson, J.R. and Daniels, P.W. (eds) (2007) *The Handbook of Service Industries*. Cheltenham: Edward Elgar.

Buck, N., Gordon, I., Harding, A. and Turok, I. (2005) *Changing Cities: Rethinking Urban Competitiveness, Cohesion, and Governance*. Basingstoke: Palgrave Macmillan.

Bunnell, T. and Das, D. (2010) 'Urban pulse – a geography of serial seduction: Urban policy transfer from Kuala Lumpur to Hyderabad', *Urban Geography*, 31(3): 277–84.

Burgers, J. (2002) *De Gefragmenteerde Stad*. Amsterdam: Boom.

Burgers, J. (2006) 'De stad als speelplaats', *Sociologie*, 2(1): 53–70.

Caldeira, T. (2000) *City of Walls: Crime, Segregation and Citizenship in São Paolo*. Berkeley, CA: University of California Press.

Caldwell, M.L. (2004) *Not by Bread Alone: Social Support in the New Russia*. Berkeley, CA: University of California Press.

Calhoun, C. (1995) *Critical Social Theory. Culture, History, and the Challenge of Difference*. Malden: Blackwell Publishers.

Calthorpe, P. and Fulton, W. (2001) *The Regional City: Planning for the End of Sprawl*. Washington, DC: Island Press.

Cambridge (2010) 'The resilient region', *Cambridge Journal of Regions, Economy and Society*. Special Issue 3(1).

Campanella, T.J. (2008) *Concrete Dragon: China's Urban Revolution and What it Means for the World*. New York: Princeton Architectural Press.

Carlino, G.A., Chatterjee, S. and Hunt, R.M. (2007) 'Urban density and the rate of invention', *Journal of Urban Economics*, 61(3): 389–419.

Castells, M. and Hall, P. (1994) *Technopoles of the World: The Making of 21st Century Industrial Complexes*. London and New York: Routledge.

Castells, M. and Portes, A. (1989) 'World Underneath: The Origins, Dynamics and Effects of the Informal Economy', in A. Portes, M. Castells and L.A. Benton (eds) *The Informal Economy: Studies in Advanced and Less Developing Countries*. Baltimore: Johns Hopkins University Press.

Castree, N., Coe, N., Ward, K. and Samers, M. (2004) *Spaces of Work: Global Capitalism and Geographies of Labour*. London: Sage.

Catungal, J.-P., Leslie, D. and Hii, Y. (2009) 'Geographies of displacement in the creative city: The case of Liberty Village, Toronto', *Urban Studies* Special Theme issue on *Trajectories of the New Economy*, 46(5&6): 1095–114.

Centre for Cities (2014) *Cities Outlook 2014*. Available at: www.centreforcities.org

Chakrabarty, D. (2000) *Provincializing Europe: Postcolonial Thought and Historical Difference*. Princeton, NJ: Princeton University Press.

Chan, A.H.N. (2000) 'Middle-Class Formation and Consumption in Hong Kong', in B.H. Chua (ed.) *Consumption in Asia: Lifestyles and Identities*. New York: Routledge. pp. 98–134.

Chant, S. (2008) 'The Informal Sector and Employment', in V. Desai and R.B. Potter (eds) *The Companion to Development Studies*. 2nd edition. London: Hodder. pp. 216–24.

Chen, M. (2006) 'Rethinking the Informal Economy: Linkages with the Formal Economy and the Formal Regulatory Environment', in B. Guha-Khasnobis, R. Kanbur and E. Ostrom (eds) *Linking the Formal and Informal Economy: Concepts and Policies*. Oxford: Oxford University Press. pp. 75–92.

Chen, M. (2008) 'Addressing poverty, reducing inequality', *Poverty in Focus*, 16: 6–7. Brasilia: UNDP International Poverty Centre.

Cheshire, P.C. and Magrini, S. (2006) 'Population growth in European cities: Weather matters – but only nationally', *Regional Studies*, 40(1): 23–37.

Childe, V.G. (1950) 'The urban revolution', *The Town Planning Review*, 21(1): 3–17.

Chordá, I.M. (1996) 'Towards the maturity stage: An insight into the performance of French technopoles', *Technovation*, 16(3): 143–52.

Christopherson, S., Mitchie, J. and Tyler, P. (2010) 'Regional resilience: Theoretical and empirical perspectives', *Cambridge Journal of Regions, Economy and Society*, 3(1): 3–10.

Clark, J. and Christopherson, S. (2009) 'Integrating investment and equity: A critical regionalist agenda for a progressive regionalism', *Journal of Planning Education and Research*, 28(3): 341–54.

Clarke, S.E. and Gaile, G.L. (1998) *The Work of Cities*. Minneapolis: University of Minnesota Press.

Cochrane, A.D. (2000) 'The Social Construction of Urban Policy', in G. Bridge and S. Watson (eds) *A Companion to the City*. Oxford: Blackwell Publishers.

Cochrane, A. (2007) *Understanding Urban Policy: A Critical Approach*. Oxford: Blackwell.

Cochrane, A., Peck, J. and Tickell, A. (1996) 'Manchester plays games: Exploring the local politics of globalisation', *Urban Studies*, 33(8): 1319–36.

Coe, N., Dicken, P. and Hess, M. (2008) 'Global production networks: Realising the potential', *Journal of Economic Geography,* 8: 271–95.

Coe, N. and Kelly, P. (2002) 'Languages of labour: Representational strategies in Singapore's labour control regime', *Political Geography,* 21: 341–71.

Coffey, W. (1996) 'The Newer International Division of Labour', in P.W. Daniels and W.F. Lever (eds) *The Global Economy in Transition.* Harlow: Longman. pp. 464–84.

Comaroff, J.L. and Comaroff, J. (2009) *Ethnicity Inc.* Chicago: Chicago University Press.

Convery, P. (2009) 'Welfare to Work – From special measures to 80 per cent employment', *Local Economy,* 24(1): 1–27.

Cooke, P. (2002) *Knowledge Economies. Clusters, Learning and Cooperative Advantage.* London: Routledge.

Cooke, P. and Morgan, K. (1998) *The Associational Economy – Firms, Regions, and Innovation.* Oxford: Oxford University Press.

Coombes, M. and Bond, S. (2008) *Travel-to-Work Areas: the 2007 review.* London: ONS.

CORDIS (Community and Development Information Service), n.d. ERAWATCH of the European Commission. Available at: http://cordis.europa.eu/erawatch/index.cfm (accessed 1 November 2010).

Corey, K.E. and Wilson, M.I. (2006) *Urban and Regional Technology Planning: Planning Practice in the Global Knowledge Economy.* London and New York: Routledge.

Corey, K.E. and Wilson, M.I. (2010) 'Benchmarking IT Cities', in K. Seetharam and B. Yuen (eds) *Developing Living Cities: From Analysis to Action.* Singapore: World Scientific. pp. 127–53.

Cornwall, A. (2004) Spaces for transformation? Reflections on issues of power and difference in participation in development, in S. Hickey and G. Mohan (eds) *Participation: From Tyranny to Transformation. Exploring New Approaches to Participation in Development.* London: Zed Books.

Cornwall, A. and Brock, K. (2005) 'What do buzzwords do for development policy? A critical look at "participation", "empowerment" and "poverty reduction"', *Third World Quarterly,* 26(7): 1043–60.

Cote, J. (2000) *Arrested Adulthood.* New York: New York University Press.

CPRE-WM [Campaign to Protect Rural England – West Midlands] (2007) *What Price West Midlands Green Belts?* Birmingham: CPRE-WM.

Cremers, J. and Janssen, J. (2006) *Shifting Employment: Undeclared Labour in Construction.* Brussels: CLR International.

Crisp, R., Batty., E., Cole, I. and Robinson, D. (2009) *Work and Worklessness in Deprived Neighbourhoods: Policy Assumptions and Personal Experiences.* York: Joseph Rowntree Foundation.

Cross, J. and Morales, A. (2007) (eds) *Street Entrepreneurs: People, Place and Politics in Local and Global Perspective.* London: Routledge.

Cross, J.C. (2000) 'Street vendors, modernity and postmodernity: Conflict and compromise in the global economy', *International Journal of Sociology and Social Policy,* 20(1): 29–51.

Cross, J.C. and Morales, A. (2007) (eds) *Street Entrepreneurs: People, Place and Politics in Local and Global Perspective*. London: Routledge.

Crouch, C. (2004) *Post-Democracy*. Cambridge: Polity Press.

Cumbers, A., Helms, G. and Keenan, M. (2009) *Beyond Aspiration: Young People and Decent Work in the De-industrialised City*. University of Glasgow: Department of Geographical and Earth Sciences and Department of Urban Studies.

Curran, W. (2007) 'From the frying pan to the oven: Gentrification and the experience of industrial displacement in Williamsburg, Brooklyn', *Urban Studies*, 44(8): 1427–40.

Currid, E. (2007) 'How art and culture happen in New York', *Journal of the American Planning Association*, 73(4): 454–67.

Currier, J. (2008) 'Art and power in the new China: An exploration of Beijing's 798 District and its implications for contemporary urbanism', *Town Planning Review*, 79(2–3): 237–66.

Curtis, H. (2002) *MTIV: Process, Inspiration and Practice for the New Media Designer*. Indianapolis: New Riders Publishing.

Daniels, P.W. and Moulaert, F. (eds) (1991) *The Changing Geography of Advanced Producer Services. Theoretical and Empirical Perspectives*. London and New York: Belhaven Press.

Daniels, P.W., Ho, K.C. and Hutton, T.A. (2005) *Service Industries and Asia-Pacific Cities: New Development Trajectories*. London: Routledge.

Daniels, P.W., Ho, K.C. and Hutton, T.A. (2011) *New Economic Spaces in Asian Cities: From Industrial Restructuring to the Cultural Turn*. London and New York: Routledge.

Davezies, L. (2008) *La République et ses Territoires; La Circulation Invisible des Richesses*. Paris: Seuil.

Davies, J. (2004) 'Conjuncture or disjuncture? An institutionalist analysis of local regeneration partnerships in the UK', *International Journal of Urban and Regional Research*, 28(3): 570–85.

Davis, M. (2005) 'A clean sweep. "Slum clearance" often means attacks on the poor', *The Socialist Review*, December. Available at: www.socialistreview.org.uk/article. php?articlenumber=9618 (accessed 15 February 2011).

Davis, M. (2006) *Planet of Slums*. London: Verso.

Davis, R.D. and Weinstein, D.E. (2002) 'Bones, bombs, and break points: The geography of economic activity', *American Economic Review*, 92(5): 1269–89.

Dear, M. and Flusty, S. (1998) 'Postmodern Urbanism', *Annals of the Association of American Geographers*, 88(1): 50–72.

Deas, I. (2013) 'Towards post-political consensus in urban policy? Localism and the emerging agenda for regeneration under the Cameron government', *Planning Practice and Research*, 28(1): 65–82.

Deas, I. (2014) 'The search for territorial fixes in subnational governance: City-regions and the disputed emergence of post-political consensus in Manchester, England', *Urban Studies* 51(11): 2285–314.

Deas, I. and Lord, A. (2006) 'From a new regionalism to an unusual regionalism? The emergence of non-standard regional spaces and lessons for the territorial reorganisation of the state', *Urban Studies*, 43: 1847–77.

de Haas, H. (2006) 'Migration, remittances and regional development in Southern Morocco', *Geoforum*, 35: 565–80.

De Roo, G. and Porter, G. (eds) (2007) *Fuzzy Planning: The Role of Actors in a Fuzzy Governance Environment*. Aldershot: Ashgate.

de Souza Briggs, X. (2008) *Democracy As Problem Solving: Civic Capacity In Communities Across The Globe*. Cambridge, MA: MIT Press.

DESA [Department of Economic and Social Affairs of the United Nations] (2008) *An Overview of Urbanization, Internal Migration, Population Distribution and Development in the World*. New York: United Nations.

de Soto, H. (1989) *The Other Path*. London: Harper & Row.

del Rio, V. (1992) 'Urban design and conflicting images of Brazil. Rio de Janeiro and Curitiba', *Cities*, 9(4): 270–9.

Derrida, J. (1967) *Of /grammatology*. Baltimore: Johns Hopkins University Press.

Devas, N. (2004) 'Conclusions: Urban Governance, Voice and Poverty', in N. Devas (ed.) *Urban Governance, Voice and Poverty in the Developing World*. London: Earthscan. pp. 186–99.

Dicken, P. (2002) 'Global Manchester: From Globaliser to Globalised', in J. Peck and K. Ward (eds) *City of Revolution: Restructuring Manchester*. Manchester: Manchester University.

Dicken, P. (2007) *Global Shift*. 5th edition. London: Sage.

Dicken, P. (2010) *Global Shift – Mapping the Changing Contours of the World Economy*. 6th edition. London: Sage.

Dickinson, R. (1964) *City and Region – A Geographical Representation*. London: Routledge & Kegan Paul.

Dicks, B. (2003) *Culture on Display: The Production of Contemporary Visitability*. London: Oxford University Press.

Dolphin, T. (2009) *The Impact of the Recession on Northern City-Regions*. Newcastle: IPPR North.

Donald, S.H., Kofman, E. and Kevin, C. (eds) (2009) *Branding Cities. Cosmopolitanism, Parochialism, and Social Change*. London and New York: Routledge.

Douglass, M. (2005) 'Local city, capital city or world city? Civil society, the (post-) development state and the globalisation of urban space in Pacific Asia', *Pacific Affairs*, 78: 543–58.

Downs, A. (2004) *Growth Management and Affordable Housing: Do They Conflict?* Washington, DC: Brookings Institution Press.

Drake, G. (2003) 'This place gives me space: Place and creativity in the creative industries', *Geoforum*, 34: 511–24.

Dunning, J.H. (ed.) (2000) *Regions, Globalization, and the Knowledge-based Economy*. Oxford: Oxford University Press.

Duranton, G. and Puga, D. (2004) 'Micro-foundations of urban agglomeration economies', in J.V. Henderson and J-F. Thissen (eds) *Handbook of Urban and Regional Economics*. Amsterdam: Elsevier. Volume 4, pp. 2063–117.

Duyvendak, J.W. (2011) *The Politics of Home. Belonging and Nostalgia in Western Europe and the United States*. Basingstoke: Palgrave Macmillan.

Earle, L. (2009) 'Occupying the illegal city: Urban social movements and transgressive citizenship in São Paulo'. PhD thesis. London School of Economics.

Eaton, J. and Eckstein, Z. (1997) 'Cities and growth: Theory and evidence from France and Japan', *Regional Science and Urban Economics*, 27: 701–31.

Economist Intelligence Unit (EIU) (2004) 'Scattering the seeds of invention: The globalisation of research and development', Available at: http://graphics.eiu.com/files/ad_pdfs/RnD_GLOBILISATION_WHITEPAPER.pdf (accessed 4 March 2011), London: EIU.

Eddington (2006) *The Eddington Transport Study*. London: HM Treasury.

Edensor, T., Leslie, D., Millington, S. and Rantisi, N. (eds) (2009) *Spaces of Vernacular Creativity. Rethinking the Cultural Economy*. New York and London: Routledge.

Engels, F. (1844; 1969) *The Condition of the Working Class in England*. Frogmore: Panther.

Escobar, A. (1995) *Encountering Development: The Making and Unmaking of the Third World*. Princeton, NJ: Princeton University Press.

Etherington, D. and Jones, M. (2009) 'City-regions: New geographies of uneven development and inequality', *Regional Studies*, 43: 247–66.

Etzkowitz, H. and Leydesdorff, L. (2000) 'The dynamics of innovation: From National Systems and "Mode 2" to a Triple Helix of university–industry–government relations', *Research Policy*, 29(2): 109–23.

European Commission (2007) *State of European Cities*. Brussels: Directorate-General Regional Policy.

Eurostat (2009) *Eurostat Regional Statistics*. Available at: http://epp.eurostat.ec.europa.eu/portal/page/portal/region_cities/regional_statistics/data/main_tables (accessed November 2009).

Evans, G. (2004) 'Cultural Industry Quarters: From Pre-Industrial to Post-Industrial Production', in D. Bell and M. Jayne (eds) *City of Quarters: Urban Villages in the Contemporary City*. Aldershot: Ashgate.

Evans, G. (2009) 'Creative cities, creative spaces and urban policy', *Urban Studies* 45(5–6): 1003–40.

Evans, P. (2008) 'Is an alternative globalization possible?', *Politics and Society*, 36(2): 271–305.

Fan, P. (2006) 'Catching up through developing innovation capability: Evidence from China's telecom-equipment industry', *Technovation*, 26(3): 359–68.

Fan, P. (2011) 'Innovation capacity and economic development: China and India', *Economic Change and Restructuring*, 44: 49–73.

Fan, P. and Wan, G. (2008) 'Innovation Capability for Economic Development: The Chinese Experience in the Reform Era', in A. Sweetman and J. Zhang (eds) *Economic Transitions with Chinese Characteristics: Thirty Years of Reform and Opening Up*. Montreal and Kingston: The School of Policy Studies, Queen's University at Kingston. pp. 1–23.

Fan, P. and Watanabe, C. (2006) 'Promoting industrial development through technology policy: Lessons from Japan and China', *Technology in Society*, 28: 303–20.

Fan, P. and Watanabe, K. (2008) 'The rise of the Indian biotech industry and innovative domestic companies', *International Journal of Technology and Globalization*, 4(2): 148–69.

Featherstone, M. (1991) *Consumption Culture and Postmodernism*. London: Sage.

Fernandes, E. (2010) 'Participatory Budgeting Processes in Brazil – Fifteen Years Later', in C. Kihato, M. Massoumi, B. Ruble, P. Subrirós and A. Garland (eds) *Urban Diversity: Space, Culture, and Inclusive Pluralism in Cities Worldwide*. Washington, DC: Woodrow Wilson Centre & Johns Hopkins University Press.

Fernandez-Kelly, P. (2006) 'Introduction', in P. Fernandez-Kelly and J. Shefner (eds) *Out of the Shadows: Political Action and the Informal Economy in Latin America*. Pennsylvania: Penn State Press.

Fielding, A. (1991) 'Migration and social mobility: South East England as an escalator region', *Regional Studies*, 26: 1–15.

Fine, B. (1999) 'The developmental state is dead – Long live social capital?', *Development and Change*, 30(1): 1–19.

Firey, W. (1945) 'Sentiment and symbolism as ecological variables', *American Sociological Review*, 10: 140–8.

Florida, R. (2002) *The Rise of the Creative Class: And How it's Transforming Work, Leisure, Community and Everyday Life*. New York: Basic Books.

Florida, R. (2005) *Cities and the Creative Class*. New York and London: Routledge.

Forsyth, A. and Crewe, K. (2010) 'Suburban technopoles as places: The international campus-garden-suburb style', *Urban Design International*, 15(3): 165–82.

Fortin, B., Garneau, G., Lacroix, G., Lemieux, T. and Montomarquette, C. (1996) *L'Économie Souterraine au Quebec: Mythes et Realites*. Laval: Presses de l'Universite Laval.

Foster, V. and Briceno-Garmendia, C. (2010) *Africa's Infrastructure: A Time for Transformation*. Washington, DC: World Bank.

Freeman, C. (1987) *Technology and Economic Performance: Lessons from Japan*. London: Pinter Publishers.

Freeman, J. (2008) 'Great, good and divided: The politics of public space in Rio de Janeiro', *Journal of Urban Affairs*, 30(5): 529–56.

Friedmann, J. (1992) *Empowerment. The Politics of Alternative Development*. London: Blackwell.

Friedmann, J. (1996) 'Rethinking poverty: Empowerment and citizen rights', *International Social Science Journal*, 148: 161–72.

Friedmann, J. (2002) 'The good city: In defense of utopian thinking', *International Journal of Urban and Regional Research*, 24(2): 460–72.

Friedmann, J. (2010) 'Place and place-making in cities: A global perspective', *Planning Theory and Practice*, 11(2): 149–65.

Friedmann, J. and Wolff, G. (1982) 'World city formation: An agenda for research and action', *International Journal of Urban and Regional Research*, 6: 309–44.

Fröbel, F., Heinrichs, J. and Kreye, O. (1980) *The New International Division of Labour*. Cambridge: Cambridge University Press.

Fröbel, F., Heinrichs, J. and Kreye, O. (2000) 'The New International Division of Labor in the World Economy' (1980), in J. T. Roberts, and A. Hite (eds) *From Modernization to Globalization: Perspective on Development and Social Change*. Oxford: Blackwell. pp. 257–73.

Fujita, M. and Thisse, J.F. (2000) 'The Formation of Economic Agglomerations: Old Problems and New Perspectives', in J.M. Huriot and J.F. Thisse (eds) *Economics of Cities*. Cambridge: Cambridge University Press. pp. 3–73.

Gabaix, X. and Ioannides, Y.M. (2004) 'The Evolution of City Size Distributions', in J.V. Henderson and J.-F. Thisse (eds) *Handbook of Regional and Urban Economics: Cities and Geography*. North Holland: Elsevier. Ch. 53, pp. 2341–75.

Gabardi, W. (2001) *Negotiating Postmodernism*. Minneapolis: University of Minnesota Press.

Gallin, D. (2001) 'Propositions on trade unions and informal employment in time of globalization', *Antipode*, 19(4): 531–49.

Garcia, B. (2005) 'Deconstructing the City of Culture: The long-term cultural legacies of Glasgow 1990', *Urban Studies*, 42(5–6): 841–68.

Garreau, J. (1991) *Edge City: Life on the New Frontier*. New York: Doubleday.

Gaventa, J. (2006) 'Triumph, deficit or contestation? Deepening the "Deepening Democracy" debate', *IDS Working Paper*, No. 264. Brighton: IDS.

Geddes, M. (2005) 'Neoliberalism and local governance – Cross-national perspectives and speculations', *Policy Studies*, 26(3/4): 360–77.

Geddes, M. (2006) 'Partnership and the limits to local governance in England: Institutionalist analysis and neoliberalism', *International Journal of Urban and Regional Research*, 30(1): 76–97.

Geddes, M. (2010) 'Building and contesting neoliberalism at the local level: Reflections on the symposium and on recent experience in Bolivia', *International Journal of Urban and Regional Research*, 34(1): 163–73.

Geertz, C. (1963) *Old Societies and New States: The Quest for Modernity in Asia and Africa*. Glencoe, IL: Free Press.

Geertz, C. (1973) *Thick Description: Toward an Integrative Theory of Culture*. New York: Basic Books.

Gershuny, J. (2000) *Changing Times: Work and Leisure in Post-Industrial Society*. Oxford: Oxford University Press.

Gertler, M.S. (2010) 'Rules of the game: The place of institutions in regional economic change', *Regional Studies*, 41: 1–15.

Gerxhani, K. (2004) 'The informal sector in developed and less developed countries: A literature survey', *Public Choice*, 120(2): 267–300.

Ghose, A.K., Majid, N. and Ernst, C. (2008) *The Global Employment Challenge*. Geneva: International Labour Organisation.

Gibbs, D. and Krueger, R. (2005) 'Exploring local capacities for sustainable development', *Geoforum*, 36: 407–09.

Gibbs, D. and Krueger, R. (2007) 'Containing the Contradictions of Rapid Development: New Economic Spaces and Sustainable Urban Development', in R. Krueger and D. Gibbs (eds), *The Sustainable Development Paradox: Urban Political Economy in the United States and Europe*. New York: Guilford. pp. 95–122.

Gibson-Graham, J.K. (1996) *The End of Capitalism as We Knew It? A Feminist Critique of Political Economy*. Oxford: Blackwell.

Gibson-Graham, J.K. (2006) *A Post-Capitalist Politics*. Minneapolis: University of Minnesota Press.

Gilbert, L. and Dikeç, M. (2008) 'Right to the City: Politics of Citizenship', in K. Goonewardena, S. Kipfer, R. Milgrom and C. Schmid (eds) *Space, Difference, Everyday Life. Reading Henri Lefebvre*. New York and London: Routledge. pp. 250–63.

Gillette, H. (2005) *Camden After the Fall: Decline and Renewal in a Post-Industrial City*. Philadelphia: University of Pennsylvania Press.

Gimeno Martinez, J. (2007) 'Selling avant-garde: How Antwerp became a fashion capital (1990–2002)', *Urban Studies*, 44(12): 2449–64.

Girard, L.F., Forte, B., Cerreta, M., De Toro, P. and Forte, F. (eds) (2003) *The Human Sustainable City: Challenges and Perspectives from the Habitat Agenda*. Ashgate: Aldershot.

Girardet, H. (2006) *Creating Sustainable Cities*. Totnes: Green Books.

Giroux, H.A. (1994) 'Paulo Freire and the Rise of the Border Intellectual', in *Disturbing Pleasures: Learning Popular Culture*. New York and London: Routledge. pp. 141–52.

Glaeser, E.L. (2000) 'The New Economics of Urban And Regional Growth', in G.L. Clark, M.P. Feldman and M.S. Gertler (eds) *Oxford Handbook of Economic Geography*. Oxford: Oxford University Press. pp. 83–98.

Glaeser, E. (2005a) 'Urban colossus: Why is New York America's largest city?', *Economic Policy Review*, Federal Reserve Bank of New York: 7–24. Available at: http://www.newyorkfed.org/research/epr/05v11n2/0512glae.pdf

Glaeser, E. (2005b) 'Reinventing Boston 1630–2003', *Journal of Economic Geography*, 5: 119–53.

Glaeser, E. (2011) *The Triumph of the City: How Our Greatest Invention Makes Us Richer, Smarter, Greener, Healthier and Happier*. London and New York: Penguin Press.

Glaeser, E.L. and Gottlieb, J.D. (2006) 'Urban resurgence and the consumer city' *Urban Studies* 43(8): 1275–99.

Glaeser, E.L., Kallal, H.D., Scheinkman, J.A. and Shleifer, A. (1992) 'Growth of cities', *Journal of Political Economy*, 100: 1126–52.

Glaeser, E. and Saiz, A. (2004) 'The rise of the skilled city', *Brookings-Wharton Papers on Urban Affairs*. Available at: http://www.jstor.org/pss/25067406.

Glaeser, E., Saiz, J. and Kolko, S. (2001) 'Consumer City', *Journal of Economic Geography*, 1: 27–50.

Glaser, B. and Strauss, A. (1967) *The Discovery of Grounded Theory*. New York: Aldine.

Glass, R. (1963) 'Introduction' to *London: Aspects of Change*. London: Centre for Urban Studies.

Glick, P. and Rouband, F. (2006) 'Export processing zone expansion in Madagascar: What are the labour market and gender impacts?', *Journal of African Economies*, 15: 722–56.

Gold, J. and Gold, M. (2008) 'Olympic cities: Regeneration, city rebranding and changing urban agendas', *Geography Compass*, 2(1): 300–18.

Goldschmidt-Clermont, L. (2000) *Household Production and Income: Some Preliminary Issues*. Geneva: Bureau of Statistics, International Labour Office.

Gomez, M.V. (1998) 'Reflective images: The case of urban regeneration in Glasgow and Bilbao', *International Journal of Urban and Regional Research*, 22(1): 106–21.

Gong, Y. (2003) 'Research on the optimization of industrial structure in the economic development of Shanghai', *Journal of Shanghai University of Finance and Economics,* October, 5(5): 47–56 (in Chinese).

Goos, M. and Manning, A. (2007) 'Lousy and lovely jobs: The rising polarisation of work in Britain', *The Review of Economics and Statistics*, 89: 118–33.

Gordon, I. (2008) 'Energy and the built environment', *Energy Policy*, 36: 4652–6.

Gordon, I. and Turok, I. (2005) 'How Urban Labour Markets Matter', in N. Buck, I. Gordon, A. Harding and I. Turok (eds) *Changing Cities: Rethinking Urban Competitiveness, Cohesion and Governance*. Basingstoke: Palgrave Macmillan. pp. 242–64.

Goss, S. (2007) 'Re-imagining the Public Realm', in G. Hassan (ed.) *After Blair: Politics After the New Labour Decade*. London: Lawrence and Wishart.

Gottmann, J. (1961) *Megalopolis. The Urbanized Northeastern Seaboard*. New York: Twentieth Century Fund.

Grabher, G. (2002a) 'The project ecology of advertising: Tasks, talents and teams', *Regional Studies*, 36(3): 245–62.

Grabher, G. (2002b) 'Fragile sector, robust practice: Project ecologies in new media', *Environment and Planning A*, 34: 1911–26.

Graham, S. and Guy, S. (2002) 'Digital space meets urban place: Sociotechnologies of urban restructuring in downtown San Francisco', *City*, 6(3): 369–82.

Graham, S. and Marvin, S. (2001) *Splintering Urbanism: Networked Infrastructure, Technological Mobilities and the Urban Condition*. London: Routledge.

Grant, U. (2008) 'Opportunity and exploitation in urban labour markets', Briefing Paper 44. London: Overseas Development Institute.

Greenberg, M. (2008) *Branding New York. How a City in Crisis Was Sold to the World*. New York: Routledge.

Greenstein, R. and Sungu-Eryilmaz, Y. (eds) (2004) *Recycling the City: The Use and Reuse of Urban Land*. Cambridge, MA: Lincoln Institute of Land Policy.

Grimshaw, D., Beynon, H., Rubery, J. and Ward, K. (2002) 'The restructuring of work in large service sector organisations: "Delayering", upskilling and polarisation', *The Sociological Review*, 50: 89–116.

Gu, S. (1999) *China's Industrial Technology*. Tokyo: United Nations University, Institute for New Technology and the UNU Press.

Guarneros-Meza, V. (2009) 'Mexican urban governance: How old and new institutions coexist and interact', *International Journal of Urban and Regional Research*, 33(2): 463–82.

Guarneros-Meza, V. and Geddes, M. (2010) 'Local governance and participation under neoliberalism: Comparative perspectives', *International Journal of Urban and Regional Research*, 34: 115–29.

Hall, P. (1988) 'The Geography of the Fifth Kondratieff', in P. Massey and J. Allen (eds) *Restructuring Britain: Uneven Development: Cities and Regions in Transition*. London: Hodder and Stoughton.

Hall, P. (1998) *Cities in Civilisation: Culture, Innovation and Urban Order*. London: Weidenfield.

Hall, P. (2000) 'Creative cities and economic development', *Urban Studies*, 37(4): 639–49.

Hall, P. (2001) 'Global City-Regions in the Twenty-first Century', in A.J. Scott (ed.) *Global City-Regions. Trends, Theory, Policy*. Oxford: Oxford University Press. pp. 59–77.

Hall, P. (2003) 'The Sustainable City in an Age of Globalization', in L.F. Girard, B. Forte, M. Cerreta, P. De Toro and F. Forte (eds) *The Human Sustainable City: Challenges and Perspectives from the Habitat Agenda*. Aldershot: Ashgate. pp. 55–69.

Hall, P.G. (1966) *The World Cities*. London: Weidenfeld & Nicolson.

Hall, P.G. (2006) 'The Polycentric City', PowerPoint Presentation, The Bartlett School, University College London.

Hall, P. and Pain, K. (2006) *The Polycentric Metropolis: Learning from Mega-City Regions in Europe*. London and Sterling, VA: Earthscan.

Hall, P. and Pfeiffer, U. (2000) *Urban 21: World Report on the Urban Future 21*. Berlin: Federal Ministry of Transport, Building and Housing.

Hall, T. and Hubbard, Ph. (eds) (1998) *The Entrepreneurial City: Geographies of Politics, Regime and Representation*. Chichester: John Wiley & Sons.

Hamann, R., Pienaar, S., Boulogne, F. and Kranz, N. (2009) 'What makes cross-sector partnerships successful? A comparative case study analysis of diverse partnership types in an emerging economy', Unpublished paper. Cape Town: Graduate School of Business, University of Cape Town.

Hambleton, R. and Sweeting, D. (2004) 'U.S.-style leadership for English local government?', *Public Administration Review*, 64(4): 474–88.

Hamnett, C. (1994) 'Socio-economic change in London: Professionalization not polarization', *Built Environment*, 20: 192–203.

Hamnett, C. (1996) 'Social polarisation, economic restructuring and welfare state regimes', *Urban Studies*, 31: 401–24.

Handy, C. (2004) 'Partnership and Trust', in S. Stern and E. Seligman (eds) *The Partnership Principle: New Forms of Governance in the 21st Century*. London: Archetype. pp. 96–104.

Hannigan, J. (1998) *Fantasy City. Pleasure and Profit in the Postmodern Metropolis*. New York and London: Routledge.

Harrison, B. (1992) 'Old wine in new bottles', *Regional Studies*, 26: 469–83.

Harrison, B. (1994) *Lean and Mean – The Changing Landscape of Corporate Power in the Age of Flexibility*. New York: Basic Books.

Harrison, P. (2006) 'Integrated Development Plans and Third Way Politics', in U. Pillay, R. Tomlinson and J. du Toit (eds) *Democracy and Delivery: Urban Policy in South Africa*. Pretoria: HSRC Press.

Harrison, J. (2008) 'Stating the production of scales – centrally orchestrated regionalism, regionally orchestrate centralism', *International Journal of Urban and Regional Research*, 32: 922–41.

Harrison, J. (2012) 'Life after regions? The evolution of city-regionalism in England', *Regional Studies*, 46: 1243–59.

Harrison, J. and Growe, A. (2014a) 'From places to flows? Planning for the new "regional world" in Germany', *European Urban and Regional Studies*, 21(1): 21–41.

Harrison, J. and Hoyler, M. (2014a) 'Governing the new metropolis', *Urban Studies*, 51(11): 2249–66.

Harrison, J. and Growe, A. (2014b) 'When regions collide: in what sense a new "regional problem"?', *Environment and Planning A* (in press).

Harrison, J. and Hoyler, M. (eds) (2014b) *Megaregions: Globalization's New Urban Form?* Cheltenham: Edward Elgar.

Harrison, J. (2007) 'From competitive regions to competitive city-regions: A new orthodoxy, but some old mistakes', *Journal of Economic Geography*, 7(3): 311–32.

Hart, K. (1973) 'Informal Income Opportunities and Urban Employment in Ghana', in R. Jolly, E. de Kadt, H. Singer and F. Wilson (eds) *Third World Employment*. Harmondsworth: Penguin. pp. 66–70.

Hartley, J. (ed.) (2005) *Creative Industries*. Oxford: Blackwell.

Harvey, D. (1982) *The Limits to Capital*. Oxford: Blackwell.

Harvey, D. (1989a) 'From managerialism to entrepreneurialism: The transformation of urban governance in late capitalism', *Geografiska Annaler Series B Human Geography*, 71(1): 3–17.

Harvey, D. (1989b) *The Condition of Post-Modernity: An Enquiry into the Origins of Cultural Change*. Oxford: Blackwell.

Harvey, D. (1996) *Justice, Nature and the Geography of Difference*. London: Blackwell.

Harvey, D. (2005) *A Brief History of Neoliberalism*. Oxford: Oxford University Press.

Harvey, D. (2010) *The Enigma of Capital and Crises of Capitalism*. Oxford: Oxford University Press.

Haughton, G. and McManus, P. (2011) 'Neoliberal experiments with urban infrastructure: The cross city tunnel, Sydney', *International Journal of Urban and Regional Research*, 36(1): 90–105.

Haywood, S.F. (2005) 'The China Syndrome and the Environmental Kuznets Curve', *American Enterprise Institute for Public Policy Research* (November–December).

Hemelryk Donald, S., Kofman, E. and Kevin, C. (2009) *Branding Cities: Cosmopolitanism, Parochialism, and Social Change*. London: Routledge.

Healey, P. (2000) 'Planning in Relational Space and Time: Responding to New Urban Realities', in A.G. Bridge and S. Watson (eds) *Companion to the City*. Oxford: Blackwell. pp. 517–30.

Healey, P. (2007) *Urban Complexity and Spatial Strategies: Towards a Relational Planning for Our Times*. London: Routledge.

Helms, G. and Cumbers, A. (2006) 'Regulating the new urban poor: Local labour market control in an old industrial city', *Space and Polity*, 10: 67–86.

Henderson, H. (1999) *Beyond Globalisation: Shaping a Sustainable Global Economy*. London: Kumarian Press.

Henderson, V., Kuncoro, A. and Turner, M. (1995) 'Industrial development in cities', *Journal of Political Economy*, 105(3): 1067–90.

Herod, A. (2000) 'Implications of just-in-time production for union strategy: Lessons from the 1998 General Motors-United Auto Workers' dispute', *Annals of the Association of American Geographers*, 90: 521–47.

Herod, A. (2001) *Labour Geographies: Workers and the Landscapes of Capitalism*. New York: Guilford.

Heynen, N., Kaika, M. and Swyngedouw, E. (eds) (2006) *In the Nature of Cities: Urban Political Ecology and the Politics of Urban Metabolism*. London: Routledge.

Hietala, M. and Clark, P. (2013) 'Creative Cities', in P. Clark (ed.) *The Oxford Handbook of Cities in World History*. Oxford: Oxford University Press. pp. 720–38.

Highmore, B. (2005) *Cityscapes. Cultural Readings in the Material and Symbolic City*. Basingstoke: Palgrave Macmillan.

HM Treasury (2006) *Devolving Decision Making: 3 – Meeting the Regional Economic Challenge: The Importance of Cities to Regional Growth*. London: HM Treasury.

Ho, K.C. (2005) 'Service Industries and Occupational Change: Implications for Identity, Citizenship and Politics', in P.W. Daniels, K.C. Ho and T.A. Hutton (eds) *Service Industries and Asia-Pacific Cities: New Development Trajectories*. London and New York: Routledge-Curzon. pp. 93–110.

Ho, K.C. (2009) 'The neighbourhood in the creative economy: Policy, practice and place in Singapore', *Urban Studies*, 45(5–6): 1187–201.

Hobday, M. (1995) *Innovation in East Asia: The Challenge to Japan*. Cheltenham: Elgar.

Holcomb, B. (1993) 'Revisioning Place: De- and Re-constructing the Image of the Industrial City', in G. Kearns and C. Philo (eds) *Selling Places. The City as Cultural Capital, Past and Present*. Oxford and New York: Pergamon Press. pp. 133–44.

Hooghe, L. and Marks, G. (2003) 'Unraveling the central state, but how? Types of multi-level governance', *American Political Science Review*, 97(2): 233–43.

Howley, P., Scott, M. and Redmond, D. (2009) 'Sustainability versus liveability: An investigation of urban satisfaction', *Journal of Environmental Planning and Management*, 52(6): 847–64.

Hoyler, M. (2010) 'German Cities', in P.J. Taylor, P. Ni, B. Derudder, M. Hoyler, J. Huang and F. Witlox (eds) *Global Urban Analysis – A Survey of Cities in Globalization*. London: Earthscan. pp. 224–30.

Hu, A.G. (2007) 'Technology parks and regional economic growth in China', *Research Policy*, 36: 76–87.

Hubbard, Ph. (1996) 'Urban design and city regeneration: Social representations of entrepreneurial landscapes', *Urban Studies*, 33(8): 1441–61.

Hubbard, Ph. (2004) 'Revenge and injustice in the neoliberal city: Uncovering masculinist agendas', *Antipode, a Radical Journal of Geography*, 36(4): 665–86.

Hubbard, Ph. (2006) *City*. New York and London: Routledge.

Huber, F. (2010) 'Do clusters really matter for innovation practices in information technology? Questioning the significance of technological knowledge spillovers', *Danish Research Unit for Industrial Dynamics*. DRUID Working Paper No. 10–21. Aalborg: Aalborg University.

Hübner, K. (ed.) (2005) *The New Economy in Transatlantic Perspective. Spaces of Innovation*. New York and London: Routledge.

Hudson, R. (2005) *Economic Geographies: Circuits, Flows and Spaces*. London: Sage.

Hudson, R. (2009) 'From knowledge-based economy to ... knowledge-based economy. Reflections on changes in the economy and development policies in the North East of England', *Regional Studies*, 45 (7): 997–1017.

Huggins, R. (2000) 'The success and failure of policy-implanted inter-firm network initiatives: Motivations, processes and structure', *Entrepreneurship and Regional Development*, 12: 111–35.

Huggins, R. (2008) 'The evolution of knowledge clusters: Progress and policy', *Economic Development Quarterly*, November, 22(4): 277–89.

Huggins, R. and Izushi, H. (2002) 'The digital divide and ICT learning in rural communities: Examples of good practice service delivery', *Local Economy*, 17(2): 111–22.

Huggins, R. and Izushi, H. (2007) *Competing for Knowledge: Creating, Connecting, and Growing*. London and New York: Routledge.

Huggins, R. and Luo, S. (2008) 'Regional Evolution and Knowledge Diffusion: Evidence from China's Three Leading Regions', in R. Huggins, H. Izushi, W. Davies, and S. Luo. *World Knowledge Competitiveness Index 2008*. Chapter 8. [Online] Cardiff: Centre for International Competitiveness. Available at: http://cforic.org (accessed 14 November 2010).

Huggins, R., Demirbag, M. and Ratcheva, V.I. (2007) 'Global knowledge and R&D foreign direct investment flows: Recent patterns in Asia Pacific, Europe and North America', *International Review of Applied Economics*, July, 21(3): 437–51.

Huggins, R., Izushi, H., Davies, W. and Luo, S. (2008) *World Knowledge Competitiveness Index 2008*. [Online] Cardiff: Centre for International Competitiveness. Available at: http://cforic.org (accessed 14 November 2010).

Hutton, T.A. (2004) 'Service industries, globalization, and urban restructuring within the Asia-Pacific: New development trajectories and planning responses', *Progress in Planning*, 62: 1–74.

Hutton, T.A. (2008) *The New Economy of the Inner City: Restructuring, Regeneration and Dislocation in the Twenty-First-Century Metropolis*. London and New York: Routledge.

Hutton, T.A. (2010) *The New Economy of the Inner City: Restructuring, Regeneration and Dislocation in the Twenty-First-Century Metropolis*. London and New York: Routledge.

Hutton, T. (2011) 'The Cultural Turn and Urban Development in Asia', in P. Daniels, K. Ho and T. Hutton (eds) *New Economic Spaces in Asian Cities: From Industrial Restructuring to the Cultural Turn*. London: Taylor & Francis. pp. 31–50.

ILO [International Labour Office] (2002) *Decent Work and the Informal Economy*. Geneva: International Labour Organization.

ILO [International Labour Office] (2010) *World Social Security Report 2010–2011: Providing Coverage in Times of Crisis and Beyond*. Geneva: International Labour Organization.

Imrie, R. and Raco, M. (1999) 'How new is the new local governance? Lessons from the United Kingdom', *Transactions of the Institute of British Geographers*, 24(1): 45–63.

Indergaard, M. (2004) *Silicon Alley: The Rise and Fall of a New Media District*. New York and London: Routledge.

Industrial Communities Alliance (2009) *The Impact of Recession on Unemployment in Industrial Britain*. Barnsley: Industrial Communities Alliance.

International Telecommunications Union (2010) *Measuring the Information Society*. [Online] Geneva: International Telecommunications Union. Available at: http://www.itu.int/ITU-D/ict/publications/idi/2010/Material/MIS_2010_without_annex_4-e.pdf (accessed 5 March 2011).

Internet World Stats (2010) *Usage and Population Statistics* [Online]. Published 30 June 2010 and 30 September 2010. Available at: http://www.internetworldstats.com/ (accessed 25 October 2010).

Irazábal, C. (2005) *City Making and Urban Governance in the Americas: Curitaba and Portland*. Aldershot: Ashgate.

Iwata, N. and del Rio, V. (2004) 'The image of the waterfront in Rio de Janeiro. Urbanism and social representation of reality', *Journal of Planning Education and Research*, 24(2): 171–83.

Izushi, H. and Aoyama, Y. (2006) 'Industry evolution and cross-sectoral skill transfers: A comparative analysis of the video game industry in Japan, the United States, and the United Kingdom', *Environment and Planning A*, October, 38(10): 1843–61.

Jacob, J. (2003) 'Alternative Lifestyle Spaces', in A. Leyshon, R. Lee and C.C. Williams (eds) *Alternative Economic Spaces*. London: Sage.

Jacobs, J. (1961) *The Death and Life of Great American Cities*. New York: Random House.

Jacobs, J. (1969) *The Economy of Cities*. New York: Random House.

Jenks, M., Burton, E. and Williams, K. (eds) (1996) *The Compact City: A Sustainable Urban Form?* London: Spon.

Jessop, B. (1998) 'The Narrative of Enterprise and the Enterprise of Narrative: Place Marketing and the Entrepreneurial City', in T. Hall and P. Hubbard (eds), *The Entrepreneurial City: Geographies of Politics, Regime and Representation*. Chichester: John Wiley & Sons.

Jessop, B. (2000) 'The crisis of the national spatio-temporal fix and the tendential ecological dominance of globalizing capitalism', *International Journal of Urban and Regional Research*, 24(2): 323–48.

Jessop, B. (2002) 'Liberalism, neo-liberalism, and urban governance: A state-theoretical perspective', *Antipode*, 34(3): 451–72.

Jhabvala, R., Sudarshan, R.M. and Unni, J. (2003) (eds) *Informal Economy Centrestage: New Structures of Employment.* London: Sage.

Johnson, C. (1982) *MITI and the Japanese Miracle.* Stanford, CA: Stanford University Press.

Jonas, A. (1996) 'Local labour market control regimes: Uneven development and the social regulation of production', *Regional Studies*, 30: 323–38.

Jonas, A. and While, A. (2007) 'Greening the Entrepreneurial City: Looking for Spaces of Sustainability Politics in the Competitive City', in R. Krueger and D. Gibbs (eds) *The Sustainable Development Paradox: Urban Political Economy in the United States.* London: The Guilford Press. pp. 123–59.

Jütting, J.P. and de Laiglesia, J.R. (2009) (eds) *Is Informal Normal? Towards More and Better Jobs in Developing Countries.* Paris: OECD.

Kamal-Chaoui, L. and Roberts, A. (eds) (2009) *Competitive Cities and Climate Change.* Paris: OECD. OECD Regional Development Working Papers No. 2.

Kanai, M. and Ortega-Alcázar, I. (2009) 'The prospects for progressive culture-led urban regeneration in Latin America: Cases from Mexico City and Buenos Aires', *International Journal of Urban and Regional Research*, 33(2): 483–501.

Kargon, R. and Molella, A. (2008) *Invented Edens. Techno-cities of the Twentieth Century.* Boston: MIT Press.

Kavaratzis, M. (2005) 'Place branding: A review of trends and conceptual models', *The Marketing Review*, 5: 329–42.

Kearns, G. and Philo, C. (1993) *Selling Places. The City as Cultural Capital, Past and Present.* Oxford and New York: Pergamon Press.

Keeble, D.E. (1989) 'High-technology industry and regional development in Britain: The case of the Cambridge phenomenon', *Environment and Planning C: Government and Policy*, 7: 153–72.

Kelly, P.F. (2002) 'Spaces of labour control: Comparative perspectives from South East Asia', *Transactions of the Institute of British Geographers*, NS 27: 395–411.

Kelly, P.F. (2009) 'From global production networks to global reproduction networks: Households, migration and regional development in Cavite, the Philippines', *Regional Studies*, 43: 449–62.

Kennedy, L. (2007) 'Regional industrial policies driving peri-urban dynamics in Hyderabad, India', *Cities*, 24(2): 95–109.

Kim, L. (1998) *From Imitation to Innovation: Dynamics of Korea's Technological Learning.* Boston: Harvard Business School Press.

Kim, H.H., Moon, J.Y. and Yang, S. (2004) 'Broadband penetration and participatory politics: South Korea case', *Proceedings of the 37th Hawaii International Conference on System Sciences.* pp. 1–10.

Kim, P. (2006) 'Is Korea a strong internet nation?', *The Information Society,* 22: 41–4.

Kipfer, S. and Keil, R. (2002) 'Toronto Inc? Planning the competitive city in the New Toronto', *Antipode, A Radical Journal of Geography,* 34(2): 227–64.

Kjaer, A.M. (2009) 'Governance and the Urban Bureaucracy', in J. Davies and D. Imbroscio (eds) *Theories of Urban Politics.* London: Sage.

Koh, F.C.C., Koh, W.T.H. and Tschang, F.T. (2005) 'An analytical framework for science parks and technology districts with an application to Singapore', *Journal of Business Venturing,* 20: 217–39.

Kong, L. (2009) 'Making sustainable creative/cultural space in Shanghai and Singapore', *The Geographical Review,* 91(1): 1–22.

Kong, L. and O'Connor, J. (eds) (2009) *Creative Economies, Creative Cities: Asian-European Perspectives.* Dordrecht, Heidelberg, London, New York: Springer.

Knight, R. and Gappert, G. (1989) 'Preface', in R. Knight and G. Gappert (eds) *Cities in a Global Society.* London: Sage. pp. 11–14.

Krätke, S. (2000) 'Berlin – The metropolis as a production space', *European Planning Studies* 8(1): 7–27.

Krätke, S. (2002) *Medienstadt. Urbane Cluster und globale Zentren der Kulturproduktion.* [*Media City. Urban Clusters and Global Centres of Cultural Production*]. Opladen: Leske & Budrich.

Krätke, S. (2007) 'Metropolization of the European economic territory as a consequence of increasing specialization of urban agglomerations on the knowledge economy', *European Planning Studies,* 15(1): 1–28.

Krätke, S. (2010a) 'Regional knowledge networks. A network analysis approach to the interlinking of knowledge resources', *European Urban and Regional Studies,* 17(1): 83–97.

Krätke, S. (2010b) '"Creative Cities" and the rise of the dealer class: A critique of R. Florida's approach to urban theory', *International Journal of Urban and Regional Research,* 34(4): 835–53.

Krätke, S. (2011) *The Creative Capital of Cities: Interactive Knowledge Creation and the Urbanization Economies of Innovation.* Oxford and Malden, MA: Blackwell-Wiley.

Krätke, S. and Brandt, A. (2009) 'Knowledge networks as a regional development resource: A detailed network analysis of the interlinks between scientific institutions and regional firms in the metropolitan region of Hannover, Germany', *European Planning Studies,* 17(1): 43–63.

Krueger, R. and Agyeman, J. (2005) 'Sustainability schizophrenia or "actually existing sustainabilities?" toward a broader understanding of the politics and promise of local sustainability in the US', *Geoforum,* 36: 410–17.

Krueger, R. and Gibbs, D. (eds) (2007) *The Sustainable Development Paradox: Urban Political Economy in the United States.* London: The Guilford Press.

Krueger, R. and Gibbs, D. (2008) 'Third wave sustainability: Smart growth and regional development in USA', *Regional Studies,* 49: 1263–74.

Krugman, P. (1991) 'Increasing returns and economic geography', *Journal of Political Economy,* 99(3): 483–99.

Krugman, P. (1996) 'Confronting the mystery of urban hierarchy', *Journal of the Japanese and International Economies*, 10: 399–418.

Kundu, A. (2007) 'Dynamics of Growth and Process of Degenerated Peripheralization in Delhi: An Analysis of Socio-economic Segmentation and Differentiation in Micro-environments', in P.J. Marcotullio and G. McGranahan (eds) *Scaling Urban Environment Challenges: From Local to Global and Back*. London: Earthscan. pp. 156–78.

Lake, R. (2000) 'Contradictions in the Local State: Local Implementation of the U.S. Sustainability Agenda in the USA', in N. Low, B. Gleeson, I. Elander and R. Lidskog (eds) *Consuming Cities: The Urban Environment in the Global Economy after the Rio Declaration*. London: Routledge. pp. 70–90.

Lal, D. (1995) 'India and China: contrasts in economic liberalization', *World Development*, 23(9): 1475–94.

Lall, S. and Teubal, M. (1998) 'Market-stimulating technology policies in developing countries: A framework with examples from East Asia', *World Development*, 26(8): 1369–85.

Landry, C. (2000) *The Creative City. A Toolkit for Urban Innovators*. London: Earthscan.

Landry, C. (2008) *The Creative City: A Toolkit for Urban Innovators*, 2nd edition. London: Earthscan.

Lang, E.L. and Danielson, K.A. (2006) 'Review roundtable: Is New Orleans a resilient city?', *Journal of the American Planning Association*, 72(2): 245–57.

Lash, S. and Urry, J. (1994) *Economies of Signs and Space*. London: Sage.

Latouche, S. (1993) *In the Wake of Affluent Society: An Exploration of Post-Development*. London: Zed.

Lau, T.Y., Kim, S.W. and Atkin, D. (2005) 'An examination of factors contributing to South Korea's global leadership in broadband adoption', *Telematics and Informatics*, 22: 349–59.

Leaf, M. (1996) 'Building the road for the BMW: Culture, vision and the extended metropolitan region of Jakarta', *Environment and Planning A*, 28: 1617–35.

Leaf, M. (2005) 'The Bazaar and the Normal: Informalization and Tertiaritization in Urban Asia', in P.W. Daniels, K.C. Ho and T.A. Hutton (eds) *Service Industries and Asia-Pacific Cities: New Development Trajectories*. London: Routledge.

Ledeneva, A.V. (2006) *How Russia Really Works: The Informal Practices that Shaped Post-Soviet Politics and Business*. Ithaca, NY: Cornell University Press.

Lee, H., O'Keefe, R.M. and Yun, K. (2003) 'The growth of broadband and electronic commerce in South Korea: Contributing factors', *The Information Society*, 19: 81–93.

Lee, W.H. and Yang, W.T. (2000) 'The cradle of Taiwan high technology industry development – Hsinchu Science Park (HSP)', *Technovation*, 20: 55–9.

Leitner, H., Sheppard, E.S., Sziarto, K. and Maringanti, A. (2007) 'Contesting Urban Futures: Decentering Neoliberalism', in H. Leitner, J. Peck and E.S. Sheppard (eds) *Contesting Neoliberalism Urban Frontiers*. New York: The Guilford Press. pp. 1–25.

Leunig, T. and Swaffield, J. (2007) *Cities Unlimited: Making Urban Regeneration Work*. London: Policy Exchange.

Lewis, A. (1959) *The Theory of Economic Growth*. London: Allen and Unwin.

Lewis, P.G. and Neiman, M. (2009) *Custodians of Place: Governing the Growth and Development of Cities*. Washington, DC: Georgetown University Press.

Lewis, R. (2008) *Chicago-Made: Factory Networks in the Industrial Metropolis*. Chicago: University of Chicago Press.

Ley, D.F. (1996) *The New Middle Class and the Remaking of the Central City*. Oxford: Oxford University Press.

Ley, D.F. (2005) 'The Social Geography of the Service Economy in Global Cities', in P.W. Daniels, K.C. Ho and T.A. Hutton (eds) *Service Industries and Asia-Pacific Cities: New Development Trajectories*. London and New York: Routledge-Curzon. Chapter 4, pp. 77–92.

Leyshon, A., Lee, R. and Williams, C.C. (2003) (eds) *Alternative Economic Spaces*. London: Sage.

Li, W. (ed.) (2006) *From Urban Enclave to Ethnoburb: New Asian Communities in Pacific Rim Countries*. Honolulu, HI: University of Hawaii Press.

Lin, C.Y. (1997) 'Technopolis development: An assessment of the Hsinchu experience', *International Planning Studies*, 2(2): 257–72.

Lindell, I. (2010) 'Introduction: The Changing Politics of Informality – Collective Organizing, Alliances and Scales of Engagement', in I. Lindell (ed.) *Africa's Informal Workers*. London and New York: Zed Books.

Lloyd, R. (2006) *Neo-Bohemia: Art and Commerce in the Postindustrial City*. New York and London: Routledge.

Logan, J. (ed.) (2008) *Urban China in Transition*. Wiley-Blackwell.

Lorenzen, M. and Frederiksen L. (2008) 'Why do Cultural Industries Cluster? Localization, Urbanization, Products and Projects', in P. Cooke and L. Lazzeretti (eds) *Creative Cities, Cultural Clusters and Local Economic Development*. Cheltenham: Edward Elgar. pp. 155–79.

Lovering, J. (2001) 'The coming regional crisis (and how to avoid it)', *Regional Studies*, 35(4): 349–54.

Low, A. (2010) 'S'pore, Guangzhou sign Knowledge City deal', *The Straits Times*. [Online] Available at: http//asianewsnet.net/home/news.php?id=15487&sec=2 (accessed 15 November 2010).

Lowndes, V. (2001) 'Rescuing Aunt Sally: Taking institutional theory seriously in urban politics', *Urban Studies*, 38(11): 1953–71.

Lupton, R. (2003) *Poverty Street: The Dynamics of Neighbourhood Decline and Renewal*. Bristol: The Policy Press.

Lury, C. (2002) 'Style and the Perfection of Things', in J. Collins (eds) *High-Pop: Making Culture into Popular Entertainment*. London: Blackwell.

Lyon, M. and Snoxall, S. (2005) 'Sustainable urban livelihoods and marketplace social capital: Crisis and strategy in petty trade', *Urban Studies*, 42: 1301–20.

MacKinnon, D., Cumbers, A. and Shaw, J. (2008) 'Re-scaling employment relations: Key outcomes of change in the privatised rail industry', *Environment and Planning A*, 40: 1347–69.

MacLeod, G. and Goodwin, M. (1999) 'Space, scale and state strategy: Rethinking urban and regional governance', *Progress in Human Geography,* 23(4): 503–27.

Magnaghi, A. (2000) *The Urban Village.* London: Zed Books.

Mahmood, I.P., and Singh, J. (2003) 'Technological dynamism in Asia', *Research Policy,* 32: 1031–54.

Malecki, E.J. (1997) *Technology and Economic Development: The Dynamics of Local, Regional and National Competitiveness.* 2nd edition. Harlow: Longman.

Malinowski, B. (1948 [1926]). *Magic, Science and Religion, and Other Essays.* New York: Doubleday Anchor Book.

Maloney, W.F. (2004) 'Informality revisited', *World Development,* 32(7): 1159–78.

Manor, J. (2004) 'Democratisation with inclusion: Political reforms and people's empowerment at the grassroots', *Journal of Human Development,* 5(1): 5–29.

Marcelli, E., Williams, C.C. and Joassart, P. (2009) (eds) *Informal Work in Developed Nations.* London: Routledge.

Marcotullio, P.J. (2007) 'Variations of Urban Environmental Transitions: The Experiences of Rapidly Developing Asia-Pacific Cities', in P.J. Marcotullio and G. McGranahan (eds), *Scaling Urban Environment Challenges: From Local to Global and Back.* London: Earthscan. pp. 45–68.

Marcotullio, P.J. and McGranahan, G. (2007) *Scaling Urban Environment Challenges: From Local to Global and Back.* London: Earthscan.

Marcuse, P. (2000) 'Cities in Quarters', in G. Bridge and S. Watson (eds) *A Companion to the City.* Oxford: Blackwell.

Marcuse, P. and van Kempen, R. (eds) (2000) *Globalizing Cities. A New Spatial Order?* Oxford: Blackwell.

Markusen, A. (2006) 'Urban development and the politics of a creative class: Evidence from a study of artists', *Environment and Planning A,* 38(10): 1921–40.

Markusen, A. and Schrock, G. (2004) 'The Artistic Dividend: Urban artistic specialization and economic development implications', presentation to the North American Regional Science Association Annual Meeting: Seattle, WA. October.

Markusen, A. and Schrock, G. (2006) 'The artistic dividend: Urban artistic specialisation and economic development implications', *Urban Studies,* 43(10): 1661–86.

Marlet, G. and van Woerkens, C. (2007) 'The Dutch creative class and how it fosters urban employment growth', *Urban Studies,* 44(13): 2605–26.

Marshall, A. (1920) *Principles of Economics.* London: MacMillan.

Martin, J.E. (1964) 'The Industrial Geography of Greater London', in: R. Clayton (ed.) *The Geography of Greater London.* London: George Philip & Son Limited.

Martin, R. (2000) Local Labour Markets: Their Nature, Performance and Regulation', in G. Clark, M. Feldmann and M. Gertler (eds) *The Oxford Handbook of Economic Geography.* Oxford: Oxford University Press. pp. 455–76.

Martin, R. (2010) 'Roepke lecture in Economic Geography – rethinking regional path dependence: beyond lock-in to evolution', *Economic Geography,* 86(1): 1–27.

Martine, G. et al. (2008) *The New Global Frontier: Urbanisation, Poverty and Environment in the 21st Century.* London: Earthscan.

Martinez-Alier, J. (2003) 'Urban "Unsustainability" and Environmental Conflict', L.F. Girard, B. Forte, M. Cerreta, P. De Toro and F. Forte (eds) *The Human Sustainable City: Challenges and Perspectives from the Habitat Agenda*. Aldershot: Ashgate. pp. 89–105.

Maskell, P. and Kebir, L. (2006) 'What qualifies as a cluster theory?', in B. Ashiem, P. Cooke and R. Martin (eds) *Clusters and Regional Development: Critical Reflections and Explorations*. London: Routledge. pp. 30–49.

Massey, D. (1984) *Spatial Divisions of Labour. Social Structures and the Geography of Production*. 2nd edition. Basingstoke: Macmillan.

Massey, D. (2007) *World City*. Cambridge and Malden, MA: Polity Press.

Massey, D. and Meegan, R. (1981) 'Industrial Restructuring Versus the Cities', in A Evans and D. Eversley (eds) *The Inner City: Employment and Industry*. London: Heinemann.

Matthiessen, C.W., Schwarz, A.W. and Find, S. (2006) 'World cities of knowledge: Research strength, networks and nodality', *Journal of Knowledge Management*, 10(5): 14–25.

May, J., Wills, J., Datta, K., Evans, Y., Herbert, J. and McIlwaine, C. (2007) 'Keeping London working: Global cities, the British state and London's new migrant division of labour', *Transactions of the Institute of British Geographers*, NS 32: 151–67.

McDowell, L., Batnitzky, A. and Dyer, S. (2009) 'Precarious work and economic migration: Emerging immigrant divisions of labour in Greater London's service sector', *International Journal of Urban and Regional Research*, 33: 3–25.

McCann, E. (2007) 'Inequality and politics in the creative city-region: Questions of livability and state strategy', *International Journal of Urban and Regional Research*, 31(1): 188–96.

McCann, E. (2011) 'Urban policy mobilities and global circuits of knowledge: Toward a research agenda', *Annals of the Association of American Geographers*, 101(1): 107–30.

McCann, E. and Ward, K. (2011) 'Introduction. Urban Assemblages: Territories, Relations, Practices and Power', in E. McCann and K. Ward (eds) *Mobile Urbanism: Cities and Policymaking in the Global Age*. Minneapolis: University of Minnesota Press.

McDonald, D. and Pape, J. (eds) (2002) *Cost Recovery and the Crisis of Service Delivery in South Africa*. Pretoria: HSRC Press.

McDonald, J.F. (2008) *Urban America: Growth, Crisis, and Rebirth*. New York and London: M.E. Sharpe.

McGee, T. (1991) 'The Emergence of *Desakota* Regions in Asia: Expanding a Hypothesis', in N. Ginsburg, B. Koppel and T.G. McGee (eds) *The Extended Metropolis: Settlement Transition in Asia*. Hawaii: University of Hawaii Press.

McGranahan, G. (2007) 'Urban Transitions and the Spatial Displacement of Environmental Burdens', in P.J. Marcotullio and G. McGranahan (eds), *Scaling Urban Environment Challenges: From Local to Global and Back*. London: Earthscan. pp. 18–44.

McGranahan, G., Jacobi, P., Songsore, J., Surjadi, C. and Kjellén, M. (2001) *The Citizens at Risk: From Urban Sanitation to Sustainable Cities*. London: Earthscan.

McManus, P. (2004) *Vortex Cities to Sustainable Cities: Australia's Urban Challenge*. Sydney: University of New South Wales Press.

McNeill, D. (2009) *The Global Architect: Firms, Fame and Urban Form*. London: Routledge.

Meegan, R., Kennett, P., Jones, G. and Croft, J. (2014) 'Global economic crisis, austerity and neoliberal urban governance in England', *Cambridge Journal of Regions, Economy and Society*, 7: 137–53.

Mehrotra, S. and Biggeri, M. (2007) (eds) *Asian Informal Workers: Global Risks, Local Protection*. London: Routledge.

Meléndez, E., Theodore, N. and Valenzuela, A. (2009) 'Day Laborers in New York's Informal Economy', in E. Marcelli, C.C. Williams and P. Joassart (eds) *Informal Work in Developed Nations*. London: Routledge. pp. 135–52.

Menegat, R. (2002) 'Participatory democracy and sustainable development: integrated urban environmental management in Porto Alegre', *Environment and Urbanization*, 14(2): 181–206.

Merrifield, A. (2002) 'Henri Lefebvre: The Urban Revolution', in *MetroMarxism*. London: Routledge.

Meusburger, P., Funke J. and Wunder E. (eds) (2009) *Milieus of Creativity. An Interdisciplinary Approach to Spatiality of Creativity*. Heidelberg: Springer Science.

Miles, S. (2003) 'Researching Young People as Consumers', in A. Bennett, M. Cieslik and S. Miles (eds) *Researching Youth*. New York: Palgrave. pp. 170–85.

Miller, M. and Kroll, L. (2010) 'World's Billionaires 2010', Forbes.com. Available at: http://finance.yahoo.com (accessed 11 March 2010).

Mintrom, M. and Norman, P. (2009) 'Policy entrepreneurship and policy change', *Policy Studies Journal*, 37(4): 649–67.

Miraftab, F. (2003) 'The perils of participatory discourse: Housing policy in post-apartheid South Africa', *Journal of Planning Education and Research*, 22(3): 226–39.

Miraftab, F. (2004) 'Making neo-liberal governance: The disempowering work of empowerment', *International Planning Studies*, 9(4): 239–59.

Mitlin, D. (2000) 'Addressing urban poverty: increasing incomes, reducing costs, and securing representation', *Development in Practice*, 10(2): 204–15.

Molotch, H. (1976) 'The city as a growth machine: Toward a political economy of place', *The American Journal of Sociology*, 82(2): 309–32.

Mooney, G. (2004) 'Cultural policy as urban transformation? Critical reflections on Glasgow, European City of Culture, 1990', *Local Economy*, 19(4): 327–40.

Morgan, K. (1997) 'The learning region – institutions, innovation and regional renewal', *Regional Studies*, 31: 491–503.

Moser, C. (2008) 'Assets and Livelihoods: A Framework for Asset-Based Social Policy', in C. Moser and A. Dani (eds) *Assets, Livelihoods and Social Policy*. Washington, DC: World Bank. pp 43–84.

Mouffe, C. (2005) *On the Political*. London: Routledge.

Moulaert, F. (2000) *Globalization and Integrated Area Development in European Cities*. Oxford: Oxford University Press.

Mulgan, G. (2010) *The Birth of the Relational State*, London: The Young Foundation. Available at: http://www.youngfoundation.org/files/images/the_relational_state_3_0.pdf (accessed 18 March 2011).

Muth, R. (1969) *Cities and Housing*. Chicago: University of Chicago.

Myers, G. (2011) *African Cities: Alternative Visions of Urban Theory and Practice*. London: Zed Books.

Mykhnenko, V. and Turok, I. (2008) 'East European cities: Patterns of growth and decline, 1960–2005', *International Planning Studies*, 13(4): 311–42.

Narayan, D. and Kapoor S. (2008) 'Beyond Sectoral Traps: Creating Wealth for the Poor', in *Assets, Livelihoods and Social Policy*. Washington, DC: World Bank. pp. 299–321.

Nathan, M. and Urwin, C. (2005) *City People: City Centre Living in the UK*. London: IPPR Centre for Cities.

National Bureau of Statistics (2009) *China Statistical Yearbook 2008*. Beijing: National Bureau of Statistics.

National Research Council (2010) *S&T Strategies of Six Countries: Implications for the United States*. Washington, DC: The National Academies Press.

National Science Board (2010) *Science and Engineering Indicators 2010*. Arlington, VA: National Science Foundation.

Nature (2010) 'Science and the city' *Nature*, 467 (7318), 899–918. Available at: http://www.nature.com.proxy2.cl.msu.edu/nature/journal/v467/n7318/index.html [accessed 3 December, 2010].

Neill, W.J.V. (2001) 'Marketing the urban experience: Reflections on the place of fear in the promotional strategies of Belfast, Detroit and Berlin', *Urban Studies*, 38: 815.

New York Times (2 October 2009) 'Do Olympic Host Cities Ever Win? Room for Debate'. Available at: http://roomfordebate.blogs.nytimes.com/2009/10/02 (accessed 15 February 2011).

New York Times (19 July 2009) 'Bogotá's Buses Offer a Lesson in Climate Change'. p. 2.

Newton, P.W. (2008) (ed.) *Transitions: Pathways Towards Sustainable Urban Development in Australia*. Dordrecht: Springer.

Newton, P. (2010) 'Beyond greenfields and brownfields: The challenge of regenerating Australia's Greyfield Suburbs', *Built Environment* 36: 81–104.

Ng, E. (ed.) (2010) *Designing High Density Cities for Social and Environmental Sustainability*. London: Earthscan.

Nicholls, W. (2011) 'The Los Angeles School: Difference, politics, city', *International Journal of Urban and Regional Research*, 35(1): 189–206.

Nichols, T., Cam, S., Grace Chou, Wen-chi., Chun, S., Zhao, W. and Feng, T. (2004) 'Factory regimes and the dismantling of established labour in Asia: A review of cases from large manufacturing plants in China, South Korea and Taiwan', *Work, Employment and Society*, 18: 663–85.

Nitsch, V. (2003) 'Does history matter for urban primacy? The case of Vienna', *Regional Science and Urban Economics,* 33(4): 401–18.

Novy, A. and Leubolt, B. (2005) 'Participatory budgeting in Porto Alegre: social innovation and the dialectical relationship of state and civil society', *Urban Studies,* 42(11): 2023–36.

O'Brien, D. (2011) 'Who is in charge? Liverpool, European Capital of Culture 2008 and the governance of cultural planning', *Town Planning Review,* 82(1): 45–59.

Odell, K.A. and Weiman, D.F. (1998) 'Metropolitan development, regional financial centers, and the founding of the fed in the lower south', *The Journal of Economic History,* 58(1): 103–25.

Office of the Deputy Prime Minister (2006) *A Framework for City-Regions.* Urban research summary No. 20. [Pdf] Wetherby: Office of the Deputy Prime Minister. Available at: http://www.communities.gov.uk/publications/regeneration/framework6 (accessed 31 October 2010).

Oh, D.S. (2002) 'Technology-based regional development policy: Case study of Taedok Science Town, Taejon Metropolitan City, Korea', *Habitat International,* 26: 213–28.

Ohmae, K. (1995) *The End of the Nation-State – The Rise of Regional Economies.* London: HarperCollins.

Oliver, A. and Ebers, M. (1998) 'Networking network studies', *Organization Studies,* 19: 549–83.

Osborne, D. and Gaebler, T. (1993) *Reinventing Government: How the Entrepreneurial Spirit is Transforming the Public Sector.* New York: Addison-Wesley Publishing Company.

Osirim, M.J. (2009) *Enterprising Women in Urban Zimbabwe: Gender, Micro-Business and Globalization.* Bloomington: Indiana University Press.

Ossman, S. (1994) *Picturing Casablanca. Portraits of Power in a Modern City.* Berkeley, CA: University of California Press.

Oswalt, P. (ed.) (2006) *Shrinking Cities,* Vol. 1. International Research. Ostfildern-Ruit, Germany: Hatje Cantz Verlag.

Paddison, R. (1993) 'City marketing, image reconstruction and urban regeneration', *Urban Studies,* 30(2): 339–50.

Paddison, R. (2009) 'Some reflections on the limitations to public participation in the post-political city', *L'Éspace Politique,* 8(2): 1–15.

Paddison, R. and Miles, S. (eds) (2007) *Culture-Led Urban Regeneration.* London: Routledge.

Pahl, R.E. (1984) *Divisions of Labour.* Oxford: Blackwell.

Pain, K. (2011) 'Spatial Transformations of Cities: Global City-Region? Mega City-Region', in P.J. Taylor, M. Hoyler, B. Derudder and F. Witlox (eds) *International Handbook of Globalization and World Cities.* London: Elgar.

Paniccia, I. (2006) 'Cutting Through the Chaos: Towards a New Typology of Industrial Districts and Clusters', in B. Ashiem, P. Cooke and R. Martin (eds) *Clusters and Regional Development: Critical Reflections and Explorations.* London: Routledge. pp: 69–89.

Parker, R. (2007) 'Networked governance or just networks? Local governance of the knowledge economy in Limerick (Ireland) and Karlskrona (Sweden)', *Political Studies*, 55: 113–32.

Parkinson, M., Champion, T., Evans, R. et al. (2006) *State of the English Cities*. London: ODPM.

Parnell, S. and Pieterse E. (2010) 'Realising the "right to the city": Institutional imperatives for tackling urban poverty', *International Journal for Urban and Regional Research*, 34(1) 146–62.

Parnell, S., Pieterse, E. and Watson, V. (2009) 'Planning for cities in the global south: A research agenda for sustainable human settlements', *Progress in Planning*, 72(2): 233–41.

Pastor, M. (2001) 'Common ground at ground zero? The new economy and the new organizing in Los Angeles', *Antipode*, 33(2): 260–89.

Pastor, M., Benner, C. and Matsuoka, M. (2009) *This Could Be the Start of Something Big: How Social Movements for Regional Equity are Reshaping Metropolitan America*. Cornell: Cornell University Press.

Pavlinek, P. and Pickles, J. (2000) *Environmental Transitions: Transformations and Ecological Defence in Central and Eastern Europe*. London: Routledge.

Pavlovskya, M. (2004) 'Other transitions: Multiple economies of Moscow households in the 1990s', *Annals of the Association of American Geographers*, 94: 329–51.

Peck, J. (1996) *Work-Place: The Social Regulation of Labour Markets*. New York: Guilford.

Peck, J. (1998) 'Workfare: A geopolitical etymology', *Environment and Planning D: Society and Space*, 16(1): 133–61.

Peck, J. (2000) 'Places of Work', in E. Sheppard and T. Barnes (eds) *A Companion to Economic Geography*. Oxford: Blackwell. pp. 133–48.

Peck, J. (2005) 'Struggling with the creative class', *International Journal of Urban and Regional Research*, 24(4): 740–70.

Peck, J. (2011) 'Geographies of policy: From transfer-diffusion to mobility-mutation', *Progress in Human Geography*, doi: 10.1177/0309132510394010.

Peck, J. (2012) 'Austerity urbanism', *City*, 16(6): 626–55.

Peck, J. and Tickell, A. (2002) 'Neoliberalizing space', *Antipode*, 34(3): 380–404.

Peck, J. and Ward, K. (2002) 'Placing Manchester', in J. Peck and K. Ward (eds) *City of Revolution: Restructuring Manchester*. Manchester: Manchester University.

Perlman, J. (2006) 'The metamorphosis of marginality: four generations in the favelas of Rio de Janeiro', *The Annals of the American Academy of Political and Social Science*, 606: 154–77.

Perlman, J. (2010) *Favela: Four Decades of Living on the Edge in Rio de Janeiro*. New York: Oxford University Press.

Petersen, P. (1981) *City Limits*. Chicago: University of Chicago Press.

Pfau-Effinger, B. (2009) 'Varieties of undeclared work in European societies', *British Journal of Industrial Relations*, 47(1): 79–99.

Phelps, N.A. and Parsons, N. (2003) 'Edge urban geographies: Notes from the margins of Europe's capital cities', *Urban Studies*, 40(9): 1725–49.

Phillips, S.A.M. and Yeung, W.C. (2003) 'A Place for R&D? The Singapore Science Park', *Urban Studies*, 40(6): 707–32.

Pierre, J. and Peters, G. (2000) *Governance Politics and the State*. New York: St. Martin's Press.

Pieterse, E. (2000) 'Participatory Urban Governance. Practical Approaches, Regional Trends and UMP Experiences.' Vol. 25, Urban Management Programme Formal Series. Nairobi: Urban Management Programme.

Pieterse, E. (2005) 'Transgressing the Limits of Possibility: Working Notes on a Relational Model of Urban Politics', in A. Simone and A. Abouhani (eds) *Urban Processes and Change in Africa*. London: Zed Books.

Pieterse, E. (2008a) *City Futures: Confronting the Crisis of Urban Development*. London: Zed Books.

Pieterse, E. (2008b) 'Empowerment', in S. Robins and N. Shepard (eds) *South African Keywords*. Johannesburg: Jacana.

Pieterse, E. (2014) 'Inclusivity', in: R. Paddison and T. Hutton (eds), *Cities and Economic Change*. London: Sage.

Piore, M. and Sabel, C. (1984) *The Second Industrial Divide – Possibilities for Prosperity*. New York: Basic Books.

Plaza, B. (1999) 'The Guggenheim-Bilbao effect: A reply to Maia V. Gomez "Reflective Images: the case of urban regeneration – Glasgow and Bilbao"', *International Journal of Urban and Regional Research*, 23(3): 589–92.

Plummer, P. and Taylor, M. (2001a) 'Theories of local economic growth (Part 1): Concepts, models, and measurement', *Environment and Planning A*, 33: 219–36.

Plummer, P. and Taylor, M. (2001b) 'Theories of local economic growth (Part 2): Model specification and empirical validation', *Environment and Planning A*, 33: 385–98.

Polèse, M. (2009) *The Wealth and Poverty of Regions: Why Cities Matter*. Chicago: University of Chicago Press.

Polèse, M. and Denis-Jacob, J. (2010) 'Changes at the top. A cross-country examination over the 20th century of the rise (and fall) in rank of the top cities in national urban hierarchies', *Urban Studies*, 47(9): 1843–60.

Polèse, M. and Shearmur, R. (2004) 'Culture, language and the location of high-order service functions: The case of Montreal and Toronto', *Economic Geography*, 80(4): 329–50.

Polèse, M. and Shearmur, R. (2006) 'Why some regions will decline: a Canadian case study with thoughts on local economic development', *Papers in Regional Science*, 85(1): 23–46.

Pollert, A. (1991) *Farewell to Flexibility*. Oxford: Blackwell.

Porritt, J. (2007) *Capitalism as if the World Matters*. London: Earthscan.

Portes, A. (1994) 'The Informal Economy and its Paradoxes', in N.J. Smelser and R. Swedberg (eds) *The Handbook of Economic Sociology*. Princeton, NJ: Princeton University Press.

Portney, K. (2003) *Taking Sustainable Cities Seriously*. Cambridge, MA: MIT Press.

Posner, M. (2011) Interview with Niall Ferguson, 'Europe and the Collapse of the West', *Globe and Mail*, 4 November.

Potts, D. (2009) 'The slowing of sub-Saharan Africa's urbanization: Evidence and implications for urban livelihoods', *Environment and Urbanization*, 21(1): 253–9.

Powell, W. (1991) 'Neither Market Nor Hierarchy: Network Forms of Organization', in G. Thompson, J. Frances, R. Levacic and J. Mitchell (eds) *Markets, Hierarchies and Networks: The Coordination of Social Life*. London: Sage and Open University. pp. 265–75.

Power, A., Plöger, J. and Winkler, A. (2010) *Phoenix Cities: Learning from Seven Recovering European Cities*. Bristol: The Policy Press.

Pratt, A.C. (2009) 'Urban Regeneration: From the arts "feel good" factor to the cultural economy. A case study of Hoxton, London', *Urban Studies* 46(5–6): 1041–61.

Pratt, A.C. and Hutton, T.A. (2013) 'Reconceptualising the relationship between the creative economy and the city: Learning from the financial crisis', *Cities*, 33: 86–95.

Pred, A. (1977) *City Systems in Advanced Economies*. New York: John Wiley.

Provo, J. (2009) 'Risk-averse regionalism: The cautionary tale of Portland, Oregon, and affordable housing', *Journal of Planning Education and Research*, 28(3): 368–81.

Purcell, M. (2008) *Recapturing Democracy: Neoliberalization and the Struggle for Alternative Urban Futures*. New York and London: Routledge.

Putnam, R. (1993) *Making Democracy Work: Civic Traditions in Modern Italy*. Princeton, NJ: Princeton.

Raco, M. (2005) 'Sustainable development, rolled-out neo-liberalism and sustainable communities', *Antipode*, 324–46.

Rakodi, C. (2002) 'A Livelihoods Approach – Conceptual Issues and Definitions', in C. Rakodi and T. Lloyd-Jones (eds) *Urban Livelihoods. A People-Centred Approach to Reducing Poverty*. London: Earthscan. pp. 3–22.

Rakodi, C. (2004) 'Tackling Urban Poverty: Principles and Practices in Project and Programme Design in Kenya', in R. Zetter and M. Hamza (eds) *Market Economy and Urban Change: Impacts in the Developing World*. London: Earthscan. pp. 97–121.

Rantisi, N. (2002) 'The competitive foundations of localized learning and innovation: the case of the women's garment industry in New York City', *Economic Geography*, 78: 441–62.

Rappaport, J. (2003) 'U.S. urban decline and growth, 1950 to 2000', *Federal Reserve Bank of Kansas City Economic Review*, Third Quarter: 15–44. Available at: www.kc.frb.org

Rappaport, J. (2007) 'Moving to nice weather', *Regional Science and Urban Economics*, 37(3): 375–98.

Rappaport, J. (2009) 'The increasing importance of quality of life', *Journal of Economic Geography*, 9: 779–804.

Rappaport, J. and Sachs, J. (2003) 'The United States as a coastal nation', *Journal of Economic Growth*, 8: 5–46.

Raspe, O. and van Oort, F. (2006) 'The knowledge economy and urban economic growth', *European Planning Studies*, 14(9): 1209–34.

Ravallion, M. Chen, S. and Sangraula, P. (2007) *New Evidence of the Globalization of Poverty.* Washington, DC: World Bank.

Ren, H. (2007) 'The Landscape of Power: Imagineering Consumer Behaviour at China's Theme Parks', in S. Lukas (ed.) *The Themed Space: Locating Culture, Nation and Self.* Lexington Books.

Richards, G. and Wilson, J. (2004) 'The impact of cultural events on city image: Rotterdam, Cultural Capital of Europe 2001', *Urban Studies*, 41(10): 1931–51.

Riddell, B. (1997) 'Structural adjustment programmes and the city in tropical Africa', *Urban Studies*, 34: 1297–307.

Rigg, J. (1997) *Southeast Asia: The Human Landscape of Modernization and Development.* London: Routledge.

Robertson, J. (1991) *Future Wealth: A New Economics for the 21st Century.* London: Cassells.

Robinson, J. (2002) 'Global and world cities: A view from off the map', *International Journal of Urban and Regional Research*, 26: 531–54.

Robson, B., Lymperopoulou, K. and Rae, A. (2008) 'People on the move: Exploring the functional roles of deprived neighbourhoods', *Environment and Planning A*, 40(11): 2693–714.

Rogers, E.M. (1976) 'Communication and development: The passing of the dominant paradigm', *Communication Research*, April, 3(2): 213–40.

Rogerson, R.J. (1999) 'Quality of life and city competitiveness', *Urban Studies*, 36(5–6): 969–85.

Romer, P. (1986) 'Increasing returns and long-run growth', *Journal of Political Economy*, 94: 1002–37.

Rose, R. (2005) *Insiders and Outsiders: New Europe Barometer 2004.* Glasgow: University of Strathclyde Studies in Public Policy No. 404.

Rosenthal, S. and Strange, W. (2004) 'Evidence on the Nature and Sources of Agglomeration Economies', in V. Henderson and J. Thisse (eds) *Handbook of Urban and Regional Economics.* Volume 4. Amsterdam: Elsevier. pp. 2119–71.

Ross, R.J.S. (2004) *Slaves to Fashion: Poverty and Abuse in the New Sweatshops.* Ann Arbor, MI: University of Michigan Press.

Roy, A. and AlSayyad, N. (2004) *Urban Informality.* Lantham, MA: Lexington Books.

Ruchelman, L.I. (2007) *Cities in The Third Wave. The Technological Transformation of Urban America.* (2nd edition). Lanham, MD: Rowman and Littlefield Publishers Inc.

Russell, B. and Tithe, M. (2008) 'The next division of labour: Work skills in Australian and Indian call centres', *Work, Employment and Society*, 22: 615–34.

Rutherford, T. and Gertler, M. (2002) 'Labour in "lean" times: Geography, scale and national trajectories of workplace change', *Transactions of the Institute of British Geographers*, NS 27: 195–212.

Sabel, C. (1989) 'Flexible Specialization and the Re-emergence of Regional Economies', in P. Hirst and J. Zeitlin (eds) *Reversing Industrial Decline? Industrial Structure and Policy in Britain and her Competitors.* Oxford: Berg. pp. 17–70.

Sasaki, M. (2010) 'Urban regeneration through cultural creativity and social inclusion: Rethinking creative city theory through a Japanese case study', *Cities*, 27(1): 3–9.

Sassen, S. (1991) *The Global City: New York, London, Tokyo*. Princeton, NJ: Princeton University Press.

Sassen, S. ([1991] 2001) *The Global City: New York, London, Tokyo*. (2nd edition). Princeton, NJ: Princeton University Press.

Sassen, S. (1997a) 'New Employment Regimes in Cities', in F. Moulaert and A.J. Scott (eds) *Cities, Enterprise and Society on the Eve of the 21st Century*. London and Washington: Pinter.

Sassen, S. (1997b) *Informalisation in Advanced Market Economies*, Issues in Development Discussion Paper 20. Geneva: International Labour Office.

Sassen, S. (2000a) *Cities in a World Economy*. London and New York: Sage.

Sassen, S. (2000b) 'New frontiers facing urban sociology at the millennium', *British Journal of Sociology*, 51(1): 143–59.

Sassen, S. (ed.) (2002) *Global Networks, Linked Cities*. New York: Routledge.

Sassen, S. (2008) 'Two stops in today's new global geographies: Shaping novel labour supplies and employment regimes', *CEPAL – Serie Mujer y Desarrollo*, No. 96. Santiago: United Nations.

Satterthwaite, D., Montgomery, M. and Reed, H. (2003) 'Diversity and Inequality', in M.R. Montgomery, R. Stren, B. Cohen and H. Reed (eds) *Cities Transformed: Demographic Change and its Implications in the Developing World*. Washington, DC: The National Academies Press. pp. 155–98.

Sauvy, A. (1984) *Le Travail Noir et l'Économie de Demain*. Paris: Calmann-Levy.

Savitch, H.V. and Kantor, P. (1995) 'City business: An international perspective on marketplace politics', *International Journal for Urban and Regional Research*, 19(4): 495–512.

Saxenian, A.L. (2006) *The New Argonauts: Regional Advantage in a Global Economy*. Cambridge, MA: Harvard University Press.

Scott, A.J. (1988a) *New Industrial Spaces – Flexible Production Organization and Regional Development in North America and Western Europe*. London: Pion.

Scott, A.J. (1988b) *Metropolis. From the Division of Labor to Urban Form*. Berkeley and Los Angeles: University of California Press.

Scott, A.J. (1993) *Technopolis: High-Technology Industry and Regional Development in Southern California*. Los Angeles: University of California Press.

Scott, A.J. (1997) 'The cultural economy of the city', *International Journal of Urban and Regional Research*, 21: 323–39.

Scott, A.J. (1998) *Regions and the World Economy – The Coming Shape of Global Production, Competition, and Political Order*. Oxford: Oxford University Press.

Scott, A.J. (2000) *The Cultural Economy of Cities: Essays on the Geography of Image-Producing Industries*. London: Sage.

Scott, A.J. (ed.) (2001a) *Global City-Regions – Trends, Theory, Policy*. Oxford: Oxford University Press.

Scott, A.J. (2001b) 'Globalization and the rise of city-regions', *European Planning Studies*, 9(7): 813–26.

Scott, A.J. (2008) *Social Economy of the Metropolis. Cognitive-Cultural Capitalism and the Global Resurgence of Cities*. Oxford: Oxford University Press.

Seetharam, K. and Yuen, B. (eds) (2010) *Developing Living Cities: From Analysis to Action*. Singapore: World Scientific.

Segal, Quince and Wicksteed (2000) *The Cambridge Phenomenon Revisited*. Cambridge: Segal, Quince and Wicksteed.

Seltzer, E. (2004) 'It's Not an Experiment: Regional Planning at Metro, 1990 to the present', in C. Ozawa (ed.) *The Portland Edge: Challenges and Success in Growing Communities*. Washington, DC: The Island Press. pp. 35–60.

Selwyn, T. (ed.) (1996) *The Tourist Image. Myths and Myth Making in Tourism*. Chichester and New York: John Wiley & Sons.

Shearmur, R.G. and Hutton, T.A. (2011) 'Canada's Changing City-Regions: The expanding metropolis', in L.S. Bourne, T.A. Hutton, R.G. Shearmur and J. Simmons (eds) *Canadian Urban Regions: Trajectories of Growth and Change*. Toronto: Oxford University Press. pp. 99–124.

Sheller, M. and Urry, J. (eds) (2004) *Tourism Mobilities. Places To Play, Places In Play*. London and New York: Routledge.

Shen, X. (1999) *The Chinese Road to High Technology: A Study of Telecommunication Switching Technology in the Economic Transition*. Houndmills: Palgrave Macmillan Ltd.

Shevchenko, O. (2009) *Crisis and the Everyday in Post-Socialist Moscow*. Bloomington: Indiana University Press.

Short, J. (1999) 'Urban imagineers: boosterism and the representations of cities', in: A. Jonas and D. Wilson (eds) *The Urban Growth Machine: Critical Perspectives Two Decades Later*. Albany, NY: State University of New York Press. pp. 37–54.

Short, J. and Kim, Y. (1998) 'Urban Crises/Urban Representations: Selling the City in Difficult Times', in T. Hall and P. Hubbard (eds) *The Entrepreneurial City: Geographies of Politics, Regime and Representation*. Chichester: John Wiley & Sons.

Shorthose, J. and Strange, G. (2004) 'The new cultural economy, the artist and the social configuration of autonomy', *Capital and Class*, 84: 43–59.

Siebenhaar, K. (2006) 'The myth of Berlin: The imagined and the staged city', *European Studies*, 23: 227–35.

Simmie, J. (2002) 'Knowledge spillovers and reasons for the concentration of innovative SMEs', *Urban Studies*, 39: 885–902.

Simmie, J. (2003) 'Innovation and urban regions as national and international nodes for the transfer and sharing of knowledge', *Regional Studies*, 37(6–7): 607–20.

Simmie, J., Carpenter, J. Chadwick, A. Martin, R. and Wood P. (2006) *The State of English Cities: The Competitive Economic Performance of English Cities*. London: Department for Communities and Local Government. Available at: www.communities.gov.uk

Simmie, J. and Martin, R. (2010) 'The economic resilience of regions: Towards an evolutionary approach', *Cambridge Journal of Regions, Economy and Society*, 3(1): 27–43.

Simone, A. (2010) *City Life from Jakarta to Dakar: Movements at the Crossroads.* London: Routledge.

Simone, A. and Pieterse, E. (1993) 'Civil society in an internationalised Africa', *Social Dynamics*, 19(2): 40–69.

Sites, W. (2007) 'Contesting the Neo-liberal City? Theories of Neo-liberalism and Urban Strategies of Contention', in H. Leitner, J. Peck and E. Sheppard (eds) *Contesting Neo-liberalism: Urban Frontiers*. New York: Guilford Press. pp. 116–38.

Skelcher, C. (2005) 'Jurisdictional integrity, polycentrism, and the design of democratic governance', *Governance*, 18(1): 89–110.

Smith, A. (2004) 'Regions, territories and diverse economies in the "new Europe"'. *European Urban and Regional Studies*, 11: 9–25.

Smith, M.P. (2001) *Transnational Urbanism: Locating Globalisation*. Oxford and Malden, MA: Blackwell.

Smith, N. (1996) *The New Urban Frontier: Gentrification and the Revanchist City.* London: Routledge.

Smith, A. and Stenning, A. (2006) 'Beyond household economies: Articulations and spaces of economic practice in postsocialism', *Progress in Human Geography*, 30(2): 1–14.

Smith, N. and Williams, P. (eds) (1986) *Gentrification of the City*. Boston: Allen & Unwin.

Snow, D.A., Morrill, C. and Anderson, L. (2003) 'Elaborating analytic ethnography: Linking fieldwork and theory', *Ethnography*, 4(2): 181–200.

Snyder, K.A. (2004) 'Routes to the informal economy in New York's East village: Crisis, economics and identity', *Sociological Perspectives*, 47(2): 215–40.

Soja, E. (2000) *Postmetropolis. Critical Studies of Cities and Regions*. Oxford: Blackwell.

Soja, E. (2010) *Seeking Spatial Justice*. Minneapolis: University of Minnesota Press.

Sorensen, A. (2011) 'Uneven processes of institutional change: Path dependence, scale and the contested regulation of urban development in Japan', *International Journal of Urban and Regional Research*, 35(4): 712–34.

Southern, R. (2002) 'Understanding multi-sectoral regeneration partnerships as a form of local governance', *Local Government Studies*, 28(2): 16–32.

Standing, G. (2009) *Work after Globalisation: Building Occupational Citizenship*. Cheltenham: Edward Elgar Publishing Ltd.

Stephenson, K. (2004) 'Towards a Theory of Government', in H. McCarthy, P. Miller and P. Skidmore (eds) *Network Logic: Who Governs in an Interconnected World?*, London: Demos. pp. 37–48. Available at: http://www.drkaren.us/pdfs/network logic03stephenson%5B1%5D.pdf (accessed 25 March 2011).

Stiglitz, J.E. (2008) 'Making globalization work – The 2006 Geary Lecture', *The Economic and Social Review*, 39(3): 171–90.

Stone, C. (2008) 'Political Leadership in Urban Politics', in M. Orr and V. Johnson (eds) *Power in the City: Clarence Stone and the Politics of Inequality*. Kansas: University of Kansas Press. pp. 136–57.

Storper, M. (1997) *The Regional World – Territorial Development in a Global Economy*. New York: Guilford Press.

Storper, M. (2005) 'Society, Community, and Economic Development', in S. de Paula and G.A. Dymski (eds) *Reimagining Growth: Towards a Renewal of Development Theory*. London and New York: Zed Books. pp. 198–229.

Storper, M. (2013) *Keys to the City*. Princeton, NJ: Princeton University Press.

Storper, M. and Scott, A.J. (1990) 'Work organisation and local labour markets in an era of flexible production', *International Labour Review*, 129: 573–91.

Storper, M. and Venables, A.J. (2004) 'Buzz: Face-to-face contact and the urban economy', *Journal of Economic Geography*, 4(4): 351–70.

Storper, M. and Walker, R. (1989) *The Capitalist Imperative: Territory, Technology and Industrial Growth*. Oxford: Blackwell.

Sun, Y., Zedtwitz, M.V. and Simon, D.F. (2007) 'Globalization of R&D and China: An introduction', *Asia Pacific Business Review*, 13(3): 311–19.

Surborg, B. (2006) 'Advanced services, the new economy and the built environment in Hanoi', *Cities*, 23(4): 239–49.

Surborg, B. (2011) *The Production of the World City: Extractive Industries in a Global Urban Economy*. Doctoral Dissertation. Vancouver: Department of Geography, University of British Columbia.

Swann, G.M.P. (1999) 'The Internet and the Distribution of Economic Activity', in S. Macdonald and J. Nightingale (eds) (2000) *Information and Organization: A Tribute to the Work of Don Lamberton*. Amsterdam: Elsevier Science BV. pp. 183–95.

Swedberg, R. (1991) 'Major traditions in economic sociology', *Annual Reviews of Sociology*, 17: 251–76.

Swyngedouw, E. (2009) 'The antinomies of the post-political city: In search of a democratic politics of environmental production', *International Journal of Urban and Regional Research*, 33(3): 601–20.

Tallon, A. (2010) *Urban Regeneration in the UK*. London: Routledge.

Tan, W. and Klaasen, I. (2007) 'Exploring 24/7 environments', *Town Planning Review*, 78(6): 699–723.

Tannerfeldt, G. and Ljung, P. (2006) *More Urban Less Poor: An Introduction to Urban Development and Management*. London: Earthscan.

Taylor, P.J. (2004) *World City Network. A Global Urban Analysis*. London and New York: Routledge.

Taylor, P.J. (2010) 'Advanced Producer Service Centers in the World Economy', in P.J. Taylor, P. Ni, B. Derudder, M. Hoyler, J. Huang and F. Witlox (eds) *Global Urban Analysis: A Survey of Cities in Globalization*. London: Earthscan. Available at: http://www.lboro.ac.uk/gawc/rb/rb349.html (accessed 4 December 2010).

Taylor, P. and Bain, M. (2005) '"India calling to the far away towns": The call centre labour process and globalisation', *Work, Employment and Society*, 19: 261–82.

Taylor, P.J. and Walker, D.R.F. (2004) 'Urban hinterworlds revisited', *Geography*, 89(2): 145–51.

Taylor, P.J., Derudder, B., Saey, P. and Witlox, F. (2007) 'Introduction: Cities in Globalization', in *Cities in Globalization – Practices, Policies, and Theories*. London: Routledge. pp. 13–18.

Taylor, P.J., Ni, P., Derudder, B., Hoyler, M., Huang, J. and Witlox, F. (eds) (2010) *Global Urban Analysis – A Survey of Cities in Globalization*. London: Earthscan.

Teo, P. (2003) 'The limits of imagineering: A case study of Penang', *International Journal of Urban and Regional Research*, 27(3): 545–63.

Timberlake, M. (ed.) (1985) *Urbanization in the World-Economy*. Orlando, FL: Academic Press.

Tödtling, F., Lehner, P. and Trippl, M. (2006) 'Innovation in knowledge-intensive industries. The nature and geography of knowledge links', *European Planning Studies*, 14(8): 1035–58.

Trigilia, C. (2002) *Economic Sociology: State, Market, and Society in Modern Capitalism*. Oxford: Blackwell Publishing.

Tsukamoto, T. (2012) 'Neoliberalization of the developmental state: Tokyo's bottom-up politics and state rescaling in Japan', *International Journal of Urban and Regional Research*, 36(1): 71–89.

Turner, S. (2009) 'Hanoi's ancient quarter traders: Resilient livelihoods in a rapidly transforming city', *Urban Studies*, 45(5–6): 1203–21.

Turok, I. (2005) *Full Employment Strategies for Cities: The Case of Glasgow. Local Economic and Employment Development Programme*. Paris: OECD.

Turok, I. (2007) 'Urban Policy in Scotland: New Conventional Wisdom, Old Problems?', in M. Keating (ed.) *Social Democracy in Scotland*. Brussels: Peter Lang. pp. 141–68.

Turok, I. (2008) 'A new policy for Britain's cities: Choices, challenges and contradictions', *Local Economy*, 23(2): 149–66.

Turok, I. (2009a) 'The distinctive city: Pitfalls in the pursuit of differential advantage', *Environment and Planning A*, 41(1): 13–30.

Turok, I. (2009b) 'Limits to the mega-city region: Conflicting local and regional interests' *Regional Studies*, 43(6): 845–62.

Turok, I. and Mykhnenko, V. (2007) 'The trajectories of European cities, 1960–2005', *Cities*, 24(3): 165–82.

Turok, I. (2014) 'Linking Urbanization and Development in Africa's Economic Revival', in S. Parnell and E. Pieterse (eds) *Africa's Urban Revolution*. London: Zed Books. pp. 60–81.

Turok, I. (2010) 'Inclusive Growth: Meaningful Goal or Mirage', in A. Pike, A. Rodriguez-Pose and J. Tomaney (eds) *Routledge Handbook of Local and Regional Development*. London: Routledge. pp. 74–86.

Turok, I. (2014) 'Redundant and Marginalized Spaces', in R. Paddison and T. Hutton (eds), *Cities and Economic Change*. London: Sage.

Turok, I. and Bailey, N. (2004) 'Glasgow's Recent Trajectory: Partial Recovery and its Consequences', in D. Newlands, M. Danson and J. McCarthy (eds) *Divided Scotland: The Nature, Causes and Consequences of Economic Disparities Within Scotland*. Aldershot: Ashgate. pp. 35–59.

Turok, I. and Edge, N. (1999) *The Jobs Gap in Britain's Cities*. Bristol: Policy Press.

UNCHS (1976) *The Vancouver Declaration on Human Settlements*. Habitat: United Nations Conference on Human Settlements.

UNDP [United Nations Development Programme] (1991) *Cities, People & Poverty. Urban Development Cooperation for the 1990s*. New York: United Nations Development Programme.

UNESCO (2010) *UNESCO Science Report 2010*, Chapter 18 China, 2010, UNESCO, http://unesdoc.unesco.org/images/0018/001899/189958e.pdf

UNFPA (United Nations Population Fund) (2007) *State of the World Population*. New York: UNFPA.

UN-Habitat (2008) *State of the World's Cities 2008/9: Harmonious Cities*. London: Earthscan.

UN-Habitat (2009) *Planning Sustainable Cities: Policy Directions Global Report on Human Settlements 2009*. London: Earthscan.

UN-Habitat (2010a) *State of the World's Cities 2010/2011: Bridging the Urban Divide. Overview and Key Findings*. London: Earthscan.

UN-Habitat (2010b) *State of China's Cities 2010/2011*. [Online] Beijing: UN-Habitat, China Science Center of International Eurasian Academy of Sciences and China Association of Mayors. Available at: http://www.unhabitat.org/pmss/listItemDetails.aspx?publicationID=3012 (accessed 16 November 2010).

UN-Habitat (United Nations Human Settlements Programme) (2011) *State of the World's Cities Report 2010/11*. New York: UN-Habitat.

United Nations Conference on Trade and Development (2010) *Creative Economy: A Feasible Development Option*. Paris: UNCTAD.

UNRISD [United Nations Research Institute for Social Development] (2010) *Combating Poverty And Inequality. Structural Change, Social Policy and Politics*. Geneva: UNRISD.

Unni, J. and Rani, U. (2003) 'Employment and Income in the Informal Economy: A Micro-Perspective', in R. Jhabvala, R.M. Sudarshan and J. Unni (eds) *Informal Economy Centrestage: New Structures of Employment*. London: Sage. pp. 39–61.

Unsworth, R. (2007) 'City living and sustainable development', *Town Planning Review*, 78(6): 725–47.

Unsworth, R. (2011) 'The Future of City-Living as Eco-Localisation', Research Paper, Leeds Sustainable Development Group, Leeds University: UK.

Urban Task Force (1999) *Towards an Urban Renaissance: Final Report*. London: Stationery Office.

Urban Task Force (2005) *Towards a Strong Urban Renaissance*. London: Urban Task Force.

Urry, J. (2002) *The Tourist Gaze*. London: Sage.

Vale, L. J. and Campanula, T. J. (eds) (2005) *The Resilient City: How Modern Cities Recover from Disaster*. New York: Oxford University Press.

van den Berg, M. (2012) 'Femininity as a city marketing strategy. Gender bending Rotterdam', *Urban Studies*, 49(1): 153–68.

van der Horst, H. (2003) 'Multicultural Theming in the Netherlands: Pacifying, Essentializing and Revanchist Effects', in S. Ingram and Reisenleitner, M. (eds) *Placing History: Themed Environments, Urban Consumption and the Public Entertainment Sphere*. Vienna: Turia & Kant. pp. 175–200.

van Liempt, I. and Rath, J. (2009) 'Problematic areas or places of fun? Ethnic place marketing in the multicultural city of Rotterdam', in J.W. Duyvendak, F. Hendriks and M. van Niekerk (eds) *City in Sight. Dutch Dealings with Urban Change.* Amsterdam: Amsterdam University Press. pp. 81–99.

Van Noorden, R. (2010) 'Building the best cities for science', *Nature,* 7318: 906–8.

Vermander, B. (2007) 'Territory, identity and social representations. Analyzing political mythologies', *eRenlaiMagazine,*www.erenlai.com/index.php?aid=670& lan=3

Vettoretto, L. (2009) 'A preliminary critique of the best and good practices approach in European spatial planning and policy-making', *European Planning Studies,* 17(7): 1067–83.

Wachsmuth, D. (2014) 'City as ideology: reconciling the explosion of the city form with the tenacity of the city concept', *Environment and Planning D: Society and Space,* 32(1): 75–90.

Walcott, S. (2001) 'Growing global: Learning locations in the life sciences', *Growth and Change,* 32(4): 511–32.

Walcott, S.M. and Heitzman, J. (2006) 'High technology clusters in India and China: Divergent paths', *Indian Journal of Economics and Business,* September, 18: 113–30.

Walker, R. and Storper, M. (1983) 'The theory of labour and the theory of location', *International Journal of Urban and Regional Research,* 7: 1–44.

Walks, A. (2011) 'Economic Restructuring and Trajectories of Socio-Spatial Restructuring in the Twenty-First-Century Canadian City', in L.S. Bourne, T.A. Hutton, R. Shearmur and J. Simmons (eds) *Canadian Urban Regions: Trajectories of Growth and Change.* Toronto: Oxford University Press. Chapter 6. pp. 125–59.

Wall, R. (2010) 'Southern African Cities', in P.J. Taylor, P. Ni, B. Derudder, M. Hoyler, J. Huang and F. Witlox (eds) *Global Urban Analysis – A Survey of Cities in Globalization.* London: Earthscan. pp. 318–23.

Walsh, K. (2007) 'China R&D: A high-tech field of dreams', *Asia Pacific Business Review,* 13(3): 321–35.

Walton, J. (1992) 'Making the Theoretical Case', in C.C. Ragin and H. Becker (eds) *What is a Case? Exploring the Foundations of Social Inquiry.* Cambridge: Cambridge University Press. pp. 121–38.

Wang, S., Wu, Y. and Li, Y. (1998) 'Development of technopoles in China', *Asia Pacific Viewpoint,* December, 39(3): 281–301.

Ward, K. (2006) '"Policies in motion", urban management and state restructuring: The trans-local expansion of business improvement districts', *International Journal of Urban and Regional Research,* 30(1): 54–75.

Ward, K. (2010) 'Towards a relational comparative approach to the study of cities', *Progress in Human Geography,* 34: 471–87.

Ward, S. (1998) *Selling Places: The Marketing and Promotion of Towns and Cities 1850–2000.* Abingdon: Taylor & Francis.

Warde, A. (1994) 'Consumption, identity-formation and uncertainty', *Sociology,* 28(4): 877–98.

Warf, B. (2007) 'Geographies of the tropical internet', *Singapore Journal of Tropical Geography,* 28: 219–38.

Warf, B. and Vincent, P. (2007) 'Multiple geographies of the Arab internet', *Area*, 39(1): 83–96.

Watson., M. and Shove, E. (2005) 'Doing it yourself: Products, competence and the meaning in the practices of D-I-Y'. Paper presented at the European Sociological Association Conference; Torun-Poland, September 2005.

Wei, Y.H.D. (2007) 'Regional development in China: Transitional institutions, embedded globalization, and hybrid economies', *Eurasian Geography and Economics*, 48(1): 16–36.

Weiss-Sussex, G. (2006) 'Berlin literature and its use in the marketing of the "New Berlin"', *European Studies*, 23: 237–58.

West, J. (2001) 'The mystery of innovation: Aligning the triangle of technology, institutions and organization', *Australian Journal of Management*, August, 26: 21–43.

West Midlands Regional Assembly (2007) *West Midlands Regional Spatial Strategy: Phase Two Revision – Draft*. Birmingham: West Midlands Regional Assembly.

Wheeler, S.M. (2002) 'The new regionalism: Key characteristics of an emerging movement', *Journal of the American Planning Association*, 68(3): 267–78.

While, A., Jonas, A.E.G. and Gibbs, D.C. (2004) 'The environment and the entrepreneurial city: Searching for the urban "sustainability fix" in Leeds and Manchester', *International Journal of Urban and Regional Research*, 28(3): 549–69.

Whitehead, C. (2009) *The Density Debate: A Personal View*. London: LSE.

Whitehead, M. (2003) '(Re)Analysing the sustainable city: Nature, urbanization and the regulation of socio-environmental relations in the UK', *Urban Studies*, 40(7): 1183–206.

Whitehead, M. (2005) 'Between the marvellous and the mundane: Everyday life in the socialist city and the politics of the environment', *Society and the Space*, 23(2): 273–94.

Whitehead, M. (2006) 'Spatializing the ecological leviathan: States, nature and the production of regional space', *GeografiskaAnnaler: Series B – Human Geography* (with M. Jones and R. Jones), March.

Whitfield, M. (2010) 'Brazil getting extreme makeover in preparation for Olympics', *Miami Herald*, 21 August 2010. Available at: www.miamiherald.com/2010/08/21 (accessed 15 February 2011).

Wiechmann, T. (2008) 'Errors expected – Aligning urban strategy with demographic uncertainty in shrinking cities', *International Planning Studies*, 13: 431–46.

Williams, C.C. (2004a) *Cash-in-Hand Work: The Underground Sector and Hidden Economy of Favours*. Basingstoke: Palgrave Macmillan.

Williams, C.C. (2004b) 'Rethinking the "economy" and uneven development: Spatial disparities in household coping capabilities in contemporary England', *Regional Studies*, 38(5): 507–18.

Williams, C.C. (2005) *A Commodified World? Mapping the Limits of Capitalism*. London: Zed.

Williams, C.C. (2006) *The Hidden Enterprise Culture: Entrepreneurship in the Underground Economy*. Cheltenham: Edward Elgar.

Williams, C.C. (2007) *Re-thinking the Future of Work: Directions and Visions.* Basingstoke: Palgrave Macmillan.

Williams, C.C. (2008) 'Rethinking the motives of do-it-yourself (DIY) consumers', *International Review of Retail, Distribution and Consumer Research*, 18(3): 311–23.

Williams, C.C. (2009) 'Formal and informal employment in Europe: Beyond dualistic representations', *European Urban and Regional Studies*, 16(2): 147–59.

Williams, C.C. and Round, J. (2007) 'Rethinking the nature of the informal economy: some lessons from Ukraine', *International Journal of Urban and Regional Research*, 31(2): 425–41.

Williams, C.C. and Round, J. (2008) 'Evaluating the penetration of capitalism in post-socialist Moscow', *The American Journal of Economics and Sociology*, 67(2): 359–79.

Williams, C.C. and Windebank, J. (1998) *Informal Employment in the Advanced Economies: Implications for Work and Welfare.* London: Routledge.

Williams, C.C. and Windebank, J. (2002) 'The uneven geographies of informal economic activities: A case study of two British cities', *Work, Employment and Society*, 16(2): 231–50.

Williams, C.C. and Windebank, J. (2003) 'The slow advance and uneven penetration of commodification', *International Journal of Urban and Regional Research*, 27: 250–64.

Williams, G. (2004) 'Evaluating participatory development: Tyranny, power and (re)politicisation', *Third World Quarterly*, 25(3): 557–78.

Willis, R. (2008) *The Proximity Principle.* London: CPRE.

Willis, K.D. (2008) 'Migration and Transnationalism', in V. Desai and R.B. Potter (eds) *The Companion to Development Studies.* 2nd edition. London: Hodder. pp. 212–16.

Wills, J., Datta, K., Evans, Y., Herbert, J., May, J. and McIlwane, C. (2010) *Global Cities at Work: New Migrant Divisions of Labour.* London and New York: Pluto Press.

Wilson, E. (1991) *The Sphinx in the City. Urban Life, the Control of Disorder, and Women.* Berkeley, CA: University of California Press.

Wilson, M.I. and Corey, K.E. (2008) 'The ALERT Model: A Planning-Practice Process for Knowledge-Based Urban and Regional Development', in T. Yigitcanlar, K. Velibeyoglu and S. Baum (eds) *Knowledge-Based Urban Development: Planning and Applications in the Information Era.* Hershey and New York: Information Science Reference.

Wilson, M.I., Kellerman, A. and Corey, K.E. (2013) *Global Information Society: Technology, Knowledge, and Mobility.* Lanham: Rowman & Littlefield.

Wilson, P.A. (1995) 'Embracing locality in local economic development', *Urban Studies*, 32(4–5): 645–58.

Wolfe, D.A. and Gertler, M.S. (2004) 'Clusters from the inside and out: Local dynamics and global linkages', *Urban Studies*, May, 41(5/6): 1071–93.

Wonders, N. and Michalowski, R. (2001) 'Bodies, borders and sex tourism in a globalized world: A tale of two cities – Amsterdam and Havana', *Social Problems*, 48(4): 545–71.

Wong, P.K. and Ng, C.Y. (eds) (2001) *Industrial Policy, Innovation and Economic Growth: The Experience of Japan and the Asian NIEs*. Singapore: Singapore University Press.

Woolley, R., Turpin, T., Marceau, J. and Hill, S. (2008) 'Mobility matters: Research training and network building in science', *Comparative Technology Transfer and Society*, December, 6(3): 159–86.

World Bank (1991) *Urban Policy and Economic Development: An Agenda for the 1990s*. Washington, DC: The World Bank.

World Bank (2000) *Cities in Transition*. Washington, DC: World Bank.

World Bank (2006) *World Development Indicators CD Rom 2006*. Washington, DC: World Bank.

World Bank (2007) *World Development Report 2007: Development and the Next Generation*. Washington, DC: World Bank.

World Bank (2009) *World Development Report 2009: Reshaping Economic Geography*. Washington, DC: World Bank.

World Bank (2010) *World Development Indicators*. Available at: http://databank.worldbank.org/ (accessed 9 November 2010).

Wratten, E. (1995) 'Conceptualising Urban Poverty', *Environment and Urbanization*, 7(1): 11–36.

Wright, M.W. (2006) *Disposable Women and Other Myths of Global Capitalism*. New York: CRC Press.

Wu, F. and Yeh, A.G.-O. (1999) 'Urban spatial structure in a transitional economy: The case of Guangzhou, China', *Journal of the American Planning Association*, 65(4): 377–94.

Yamamoto, K. (2010) 'The agglomeration structure of the animation industry in East Asia: A case study of Tokyo, Seoul, and the Shanghai region', *Science Reports of Tohoku University, 7th Series (Geography)*, 57(1/2): 43–61.

Yeoh, B.S. (1999) 'Global/globalizing cities', *Progress in Human Geography*, 23(4): 607–16.

Yeoh, B.S.A. (2005) 'The global cultural city? Spatial imagineering and politics in the (multi)cultural marketplaces of South-east Asia', *Urban Studies*, 42(5/6): 945–58.

Yeung, H.W.C. (2002) 'Towards a relational economic geography: Old wine in new bottles?' 98th Annual Meeting of the Association of American Geographers. Los Angeles, California, 19–23 March.

Yeung, H.W.C. (2005) 'Rethinking relational economic geography', *Transactions of the Institute of British Geographers*, 30: 37–51.

Yeung, H.W.C. and Lin, G.C.S. (2003) 'Theorizing economic geographies of Asia', *Economic Geography*, April, 79(2): 107–28.

Yigitcanlar, T., Velibeyoglu, K. and Fernandez, C.M. (2008) 'Rising knowledge cities: The role of urban knowledge precincts', *Journal of Knowledge Management*, 12(5): 8–20.

Young, C., Diep M. and Drabble, S. (2006). 'Living with Difference? The "Cosmopolitan City" and Urban Reimaging in Manchester, UK'. *Urban Studies*, 43(10): 1687–714.

Young, M. and Willmott, P. (1957) *Family and Kinship in East London*. London: Routledge & Kegan Paul.

Yuan, Z. (2005) 'Features and impacts of the internationalization of R&D by transnational corporations: China's case', in UNCTAD (ed.) 24–26 January 2005, *Globalization of R&D and Developing Countries: Proceedings of the Expert Meeting, Geneva*. New York and Geneva: United Nations. pp. 109–15.

Zhou, Q. and Yang, A. (2010) 'Cheating in certification of high-tech companies', *New Century*. [Online] Available at: http://news.sciencenet.cn/html-news/2010/8/235447-2.shtm (accessed 3 August 2010) (in Chinese).

Zhou, Y. (2008) *The Inside Story of China's High-Tech Industry: Making Silicon Valley in Beijing*. Lanham: Rowman & Littlefield.

Zimmerman, J. (2008) 'From brew town to cool town: Neoliberalism and the creative city development strategy in Milwaukee', *Cities*, 25(4): 230–42.

Zukin, S. (1980) 'A decade of new urban sociology', *Theory and Society*, 9(4): 575–601.

Zukin, S. (1991) *Landscapes of Power: From Detroit to Disney World*. Berkeley, CA: University of California Press.

Zukin, S. (1995) *The Cultures of Cities*. Malden and Oxford: Blackwell Publishing.

Index